Canada's Voice

Canada's Voice

The Public Life
of John Wendell Holmes

ADAM CHAPNICK

UBC Press • Vancouver • Toronto

20 19 18 17 16 15 14 13 12 11 10 09   5 4 3 2 1

Printed in Canada with vegetable-based inks on FSC-certified ancient-forest-free paper (100 percent post-consumer recycled) that is processed chlorine- and acid-free.

Library and Archives Canada Cataloguing in Publication

Chapnick, Adam, 1976-
  Canada's voice : the public life of John Wendell Holmes / Adam Chapnick.

Includes bibliographical references and index.
ISBN 978-0-7748-1671-7 (bound); ISBN 978-0-7748-1672-4 (pbk.); ISBN 978-0-7748-1673-1 (e-book)

  1. Holmes, John W., 1910-1988. 2. Canada – Foreign relations – 20th century. 3. Diplomats – Canada – Biography. 4. Canadian Institute of International Affairs – Officials and employees – Biography. I. Title.

| FC601.H64 C43 2009 | 327.710092 | C2009-901139-5 |

Canadä

UBC Press gratefully acknowledges the financial support for our publishing program of the Government of Canada through the Book Publishing Industry Development Program (BPIDP), and of the Canada Council for the Arts, and the British Columbia Arts Council.

This book has been published with the help of a grant from the Canadian Federation for the Humanities and Social Sciences, through the Aid to Scholarly Publications Programme, using funds provided by the Social Sciences and Humanities Research Council of Canada.

UBC Press
The University of British Columbia
2029 West Mall
Vancouver, BC V6T 1Z2
604-822-5959 / Fax: 604-822-6083
www.ubcpress.ca

To Alana

Contents

Contents

Preface

It is hard to imagine a person who embodied the ideals of postwar Canadian foreign policy more than John Wendell Holmes. From his tireless work ethic, to his fierce loyalty to family and friends, to his commitment to peaceful forms of conflict resolution, to his unyielding desire to make a difference in the world, he approached life and country in a way that would make citizens of any political stripe proud. As a boy growing up in early twentieth-century London, Ontario, he was a successful student, widely respected for his contributions inside and outside the classroom. After a brief career as a high school teacher and then administrator for the Canadian Institute of International Affairs (CIIA), he entered public life and quickly became an exceptional diplomat, recognized around the world for his thoughtfulness, humility, and dedication. At the age of fifty he returned to the CIIA, this time as its president and then director general, and he expanded the depth and breadth of published research on Canadian foreign relations exponentially. In the late 1960s, he added to his responsibilities a part-time professorship at the University of Toronto and evolved to become a brilliant teacher and mentor to countless future scholars and policy practitioners. Throughout this period, he was also internationally revered as an esteemed commentator on global politics. In his final years, he was as much a prophet as an analyst, boldly calling on the international community to pay greater attention to issues such as environmental degradation and the spread of pandemic diseases well before such ideas were common within the mainstream foreign policy discourse.

Those who knew him recall his wry sense of humour, the twinkle in his eye, and the genuine interest he took in them as people, regardless of age or pedigree. He was a calming presence, a confidence builder, and an inspiration. Through his public service, his teaching, his writing, and his friendships, he did more than any other man or woman of his generation to influence how Canadians saw themselves on the world stage. He played an equally crucial role in shaping the way that diplomats, scholars, and statespeople abroad understood Ottawa and its citizens. For students and practitioners of international affairs at home and around the world, he was Canada's voice.

Paradoxically, John Holmes was an immensely private man. "You should start your biography with an apology," said one former associate when I asked him about his memories. "John would have been upset if he'd known that someone was writing a book about him." Others disagreed, but the late Geoffrey Pearson was probably right. Holmes kept even his closest friends and family members at a certain distance, never revealing his whole self to any one of them at a given time. There were aspects of his life, both personal and professional, that he preferred to keep private, and this might well explain why, unlike so many of his contemporaries in the public service, he never published a complete memoir. It was as if the private John Holmes was a different man: he compartmentalized his feelings so effectively that his personal circumstances rarely had any obvious, meaningful impact on his public achievements. This book therefore does not explore his private life and activities in significant depth. Nonetheless, Holmes was also a professor trained in history. He believed in rigorous research, in exploring every side of a story, and in presenting the results in a balanced and even-handed manner. He would have understood that certain aspects of his personal experience, no matter how much he would have preferred they go undocumented, were indeed germane to an assessment of his public career, and he would have tolerated the retelling of the events surrounding his controversial departure from the Department of External Affairs.

As much as he is recalled today with affection, this biography does not seek to canonize John Holmes. Just as Canada has never been a perfect international citizen, Holmes was not a flawless human being. And, like his country, he, too, had secrets that he preferred to forget, or at least not to share. This story is nonetheless about a man who served Canada with distinction and who, in so doing, touched more lives than he ever could have imagined. No serious student of Canadian foreign policy, and of the way that Canadians see themselves in the world, can ignore his impact.

For much of the twentieth century, Canadians with an interest in global affairs chose well in allowing him to serve as their national conscience and international ambassador. His voice was theirs: when it was heard, and it was heard loudly and often, at home and overseas, they had every reason to feel proud.

I first contemplated a biography of Mr. Holmes as a doctoral candidate working on a history of Canada and the founding of the United Nations. It did not take long to recognize how important he had been not just to the story itself but also to the way that it has since been documented and remembered. He was an integral member of the cadre of civil servants who dominated the Canadian public arena during the nation's formative years as a world player. Once retired, he was the most prolific commentator on that period and on future directions in Canadian foreign policy. It was only later that I learned how many others he had affected through his teaching and mentorship, but this discovery was hardly surprising: it is difficult to open a leading textbook on Canadian external relations without coming across a dedication to John Holmes. Foreign policy experts who were not his students – and their numbers are limited – also almost inevitably knew him as a mentor or a colleague. I am too young to have met Mr. Holmes, and I can only imagine what it would have been like to discuss and share ideas with one of Canada's pre-eminent public intellectuals. It therefore is my hope that this work will be of interest not only to Mr. Holmes' living contemporaries and immediate successors but also to future generations of scholars, commentators, and public servants who face the tremendous challenge of continuing to question, explore, and attempt to improve the way that Canada and Canadians behave on the world stage. This book is not a step-by-step account of the history of Canadian external relations during John Holmes' most influential years. Rather, it is a story of how one man, working within and outside of the political process, forever changed the way that we understand Canada and its place in the world. At a time in the history of Canadian foreign policy when we lack the universally appealing heroic figures that were so prominent in the early Cold War era, it is worth reflecting on the qualities and contributions that made those individuals so memorable. John Holmes' life story allows us to do just that.

Acknowledgments

Erica Berman inspires me to continue to strive to succeed as a scholar and a person. The addition of Alana Leigh Berman Chapnick to our family has made that process even more rewarding.

The Chapnick and Berman families have continued to offer their unquestioned support, as have the Rossmans, still the keepers of my home away from home in Ottawa.

Before it was submitted for review, Barbara Falk, Gayle Fraser, Norman Hillmer, Ann and Nancy Skinner, and Denis Stairs read and commented on a draft of this manuscript and Abe Rotstein helped revise a particular section. I asked for their guidance because of my respect for them as people and my regard for their intellect. Their sincere feedback, as well as the comments provided by UBC Press' anonymous reviewers, has made this book a much better product.

The support of all of my colleagues at the Canadian Forces College, and of Peter Foot in particular, made it much easier to research and write peacefully.

The research for this book began during a postdoctoral fellowship that I held at Carleton University and then at the University of Toronto. Robert Bothwell and John English were instrumental in helping me secure the funding, and the departments of history at both institutions were very supportive. A special thanks to Jane Abray, Vicky Dingillo, and Margaret MacMillan, who assisted in my transfer of the fellowship to Toronto after the first year.

Each one of the over 150 people who agreed to speak with me about their memories of John Holmes deserve personal thanks. Many not only gave of their time and of their private letters and photographs but also helped connect me with others whom I would not have found otherwise. In order to protect their privacy, I have generally not made specific references to their insights in my notes, but I would like to recognize Wendy Woytasik-Karr for her selfless efforts to help me secure appropriate photographs.

Although I did not interview them formally, Stephen Azzi, Laura Brandon, Greg Donaghy, Paulette Dozois, Mary Halloran, Gary Kinsman, Hector Mackenzie, Christopher McCreery, Peter Neary, June Rogers, Chuck Ruud, Nancy Snellgrove, Kevin Spooner, and Ryan Touhey also provided comments and advice. Megan Sproule-Jones' helpful comments and suggestions as she created the index went beyond the call of duty.

At different points during the course of my research, I relied on the assistance of Darin Abseh, Kaitlin Bardswich, Heather Dichter, Margo Horoszko, Véronique LaRue Constantineau, Shivma Maharaj, David Meren, Noelle Morris, and Michael Yuzdepski to track down files, organize data, and translate difficult passages of text.

My access to the Holmes Papers at the Trinity College Archives and at the CIIA Library would not have been possible, nor as rewarding, without the help and support of Charles Beer, Walter Eisenbeis, Marion Magee, Henry Pilon, and Sylvia Lassam.

The archivists and holders of institutional memory whom I met across Canada, the United States, and Great Britain were almost uniformly gracious, thorough, and immensely helpful. Although I have almost certainly forgotten some of them, those who made a particular difference include Charles Boyd at Pickering College; Anne Daniels at the University of Western Ontario Archives; Clare Everett-Allen, Richard High, and Karen Mee from Leeds University Library; Jane Gorjevsky of the Carnegie Corporation; Ana Grant at Bishop's University Archives; Heather Home at the Queen's University Archives; Marie Korey of Massey College; Jane Lynch from the University of Toronto's Interlibrary Loan Department; Don McLeod at the Canadian Lesbian and Gay Archives; Joelle Miller of the Rockefeller Archive Center (who went above and beyond the call of duty to locate a number of obscure files); Michael Moir at the Clara Thomas Archives and Special Collections, York University; Robert Paul at the Diefenbaker Centre; Elizabeth Seitz and Selina Coward at the University of Regina, Archives and Special Collections; Peter Telford of the Alumni Association of London South Collegiate Institute; Garron Wells and the staff at the University of Toronto Archives; Erwin Wodarczak at the University of British Columbia Archives; all of the staff at the reference and archives desks at Library and Archives Canada; all of the staff with whom I dealt at the Thomas Fisher Rare Books Library; and the UN Reference Team at the Dag Hammarskjöld Library.

Funding for the research for this book was provided in part by a post-doctoral fellowship from the Social Sciences and Humanities Research Council and from a variety of research sources at the Canadian Forces College and the Royal Military College of Canada.

Lloyd Axworthy, Peter Dobell, and Alan Henrikson generously allowed me to quote directly from their personal letters.

Finally, it is hard to imagine that there could be a better academic editor than Emily Andrew, and I am indebted to her and the rest of the excellent team at UBC Press (including, in particular, Holly Keller, Randy Schmidt, Megan Brand, and copy editor Joanne Richardson) for standing by this project through the review process and beyond.

Abbreviations

ACUNS	Academic Council on the United Nations System
ATIP	Access to Information and Privacy Act
BUA	Bishop's University Archives
CBC	Canadian Broadcasting Corporation
CCA	Carnegie Corporation Archives
CCF	Co-operative Commonwealth Federation
CIIA	Canadian Institute of International Affairs
CIS	Centre for International Studies, University of Toronto
CN	Canadian National (freight railroad)
CPY	Yugoslav Communist Party
CSIS	Canadian Security and Intelligence Services
CUSO	Canadian University Services Overseas
DC	John G. Diefenbaker Centre for the Study of Canada
DCER	*Documents on Canadian External Relations*
DEA	Department of External Affairs
FBI	Federal Bureau of Investigation
FSO	Foreign Service Officer
ICJ	International Court of Justice
IHR	Institute of Historical Research
IIA	International Institute of Agriculture
IJC	International Joint Commission
IPR	Institute of Pacific Relations
KGB	Committee for State Security (of the former Soviet Union)
LAC	Library and Archives Canada

LSR	League for Social Reconstruction
MAD	Mutual Assured Destruction
MP	Member of Parliament
NATO	North Atlantic Treaty Organization
NDC	National Defence College
NORAD	North American Air Defence Command
OAS	Organization of American States
OC	Order of Canada
OPEC	Organization of Petroleum Exporting Countries
PCO	Privy Council Office
PHP	post-hostilities problems
PLO	Palestine Liberation Organization
PPP	People's Progressive Party
PSC	Public Service Commission
RAC	Rockefeller Archive Center
RCMP	Royal Canadian Mounted Police
RIK	Ronald Ian King
SM	Medal of Service (of the Order of Canada)
SSEA	secretary of state for external affairs
U of T	University of Toronto
UBC	University of British Columbia
UN	United Nations (Organization)
UNA	United Nations Association
UNAEC	United Nations Atomic Energy Commission
UNEF	United Nations Emergency Force
UNITAR	United Nations Institute for Training and Research
UNOGIL	United Nations Observation Group in Lebanon
URA	University of Regina
USSEA	under-secretary of state for external affairs
UWOA	University of Western Ontario Archives
WIB	Wartime Information Board

Canada's Voice

I

The Early Years

H alley's Comet can be seen from the earth once every seventy-five years. In 1910, it was at its most visible on 18 May. Exactly one month later, in a small London, Ontario, hospital, John Wendell Holmes was born with the mark of the comet on his back, or so his doctor, with a smile, liked to describe his birthmark. This playful optimism fit the family household. The father, Wendell Holmes, was the son of a minister. Reverend John Holmes, of English and Irish stock, had been ordained into the Bible Christian Church in 1871 and served there until it merged with the United Methodist Free Churches and the Methodist New Connexion to form the United Methodist Church in 1907. Eighteen years later, the Methodists joined with a number of others to form the United Church of Canada. The Reverend Holmes first worked in Prince Edward Island before moving to London, where his family settled. His wife was Jane (Jennie) Greenway, sister of Thomas, Manitoba's first Liberal premier and the family's first national celebrity.

The Holmeses believed in the social gospel. The children went to services every Sunday, after which they visited with their grandparents: their mother's side one week, and their father's the next. Wendell himself became one of London's great success stories, a book seller who began his career at the old Methodist Book Room (it later became Ryerson Press) and then went out on his own, selling his wares in corner stores and pharmacies. Over time, he was able to purchase three shops in southwestern Ontario. His achievements can be credited to his humility. He was skilful with his customers, self-effacing, and socially conscious. When the Depression came and many of his patrons could no longer afford to indulge in the luxury of buying books, he lent out his stock as if he were running a library. He was also a consensus builder, famous for saying to his children, "Well, I'd like to hear the other fellow's point of view."[1]

Wendell Holmes married Helen Morton. She was five years his junior and hailed from Ayrshire, Scotland. The second of eight children, Helen had moved with her stonemason father to Canada at the age of four in search of a better life. She was in many ways her husband's opposite: reserved, emotionally remote, even difficult at times. It made sense that she filled the role of family disciplinarian, the undisputed matriarch. She "had a high and quick intelligence and intellectual curiosity, spent too much time on house-cleaning and too little time with the books she loved," wrote her son several years after her death. Self-educated and a voracious reader, she kept her wit and quick tongue largely to herself. She was much less religious than her husband – "cleanliness for her was more important than godliness" – but believed nonetheless that people would be judged by the way they lived and how they treated others.[2] Together, she and her husband shared an allegiance to Canada's Liberal Party, a commitment to their family, and a loyalty to the British Empire common to most in their town in the late nineteenth century.

There were four children. First came Helen (Buzz) in 1908. John, whom they immediately called Jack, arrived next in 1910, and the twins, Elizabeth and Isobel, followed two years later. They were a close family and grew larger through the addition of the Riddles, the Beers, and the Skinners. They bonded on the shores of Sauble Beach in the summers and then back in London over Christmas, when an extra effort was made to gather everyone together to sing, watch plays put on by the children, and compete in the famous Christmas musical quiz. Humour was rampant, as the Holmeses, and Jack in particular, had a penchant for espousing Holmes-spun wisdom through puns.

Jack himself was a curious child and was clearly his mother's son. In his earliest years, he followed her around while reading from the endless supply of material that his father brought home from the shops. In spite of their lack of formal schooling, his parents seem to have passed on to him the habits of an absent-minded and captivated academic. It was normal for him to bump into his mother while walking through the house with a book in his hands. Later, when he received his first tape recorder, he also chased her with a microphone. "Oh, Jack, put that thing away," she often said in loving anger. She was the only one who could speak to him like that, the only member of the family clever enough to intimidate him just a bit. Over time, it became clear that he had acquired both his father's warmth and commitment to family and his mother's pure intelligence and emotional detachment. He was a man whom everyone felt they knew well until they thought about it and realized that, while they admired him immensely, they hardly knew him at all.[3]

Jack's parents loved to travel and shared an interest in world affairs, so it is not surprising that their son's first recorded memories come from the Great War. It was a regular topic of discussion at the dinner table, especially once Helen's younger brother Alec went overseas. When Alec was killed at the Somme in the autumn of 1916, Helen was crushed. It was one of the rare occasions when she wept in front of her children, and the sorrow she so obviously felt when she had to inform her younger sister of their brother's death that evening made Jack cry too.

Life in the Holmes household improved in 1917. Jack sang patriotic songs in school and watched with excitement as soldiers marched proudly in the streets. As a cadet, he was dismissed from class early one day in 1918 to celebrate after the Germans had been set back. Then, on 11 November, the war ended. The neighbourhood children sang "There are smiles that make us happy" and poured confetti down from the second floor of Wendell's shop during a victory parade. That night, Jack went with his father to Victoria Park, a fifteen-acre gathering place in the heart of downtown. There, they joined crowds across North America in watching the defeated Kaiser burn in effigy. Less than twenty years later, the Imperial Order of the Daughters of the Empire would spearhead the construction of a cenotaph on that very spot. It was a haunting and disturbing experience for Jack. Along with Alec's death, it formed one of his most vivid memories of the First World War, an experience from which glamour had disappeared early on.[4]

He grew up in what he later described as a strict household. His parents were adamant that he succeed in school, and he did. London South Collegiate Institute had opened in an abandoned building across the street from Victoria Public School in 1922, and Jack was part of its second class. "We're here to win the day for the Garnet and Gray, and to London South we pledge allegiance now," the students could be heard reciting every morning. Jack flourished as a student; he was both popular and incredibly bright. He participated on the school's literary executive and edited the yearbook, the *Oracle*, in his second-to-last year. He was a leader among his peers, acting as a so-called pall-bearer when the students moved from their condemned school house into a new building not long before graduation, and encouraging expressions of pride in both London South and the British Empire. "Why can we not in our mad rush of living to-day," he wrote in the *Oracle* in 1927, "take time to honour the Empire to which all of us, whether we show it or not, are proud to be citizens. Let us not be persuaded into believing that it is smart to show no patriotism. It is in reality a very low form of discourtesy and, most of all, of ingratitude."[5] From the beginning, it seems, he used his voice to inspire and enlighten.

When he accepted the school's senior public-speaking medal from his father – the award's sponsor – he did so with pride. It was not the first time that London South had recognized his achievements. He had won an English prize the year before, along with the prestigious Confederation Medal. The latter was particularly special since it was presented to him by Edwin Pearson, a family friend and father of the diplomat who later became Jack's idol and mentor.[6]

When he finished high school, there was no doubt of what would come next. Buzz was also highly intelligent, but Jack – who remained close with all of his sisters, but especially Buzz – was the man in the family, and it was he who was sent to university. It was a tell-tale sign of the times, and the spirit of these years influenced the way that Jack thought of his sisters for the rest of his life. Although he forever saw himself as responsible for their well-being, in reality, he needed Buzz, Elizabeth, and Isobel. He relied on them for comfort, support, and a sense of family that he would not have had otherwise since he never married. They were his shield from the outside world when he needed to escape, and they welcomed him lovingly whenever he returned from his studies and travels.

For his undergraduate schooling, there was only one place to go. The expanding University of Western Ontario was close to home. Led by President William Sherwood Fox, the university viewed high-quality teaching as its foremost obligation and was the obvious choice of most southern Ontarian undergraduates. It was 1928, the economy was good, Western was about to complete construction of the J.W. Little Memorial Stadium (a symbol of pride across the township), and Jack's prospects were limitless.[7] He became a part of the class of Arts '32 and posed for his first school yearbook photo dressed sharply in a jacket and tie alongside five women and three other young men.[8]

The five-foot-ten, good-looking, brown-haired, brown-eyed youth embraced university life. He was elected class president and began eight months residence at one of the university's newly established inter-faculty fraternities, Sigma Kappa Sigma, so that he could pledge the following year. The administration at Western insisted that acceptance into the fraternity be dependent on high academic achievement, and Jack's fresh-man grades, largely firsts, two seconds, and a third in modern German literature, easily gained him admission. Now a member of one of the most respected clubs on campus, and exposed to the university's brightest from across the disciplines and faculties, Jack Holmes thrived. He continued in politics and was elected to the student administrative assembly. Prefect E.J. Wright credited its accomplishments that year, which included the establishment of the University Students' Commission – an undergradu-ate inter-faculty group – to "the splendid co-operation that existed, and the willingness to work that was so noticeable in the 1929-30 governing body."[9]

Jack also found time to pursue his interest in theatre, performing the parts of Benedick in Shakespeare's *Much Ado About Nothing*, Krogstad in Ibsen's *A Doll's House*, and, later, Shylock in *The Merchant of Venice*. The shows were collaborations between the Player's Club and the Hesperian Club on campus, both of which counted Jack among their members. He was on staff at the student newspaper, the *Gazette*, and even published the only issue of the *Hesperian*, Western's first literary magazine, all the while keeping up with his school work. Jack received all firsts in his second year, save a B in economics, and won Wyatt Scholarships in English and history for finishing at the top of his class in both of his major subjects.

The awards made it easier for him to ignore the economic crisis that was overtaking the Western world. The greatest depression of modern times was especially punishing to Canadians. Unemployment rates jumped from 5 percent to over 30 percent in just four years. The stock market col-lapsed and prices fell. Automobile production dropped by three-quarters, and drought and crop failures led to an agricultural crisis. As his father's business struggled, and families around him lost everything, Jack Holmes remained focused on his own personal development at the University of Western Ontario, comfortably entrenched in an academic bubble.

This all began to change in the fall of 1930 as he evolved from active member of the university community to genuine student leader. He be-came president of the Player's Club, expanded its membership, and, in its most productive month, produced three separate one-act performances. He remained involved with the Hesperians and took over as editor and "pen-pusher" of the *Gazette*. It was this last responsibility that engaged him the most. The year began controversially when, just days after he had secured prized advertisement dollars from the Grand Theatre, a group of young students, in the midst of Initiation Day, burst into the theatre without paying. Within hours, the proprietor had retracted his financial commitment, leading the new editor to comment in one of his first columns: "Remember that still more than the actual money has been lost to the student body, we have lost the good-will and respect of one of that group who have done so much for us; namely the business men of London."[10]

In spite of his anger and clear disappointment, there was a professionalism to Jack's approach that garnered him respect among his peers. Within weeks, he was proposing to publish a new literary supplement, in the spirit of the now-defunct *Hesperian*. The literary magazine was produced as a Christmas issue, shortly before the editor took a two-month leave of absence. Although it appears that he was ill, his school work certainly did not suffer, and he did not provide an explanation in the paper for his departure.

At the end of the year, Jack wrote a summary of his *Gazette* experience for the university's yearbook, *Occidentalia*:

> Pausing a moment in retrospection to review the epochal changes of a fast fleeting year, we experienced a gratifying sensation of satisfaction ... It was apparent that a policy of retrenchment at this time meant regression. Thus there blossomed forth from the snowy campus heights the spirit of the old Gazette in new resplendent raiment. Blown before the winds of progress, down the hill to oblivion, disappeared the little old paper. In its place there appeared the new University of Western Ontario Gazette, adopting for its slogan, "More than a newspaper" ...
>
> The need for an undergraduate publication is indisputable. It furnishes the medium through which the initiated may learn that excellence of technique that will stand him in good stead in future years. There he may learn simplicity and precision of expression and that great necessity, namely, clear thinking.
>
> We, who have had the privilege of serving the Gazette this year, have derived from our services, not merely intellectual and literary remuneration, but also a very keen sense of pleasure. May you, who are successors, fare likewise.
>
> *To you we fling the torch,*
> *Be yours to hold it high.*[11]

As he was preparing to leave the *Gazette* and focus on his final year as an undergraduate, the administration at the university experienced both public success and fiscal turmoil. In 1931, for the first time a Western student won a prestigious Rhodes Scholarship. In the midst of this great achievement, however, the Depression began to affect the school's bottom line. Grants from both the City of London and the Province of Ontario were reduced, and in 1932 faculty members were forced to accept a reduction in pay along with an increased workload. In spite of student demands for more learning space, plans for further expansion were delayed indefinitely.

Jack also finally felt the effects of the Depression personally. It is not clear whether it was the fault of his apparent incapacitation or his lack of involvement in university athletics, but, although he once again received Wyatt scholarships in English and history, he does not seem to have applied for a Rhodes. With that, he gave up his best chance for paid education abroad (and an ideal opportunity to avoid facing the economic crisis at home).

Jack was not yet certain of what he wanted to do for a living, and by the fall of 1931 he had begun to take journalism more seriously as a possible option. In 1930, on a whim, he mailed a copy of the *Hesperian* to the editor of the *Toronto Mail and Empire*, William Arthur Deacon. They had corresponded intermittently since then, and Jack began sending Deacon some of his own writing, including an essay on Walt Whitman. The editor was so impressed that he asked for three extra copies. One was for his friend, the playwright Merrill Denison. The others went to what he called "Whitmanians," one of whom had collected a wide assortment of relics and documents that had yet to be organized. Deacon thought that Jack might assemble the material into a book and offered to assist in the process. Although nothing came of the idea, Deacon's respect for the young student was beyond doubt: "Your considerable abilities are not narrow in focus," he wrote in April 1932, "and your personality and naturalness of manner positively charming. I am sure your life is going to be very successful and useful, whatever line of work you decide on."[12]

Another possible line was politics. In his third year, Jack wrote a number of academic essays on radicalism and revolution and their impact on British and French colonial policy. In a humorous "class prophesy" about his future, he was chided by fellow students Ruth Hayes and John Kevin O'Connor as the one most likely to be deported to Poland for having instigated communist riots.[13] In 1932 he consulted Deacon – fast becoming a radical himself – about how he might direct his new focus. "Speaking of socialism," he wrote, "what do you think of the L.S.R.? ... I have become quite interested in Mr. Underhill's League for Social Reconstruction. I am not yet a confirmed socialist, but it is my distrust of my own ability to decide, rather than my dislike of any of the implications of that term that keep me from being one. In the meanwhile I think that the very moderate Socialist Program of the L.S.R. and of Mr. Woodsworth would mean a tremendous political and economic progress in Canada as compared with the dithering planlessness of our two great parties."[14] Deacon expressed little confidence in the League, suggesting that it had come along too late to make a real difference in the world, and Jack's interest in active socialism faded shortly thereafter.

Another man set him upon his future path. Arthur Garrett Dorland had a PhD from the University of Toronto and was the chair of the history department at Western. He was a Quaker, whose doctoral thesis had examined the history of the Society of Friends. He brought with him to his leadership position a progressive approach to conflict resolution and a special ability to inspire his students. His impact was formidable. Fifty years later, in a speech in honour of his accomplishments, Jack explained: "He injected into my enthusiasm the moral factor. I began to see the study of history as a key to peace and social change ... He taught me to see starkly enough the nature of conflict, the ills of our society, but they were to be regarded as remediable if I and others would do something about them."[15] Jack's new goal, not all that incompatible with his progressive sympathies, was to give voice to history as a teacher. The classroom would be his forum to contribute to a more peaceful world. Dorland encouraged him to revitalize what had been known in 1926 as Western's League of Nations Society. The group began meeting again in 1931 and passed resolutions calling on the countries of the world to voluntarily disarm and then use moral pressure to stall the expansion of fascism. The club, and the increasingly difficult depression, had made Dorland's star pupil more serious and focused. In 1932, when eight students were elected to the Honour Society, recognizing invaluable service to the university in non-athletic capacities, it was *John*, not Jack, Holmes who accepted one of the commendations.

John Holmes won the University of Western Ontario's gold medal in history in 1932 and was elected class valedictorian. For the first time that year, the spring convocation ceremony was held outdoors in the J.W. Little Memorial Stadium. On 27 May, close to 2,500 faculty, staff, graduates, and their families gathered and listened intently to a youth who was fast becoming a man. His speech was full of his ever-present wit, but it was also rather dreary. "Shall we be known as the depression class that started merrily off in the blast of a big boom, and crawled out on to the desert flatness of economic prostration?" he asked. He referred to what the often heralded British reformer and former prime minister William Ewart Gladstone had once called "the responsibilities of privilege," urging his colleagues to take seriously their obligation to give back to the society that had begat them a university education. "[The great Victorian poet] Matthew Arnold has taught us that the aim of all culture is to learn and propagate the best that has been said and thought in the world," he said. "The world is sorely in need of culture in the year 1932, and we, who have spent four years preparing ourselves for the task of cultivating the world, must take ourselves a large share of the labour." There were few job prospects for him and his classmates, he admitted. To face the world after graduation, they would have to be prepared for an adventure.[16]

Young John Holmes had already learned the importance of budgeting judiciously. The Depression had instilled a conscientiousness in him that bordered on frugality. Throughout his adult life, friends and co-workers who knew him well chided him about some of his older, ragged outfits, including one particular find at a sale in England at Marks and Spencer. The button-down shirt had been reduced because of a manufacturing error: the two sleeves were cuffed differently. No matter, explained Holmes to his office colleagues: if he wore a sweater over it, no one would notice. This is not to say that he was not generous with others: John Holmes dedicated a good portion of his life and some of his income to the care of his young nieces, Ann and Nancy Skinner, who lost their father at an early age. Apart from purchasing the latest audio equipment to play his always expanding collection of classical music, however, he generally had great difficulty spending money on himself.

He was more comfortable, and indeed successful, finding work in difficult times. Summers during his years at Western and throughout most of the 1930s were spent at the leading boys' program in Canada, Camp Ahmek, working for a psychologist whose other responsibilities included serving as the director of character education at Pickering College, a private Ontario boys' boarding school. Taylor Statten, a Methodist, was fast becoming a legendary figure in boys' work. Known as "the Chief" to his colleagues and "Canada's dean of campers"[17] to historians of the period, he dedicated much of his life to providing character-building experiences for young Canadians. The stunning campground on Canoe Lake in what was called the Ahmek district of Ontario's Algonquin Park inspired comparisons by former campers to the Land of Oz. As a counsellor, or perhaps a section director (it is not clear), John Holmes slept in Pansy Palace, a log building at the lake's edge. He spent his days canoeing, swimming, and enjoying other aspects of camp craft. Ahmek also had a theatre capable of seating close to five hundred. How Holmes secured a position at such an elite program – a young Pierre Trudeau arrived in the late 1930s – is unclear, but Statten was known, according to one long-time camper and staff member, for his "uncanny ability to spot potential leaders when they were very young and inexperienced and induce them to work on his team."[18]

In 1932, Holmes applied for and was granted a University of Toronto (U of T) Alumni Federation War Memorial Fellowship to cover the costs of his Master of Arts training. In spite of the Depression, the U of T was expanding. Students like Holmes, wrote the university president in his end of year report, had come to appreciate "the value of education as a preparation and equipment for life." It was the soundest investment in their future that they could make.[19] In the fall of 1933, the U of T grew to over eight thousand students and the School of Graduate Studies increased by more than 10 percent to 731. Holmes was one of 232 MA candidates, thirty-six of whom were historians.

That September, he left home and settled in the recently built Emmanuel College residence. Not far away was Herbert Norman, the brilliant son of a missionary who had spent much of his childhood in Japan. The two became friends, and although their paths diverged, a decade later they resumed their friendship as colleagues in Canada's Department of External Affairs (DEA).

In the classroom, Holmes' focus moved from British colonial history to more distinctly Canadian and constitutional issues, and he continued to take French in conjunction with his regular course load. The result of his countless hours in the archives was a rather dry assessment of the state of border relations between Canada and the United States during the American Civil War. In retrospect, the study was more important for how it shaped his understanding of the world, and how he later communicated that understanding to others, than for its actual conclusions.[20] There were certain elements of foreign policy that could not be changed, he realized – like geography. Canada was a permanent neighbour of the United States, and this fact would forever play a significant role in its external relations. The United States would always occupy a greater part of the Canadian collective mind than the other way around, and its domestic concerns would have a perpetual effect on Canadian-American relations and on Washington's commitment to global affairs. Dealings between the two North American countries were also inherently difficult. By nature, in sharing what amounted to an illogically constructed border, they should have been in perpetual conflict. The relationship therefore could never be taken for granted.[21]

From the time he arrived in Toronto, John Holmes had intended to use his MA to gain admission to the University of London, where he hoped to study colonial and imperial history. Having only just arrived at Emmanuel College, he immediately solicited William Sherwood Fox (still Western's president), Arthur Dorland, and the managing editor of the *London Free Press*, Arthur Ford, to serve as referees for an Imperial Order of the Daughters of the Empire War Memorial Postgraduate Overseas Scholarship. Their references were glowing. President Fox called him "one of the best students that have passed through our halls." Dorland added, "a natural student, a prolific and intelligent reader with a sound instinct for source material, which combined with a nice sense of style and ability to express himself, have made his work really distinguished." Ford, the father of Robert Ford, another future member of the DEA, noted that he was "one of the most brilliant and promising students it has been my good fortune to know ... He is a young man of the highest character, cultured and literary in his tastes."[22] All of their kind words were for naught. Holmes did not win, and in the summer of 1933 he found himself instead at the University of Western Ontario's newly established French-language summer school in the small Quebec town of Trois-Pistôles.

The program was eight weeks long and cost ten dollars, plus six dollars per week for room and board. Students were chosen from among the university's finest, along with select recent graduates. It is likely that when Holmes' application to study in London was rejected, President Fox offered him a space in the fledgling program. The school's progressive outlook suited its newest addition. The founders believed that by immersing themselves in francophone culture, and speaking only French, students could learn far more about Canada's other "founding nation" than they ever could in the classroom. Save a necessary course in phonetics, formal classes were shunned in favour of addresses (in French) on contemporary topics by prominent guests, including professors, journalists, and poets. Afternoons and evenings were spent interacting with the rest of the community in sport and through discussions in shops and markets. The students sang French-Canadian songs every day and, at times, had their activities broadcast on French radio through a station in Rimouski. It was an outstanding example of the benefits to be had through cooperation between the universities and the general public.

Forty years after the fact, Holmes reflected: "It was much more than the language that I learned ... I was not just exposed to the culture of Quebec, I was happily enveloped in it. I not only learned to speak in French, I learned to laugh in French and we did an enormous amount of that. The affection and esteem I acquired for the good citizens of Trois-Pistôles has remained and would certainly survive even political estrangement."[23] The idea that cooperation was best achieved through dialogue, cultural interaction, and mutual understanding remained with him throughout his professional career.[24] Moreover, he realized, and would later regularly impress upon others, often it was the informal discussions or, in this case, the time outside of the classroom that played the most important role in resolving differences.

This strong progressive strain in his thinking, along with his previous connections with Arthur Dorland and Taylor Statten, made Pickering College, just north of Toronto in Newmarket, Ontario, a logical destination for the now twenty-three-year-old young man.[25] Pickering defined what might be termed radical Canadian civility in education in the 1930s. Founded as the Society of Friends' boarding school in 1842, it was a Quaker College, whose board chairman, Sam Rogers, garnered acclaim for spearheading a $60,000 campaign to create a mobile medical mission to support soldiers injured on both sides of the Spanish Civil War. Pacifist in nature, the institution aimed, in the words of its headmaster, Joe McCulley, "to produce cultured men who will so highly regard their civic responsibilities that they will wish to have a part in directing the changes of the future."[26]

McCulley – who went on to become deputy commissioner of penitentiaries and then the warden of Toronto's Hart House – was an imposing man: blond, six-feet tall, a Rhodes Scholar, and on a mission to change education and to affect the state of the world. The radicalism, which would hardly have seemed strange to a graduate of Trois-Pistôles, came from his belief that, while tests and exams might measure efficiency in the classroom, the best learning often took place outside – literally. Pickering taught science by taking students into the wilderness with maps and compasses. It stressed the importance of the natural environment almost fifty years before others embraced the idea.

It was also distinctly Canadian. As McCulley explained, "The Canadian culture is not a transparent or trans-oceanic form. Our roots, indeed, go deep into the tradition and history of the British peoples, and certainly our institutions of government and politics are a direct outgrowth of the centuries old struggle for democratic and political forms and a judiciary that would be above reproach. Even these, however, had to be modified because of the peculiar conditions and circumstances of Canadian life."[27] For him, Canada was a nation of immigrants: multicultural, tolerant, and full of potential. Pickering was the first independent school in the province to break the colour bar, to accept Jews as residents, and to abolish the use of the cane as a form of punishment.

The lack of pretentiousness was impressive considering the pedigrees of the masters. There was, of course, McCulley, and Statten, the assistant headmaster who also taught at the University of Toronto. Another master was the author of the Province of Ontario's senior matriculation textbook. One later coordinated rehabilitation programs for the United Nations. T. Ronald Ide, the first chair and chief executive officer of TV Ontario, spent time at Pickering. All of these men used their prestige to bring guests such as J.S. Woodsworth and the former LSR president, Frank Underhill, to the college as speakers. None of them asked for anything in return.

The staff also included Charles Ritchie – remembered today as one of Canada's most celebrated diarists – still looking more like a student than a master at the age of twenty-four. Such youthfulness could be helpful as all teachers served as advisors and counsellors for Pickering boys. Ritchie, who later became one of the leading diplomats of his time, recalls self-deprecatingly: "The boys had a sort of cult for me, treating me as something between a mascot and their own freak, in some cases their friend."[28]

This close relationship encouraged open discussions and debate, and Pickering was criticized across the province for its embrace of political controversy. McCulley did not care: "Freedom," he quoted from a principal at Manchester College in Oxford, "is a part we have to act. It is not a state that we rest in and enjoy. Your freedom lies, not in what you reject, but in what you accept, in what you affirm, in what you assert, and above all in what you create. The free man is first and foremost a creative man. He is a man whose best is always leading him on to a better."[29] Both John and Jack Holmes fit in easily at Pickering College.

The 1932-33 academic year was to be Charles Ritchie's last, and the school therefore needed a new English teacher. With his progressive beliefs, his passion for education, and his boyish enthusiasm, Master Holmes was an ideal replacement. More personally, the only other option was to enter the book-selling business, and for that he had no real interest. He settled into his $1,500 a year job in Newmarket (it was later raised to $1,800), boarding in the residence and taking his meals with the students. It was above-average pay for the period, even without his accommodations. This made the new master more comfortable than many of his fellow Western graduates, and for that he was grateful. Holmes was at the time, in his own words, "a rather mushy kind of social democratic pacifist," the perfect addition to a school that struggled throughout the decade to rationalize its dedication to reasoned discussion as the ultimate form of conflict resolution with an increasingly violent and blood-thirsty German Reich. Five years later, he continued to be pained by the failure of diplomacy to arrest international aggression.[30]

Perhaps it was Holmes' natural tendency towards indecision or maybe it was his uncertainty about his future – whatever the reason, the new master waffled between "John" and "Jack" while he was at Pickering. Regardless, the young English teacher quickly gained a reputation as a good person and a great instructor. Inside the classroom he was a harsh critic of poor grammar, but outside the classroom he encouraged his students to express themselves creatively through theatre. In Pickering's tradition, he led by example. Not only did he become the school's dramaturge and artistic director, in 1935 he also filled in as an actor on just forty-eight hours notice.

Students still recall Holmes' valiant attempts to puddle around in the craft shop, where he displayed no competence whatsoever, and his incessant puns. "We see then," he wrote in the 1934 school yearbook, "that the public enemy number one, the man who castigates the punster, is nothing but a provincial-minded Anglo-Saxon seeking compensation for his own lack of wit. He is trying to dam one of the noblest streams of our culture by designating as 'the lowest form of wit' what is really the basic form of wit. It is a sad condition, something for every right-thinking person to ponder over."[31] He joined the students for a trip to the West Indies over Easter 1936 and tolerated the adolescent pranks that they played on him incessantly.

Although happy at Pickering, John Holmes was never entirely satisfied. He still thought of returning to school and still hoped to study in England. After half a decade of teaching and living frugally, he saved enough money to do so. In the spring of 1938, he requested and was granted a leave of absence to pursue doctoral studies at the University of London. He never intended to return but was conscious of keeping every option open. His departure was greeted with regret by everyone at the school. In "Going Holmes," the editors of the school yearbook, the *Voyageur*, noted that when one student learned that Mr. Holmes was leaving, he wrote to his parents, "nothing short of a catastrophe has happened." The writers could not have agreed more: "All we can look for therefore," they explained, "is that the traditional solemnity of the British museum will be shattered, that 'father' Bunny Austin will be driven from Wimbledon, and Noel Coward will be toppled from his throne, all by the wit and skill of John W. Holmes. And to all these worthy enterprises we say 'good luck,' but come back."[32]

Holmes visited the college many times – his brother-in-law Harry Beer later became headmaster and Harry's son, Charles, is still heavily involved today – but his career as a high school teacher was over.

By late September, he was on a train through Quebec to a ship called the *Duchess of Athol* headed for Scotland. His stomach churned for much of the trip, and not only from sea-sickness – that had passed by the third day, replaced by fear of a world war. Adolf Hitler had already annexed Austria and was advocating the right of Czechoslovakia's Sudeten Germans to reunite with their brothers and sisters in greater Germany. The latter was an obvious attempt at a takeover, and while many Europeans feared the worst, the Western Allies were not yet prepared to fight. Instead, Britain's prime minister, Neville Chamberlain, flew to Munich. Along with the leaders of Italy and France, he agreed to allow Hitler to take over the Sudetenland in exchange for a promise from the German chancellor to leave the rest of Czechoslovakia untouched. Together, Chamberlain declared, the Allies had made peace with honour, peace for our time.

The reaction on the ship was ecstatic. Holmes joined other students in raiding the first class section and celebrating with champagne. All the while, however, he retained a degree of his ever-present caution. He wrote home: "I haven't quite figured out yet whether Mr. Chamberlain is going to be right in the long run. All I know is that I am joining most hastily in the mass sigh of incredible relief."[33] There was for him still too great a possibility of war. Peace could be assured only when people had changed their ways of thinking. Sir Frederick Banting, the Canadian Nobel Prize winner and co-discoverer of insulin, who happened to be aboard the same ship, was more optimistic and less restrained. The students had to put him to sleep after he celebrated with too much enthusiasm. Banting later perished in an air disaster in Newfoundland while working as a liaison officer between the British and the Americans during the conflict.

Following a brief stay with family in Scotland, Holmes arrived at the University of London's King's College with mixed feelings. After touring the city's upscale West End, his romantic vision of an older, slower metropolis was replaced by an acknowledgment of the modernity of one of the largest industrialized centres in the world. It was not quite New York, and for this he was grateful – the hectic nature of that American city always left him slightly uncomfortable – but it took some adjusting before he was fully at ease.[34]

Mary Greey, later Mary Graham, helped his transition. She was, he learned, a close friend of Lester Pearson, and their friendship was one of many that kept him happy and occupied over the next year. She recalls

Holmes as an outstanding dancer and a disarmingly charming companion who was comfortable in London's social scene. His light tweed jackets made him look like an Englishman, he loved the theatre, enjoyed long walks in England's delightful countryside, and fascinated young and old alike during intellectual discussions (often about history) over tea. He kept up-to-date on current events by reading vociferously (the London press as it was published and the *Globe and Mail* when it arrived in the post from his father). He wrote letters home every week, often more than once, and took an interest in the progress of his growing family. All the while, however, he kept his distance, sharing his time among various social circles and never getting close enough to any one person to begin a serious relationship.

At school, he planned to study with Vincent Harlow, a recent arrival from Oxford who had joined the Department of Imperial History. Professor Harlow immediately set his new student to work reading background material, delaying a decision on the focus of Holmes' thesis until he had a real sense of the young man's ability. The relationship, though civilized, was brief. When Harlow failed to arrive for class the following week, an apparently typical occurrence among some of the university's senior professors, Holmes entered into a fascinating discussion with one of his assistants. Within a matter of minutes, he had been convinced to transfer to University College where he could study under H. Hale Bellot, Commonwealth Professor of American History. Harlow took the decision well – he had too many students already – kept a space for Holmes in his seminar and even obtained for him an invitation to another in diplomatic history. Holmes set to work on a study of the relations of British North America and the West Indies with the United States during the American Civil War.[35]

Unlike Harlow, Bellot had a clear plan for Holmes' time at University College. He was to spend two years in London fulfilling his residency requirement, doing research, and reaping the full benefits of the British postgraduate experience by reading, writing, and associating actively within the academic community. His study would draw heavily on newspaper accounts, public and private letters, and the limited secondary material available. Once the two years had passed, Holmes would return to North America to examine the Canadian and American records before coming back to London briefly for what was called his viva voce, or oral defence.

The schedule suited Holmes' tastes and interests. Bellot had given him the freedom to continue to indulge his journalistic fancy – he published in the literary supplement to the *Gazette* back at home and in the *London Free*

Press while he was away – and encouraged his activities with the Institute of Historical Research (IHR), a social hub for young London historians. Holmes co-founded a Commonwealth group within the IHR to discuss the future of the former empire. The participants were more progressive than were those of the Old Royal Empire Society. Their meetings provided a place for over twenty students from Bermuda, Ceylon, Jamaica, South Africa, India, and a number of other colonies and countries to socialize and learn about each other's history and culture in a friendly and supportive environment.[36]

The students shared their collective disgust when they learned of the pogroms against German Jews that November. Holmes called them massacres in his letters home and privately condemned the rather casual British response. "This country, I am afraid," he wrote his sister Elizabeth, "has lost its nerve and its morale and only a complete cynicism and fatalism prevail. I'm glad I'm just visiting."[37] His idealism was nurtured in the Commonwealth Group, where British pretensions and frowning upon the lower classes were rejected as illiberal, snobbish, and heartless. Holmes' old Quaker mentors would have been welcome here, and he himself felt comfortable.

He returned to Canada for Christmas and spent what became a working holiday visiting with family and reading extensively at the Ontario Archives. When he was not deep into the newspapers of the 1860s, or setting the famous Christmas quiz, he was making plans for the rest of his doctoral experience. Money was short, and although he very much wanted to spend a year at Harvard, Yale, or Cornell completing the research for his dissertation, since none of these schools seemed able to offer him a fellowship, he considered a temporary return to Pickering. The school had made him a tempting offer, and its location just outside of Toronto would have allowed him to continue to pursue his studies, albeit more slowly. But Holmes did not want to live in Newmarket again, and he was not the type to make decisions based on money alone. Upon his arrival in London, he applied for a British Council Dominion Scholarship and set back to work on his thesis. "My single ambition," he wrote on his application, "is to return to Canada and resume teaching in either a secondary school or a university."[38]

It was here in London in early 1939 that Holmes had his first experience as an expert on Canadian foreign policy. On behalf of the University College Historical Society, his friend and senior colleague, Robin Humphreys, invited him to give a lecture on Canada's international role. While Holmes liked to claim that he despised public speaking, his success in high school and his comfort in the classroom demonstrated that he was a natural; and, indeed, he was quite at ease in front of an audience. The style of the talk characterized his approach to public lectures throughout the rest of his life and was one of the reasons that his voice was respected by Canadians of a variety of political inclinations. As he explained in a letter to his parents, he felt it best not to present his own viewpoint on the state of affairs; rather, he wrote, "I just tried to sum up Canada's traditional policy and then analyze the arguments for and against each of the possible policies we might follow in the future."[39] The forty-five-minute lecture provoked a spirited set of questions, which he answered with pleasure. Not long after, he accepted another invitation to speak, this time on the Empire and American foreign policy. His confidence growing, he submitted a long essay on lessons for Canada from the American Civil War to *Saturday Night*, a leading magazine at home. To his delight it was accepted, and that summer John Holmes made his public debut as a political commentator with the message that "the fundamental basis of liberal democracy is a belief in the ultimate power of reasonable persuasion rather than force."[40]

Wendell and Helen Holmes were excited and proud of their son's success, but they were also worried. The situation in Europe seemed to be deteriorating, and he was too close to the danger. The younger Holmes was much less concerned, his faith in humanity having grown stronger thanks to his experience in the Commonwealth Group. "I don't think there is any need to worry in the immediate future," he wrote home on Valentine's Day. "Even the gloomiest pessimists here feel things will be all right for this year anyway ... I really think that Canada is probably suffering a reaction from the developing American panic ... Really I don't think there is any danger of a war while Mr. Chamberlain is in power, and there is very little chance of his going out of power without a heart attack."[41] One month later, Hitler invaded the rest of Czechoslovakia, and the philosophy of appeasement became a source of political embarrassment.

German aggression did not prevent Mr. and Mrs. Holmes from crossing the Atlantic to visit their son in the spring. It was a great experience for everyone, full of travel through the country, trips to the galleries and the theatre, and visits with new friends. Holmes' mother and father met his professors, spoke with his colleagues, and left confident that he was safe and content. The vacation was a pleasant break from reality for all. By the time the Holmes parents returned to Ontario, Hitler had made overtures to Italy's fascist dictator, Benito Mussolini, and had initiated plans to take over Poland. In response, Britain and France accelerated their rearmament process in anticipation of a major war.

The chaos throughout Europe echoed in Holmes' personal life. Just weeks after Holmes' scholarship application was rejected, Professor Bellot informed him that he would be spending a term in the United States. Professor Humphreys would take over direct supervision until his return the following January.[42] With no money, no supervisor, research to be done across the Atlantic, and Europe headed for war, it was time to think seriously about returning home. Holmes began the paperwork for study leave in Canada and spent July and August travelling across England and France. He was wandering through the Loire Valley when Hitler attacked Poland, and he managed to return to London just in time to pack up his things before the conflict escalated.

He arrived at his residence the day that Britain and France declared war, an event that effectively ended his career as a graduate student. "I shall never forget those 24 hours in London," he wrote home the next day. "Like everyone else I had almost no sleep. There was a group of boys at London House all feeling quite aimless, except the doctors who had jobs. In the morning I went to the bank and took the precaution of securing all my money ... in order to pass the time I helped all day packing sandbags. We finished this job at about 4.30 and then just sat down with nothing to do but wait for the first air raid."[43]

Within days, the university had closed and Holmes left for neutral Ireland. Having all but given up on finishing his studies in London – the university itself was evacuating to Wales – he elected to make the best of what had become an extended holiday. He knew it was wrong to enjoy himself with war so close by, but Dublin was peaceful, the newspapers revealed little, and his future was uncertain. Thanks to Professor Bellot, he received a message from the vice-provost of Trinity College, University of Dublin, inviting him to continue his studies as a transfer student in Ireland, but it was too late.[44] He knew that he was coming home, and less than a week after the University of London accepted his leave application, he left Europe for New York. After a brief stop at the World's Fair he returned to Canada to contemplate his future. He had enjoyed his experience in England, but the troubling international situation made it clear that it was time to move on.

He reached London, Ontario, late enough to prevent a return to Pickering until the following year and settled back in his parents' house without a clear idea of what was to come. With little money, no job, and – perhaps because of the death of his uncle in the first war, maybe because of the pacifist influences of Pickering and the Commonwealth Group, or even possibly, as he later claimed, because of his poor eyesight – no serious thoughts of joining the military, academic work was the obvious option. He spent most of the next few months at the University of Western Ontario, researching and writing in the library. If the war continued, he could always return to Pickering. Otherwise, there was still a faint chance that he could complete his PhD.[45]

Eventually, he found a better option. The Canadian Institute of International Affairs (CIIA) was founded in 1928 as a discussion forum for citizens interested in the Empire and world affairs. Under the leadership of the workaholic Escott Reid, by 1939 it had established branches across the country and was hosting a speakers series and study sessions to keep them active. Reid and Holmes shared similar cultural backgrounds. Both were educated, in part, overseas, and neither completed his final degree. The most significant difference between the two was in temperament. Holmes had strong views but abhorred conflict; Reid was inflammatory and often unwilling to compromise. Holmes' natural humility contrasted with Reid's arrogance. Both were idealistic, but while the former restrained his idealism (and his youthful commitment to socialism) just as he did his emotions, the latter's political views (he was initially socialist and neutralist) and perpetual emotional explosions (which continued throughout his career) made him intolerable to some of his colleagues and superiors.[46]

Under Reid, the CIIA took its role in society seriously and promoted Canadian involvement in world affairs as widely as possible. After he resigned to join the DEA, the National Council of the CIIA decided to expand into the field of public education. "The greatest service we can render to our nation at a time like the present," wrote leading member Edgar J. Tarr just before the war began, "is to be an influence preventing the general development of a narrowness of national outlook which would make impossible an appreciation of the real causes of international rivalry and friction – a lack of understanding of which by Canadians would prevent Canada from playing its part, large or small, in unravelling the tangle of world affairs."[47] How it could do this without becoming a vehicle of government propaganda was not clear at first, but a $9,000 grant spread over three years from the US philanthropic Carnegie Corporation (an American organization) made finding a solution a priority.

A committee, including the chair of the National Executive, J.M. Macdonnell; the chair of the Public Education Committee, C.S. MacInnes; and the national secretary, John Baldwin; began plans for a CIIA information service. They envisioned a drastically expanded library and a publication program directed at average Canadians. The Carnegie grant could fund acquisitions, publications, and a secretary to manage the project. As they considered potential candidates, Baldwin thought of his former Camp Ahmek colleague, John Holmes. Holmes received an invitation to apply and did so immediately. A formal letter of resignation to Pickering followed shortly thereafter.[48]

On 12 July 1940, John Holmes attended a CIIA National Executive Committee meeting at which he was introduced as the new information secretary. His salary of $125 per month was considerably less than what he received at Pickering, but the job was exciting and allowed him to make a contribution to the war effort that was better suited to his attitude and temperament than was becoming a soldier. Forty-five years later, when he reflected on his decisions to join the CIIA and, later, the public service, he wrote: "In the traditional way I should say that I was bitterly disappointed and wanted to go to war, but I was not. I have no doubt that I was more useful to my country doing what I did, even if it was unheroic. Still I always recall what was said to me by my dear friend, Raleigh Parkin, who had survived War Number One … 'I know, however, what it must be like to miss the great experience of your generation.' As a commentator it has left me partially paralyzed."[49]

Holmes was added to the public education and research committees and was invited to attend the monthly gatherings of the National Council and National Executive. His first tasks included revitalizing the institute's library and founding a new, accessible publication series. Following in the tradition of his father, he took inventory, ordered new books, subscribed to a number of journals, and purchased a series of official publications. He also established a two-part clipping service, one focused on world affairs and the other on public opinion. Finally, he continued to distribute daily and weekly press releases to the more significant Canadian newspapers, expanding the scope of the practice to include the French-language media. The reputation of the institute's information service grew quickly, and American analysts studying world affairs added the CIIA to their list of resources.[50]

Working closely with the chair of the public education committee, Terry MacDermot, Holmes also drafted "Bushels to Burn," the first volume of what has since become known as the *Behind the Headlines* series. It was published that September in conjunction with the Canadian Association for Adult Education. The essay focused on the massive wheat surplus that had been harvested in Canada on account of the war. "One thing is certain," Holmes wrote. "We cannot abandon the wheat-growers, the store-keepers and bankers and school-teachers who serve them, as well as the thousands of workers in the East who make farm-machinery and binder-twine. If they cannot live on wheat, other provisions must be made for them ... All of Canada has prospered with wheat and all of Canada should share the costs in time of adversity."[51] By the fall, the CIIA had begun to distribute issues of the pamphlet across Ontario, charging ten cents per copy. At about the same time, Holmes commissioned the publication of a second set of essays for a democracy and citizenship series linked to a set of Canadian Broadcasting Corporation (CBC) broadcasts called "Citizens All," as well as for the world affairs series published by Oxford University Press.[52]

His salary was increased when he became the CIIA's permanent information secretary in November, and by early 1941 he had settled into a comfortable, regular routine. With Escott Reid no longer involved, the CIIA had become a more moderate organization, perfectly suited to the new secretary's views of the world. In May, Holmes co-authored another *Behind the Headlines* volume, "Dynamic Democracy." His essay explored the temptation to use barbarism to combat the evils of Nazism, advocating resistance to any urges to abandon the ideals and philosophy that made democracy great. "Honesty must be the basis of all international relations and of the whole civilization for which Canada fights," Holmes argued for not the last time. "Civilized countries must stand for fundamental principles greater than party policies, principles which can be fearlessly enunciated and upheld." Canada's future success hinged on the pursuit of the "middle way of democracy," an approach to world affairs that required patience, faith, and dedication to common principles of decency. As Canadians began their profound transformation from inward-looking isolationists to engaged global contributors, Holmes' commitment to an internationalism grounded in the realities of the world around him grew as well.[53]

His hard work was noticed by his superiors. When National Secretary Baldwin accepted a position in the DEA, Holmes took his place on a temporary basis. A selection committee was then struck and offered the position to Fred Soward, an academic who would also find himself in the public service for much of the war. When Soward declined, the committee turned to Holmes. His attitude towards the opportunity was mixed. In a letter to his parents, he explained that the job was "generally looked upon as an entrée into some of the country's best jobs and all the previous secretaries have moved on to big things. But," he wrote,

> I am faced with the momentous decision as to whether I want to move on to big things ... Ambition, I discover, is not an overwhelming motive in my case. I would gladly spend the rest of my life with my clippings and my

pamphlets, perhaps finding a less strenuous route to fame and fortune. I'm afraid I've reached a crucial point in my "career," and I don't like crucial points ... I am firmly convinced that the Institute is a very good thing and should go on, and, judging from the last year's financial and membership results, there are a lot of other Canadians who feel the same way. If only I could do my bit under some one else's direction.[54]

His comments might not have been entirely truthful; rather, as he did before making most significant decisions, Holmes hesitated, clinging, if only for a moment, to a nostalgic vision of his allegedly simple, hassle-free past. It was a way for him to lower his expectations of what would come next, to eliminate any exuberance that might disrupt the progress his life had made to that point. In reality, the increased salary of $2,600 per year, additional responsibilities in the shaping of Canadian public thinking about world affairs and international postwar reconstruction, and the two-year contract offered to him by the committee were all too attractive. Holmes agreed in October 1941 to become national secretary retroactive to 1 September.[55]

Although his responsibilities increased, he did not neglect his commitment to research. True to his letter home, he continued to be involved in the institute's publications series, in applying for external funding, and in arranging for guest speakers. In December 1941 he initiated plans to secure a renewal of a multi-year $20,000 grant from the Rockefeller Foundation to support the CIIA's research program. The money paid for more than half of the institute's yearly expenses.

In January 1942, the CIIA played host to one of Canada's leading civil servants, Lester (Mike) Pearson. Wendell and Helen Holmes were family friends of the Pearsons, and their sons first met the summer before when Pearson passed through the CIIA office. Like Escott Reid, Pearson had a lot in common with John Holmes. Both grew up in houses that promoted the social gospel and were strongly committed to serving their country. Both preferred negotiation to conflict, and both handled themselves well in small groups, including the media. The most significant difference between them was ambition: Pearson naturally led from the front while Holmes was more comfortable facilitating from within.

Pearson's lecture was so stirring that Holmes attempted to arrange for its publication.[56] The negotiations were unsuccessful – as a civil servant, it was awkward for Pearson to allow his talk to be distributed publicly – but the conversations were hardly wasted. The two developed a degree of mutual admiration that served both of their futures well.

As Pearson's profile in the DEA grew, so too did Holmes' at the CIIA. The national secretary began a country-wide tour of the institute's branches in February, listening patiently to organizers' complaints and encouraging the studies of reconstruction that were taking place under the auspices of the fast-expanding CIIA nationwide. In spite of the war, membership increased from 1,190 in 1939 to 1370 in 1942. Holmes' travels, which took him east before he landed in British Columbia, exposed him to some of the country's leading public figures. As his reputation grew, his visits became more popular. Stories of his work at the institute eventually reached Chicago, where he was invited to speak at the Library of International Relations. Still the keeper of the CIIA library at heart, Holmes arranged an exchange of materials with the Illinois librarians.[57]

He returned to find the internationalist and publicly focused vision of the CIIA, with its well-attended study conferences and roundtable discussions, becoming increasingly attractive to the national government. In September, Prime Minister Mackenzie King created the Wartime Information Board (WIB) with the goal of promoting Canada's global achievements and enhancing the national commitment to postwar internationalism. The WIB brought legitimacy to the CIIA's aims, and an inordinate number of government officials pledged to discuss the role of the smaller states in the future world order at Mount Tremblant that December. Tremblant had been chosen largely because this was to be a multicultural conference, with delegates from as far way as India planning to participate, and there were few prominent locations in Quebec that appeared willing to accommodate guests of what Holmes later called "various colours with different religious faiths."[58] The National Executive of the CIIA, which was sponsoring the conference through its affiliate, the Institute of Pacific Relations (IPR), asked him to lead its delegation, offering him an exciting opportunity to speak to the most esteemed and well-connected audience he had ever faced.

At almost the same time, Holmes was solicited to help establish Canada's Wartime Prices and Trade Board in Washington. The body had been created just before the onset of the Second World War to help limit inflation and prevent the social unrest that had exploded at the end of the last major conflict. In the early years of the new war, the federal civil service expanded at an unprecedented rate, drawing extensively from Canada's relatively small academic elite. As one historian has noted, "The majority of the intellectual community, the needs of modern society, and the public mood all dictated that the state continue to expand its role and that the expert adviser would be central to the expansion."[59] With the help of Wynne Plumptre, who knew Holmes from his days at the University of Toronto, the chair of the board, the youthful and determined Donald Gordon, pursued Holmes aggressively, going so far as to invite him to Ottawa for a personal meeting and then privately negotiating his release from the CIIA with some of the organization's executive. While in Ottawa, however, Holmes spoke with another professor he had met at the University of Toronto, George Glazebrook, who had recently been seconded from the university into the DEA. Glazebrook told him to delay responding to Gordon because external affairs was in the process of recruiting a number of talented academics as temporary wartime assistants, and he was near the top of the list of potential recruits.[60] Escott Reid, who had also spoken with him, concurred.

Not knowing what to do, Holmes wrote Lester Pearson. "Being considerably over age," he explained, "I had not thought of applying to the Department for a position, and, because of my work at the institute, I was not hunting for a new post. But if I am to leave here, I want to make sure that I get into the most useful kind of service. My poor eyesight means that I can join the army only in some administrative capacity, and I think personally I can accomplish more in some civilian post. I have no illusions about my capacities and don't want to suggest that I think I should be a particular blessing to any government agency, but with the present shortage of available persons, there seems to be a premium even on the dullest of us. When I say, therefore, that I should like to go wherever I am needed most, I hope you will understand that the statement is made with due modesty."[61] It was a typically Holmesian letter: cautious, modest, yet at the same time not without ambition. Certainly, he was nervous about this next step, but it appears that Holmes used these exchanges to make himself feel more comfortable with a decision that he had already made.

Pearson wrote back, noting that, although Holmes would make an excellent contribution to any government department, the best fit would be at the DEA.[62] Since appointments took time, and Donald Gordon would not wait until Holmes received confirmation that there was a spot for him in Ottawa, Pearson personally contacted the under-secretary of state for external affairs, Norman Robertson, and asked that the process be expedited. The day that Pearson's letter arrived, Robertson's assistant, Saul Rae, requested that Holmes come to Ottawa for an interview with the Civil Service Commission. Along with two members of the commission, Holmes met for an hour with Robertson, his associate under-secretary,

Hume Wrong, and a number of other well-placed foreign service officers. Holmes made an excellent impression. Although there would be a position avaiable, he was warned that civil service regulations stipulated that it would be temporary and that he would have to reapply if he wished to stay on after the war.

For Holmes, the restrictions acted as an incentive. Whether he would admit it or not, he felt most comfortable and indeed confident when he had a means of escape. "Frankly I am interested in a war job at the moment and not in a career," he wrote Pearson, knowing that since he had already been parachuted into the DEA, if he performed well he would be virtually guaranteed employment after the war.[63]

On 14 October, about two weeks after his interview, Norman Robertson offered John Holmes the post of special wartime assistant. It came with a slight reduction in pay, from the $2,600 that Holmes had been earning to $2,520, the salary of a typical foreign service officer with two years of experience. Along with the letter went another to the CIIA asking for his release while acknowledging that Holmes might need to remain with the institute through the new year to attend the conference at Mount Tremblant and support the transition to a successor. Holmes received the contract from the DEA two days later and accepted ten days after that, with the caveat that he remain in Toronto until January. The CIIA's National Executive was informed of his resignation officially at a meeting in mid-November, and his appointment as special assistant was formalized on 2 December with a 1 January 1943 start date and provision for him to arrive a few weeks late, if necessary.[64]

His experience at the IPR conference, his last major duty as the CIIA's national secretary, was mixed. The event solidified the commitment of all of Canada's major political parties to a more internationalist outlook in world affairs and set the stage for his subsequent work at the DEA. Less positively, the IPR's international membership included a number of communist sympathizers, some of whom fought with Holmes over whether the Japanese were really to blame for the attack on the United States at Pearl Harbor.[65] Their comments were noticed by the FBI, which was present at Tremblant, and there are references to John Holmes in its files.

Holmes did not forget the difficulties in Quebec, but he was on his way to Ottawa in January 1943, and he had left the CIIA in an enviable condition. Attendance at Tremblant had been record-breaking, and international interest and participation had reached unprecedented levels. His research committee published four books and three pamphlets in his final year, most of which were translated into French and distributed out of

Montreal. There were new links to the Ontario Secondary Schools Teachers' Federation. Membership had increased to 1,365. The Carnegie grant
had been renewed, and a new $20,000 Rockefeller grant to supplement
it had been secured.[66] There was a new headquarters on Bloor Street,
and morale at the institute was good. Finally, the new national secretary,
Douglas MacLennan, was well suited to the position. John Holmes exited
the CIIA with a genuine sense of accomplishment, personal momentum,
and a bright future. He had already developed an outstanding network of
friends and colleagues whose connections would contribute almost immediately to the expansion of the influence of his thinking about Canada
and the world.

2

External Affairs' New Golden Boy

I f there was ever a place for the thirty-two-year-old John Holmes to call home in early 1943 it was the East Block of Parliament Hill. Although he missed his family dearly, he had an ideal job as special wartime assistant in the Department of External Affairs, and he found his colleagues delightful. The atmosphere around him was also positive. When he arrived at the office in early February, the Second World War was turning in the Allies' favour. The Germans had surrendered at Stalingrad and the Americans had launched their first bombing raids at Wilhelmshaven. The new recruit immediately began what Charles Ritchie called "an education in public service." Led by Norman Robertson, the inhabitants of the East Block remained unpretentious in spite of their exceptional abilities. "We are not trying to be anything special," Robertson once explained. The job was to serve Canada as best they could.[1] Long hours were to be expected, stimulating intellectual discussions were mandatory, and good writing was a necessity. The officers shared a dedication to Canada, to playing a meaningful role in world affairs, and to the spirit of the British Empire. For a progressive English Canadian internationalist, it was a once-in-a-lifetime opportunity.

The department was not without its problems. There was an uneasy divide between the utopians, led by the former CIIA president Escott Reid and tolerated by Lester Pearson – both of whom had conveniently been posted to Washington – and the pragmatists, who took their instructions in Ottawa from Robertson and his associate under-secretary Hume Wrong. Although almost always respectful, and close friends outside of the office, the civil service leaders could differ significantly on the practical means of attaining their goals. There was also some personal awkwardness between Pearson and Robertson. Older and more experienced, Pearson had fully expected to be appointed under-secretary in 1941 and was at times uncomfortable working under someone he considered his junior.[2]

Then there was Mackenzie King. The aging prime minister and secretary of state for external affairs was petty. As Holmes quickly learned, it was common practice for the officers in Ottawa to work evenings and parts of each weekend – they were formally scheduled to take such shifts in addition to their assigned duties – but instead of encouraging or praising their dedication, King would famously call the office at night and on Sundays to see who was there. The prime minister was also well known for taking his most senior civil servants to expensive restaurants and forcing them to sign the bills, allowing him to continue to claim publicly that he never wasted Canadian taxpayers' hard-earned dollars. His attendance at séances during which he conversed with the dead impressed Holmes and others even less.[3] If there was one thing upon which virtually everyone in the civil service could agree, it was that their leader was hardly inspirational. Fortunately for the new recruits to external affairs, he was also remote and exercised little direct influence on their personal development.[4]

Holmes' first experiences in the department were positive. When he reported for duty, he was welcomed by Marcel Cadieux. Cadieux was well thought of by all and, as one of the few francophones in the East Block at the time, fully conscious of how it felt to be different. The two officials shared an office in the early days, and Holmes could not have had a more open and accepting companion. It was Cadieux, he recalled much later, who set out for him what he called the facts of life in the foreign service.[5] In a book on the Canadian diplomat that he published twenty years later, Cadieux explained: "Diplomats in some respects continue to be civil servants, of a special kind; they must carry out their duties in conditions which impose upon them a need to be well informed, to serve with distinction, to represent their country appropriately; at home they would not normally bear the costs of these duties. Canadian diplomats must work with the modest means at their disposal, with limited leisure time, and with somewhat special administrative responsibilities." His book describes an honourable, elite profession in which officers were role models for the people and country they represented. "Personal and professional worth, an ability to represent the varied cultural elements of the country, an attachment to democracy, a sense of the practicable – these are all components characteristic of the image of our diplomatic officers as conceived by the

Department," he wrote. This description would have resonated with John Holmes, and he quickly adapted to the rigours and high expectations of his position.[6]

Down the hall from Holmes and Cadieux was Fred Soward, a wartime assistant himself and an admirer of his new colleague's intellectual abilities. Professor Soward provided encouragement, helping Holmes gather the courage to send draft memoranda on a wide range of foreign policy issues to his superiors, whether they had asked for them specifically or not. Such behaviour was risky. When the more senior Escott Reid shared his unsolicited opinions he provoked frustration – largely because his letters were copious, long, and often unrealistic. Soward knew that Holmes was different. His clear thinking and sound writing brought him immediate respect from Wrong and Robertson.[7]

Because Holmes' application to the department had been fast-tracked, exactly what he would be doing when he arrived was not entirely clear. By default, he became executive assistant to the under-secretary of state for external affairs. As an impressionable young officer, he learned a lot from his first mentor. A former Rhodes Scholar, Norman Robertson was well respected for his mastery of not only the state of Canadian foreign policy but also virtually any government business. He had come to his position almost accidentally after the death of his own mentor, Dr. Oscar Douglas Skelton, and recognized the importance of developing a rapport with his staff, from the most experienced colleagues through to the newest administrative assistants. Holmes never forgot the way that Robertson kept track of the personal lives of his entire team. "He knew when every secretary's father died and agonized for her," he recalled thirty years later. It was a means of inspiring loyalty and dedication that the new recruit emulated throughout the rest of his life.

Criticism of Robertson's work as under-secretary has tended to focus on his deficiencies as an administrator. His desk was known to be a disaster, with piles of paper seemingly spread out aimlessly across it. Holmes understood his colleague differently. "One of the things he taught me," he once explained, "was the art of creative delay. People would come storming up and ask, 'What has happened to that memorandum I put on his desk on Thursday? Nothing's been done about it.' And I would say, 'Well, I'll try to put it on top of the pile.' It would go back – he knew exactly where it was, it was intended to be there – and a week or so later you knew why he'd put it there because the action was impulsive and it would go away."[8] Whether such a form of office management was effective is debatable, but it suited Holmes' temperament. Much to the chagrin of his future employees, he later adopted it as his own.

His job for Robertson was largely as a drafter of speeches intended for the prime minister, a testament to the trust and respect that he earned so quickly. Holmes created a first effort, Robertson revised, and, if it was good enough – usually meaning cautious enough not to offend anyone – it later made its way into the hands of the politically savvy Mackenzie King. Because of his work at the CIIA, Holmes' specific expertise was thought to be international organization. He became a reliable source of analysis and information on the evolving plans to form a successor to the failed League of Nations – the United Nations Organization. The constitutional research he had done in London also made him a credible commentator on the development of dominion status within the Commonwealth. In his speeches for King, Holmes stressed the increasingly important role of the smaller powers in world affairs, the impact of the United States on the international order, and the dangers of regionalism – themes that he returned to consistently in his later career.[9] He also never lost faith in the Commonwealth. One draft speech from his early months in the department concluded:

> The British Commonwealth has stood together in grim times for the greater good of mankind; and it may have to do so again. A time when we are trying hard to create lasting bonds between countries is no time to break the bonds which hold together the one league of nations which survived the last decade … The only reason for breaking the bonds of Commonwealth would be if they stood in the way of a larger unity. They will only do so if the Empire closes ranks, forms a front against the rest of the world, and forbids its members the right to participate freely in the cooperative effort of all nations to assure peace and prosperity.[10]

Since Robertson did not know exactly how to best employ Holmes in those first months, he often allowed Hume Wrong to borrow his assistant. Robertson and Wrong formed an intriguing partnership. Unlike the under-secretary, Wrong was hardly tactful. He was brilliant but impatient, easily frustrated by mediocrity and under-achievement. He demanded the utmost from his staff and was a harsh critic of poor writing. At the same time, he had tremendous respect for the sincerity, dedication, and capacity for hard work that Robertson put forth so consistently. The two shared a degree of dignity and integrity that was virtually unmatched in their time. Their partnership as leaders of the department was tremendously successful.

That Wrong would warm to Holmes is not surprising. Less than two weeks after the young Holmes arrived, he was asked to draft a paper on public attitudes towards the organization of the future international order and Canada's role within it. The assignment reflected the East Block's concern with the postwar world and with the shift in Canadian public sentiment from self-interested isolationism to activist internationalism. Holmes' first effort was more thorough than even Wrong could have anticipated. For the next eight months he became the department's unofficial analyst of media commentary on international organization. His suggestion that Canadians of all ages and backgrounds supported a leadership role for their country on the world stage resonated with his superiors and formed the basis of departmental recommendations from that point forward. Wrong took his famous blue pencil to Holmes' writing just like the new official had to his own students' work at Pickering, and the junior civil servant became an even better drafter for it.[11]

In July, as the Allies landed in Sicily, Wrong recruited Holmes to serve as secretary to a post-hostilities planning committee. The British had long been sharing copies of their discussions on the postwar period with Ottawa, but until that summer the department lacked a way to respond to the briefs, let alone make its own plans. As secretary to the committee that would do the bulk of Canada's postwar strategic thinking, Holmes became one of the drivers of the first formal Canadian foreign policy planning process. Throughout the next year, he attended thirty-one meetings with some of the sharpest political minds in the civil service and the military as they developed Canadian policy towards international organization, postwar defence arrangements with the United States, Newfoundland (a British colony until 1949), and a fast-emerging conflict between the Western powers and a Soviet Union that was increasingly disappointed in their unwillingness to land troops in western Europe.

Having served on both the advisory and working committees on post-hostilities problems, Holmes helped shape Canada's postwar approach to world affairs. It was a functionalist strategy, based primarily on Wrong's thinking. As a relatively small power in world affairs, Canada could not expect to have the privileges or influence of great powers like the United States or Great Britain. This explained why the post-hostilities planners responded to British memoranda instead of initiating policy discussions on their own. Nevertheless, there were still issues upon which, by reason of its wealth or perhaps its abundance of natural resources, Canada was a major player. In those cases, since it could make a significant contribution, it deserved a significant voice. Proportionality was key: the functional principle was an approach to Canadian participation in world affairs that reflected the realities of the day in a reasonable and fair manner. It became the basis of Holmes' global outlook from that point forward and later served as a guiding principle for many of his public commentaries.[12]

By the end of 1943, with Italy now at war with its former German ally, and a Nazi defeat gaining an air of inevitability, John Holmes had established himself as one of the department's rising stars. As the special wartime assistant responsible for both intra-Commonwealth affairs and post-hostilities planning, his duties included writing speeches, drafting memoranda, analyzing British foreign policy, and taking minutes during the committee meetings. Overall, Robertson wrote in his first evaluation, "He has proved to be a very valuable and industrious member of the Department."[13] The normally critical Hume Wrong had "no hesitation in reporting enthusiastically on Holmes. It is surprising how quickly and intelligently he has adapted himself to work in the Department, in view of his ... lack of experience in this sort of work. He is well-informed, most industrious, and the possessor of a good English style. He also has an [attractive] personality, gets on easily with people, and is taking just the right sort of initiative. I strongly recommend that he should be added to the permanent staff of the Department, if he is agreeable."[14]

As a sign of respect for Holmes' abilities and in recognition of his connections at the CIIA, in December, Wrong sent the young man to an exclusive institute-sponsored conference at Montebello, Quebec. His job was to continue to develop the relationship between the civil service and the internationalist intellectuals and to report back on the nature of popular thinking about the postwar. Once again, he performed admirably. John Holmes had quickly grown into the role of junior expert on Canada's current and future role in the world. He had not yet achieved the same stature as Hume Wrong or Norman Robertson, but when the London-based Charles Ritchie sent documents on British postwar thinking home to his superiors in Ottawa for consideration, Wrong made sure that his able secretary was always included on the distribution list.[15]

It is hardly surprising that some of the ideas emanating from the post-hostilities planning committee's deliberations during this period became hallmarks of Holmes' future discussions of world affairs. In January 1944, for example, the working committee issued a report on what it called international policing. Its recommendations alluded to the peacekeeping ideal that would be pursued by Lester Pearson in the years to follow and also to the external realities that would make the North Atlantic Treaty Organization a political necessity. Specifically, the committee envisioned the creation of a "United Nations Security Force" of officers from all of the member countries that would have full access to airports and airfields around the world. Staffed largely by the great powers, it would nonetheless include the smaller states, whose militaries would participate when their interests were at stake. Since their thinking was obviously idealistic (others might say visionary), the writers also foresaw the subdivision of the United Nations (UN) into regional defence spheres with organized forces acting as first-response teams in the case of smaller crises.[16] That Canada's region would have to reach beyond North America was made clear in a later study. A bilateral[17] security arrangement would leave the smaller partner vulnerable in any US-USSR military conflict, and it was therefore in Canada's best interests to establish a broader international security framework. This was the philosophy behind the North Atlantic Treaty over three years before the negotiations to found it began.[18]

As Canadian planners were contemplating the future world order in early 1944, the great powers developed actual policy. Both Britain and the United States produced detailed proposals on the shape of a new global security organization. Since Canada was not a great power, and its prime minister hardly advocated Canadian influence on security issues, the members of the East Block were not fully up-to-date on the thinking of their most significant allies. A conference of Commonwealth prime ministers scheduled for 1 May was expected to change that. As one of the department's Commonwealth and international organizations experts, Holmes was a logical choice to accompany Robertson to London. His departure was booked for 25 April. That night, there were radio reports that a plane bound for the United Kingdom had crashed, killing everyone aboard. Members of the Holmes family agonized for a number of days before they received a note explaining that their Jack had taken an earlier flight and was happily settled and renewing old friendships across the Atlantic.

The opening of the conference was awkward for the Canadian delegation. Prime Minister King's refusal to commit his country to an imperial foreign policy did not endear him to colleagues from Australia and New Zealand. Nonetheless, Australia's prime minister, John Curtin, was less dedicated to a united stance than most analysts had anticipated, and by the end of the first week the dominions were largely cooperating in their rejection of Winston Churchill's regional approach to international order. In spite of their pressure, and contrary to the advice of his closest advisors, the British prime minister refused to abandon his vision of the three leading powers – Britain, the United States, and the Soviet Union – dominating a series of geographically dispersed security councils.[19] On the morning of 11 May 1944, the dominions spoke with British foreign secretary Anthony Eden about a more universal world organization. Although Eden's positive response was almost perfectly in line with previous Canadian thinking, Mackenzie King said almost nothing.[20]

Sitting just behind him, Norman Robertson sensed that an opportunity was being missed. He immediately sent a note to the back row, where Holmes was quietly listening. The Canadian prime minister was scheduled to address the British Parliament that afternoon, and his text would have to include what he had failed to say in the morning. Holmes went to work, highlighting Canada's commitment to collective security as well as its loyalty to the British Empire. He presented the Commonwealth as an example of effective international cooperation. A late lunch that day meant that King did not have time to read the text before he delivered it. The result was what Winston Churchill referred to as "the great climax of the development and demonstration of the power of Canada," and what one Canadian journalist called "possibly one of the momentous utterances of his long political career."[21] Holmes wrote home humbly, not even mentioning that he had drafted the speech without oversight: "I must say that the P.M. was in very good form himself. He received quite an ovation, and the whole thing was really very moving."[22] It was only later in life, when he better understood his role as interpreter of Canada to the world, that he was comfortable taking credit for what he had accomplished.

His reward for the excellent work was an invitation to stay longer in London. The highlight of the period was a meeting with the Royal Family. It was an exclusive affair, which meant that there was time for personal conversations. Holmes spent five minutes speaking alone with the Queen. The content of the conversation was hardly memorable, but the way in which the Royals presented themselves was. The "ladies and gentlemen in waiting" were experts in controlling the flow of people to and from their political masters without seeming intrusive or obstructionist, he wrote to his family.[23] It was a form of behaviour management that was equally applicable in the university classroom. When he later became a professor, Holmes' students noted how they had thought at the time that their discussions had roamed freely, only to realize afterwards that their instructor had kept them on track in his own subtle way.

Upon his return to Ottawa, Holmes became Hume Wrong's right hand on questions of the future world order. He penned preliminary responses to the great power proposals at Dumbarton Oaks, the exclusive conference that established the rough blueprint for the UN, and drafted briefs on potential Canadian positions on a variety of postwar issues. Conceptually, his thinking did not change. Collective security was still preferable to regionalism and, as a result, while the UN was crucial, Canada had to limit its exposure to organizations (like the Pan-American Union) that had defence implications. The great powers had to take the lead in shaping the new world order. The middle states, while secondary actors, could never allow themselves to be taken for granted. And the functional principle had to form the basis of any discussions of representation.[24]

There was one exception. When it came to Canada's role in the future occupation of Germany, Holmes abandoned his typically neutral pragmatism for more political thinking. "It is true," he wrote to Wrong, "that, in this connection, there is no special Canadian interest distinct from that of the other United Nations; we all want to keep Germany from repeating her crimes. It might be argued that, as our interests are the same as those of the Great Powers, we might safely leave to them the formulation of policy on our behalf in the interests of efficiency. This, however, is an argument which we cannot accept. We cannot concede this principle lest it be used against us in the world security organization." Functionalism, then, was at times less a policy of principle than a means of making Canada a more prominent world actor. That it suited Canadian interests was more important than that it was inherently good policy.[25]

By October 1944, with Paris liberated and the end of the war in sight, many of Holmes' academic colleagues contemplated a return to their old lives. He himself was no different. He made subtle inquiries about a teaching position at Western, and his prospects seemed reasonably promising. At the same time, external affairs was facing a personnel shortage, and Hume Wrong did not want to lose one of his protégés. When Wrong confronted him about his future plans, Holmes hesitated. The work in Ottawa had been rewarding, but he had always avoided making a permanent commitment. If he did prolong his stay, he needed assurance that he could continue to do the type of work he was doing. A year in Lima, Peru, for example, was not at all enticing. Wrong responded with uncharacteristic flattery. There was an unspoken distinction in the department between individuals whose roles were primarily social and those who did the real political work in Ottawa, London, and Washington. Holmes was unquestionably in the latter group, and Wrong hoped to take him along to any future international meetings that discussed the UN. Moreover, if he still wanted to leave in a year or two, the DEA would not have any hard feelings and would, in fact, help him find academic work. Holmes' skills were needed, and the department's leaders wanted him to stay.[26]

The decision was easy. Even before Holmes committed formally, Norman Robertson put into motion a plan that he had been contemplating since the spring. In early October, he requested that the Treasury Board fund three new positions at the second secretary level in the Office of the High Commissioner in London. It was time to bring Charles Ritchie home, and since there was no one with his experience to serve as a replacement, Robertson planned to send two or three lower-level officers in his place. It is not coincidental that Holmes had spent much of his second and third weeks in London speaking with High Commissioner Vincent Massey, an Oxford graduate and military veteran with a high impression of himself, his country, and the British Empire. The experience was, in part, an audition. The veteran official was eccentric, and it was critical that he thought highly of those working beneath him. Holmes passed the test. "I am very glad that you are sending John Holmes to Canada House as 'a partial replacement' for Ritchie," Massey wrote to Robertson. "He will, I am sure, do well and I like him personally. I realise that there is no-one available who has the combination of qualities which Ritchie possesses – maturity of judgment, great experience, indeed all the attributes which a diplomat should have – but Holmes I think should do well and, as I have said, we shall welcome him as a member of the staff here."[27] That December, after a glowing endorsement from Norman Robertson, Mackenzie King approved Holmes' promotion to temporary second secretary, an increase in his salary to $3,300 per year, and his posting to the Office of the High Commissioner for Canada in London. The news was received positively across the Atlantic, where Holmes was referred to by one British colleague as "an excellent example of the intelligent young Canadian official of present-day Ottawa."[28]

Before he set sail for the United Kingdom, John Holmes dealt with one final project in Ottawa. Thanks to Canada's increasing interest and involvement on the world stage, the DEA was expanding more rapidly than had been anticipated. With the demand for new officials exceeding the supply of ideal applicants, the qualifications for recruits were relaxed.[29] In addition, as the department grew, it became difficult to provide new officers with the same initial guidance that Holmes had received through his talks with Marcel Cadieux. Norman Robertson was concerned, and called on Holmes and another relatively junior officer, Gordon Robertson, to develop a formal training program for new diplomats.

Holmes embraced the challenge and proposed four major innovations. First, the DEA needed a handbook, something that the meticulous Gordon Robertson could produce quite easily. Second, the East Block could set up a tutorial, or mentorship, system to mimic Holmes' experience with Cadieux. Third, a seminar series could provide background information about most of the responsibilities that officers could be asked to take on. Holmes foresaw at least twelve sessions, to be offered once per week. Each would be facilitated by a departmental specialist. Wrong, for example, would lead a workshop on how to draft letters and memoranda. Glaze-brook would brief on security. John Read, the DEA's international law expert, would advise on legal issues and implications. Holmes' old friend at the CIIA and a former principal at Toronto's prestigious private boys high school, Upper Canada College, Terry MacDermot, who was now in the Information Division, would share his wisdom on public relations strategies. Finally, organized discussion groups to brief the officers on more substantive issues of policy could be led by internal subject matter experts along with specialists from other relevant parts of the government.[30]

As Holmes prepared to leave Ottawa, Gordon Robertson transformed these ideas into the "University of the East Block," a training centre for new Canadian foreign service officers. The experiences of those who went through the program in its earlier years were mixed. Many had particularly fond memories of their introductions to the major players not only in the Canadian diplomatic world but also in Ottawa more generally through a series of "field trips" across the city and evenings of beer and sandwiches at senior officials' homes and apartments. Others recall their unprecedented access to departmental gossip. Still more found the discussions pedantic, if not useless. Regardless, the university was an institution, and it would not have existed without the efforts of John Holmes.

Holmes returned to London carrying with him a letter from a former officemate, and the man assigned to replace him as the post-hostilities planning secretary, George Ignatieff. The Russian-born son of a count and a princess whose family had escaped persecution by the communists during the civil war in 1920 was another former Rhodes Scholar and, like Holmes, was also moving up in the DEA during the beginning of what would be an illustrious career. Ignatieff had been courting a young Canadian woman, Alison Grant, but the demands of his job conspired to keep them apart, especially since Grant lived in London. He had grown impatient with the situation and hoped to resolve it through marriage. Since he could not see Grant himself, he called on his trusted friend, John Holmes, to deliver his written marriage proposal. Holmes was pleased to oblige, but Ignatieff's handwriting was so awkward that Grant could not decipher the message. It was therefore up to Holmes, the intermediary, to propose marriage on his friend's behalf. The mission was a success. George and Alison Ignatieff were married shortly after and lived a long and happy life together.[31]

The meeting with Grant was the highlight of a disturbing first week in London. Holmes arrived to find what he recalled as the lovely grey building known as Canada House, his new place of work, in a depressing state. All of the windows had been sealed and then covered with strips of tape to protect against German attacks. The next day, while taking breakfast in his flat, the windows began to shake, followed by what he described as "the most bloodcurdling of sounds – a long whistling roar." He learned only later that this was good news. Since rockets travel faster than sound, hearing them generally meant that the worst was already over. This explains why most of his neighbours had continued about their morning as if nothing had happened. It was only upon leaving his flat that he found shopkeepers sweeping masses of broken glass.

The event had a significant impact on him at two levels. He gained a new appreciation and admiration for how the British, and people more generally, dealt with the dreadfulness of war. "As I said in the first place," he wrote home, "I really do see my own experiences in proportion and I don't pretend that I know anything at all about the horrors of enemy action. But I did learn a few things about how people behave – and even how I myself behave – in such times. What I have learned about human nature is most reassuring. When you think about it, the hideousness of the rocket is terrifying. At any hour of any day anybody is apt to be blown to pieces. But people keep on going to work and getting meals and going to pictures." The British were philosophical, if not fatalistic, but they also made the best of their situation. It was an approach to crisis management that Holmes attempted to emulate throughout his life – and one that he later advocated in his public lectures and in the classroom.

The strikes also caused him to develop a genuine hatred of the enemy. In the same letter, he explained:

If I did learn a new appreciation for English people – and for Canadians who live here – I developed some new attitudes to the boys who did the firing. I recognize that our bombing has done some hideous things in Germany, and I am even prepared to admit that the Blitz on London might have some military excuse – if there ever is any excuse for the war having been let loose in the first place. But the insane and purposeless slaughter by these devilish inhuman impersonal machines made me very mad. I remember being wakened out of my sleep about three times one night by bangs and becoming conscious of the fact that in my stupor I was muttering, "I hate the Germans." It was a little silly, but I must say it expressed my subconscious. I think I can honestly say that my hate was not caused by fear that the next one would fall on me because by that time I knew that I was invulnerable, but it was caused by the hideous thought that in three parts of London there were smashed bodies littered about and screaming women under tons of debris.[32]

His strong feelings never abated, and students who heard him lecture in the 1960s still recall the tinge of bitterness that came through when he talked about the Axis Powers of the 1940s.

In the midst of the chaos, Holmes moved into the nicest workspace he would ever have – the office of the political counsellor, which overlooked Whitehall and Northumberland Avenue on the west side of Trafalgar Square. Although the view itself was grand, it was likely the scene that was most energizing. Northumberland contained a mixture of corporate buildings, government offices, and the home of the Royal Commonwealth Society. Then there was Whitehall itself, a bastion of history. Canada House was an excellent place to work, even if the back of the building was still occupied by the Royal College of Physicians, a stubborn group that refused to leave.

Initially, Holmes' job seemed fairly straightforward. Every morning he cycled or took the bus to work. Boxes of Foreign Office documents (the "red" boxes) were delivered to his office. He read the material carefully, headed to the Foreign Office to speak directly to some of the drafters of the notes for clarification, and then sent thematic reports back to Ottawa.[33] His specific focus was British foreign policy, while his colleague, Doug LePan, a military veteran and poet who quickly morphed into one of the DEA's economic experts, dealt with domestic and economic issues. Together they wrote weekly summaries for circulation at home. The two found that they had a lot in common and quickly developed a degree of trust and friendship that, for Holmes at least, was virtually unmatched during this period.

The young officers were supervised by Vincent Massey. The Canadian high commissioner was known to many as a snob, but Holmes came to see him differently. Certainly, he preferred to mix with a highbrow crowd, and indeed his interests lay almost exclusively in high culture and the less technical aspects of diplomacy, but he chose his friends carefully and tended to associate with only the most prominent and influential political players. Massey was also a skilled writer and possessed as fine a set of manners as any Canadian, two skills crucial to diplomatic success.[34] When the high commissioner asked Holmes to serve wine at one of his dinner parties, it was not an attempt to demean him. The young diplomat needed first-hand experience in how the elite conducted themselves and how to behave among them. He was too junior to be a full-fledged participant at the Massey gatherings, so acting as an attendant was the only way to learn. Finally, like Holmes, while Massey was proud of his British heritage, he was also a strong Canadian nationalist and a fierce defender of his country's independence.[35] They rarely clashed during their time together in London.

Massey's greatest skill as high commissioner was his ability to secure the right guests for his parties and then to stimulate candid dialogue that would generate intelligence that might not have been obtained otherwise. Holmes took careful notes during one particular private dinner in late February 1945 in the midst of an elite Commonwealth relations conference. The event was attended by major opinion leaders from both Canada and the United Kingdom, including editors of leading Canadian newspapers and magazines along with at least three British cabinet ministers. When the conversation shifted to relations within the Commonwealth, Holmes was shocked by what he learned. The British were less committed to imperialism than Canadians might have thought on the basis of press reports in Ottawa.[36] Massey taught Holmes that not all diplomacy was formal, that casual conversations played a critical role in the successful execution of foreign policy, and that attention to proper protocol and manners went a long way towards gaining the trust and respect of the political elite. It was largely thanks to Massey that he was able to expand his already large circle of friends in 1945. His work earned him an invitation to act as secretary (to Wrong and Massey) at a Commonwealth conference on international organization that April, the opportunity to serve as acting high commissioner for a week when Massey was away, and regular invitations to dine with the Massey family thereafter.[37]

The Canada House experience continued largely without incident through much of the spring. On 7 May 1945, Holmes received a call from Massey that ended with the matter of fact statement, "The war is over." The next day, people danced in the streets of London as the prime minister's voice was channelled through loud speakers to formally announce the ceasefire. Because Holmes' office overlooked Trafalgar Square, it soon

became the meeting point for those who wished to view the celebration
from above. Guests came in and out, including staff from Canadian
Movietone News who filmed some of their footage from his window.
Holmes watched Winston Churchill make his famous V-sign and joined
in the celebration the next day by throwing pennies to the crowds below.
Later, he, Mary Greey, and her future husband, Gerald Graham, went to
the Palace to listen to the King. Afterwards, they rejoiced in song at a pub.
Holmes joined the Masseys for a victory dinner that evening.[38]

The second secretary received positive evaluations of his analysis of
issues such as the upcoming peace treaties and Canadian policy towards
the UN throughout June and July. On 6 August 1945 he met with a visiting Lester Pearson at the Savoy Hotel. On their way out of the building,
they noticed a news bulletin. Holmes later wrote of the experience: "And
there it was. A perplexing and devastating device had been dropped on
a place called Hiroshima."[39] Neither knew how to respond, nor did they
grasp the enormity of the event right away. It was only two days later
that Holmes was able to write home convinced that there could never be
another world war.

He remained optimistic about the future largely because of his relationship with Pearson. Unlike Robertson and Wrong, whose respect for him
was manifested collegially, from the very beginning, Pearson – who shared
with Holmes a similar Methodist upbringing – treated him as a friend. As
a result, Holmes always felt closer to Pearson than to the others, even if
his admiration for Wrong and Robertson as individuals might well have
been greater. Pearson's infectious enthusiasm and tremendous capacity for
work gave him hope that even the world's most difficult problems could
be solved, and he used this positive energy as a stimulus to stay focused
during what were truly unsettling times.[40]

Unlike some of his colleagues, Pearson encouraged Holmes' idealism.
The junior civil servant therefore wrote differently depending on his
audience. Analyses sent to Hume Wrong that autumn were cloaked in
the usual caution. One well-received commentary on the future of the
Commonwealth, for example, emphasized the benefits of incremental
progress while criticizing the Australian government for its flamboyance,
its aggressiveness, and its overall ineffective public diplomacy. A note for
Pearson just ten days later had a different tone. Canada's contribution to
the UN's founding conference at San Francisco, Holmes argued, had been
exceptional, particularly since the Canadians had made a difference in
fields outside of their traditional expertise. "We are now looked upon as a
country which has sound and responsible ideas on important problems,"

he added, suggesting that it was time for a bolder role in world affairs. Later he would suggest to Pearson that Canada insist on making a significant contribution to the Pacific aspect of the postwar peace negotiations. Predictably, it was largely the material for Wrong that reached the prime minister unchanged, while the ideas for Pearson had a more significant impact on Holmes' thinking personally.[41]

By the end of the year, Holmes had risen sufficiently in the unofficial departmental hierarchy to participate in the examination process for new civil servants.[42] The DEA had begun a massive recruitment campaign in August 1944 in preparation for the expansion that would almost certainly come at war's end. The focus was on military personnel currently overseas. It was in many ways an awkward job, given that Holmes still had no guarantee that he would be able to keep his own position once the troops came home. Throughout the year there had been difficulties and confusion over his official status. His medical classification was reviewed in January 1945, and in March he received a government letter notifying him that he had unfairly benefited from his position in the DEA. From that point forward, in spite of his eyes, he would be considered eligible for military service. He would not receive any form of preferential treatment if he chose to apply for a permanent position. What is more, at the end of May he was informed by the National Selective Service that he was in fact not permitted to change employment until further notice.[43] In the end, as Norman Robertson might have predicted, the issue appeared to be much more significant than it was. On 17 January 1946, Hume Wrong took Holmes to dinner at the Travellers' Club and informed him that he and Robertson had requested jointly that Holmes be promoted to first secretary. It was a significant advancement that would typically have required six to ten years of service. Holmes had yet to complete three.[44]

The good news arrived in the midst of a difficult period in Canadian foreign policy and in the external relations of the Western world more generally. When he looked back forty years later, Holmes reflected to a colleague in Quebec: "I watched the Cold War develop from a seat in London and in Moscow in the 'forties and to me it was a history of specific events in Poland or Greece or the USA and response was to specific events rather than a kind of plague descending upon us which purported to explain all things."[45] Examining his records suggests otherwise. The Cold War crept up on him, even if the pace of the creep changed with major international crises. First, there were the discussions at the post-hostilities problems (PHP) meetings. Then there were the rumours. In June 1945 he began to hear reports of disturbing behaviour by Soviet troops in Eastern Europe.

Prisoners of war, it seemed, had been treated inhumanely – and not accidentally. He preferred not to believe the stories at first, but he could not deny the impact of the speculation, nor could he ignore the deteriorating relationship between the West and its Soviet allies as the war came to an end. As summer turned to fall, his reports to Ottawa seemed to confirm his worst fears as he focused on communism and its implications for British foreign policy.[46]

At the end of October, Holmes represented Canada House at a world youth conference in London. The United States and Great Britain chose not to allow their delegates to attend, fearing that the event was a communist gathering masquerading as something else. The Canadians felt differently, convinced that it was only through engagement, and therefore participation, that they could exercise any effective influence against communist assertions of international influence. The conference played host to over six hundred delegates from sixty-four countries and, indeed, was dominated, in terms of control and direction, by the Soviet representatives. Nevertheless, the Canadians concluded that future meetings would be worth attending since working from within remained the best means of influencing their outcomes. This approach was well received in Ottawa, and its approval helped convince Holmes that, at the strategic level, Canadian participation in the Cold War, at least in its early days, was distinct from that of its great power allies.[47]

Holmes' disappointing experience at the first meetings of the United Nations General Assembly in January 1946 – the highlight of which was almost certainly an attempt to make a phone call that was interrupted because some of the Muslim delegates had converted the phone booth into a mini mosque – and his almost entirely negative experience as a participant on the UN Atomic Energy Commission that spring did nothing to alleviate his concerns. The great power leaders in the West had become moral absolutists, he observed, while the Stalin-led communists were secretive, unreliable, and likely expansionist. Revelations of the existence of Soviet spy rings in Canada only made things worse. Because he was close to both Wrong and Massey, Holmes was included in confidential discussions about Igor Gouzenko, a Soviet defector who had smuggled documents out of the embassy in Ottawa and surrendered them to the RCMP, before the information was made public. The focus of these meetings, he explained much later, was not so much on the threat of communist ideology as it was on what was clearly Soviet paranoia and the risks and costs of provoking it. As a result, in the early Cold War period, the Canadians often paid more attention to the actions of their allies than they did to their enemies. This attempt to constrain was not evidence that Holmes and those who were sympathetic to his approach took the Soviet threat less seriously; rather, it was because they feared the ultimate power of the Soviet Union that they focused so extensively on avoiding provocation.[48]

There was no break once the controversy surrounding the Gouzenko affair began to fade. Because of his increasing responsibilities and importance, Holmes took just four and a half days of official leave in 1946 and through the first four months of 1947. What came next was a dispute over Commonwealth representation in the negotiation of the German peace settlement and in discussions of the future defence of the Pacific. Specifically, the Canadians were frustrated when their suggestions to solve the German issue – which they had to submit in writing instead of in person – were ignored by their British colleagues and when too much attention was paid to Australia's foreign minister, Herbert Evatt, when he expressed distinctly national concerns.

It was a difficult time for Great Britain. As one analyst has explained, by 1945, it "was no longer a power of the first rank." Moreover, its economic weakness made it reliant on the United States to maintain even its lesser position.[49] London's secret meetings with Evatt, from which the Canadians were excluded, were a source of frustration for Holmes and his colleagues, who held firmly that Australia's bold and undiplomatic posturing was thinly disguised bullying and detrimental to any hope of future Commonwealth unity. The Canadians had begun to recognize and accept the need for increasing flexibility among countries that would not all be on quite the same side during the evolving Cold War. The frustration with the British attitude towards Australia was even more upsetting because it was Canada that was making the real sacrifices: a dramatic $1.25 billion low-interest loan to the mother country, worth a full 10 percent of the gross national product, is the best example. As often happened in the case of the Commonwealth, the internal conflicts were eventually overcome by a shared pragmatic commitment to the spirit of the organization, one that allowed for a diversity of views and opinions, cultural difference, and international collaboration.[50]

With that, Holmes left for Italy to help close out the International Institute of Agriculture (IIA). What was meant to be an opportunity for rest and relief – the conference was a mere formality since the IIA had become redundant with the founding of the Food and Agriculture Organization in October 1945 – was instead a profoundly disturbing two weeks. Driving through the Capitol Hill, the *Piazza Venetia*, Holmes and his fellow passengers in the British embassy car were attacked and stoned by Italian protestors. The ruffians were upset at the decisions taken by the Council of Foreign Ministers to divide the former city of Trieste into two zones, neither of which was placed under Italian control. Since coming into Italian hands after the First World War, Trieste had developed into a vibrant commercial port and was expected to be a driver in Italy's postwar economic recovery. The protestors blamed the Western Allies for failing to return control of their zone to the Italian government. The car that Holmes was in had its windows smashed to pieces. His cheek was blood-ied, but his physical injuries were only superficial. Nevertheless, the attack shook him. He wrote home to his sister: "You can feel the bitterness and the disillusion. The stone which smashed the window of our car in Piazza Venetia brought me down to earth. It was a small and silly incident, but it put me in touch with the passions that are seething in this bewildered and frightening continent. Just when I am being reminded of the rich variety and the culture of European life I am driven to wonder whether Europe will survive."[51]

In his despair, Holmes could have made a number of choices. Pickering College still had space for him if he wanted to return. Just before he left for Rome he had received a letter from the CIIA asking him if he would be wiling to come back to the institute now that the war was over. Teaching at the university level was also an option: he had given lectures on inter-national affairs throughout London in the spring. But these alternatives would have required him to make life-changing decisions. He was comfort-able in the East Block (even if he had been in London for more than half of his career). He felt that he was making a tangible contribution to his country and to the world. And he could not help but admire the people for whom he worked. His disturbing introduction to the Cold War did not scare him away. Furthermore, another promotion was forthcoming. Hume Wrong wrote personally in June to confirm Holmes' rise to first secretary and the virtual guarantee of a permanent position. Officially, he reached the rank of foreign service officer (FSO) 4 on 8 July 1946, with a salary of $4,500. As for change, however – that he would not be able to stop. His increase in both status and stature meant a job with greater responsibilities. Add to that the changes taking place in Ottawa, and it was clear that he would be forced to adapt. Vincent Massey returned to Canada in May and had to be replaced. Norman Robertson was exhausted and wanted a new position. It was also time to bring Lester Pearson back to the centre of government. After a much-needed vacation, Robertson replaced Massey in London, Pearson replaced him as under-secretary of state for external affairs, and Hume Wrong took Pearson's place in Washington. All three wanted Holmes to work with them.[52]

Pearson, who, because of his new position, had the most influence in the final decision, made the first offer. It was an opportunity to take a leadership role in launching what he later called "a new regime," to be directed by Canada's just-appointed secretary of state for external affairs, Louis St. Laurent. It would be the kind of activist, internationalist East Block that Holmes had often hoped for. The thirty-six-year-old was flattered, but he was not ready for the upheaval. He was settled in London, at ease in his job, and, in spite of his persistent homesickness, he was not prepared to return to Ottawa just yet. Moreover, with the transition among the senior staff in Canada House that was about to take place, he was one of the few officers with the experience necessary to keep things running smoothly.[53] Because of the gap between Massey's departure and Robertson's arrival, he got his wish temporarily. Frederic Hudd took over as interim high commissioner and Holmes continued to serve him as he had Massey before.

Norman Robertson's eventual appearance after a brief illness was greeted with cheer. Holmes became close with the entire Robertson family; he wrote home about young Judith, able, at age five, to ask questions that would tongue-tie even the sharpest adults. He offered to take care of the family dogs when his commissioner was away. And he became good friends with Robertson's wife, Jetty. The honeymoon, of course, could not last, and Lester Pearson was serious about bringing his younger colleague home. By the end the year Holmes was preparing for the adjustment ahead. It had been months since his promotion and he had finally begun to accept the major changes in his life. He was now a full-fledged diplomat, a permanent member of the Department of External Affairs. "It doesn't make me feel very different," he wrote his sister, "although it is pleasant to feel that I have a steady and permanent job with a good income and a pension."[54]

Until the transfer to Ottawa was complete, Hume Wrong – who had been waiting for a new second secretary for over four months – held out hope that he could still get Holmes to Washington. In February 1947 he wrote Pearson, making it clear that, while Escott Reid, an experienced diplomat with years of experience as Pearson's senior assistant in Washington, was a good fit on paper, it was time for him to "diversify his experience." Truthfully, Wrong and Reid did not get along professionally, and Holmes' reporting skills made him an excellent replacement.[55] As the negotiations continued, with the staffing situation in the DEA still uncertain, even with a Cabinet exemption from a federal initiative to shrink the public service, Holmes asked for time off to see his family. Robertson advised Pearson to grant it, but made it clear that it was imperative that Holmes be returned to him afterwards. Pearson, however, saw the trip as a chance to bring his colleague back more permanently. The government was creating a joint intelligence board and Holmes was an ideal candidate to chair it.[56]

When he learned of Pearson's latest plan, Holmes was upset. Having lived through the Depression, he was always conscious of his financial situation, and he had already paid for his apartment in London through the summer of 1947. The lack of notice about his departure from Canada House also meant that his successor would be left without any real guidance or instructions. Holmes was intimidated by the new position and by the prospect of working directly under Pearson. Hume Wrong had also told him about the opening in Washington, and it appealed to him more than the prospects in Ottawa. To complicate matters, his father had had a heart attack, and he hoped to stay at home with his mother until he had assurance that Wendell Holmes would recover. The trip back to Ontario was hardly a holiday for someone who needed one.[57]

At the last moment, Norman Robertson took ill again, Dana Wilgress quickly arrived at Canada House to fill in, and Holmes was called back to London. By mid-June, he had reimmersed himself in Commonwealth affairs, most specifically in India's drive for independence.[58] Although not entirely refreshed, he knew that, as an officer abroad, he would be earning nearly twice as much as he would have been at home thanks to allowances and tax breaks. With his father less than fully recovered, this information reassured him about what he could do for his family.

His sense of relief translated into exceptional work. Holmes' personnel report from that July was glowing. It noted that the quality of his performance merited promotion from grade four to grade six. He was conscientious in everything that he did and got on with his fellow officers admirably. Personally, he was "an altogether admirable colleague – intelligent, cooperative, friendly, with judgment, zeal and personal charm." Professionally, wrote his assessor, "There is none better. His circle of friends in London is wide and useful; his initiative, sense of responsibility, and faculty of lucid statement make him a very valuable member of the staff."[59] The report appears to have travelled back to Prime Minister Mackenzie King, who, according to Hume Wrong, later mentioned Holmes explicitly in a conversation with Pearson about up-and-coming foreign service personnel. Clearly, he was one of the chosen.[60]

There were two more significant experiences in London before Holmes' time there was cut unexpectedly short. The first involved Indian independence and the resulting admission of India and Pakistan to the Commonwealth as full members. Canada was largely an observer as the debate over the independence bill travelled through the British Parliament, allowing Holmes to analyze the situation carefully without becoming too attached. He concluded that, by making non-white India a full member, the British had affirmed a conception of the Commonwealth based on what he later proudly called "the Canadian thesis." Just as they had been for him as a student in London, ties were based on culture and history rather than on any specific joint policy or approach to politics. The old dominions were independent entities, faithful to the organization by choice, not because of an imperial obligation. For Holmes, India's new status was a victory not only for the developing world but also for traditional Canadian nationalists who had maintained for years that loyalty to British institutions did not have to compromise national sovereignty or an independent Canadian identity.[61]

The second notable experience was a trip with Minister C.D. Howe to Germany from 10-12 August 1947. For Holmes and his three companions – Howe, an administrative officer from Canada House, and Frank Walker of the *Winnipeg Free Press* – the tour was revealing. From the moment that they entered the American headquarters in Frankfurt, they could not help but notice the devastation that had been inflicted upon Germany.[62] Britain had been damaged, Holmes noted, but Frankfurt had been "hacked to pieces." Virtually no buildings had been spared by the war. After a night's sleep, the group set out for the displaced persons' camps, the real purpose of their visit. At first, in the relatively rural western district of Zeilsheim, Holmes was struck by the willingness of the Jewish refugees to say anything that might get them out of Germany quickly. When the Canadian delegates asked them if they wished to immigrate to Canada they all enthusiastically answered yes. Yet their actions did not match their words: nearly all of them were headed for Palestine. Moreover, Holmes reflected in his report, "I don't think we were entirely popular in that camp." While C.D. Howe posed for a picture in front of a memorial to Jewish victims of the Holocaust (located in Eleanor Roosevelt Square), there were secretive conversations taking place in Yiddish that he could not understand. He was no more comfortable with the behaviour of some occupying Americans. He did meet a number of officials who had been moved by the unconscionable inhumanities that these refugees had suffered and were doing their utmost to make their lives easier. But there were also some whose arrogance over having defeated the Germans was appalling. Too many of the guards, he wrote, looked "upon their charges as children or, to put it bluntly, exhibits of the zoo." He was impressed when Howe exploded over the behaviour of one particular individual, reminding him that human beings deserved better.

The trip also included a tour of the Olympic stadium in Berlin and a visit to the remains of Hitler's chancellery. It had somehow survived mostly in tact, and opportunists had been removing marble and paintings. "This may be called looting," Holmes wrote, "but I see no reason why valuable materials should be left in a shell too grandiose to serve any useful purpose in the foreseeable future." He and his colleagues were able to venture as far as the outside of the bunker in which Hitler committed suicide, but they could go no further. After taking time to pay respects to the Canadian soldiers who had given their lives in Germany, the group returned home, moved and shaken.[63]

For Holmes, the trip marked the beginning of the end of a transformative period. The war, and its impact on every level of his personal and professional experience, had changed him permanently. In just three and a half years, he had evolved from special wartime assistant to the under-secretary of state for external affairs with no clearly defined role to one of the most promising young officials in Canada's foreign service. His country, which in 1943 was only beginning to embrace internationalism, had acquired a new minister of external affairs with an ambitious and committed global outlook. His mentors occupied the most powerful positions in the DEA and were looking out for him constantly. And his circle of friends, both at home and abroad, was growing. Things, it seemed, could not get much better for an official still acquiring his voice as a contemporary internationalist.

3

The Rising Star

When John Holmes returned from Germany, he knew that it was only a matter of time before he would have to leave London permanently for a new posting, but he never could have guessed where he was headed. The Soviet Union was, in one diplomat's words, "the most difficult and disagreeable post we have behind 'the iron curtain' … bleak and unenviable." Officers' families hated it, the weather was bad, and there was little to do. At the same time, it was crucial that Canada be well represented in Moscow as the Cold War became more intense, and the post called for "a good deal of balanced wisdom and an unprejudiced mind, and a patient, tolerant but sanguine disposition."[1] Dana Wilgress, a senior mandarin who had been educated in both Canada and Japan and under whom Holmes had served briefly in London, was an excellent Canadian ambassador; however, because of his expertise in international economic policy, he had been recalled to participate in the negotiations to create what became the General Agreement on Tariffs and Trade. The Cornell-educated and highly regarded Robert Ford, later a distinguished poet, took his spot, but by the fall of 1947 he was ill and in need of a transfer. The comforts of London, moreover, were welcomed both by him and his wife Tereza.

Young, bright, healthy, and unattached at thirty-seven, John Holmes was an ideal short-term replacement. Just as important from a strategic perspective, since he was still too junior to be appointed ambassador, he arrived with the rank of chargé d'affaires. The downgrading of the Canadian representative was interpreted by the Soviets as what Holmes liked to call a diplomatic insult, and that is exactly what Ottawa intended. The USSR had withdrawn its ambassador in the wake of the Gouzenko affair. Sending a more junior representative to Moscow demonstrated appropriate Canadian displeasure without severing relations completely.

When Wendell Holmes learned of the move, he worried. Ann and Nancy Skinner, daughters of John Holmes' sister Isobel, had already lost their father, and the family had long ago decided that Uncle Johnny would look after the girls' long-term well-being. Nancy had polio, and in spite of her energy and determination, she was confined to a wheelchair and at times required extra assistance. If her uncle were to spend the rest of his life travelling abroad to far-away places, it would be difficult to fulfil his family responsibilities. The younger Holmes understood the challenge and wrote to his father reassuringly. The posting was only supposed to last three months. By that point, relations with Moscow should have improved enough to justify the return of a full-fledged ambassador. Taking the difficult assignment now also enhanced Holmes' chances for greater promotions in the future. "Looking at the prospects," he wrote, "I can say I have every reason to believe that I can be an ambassador with a salary of about $15,000 a year before I am finished ... I should have a good enough margin to help Nancy or any other members of the family who need it."[2] Indeed, along with the posting came a promotion to FSO 5, an immediate increase of salary to $5,400, and another a few months later to $6,000. The man who was never going to be a career diplomat had just made a long-term commitment to the Department of External Affairs.

He was excited about the Moscow posting, but nevertheless sought official confirmation that he would be home fairly quickly. When a letter from Terry MacDermot of the personnel division noted that the plan was to bring him back either to Ottawa or to the UN mission in New York no later than early February 1948, he was ready to go.[3] He crossed by ship, of course, since only ambassadors travelled by plane. Holmes passed through Stockholm on the SS *Sestroretsk*, docking in the Soviet Union on 3 November after nine days at sea. His departure had been hurried so that he could arrive before the Baltic Sea froze over and cut off trips to the east for part of the winter. Once he reached Moscow, he travelled by car through a series of narrow cobble-stone streets to the central part of the city, where the nineteenth-century building that housed the embassy was located. As ambassadors, both Wilgress and Ford had lived in a suite on the top floor, but Holmes felt uncomfortable in such luxury and chose instead the first secretary's flat on the ground level. He had learned a bit of the native language on the trip over through a book called *Hugo's Simplified Russian*, but he could still barely communicate with some of the servants. Fortunately, the cook spoke German, and Holmes, who picked up languages quickly, had a good enough understanding to engage in a reasonable conversation.

His first impressions of his new post were mixed. The country was grey, there was no hot water (people at the embassy burned wood in a copper boiler to take a warm bath), and Tereza Ford had shipped all of the food and drink for entertainment purposes with her to London. Because it was winter, no new supplies were scheduled to arrive until April, forcing Holmes to rely on Soviet products and prices. This made keeping company expensive. There were also restrictions on his delegation. Fellow diplomats were fond of saying that they could travel only as far as one tank of gas would permit, and that included turning around and coming home. The *Burobin*, the Soviet organization assigned to look after foreign officers' needs, was notoriously slow to respond to concerns, and, to make matters worse, a chandelier that Holmes had imported from Belgium was broken by the installers shortly after it arrived. Mail was often pre-screened, the telephones in the embassy were bugged, and the Soviet secret police followed him everywhere. He never forgot the day that he departed for Easter Mass unannounced (or so he had thought) only to find that a seat in the church had already been reserved for him when he got there. Drivers waited for him out in the cold at the end of theatre productions until well after midnight, adamantly refusing to let him walk the half mile home. One time the embassy staff took a picnic lunch to the countryside only to encounter shady figures emerging from the woods to make sure that they did not venture too far from Moscow without permission. Another time the pipes froze, and, as expected, the Soviets failed to respond. In this case, Holmes was clever. He deliberately made a long-distance call on his tapped phone, letting his government know that it might have to arrange for a Westerner to come fix the problem because the Soviets were being uncooperative. Then he called the French chargé d'affaires and asked if he could stop by to take a shower. Shortly after he hung up, a plumber arrived. When it came to a choice between isolating the Western diplomats or simply making them uncomfortable, the Soviets chose isolation every time.

Not everything was so terrible. Holmes' chauffeur, Maxim Constantinovich, was knowledgeable, friendly, and happy to drive him across the city in a comfortable Buick sedan draped with a Canadian flag. The translator, receptionist, and switchboard operator, Vera Andreyevna, helped out with communications difficulties. Administrative officer George Costakis had not only assembled a collection of early twentieth-century Soviet abstract

art, but he had also mastered the Russian bureaucracy. Together they gave
Holmes a new name, Ivan Vassilievich (an apartment owner in a theatre
production that had been banned because of its criticism of Soviet society),
and while they, too, were bound to report on his activities, they treated
him with all of the respect and dignity that they could. Finally, since the
Soviets limited every embassy to the same quantity of supplies, and the
Canadian team was fairly small, Holmes' group was relatively comfortable
in terms of personal stocks of food and drink. At one point, one member
even managed to pick up the CBC on the radio.

The other Western diplomats, all of whom were suffering from the same
overall treatment, were wonderful. The Commonwealth missions, for
example, gathered every Saturday morning to commiserate and exchange
notes, and Holmes met with the Americans at least as often. The Swedes,
Norwegians, and especially the Dutch were also helpful. Holmes became
close with Vijaya Lakshmi Pandit and her daughter Nayantara Saghal of
India, who lived on Smolensky Boulevard, and Walter Bedell Smith of
the United States, who was close by at Spaso House. The journalists were
similarly forthcoming and open, and many became close colleagues as well
as trustworthy sources. Walter Cronkite, the United Press correspondent
at the time, recruited Holmes as a tennis partner and in later years was
said to have interrupted an intimate personal conversation when he saw
Holmes enter a restaurant so that he could greet the distinguished Canadian properly.

Most important, Holmes discovered "Russia" and the Russian people.
In a vivid recollection of his arrival in Moscow in 1947, he remarked on
looking out on the deck of the SS *Sestroretsk* and noticing how "the sun
came under the low black clouds and suddenly illuminated the gold dome
of St. Isaac's and the onion spires of the Admiralty and St. Peter and Paul –
gold and exotically beautiful." At that point he understood "that this was
not just the Soviet Union; it was Russia and one of the most fascinating,
one of the most attractive, and one of the most repulsive countries in the
world." "There are things I have seen and heard in Russia," he later recalled,
"which have given me more pleasure and excitement than I have experienced
anywhere else and there are Russians, red and white, for whom I have felt
a warmer glow than for any other people." His spare time in Moscow was
spent reading Russian history, learning the language, and bicycling to the
theatre. After he left, he expressed his hope "that the Russian character,
which has the great capacity for heroism, idealism, and brotherly love, as
well as for violence, arrogance, and cruelty, will, out of sheer zest for living,
triumph over the rigidity of the regime."[4]

That rigid regime – along with Winston Churchill's famous iron curtain speech and US President Harry Truman's doctrine to protect Western democracies from communist influence, which followed shortly after – demonstrated that the Cold War was turning hot. Communists were agitating across Europe and within less than a decade would be actively seeking to expand their influence into the current and former African colonies. Their secretive manner, particularly in the Soviet Union, was off-putting and made it difficult for any real negotiations to take place. As Holmes explained in an interview much later, the Canadians were isolated from the Soviet people "not by our choice but because the consequences of them associating with us were such that we would not endanger them with invitations … if we failed to see that the Russians wanted only peaceful competition with us at that time, they have themselves to a large extent to blame."[5] Radicals in the West advocated a pre-emptive strike, but most – including Holmes and the majority of Canadians – were happy to follow the patient but firm approach that Dana Wilgress, among many others, had been advocating since the end of the Second World War.[6]

Shortly after his arrival, Holmes witnessed the ugliness of the Cold War first-hand. The thirtieth anniversary of the October Revolution was a spectacle that lasted for days. Designed for both domestic and foreign audiences, it celebrated Joseph Stalin and Soviet power while at the same time attempting to demonstrate the cultural superiority of communist society. On the first evening, a Thursday, Holmes was invited to a six-hour performance at the Bolshoi Theatre, one of the few locales that would be consistently open to Western diplomats. The next morning there was a memorable parade in the Red Square. Foreign representatives were forced to stand in the cold for over an hour watching as the flags and military personnel passed by. When the first column approached, the British ambassador scratched his ear and the move was mistakenly interpreted by those around him as a salute. For the rest of the parade, every time that a column passed, the entire diplomatic audience felt obligated to take off their hats and allow the freezing rain to beat down on their mostly bare heads.

That night, coughing and sniffling, they attended a reception hosted by Foreign Minister Vyacheslav Molotov. Chairs were provided for the communist representatives, but the Westerners had to stand as Molotov heaped insults upon them and alluded to Soviet progress in developing an atomic bomb. Holmes was less than impressed with the spectacle. In one of the first of more than 350 despatches that he wrote from Moscow, he noted that the military experts he had consulted did not believe that the Soviet army was as strong as the press had claimed and that Joseph

Stalin not only failed to appear but also refused to announce the end to the rationing of bread for which much of the population had been hoping.[7]

Not long after that memorable evening, Holmes faced his first diplomatic challenge as head of post. On 12 November 1947, James Weld and Anthony Clabon, two Canadians stationed at the military mission in Germany, were stopped by Stalin's officials about 100 kilometres inside of Soviet territory in a region called Kaliningrad (Koenigsberg). When questioned, they claimed that they got lost travelling from Warsaw to Danzig (Gdansk). The Soviets were suspicious of their illegal entry into Russian territory because their arrest took place due north of Warsaw, whereas Danzig was to the northwest. Holmes heard of the problem only on the fifth day of their detainment, and on 18 November he met with officials at the Soviet ministry led by a Mr. Trukhanovsky to negotiate their release.

Trukhanovsky clearly expected a confrontation and appeared shocked when Holmes represented himself with the utmost civility. He soon abandoned his reserve, sat down, and sketched a map of Eastern Europe to demonstrate how far off-track the Canadians had gone. Holmes refused to admit that Weld and Clabon were anything but lost, but he did assure Trukhanovsky that if their release could be secured immediately, there would be a full investigation, and, if warranted, the two would be disciplined and perhaps even sent back to Canada. About a week later, they were let go without further incident.[8] For Holmes, his success, and the way that he had obtained it, was crucial. The calm, mediatory approach had worked – and with the most stubborn of opponents. Even the most reluctant of Soviet officials could be reasonable in one-on-one encounters. This success is likely one of the many reasons that Holmes advocated negotiation as a method of conflict resolution so strongly throughout his public life.[9]

Elation soon turned to disappointment as Holmes learned that his stay abroad had been extended. For strategic and diplomatic reasons, the new minister of external affairs, Louis St. Laurent, did not feel comfortable sending a full-fledged ambassador to Moscow until Molotov announced an intention to reciprocate. The Soviets were stalling, and both St. Laurent and Lester Pearson thought that replacing Holmes with another chargé d'affaires would be insulting to Moscow and therefore not worth the risk. The young diplomat would have to wait. Fortunately, Terry MacDermot appreciated his family situation and continued to lobby for his return. Also in Ottawa, Pearson confirmed with Norman Robertson that Holmes would not be sent to London. Ottawa was next, with a possible brief stopover to support the Canadian delegation at the United Nations Security Council.[10]

Holmes' experience in Moscow continued rather uneventfully until late February 1948. Just a few hours before the festivities to mark the thirtieth anniversary of the formation of the Soviet army were to begin, Western diplomats received invitations to participate. The spectacle, which included senior ranks of the army and Politburo, took place at the Bolshoi Theatre. This time Joseph Stalin did attend, and he appeared to be in good health. Thirty years later, Holmes described the experience as "like seeing Santa Claus. Aside from the physical resemblance there was the fact that one wasn't sure whether this man was the real thing. I could have taken him for my father, and Stalin was said to have many stand-ins."[11] The celebration was disturbing. The Soviets blatantly distorted history and vilified all Westerners as imperialist aggressors. Their contributions to the Second World War were virtually ignored, and their motivations for fighting the Nazis were decried as immoral. Holmes' colleagues from the United States and Great Britain eventually walked out in disgust, but he stayed. Even if the Western nations were united in their commitment to the Cold War, under his watch the Canadians could differ with their allies over tactics. He explained his behaviour the next week in a letter to Pearson. There was no denying that without the Soviet army Canadian soldiers would have suffered much more severely in the war against the Germans. Moreover, walking out was a risky, dramatic gesture, which could either be ignored or just as easily result in embarrassment. In the future, he wrote, "a less ostentatious policy of staying home is, I feel certain, preferable, although I have by no means made up my mind whether we should even go that far."[12]

He was less tolerant of what he called the cultural purges that had been taking place in the Soviet Union since the summer of 1946. The central committee of the Communist Party insisted on what was roughly translated as "socialist realism," a form of censorship of domestic artists that Holmes found disgusting. "There is one aspect of the current cultural crisis which is perhaps most depressing of all," he wrote. "Conformity enforced with terror seems to have sapped not only the artistic integrity of the artist, but also his moral integrity." Those who chose to obey the rules were producing a canon of "puritanism, anti-intellectualism, philistinism, and a kind of schoolmarmishness." For Holmes, the Soviet regime's unwillingness to welcome critical thought was its most alarming feature.[13]

In April 1948, after six months in Moscow and two months after a coup in Czechoslovakia that seemed to reaffirm Stalin's commitment to expand his influence in eastern Europe, Holmes sent a series of revealing memoranda back to the East Block. His assessment of the state of the Cold War was tinged with disappointment. Over the previous three months, letters to his family had expressed a degree of sympathy for the Soviets (particularly the Russians) and their situation. They were a desperate people, struggling to recover from a brutal war and embarrassed that the West had built itself back up so quickly. Their weakness made their proverbial bark worse than their bite, and it was likely that once they regained confidence in themselves and in their economic system relations would improve. Nonetheless, state-imposed censorship and mean-spirited government propaganda presented by the national media had him worried. "The Communists do not recognize," he wrote to Escott Reid, "that all men, not just capitalists, landlords and Grand Dukes, are corrupted by absolute power. Nor have they recognized that calculated dishonesty destroys confidence and trust on which alone a peaceful and stable national and international polity can be established. It is not surprising, therefore, that the Soviet leaders have lost sight of the goal they set out to achieve." The communists had deliberately exaggerated the Western threat in order to create a climate of fear that would foster public acceptance of increasingly hard-line measures directed at all aspects of society.[14]

In a memorandum to Pearson he elaborated. The Soviets did not want a hot war with the West. Because of their weakened economic situation, they did not think that they could win one. But they also did not want to lose the (non-nuclear) military advantage that they had established during the Second World War. They were therefore unlikely to start a war deliberately unless the West appeared to be increasing in strength so quickly that they felt that they had no choice. "If I may presume to draw one conclusion concerning Canadian policy from this report," he finished, "it is that we should in the next few months take particular care to leave the Russians grounds for retreat. Certainly we should leave them no room to advance. Whatever the risks of firmness, the risks of weakness are greater ... It seems to me, however, of desperate importance that we use our considerable influence in the coming months to prevent the United States from taking heady action without calculating the consequences."[15]

Pearson was impressed by his observations and passed them on to St. Laurent as well as to Dana Wilgress and Hume Wrong. Wilgress, the only senior mandarin who was fluent in Russian and the DEA's leading expert on the Soviet Union, praised Holmes' thoroughness, but his policy prescription differed. Rather than maintaining the dialogue with the Soviets, he proposed to "leave the Russians alone behind their Iron Curtain where their power is supreme." Wilgress went on, "I would stop talking about meetings to resolve the differences between East and West, stop explaining our policies to the Russians, and stop the foolish propaganda battles in which the Russians, having fewer inhibitions, usually come off best. I appreciate that all this places a strain upon our self-restraint that may be difficult to bear, but I agree with those who feel that we have tried to get along with the Russians and failed. The corollary I see to this is to leave them alone."[16] Although Holmes often glossed over or even ignored such comments in his later studies of the history of the time, it was clear that not everyone in the East Block believed that the moderate, mediatory approach was the right one. There was never a coherent departmental view on world order, and John Holmes' policy prescription was always much less the *Canadian* way than it was the *Holmesian* (or *Pearsonian*) one. Too many Canadians, and particularly commentators who refer to a golden age in the nation's diplomatic history, have since confused the two.[17]

By the time he had completed his analysis, the Soviets had begun to crack down even harder on the Western diplomats, leaving Holmes with little to do other than write weekly reports based on what he could learn from the media and his friends in the neighbouring embassies. His yearning to come home also intensified. Pearson wanted Holmes to join him in Paris for the meetings of the UN General Assembly and Security Council in September. Canada had recently been elected to the council and had just two years to make its mark. Holmes, Pearson felt, was one of the DEA's most reliable voices and would be particularly helpful. Holmes much preferred to return straight to Canada, but he also figured that his refusal would only increase the chances that his stay in Moscow would be extended yet again. While he awaited final confirmation, he continued to send reports to the East Block stressing his rather nuanced interpretation of the Soviet position in the Cold War. "What remains to be determined is the Soviet motive," he wrote in the spring. "The Americans are convinced that the Russians are playing a propaganda game ... I think the Americans are probably right, but I am not entirely convinced that the Russians are not after negotiations. [Perhaps they would like to] reach a modus vivendi which would give them a little peace in order to build up their resources and proceed further with their underground work."[18]

It was this appreciation of nuance that caused Holmes to predict a crisis in Yugoslavia well before it happened. After the war ended, the Federal People's Republic of Yugoslavia aligned itself, apparently quite comfortably, with its communist liberators from the Soviet Union. Holmes first detected conflict between Moscow and Belgrade in late May 1948. Although he had no evidence, he wrote to Pearson about his suspicions. One month later, when the lack of reporting from the Soviet media on the situation in Yugoslavia became obvious, Holmes reiterated concerns that were now being echoed by his colleagues in the United States and the United Kingdom. Behind the scenes, the struggles between Josip Broz Tito's Yugoslav Communist Party and the Cominform run out of Moscow were reaching their tipping point. Tito was too nationalist, and too ambitious, for Stalin's taste, and the Soviets eventually publicly castigated the people of Yugoslavia for their alleged military weakness during the war and their overall political incompetence. At the end of June, Yugoslavia was formally expelled from the Cominform by the Soviet satellites.[19]

Although Canada had a legation in Yugoslavia from February 1948, Holmes learned about all of this from the Soviet newspaper *Pravda*, which published an obviously biased account on 29 June 1948. His response was twofold, demonstrating the same cautious pragmatism that typically characterized his international briefings. He could not help but concede that the schism was good for the West. "All of this is, I think," he wrote to Ottawa, "indicative of what seems to be the crass stupidity of the Russians in handling their brothers ... It is only arrogance, stupidity, or insensitivity that leads the Russians to humiliate so proud a people as the Yugoslavs by forcing them to admit their own partisan activities during the War were of minor importance. Here, it seems likely, is the root of further trouble. The prospects of the Russians holding the loyalty of these people by love rather than by force seems small." At the same time, though, he advised his government against assuming that the crisis was indicative of an opportunity for a quick Western victory in the Cold War. Most important, he warned against opportunistically adopting Tito as an ally. The West held the moral high ground in the battle against the Soviets, and simply wiping away the history of Tito's tyranny and attacks on democracy because of the split with Stalin would be unethical and dishonest.[20]

Holmes was wrong in his assessment of a crisis in Germany that summer. In another attempt to assert itself both domestically and internationally, the Soviet Union blockaded the Allied occupied sections of Berlin in late June. The action was virtually ignored in the Moscow press, and the Russian people seemingly knew nothing about what was taking place.[21] (Perhaps this explains why Holmes' analysis was so flawed.) In his report to Ottawa, he argued convincingly that the Soviets were not ready for a hot war over Germany at that time, but his suggestion that a direct Western challenge was doomed to failure was unfounded.[22]

Mackenzie King had his own reasons for following Holmes' advice. The British had asked Canada to contribute to an American-led airlift of supplies to West Germans in need, and the aging leader interpreted the request as an attempt by London to assert its old imperialist influence. Pleas from the more internationalist leaning St. Laurent and Under-secretary Pearson made little difference. As a result, Canada's involvement was limited to an ineffective discussion at the Security Council, which convened at the end of November 1948 and extended through to the following February. Although the situation itself was intense, US President Truman's decision to airlift supplies into Berlin worked perfectly and was hardly the action of, in Holmes' terms, a "military hothead."[23]

Perhaps the faulty analysis was a sign of fatigue. The Soviets had made life particularly difficult for foreign diplomats, and Holmes was aching to return home. John Watkins, another bachelor, was set to replace him in Moscow, and Watkins' sought-after job in Ottawa as head of the European Division was open. What Holmes did not want to do was to go to Paris for UN-related work. He explained this politely to Escott Reid, focusing on his ignorance of world affairs, which had only been cultivated by his stay in Moscow. He was much more candid with his family. When he learned that Norman Robertson had hoped to bring him back to London for six weeks before dispatching him to Ottawa, he wrote of his excitement to return to the division in which he had first worked when he entered the department. "I was afraid I should get involved in United Nations affairs which I don't much like," he added.[24]

His lack of enthusiasm for the world organization was understandable. The UN's activities had been largely disappointing since 1945, hamstrung by the Soviet veto and the general inability of the great powers to cooperate. Canada, in fact, was itself already contemplating a regional security alliance to compensate for the Security Council's likely ineffectiveness against the Soviet threat. Holmes must have been disappointed when Lester Pearson not only decided to cancel the trip to London so that the departing chargé could help Watkins with what was, for every visitor to Moscow, a difficult transition but also determined that a journey to Paris would be a logical stopover before coming home. Holmes remained wary of his new assignment throughout August as he prepared to leave the USSR.[25]

On 2 September 1948, he responded to a memorandum by Reid on the place of Canada in the Cold War that was circulating among the senior members of the DEA. It was his last major commentary from his position in Moscow and reflected a view of the conflict that had been confirmed by his experience over the previous year. Both sides had made mistakes since 1945, and it was wrong to deny Western culpability, but the Soviets' errors had been much worse. It was their secrecy and unwillingness to communicate honestly that had accelerated the spiral of fear and mistrust.[26]

The following week, Holmes held a large party at the embassy to say good-bye to his friends and colleagues. Each of the twenty members of his staff received a parting gift, based on what he deemed were their genuine wants and needs: clothes, scarves, fountain pens, and even make-up. As he boarded a train for Brest-Litovsk, he wrote home, expressing feelings of nostalgia and perhaps regret. "I don't suppose I shall ever have again so many good friends and so much happy social life," he explained. Sitting down alone on the train with a large selection of Russian dolls that he had collected for his nephews and nieces, he felt "lonely and bereft." The experience in Moscow had been "unforgettable."[27] But it was over now, and he was off to advise General Andrew McNaughton on Security Council questions. His arrival was fixed for 20 September, at which point he joined the Canadian delegation at the Hotel Raphael on Kleber Avenue.

"The Great Holmes,"[28] as he was later known in the embassy in Moscow, was deeply missed when he left the Soviet Union, but he himself was pleasantly surprised by his new job. His years with the CIIA and now in the foreign service under Robertson and Massey in particular had turned him into an expert in the social aspects of diplomacy, and when it came to finding a place to reunite with old friends, there was none better than a meeting of the UN. It was, he said, like a "world-wide fraternity." He got along well with his new supervisor, General McNaughton, who lovingly referred to his team of himself, Charles Ritchie, and Holmes as the three dwarves. This was not, of course, because they were small in stature but, rather, because they were workers, never seeming to let up from their endless running around at the Palais de Chaillot.[29]

The General, as Holmes called him in his letters home, had a university degree in physics and engineering and had used his scientific training to rise quickly within the Canadian military. After spending the years from 1935 through 1939 in charge of the National Research Council, he returned to the service as the commanding officer of the First Canadian Infantry Division. For a period, he commanded the entire Canadian army until criticism of his judgment and poor health led to his resignation at the end of 1943. Still popular at home, he was appointed minister of national defence in 1944, tasked with convincing the public that conscription was necessary for complete victory in the Second World War. His failure to do so ended his brief political career. His focus returned to technical military matters, and, after the war, he became Canada's representative to the United Nations Atomic Energy Commission (UNAEC). When Holmes arrived in Paris, McNaughton was Canada's acting permanent representative to the UN while he finished his term on the UNAEC.[30]

Perhaps the only real letdown during those first weeks in Europe proper was a dinner with an ill-looking Mackenzie King. In spite of his poor health, the prime minister was his usual self, a combination of graciousness (such as when he asked for details about Holmes' experience in the Soviet Union) and utter pettiness (such as when he virtually forced his official to order the flambé – something that did not interest him in the least – simply because King wanted to see the dish light up before his eyes without having to put it on his own bill). The prime minister soon retired and was replaced in late 1948 by the much more appealing Louis St. Laurent.

During the approximately three months that he spent in Paris, Holmes was most involved with the Middle East file. Palestine had been left to the UN by the British in 1947, and a special committee had organized a partition of the land into Jewish and Arab states living side by side. The negotiations broke down, however, over who would administer the territory during the transition. Initially, the under-secretary of state for external affairs, Lester Pearson, played a leading role in attempting to secure a compromise between the British, who wanted to play no role at all, and the Americans, who expected the government in London to take the lead. In this case, the Canadian mediator was largely unsuccessful. The UN solution remained unacceptable to the neighbouring Arab states, and violence erupted across the territory. By late 1948 the UN was involved again. Both Pearson, now a member of the government, and General McNaughton actively sought a great power consensus, and Holmes' letters home noted with amazement how the three dwarves literally ran from meeting to meeting, and building to building, to find a solution.[31]

On 14 November 1948, at a little after 3:00 PM, and with a Canadian-penned UN resolution calling for an armistice finally before the General Assembly, Holmes got caught up in the excitement. As he was distributing copies of the proposal while at the same time drafting part of the General's speech, which was to be given momentarily, he grew tired and sat down to gather his thoughts. In the commotion, he forgot to look for a chair and crashed hard onto the floor. There were cameras everywhere, and they could not help but shift to Holmes temporarily. Later, colleague Gerry Riddell reflected in jest, "They'll all say that the Canadians were falling between two stools." More seriously, the situation was temporarily resolved, and not much later Israel was admitted to the UN.[32]

The Palestine experience confirmed for Holmes that Canada could indeed act as a bridge-builder among the great powers. "If it hadn't been for the Canadians," he wrote home, "Palestine would have been compromised to-day, that is absolutely certain."[33] Years later, his opinion had not changed. The "Canadian mediatory activity" on the Palestine issue, he told historian Donald Barry, "marked our entry into the political sphere." It gave McNaughton the "authority and respect" he needed to become "a real operator" on the Security Council.[34]

Secretary of State Pearson was so impressed by his protégé's perform-ance at the UN that he asked Holmes if he wanted to return to Ottawa as his personal assistant. The new position would see him working as a sort of private secretary responsible for keeping Pearson abreast of everything taking place in the DEA. (Any potential overlap or conflict between this job and the role of the under-secretary of state for external affairs was simply ignored.) The offer was intimidating. It was more re-sponsibility than Holmes had ever handled and there were others senior to him, such as Gerry Riddell and Charles Ritchie, who had been passed over as candidates. A compromise was reached. Riddell, one of the most perennially under-rated officials of the period, accepted the position and Holmes replaced him as temporary head of the UN Division in Ottawa while also agreeing to serve as acting Canadian permanent representative to the UN. He even settled into Riddell's old office in room 103 of the East Block, now a much more spacious place to work since the members of the Department of Finance, who had previously shared the area, had been moved elsewhere.[35]

Upon his return, although he was only thirty-eight, Holmes became a leader and mentor to the DEA's newest members. Shortly after their first day, he invited each group of recruits home for drinks and sandwiches. The idea was to make them feel comfortable, to allow them to understand that, while experience mattered (there was a formal hierarchy within the department), the group was a team, and everyone's ideas were valued. Lunches in Ottawa were eaten at a cantina in the basement of the East Block run largely by the blind. Officers and secretaries of all ranks bought their meals and sat down with whomever was around. One's standing in the DEA was irrelevant. There is a reason that both the secretarial staff and the former officers who served in the East Block in the late 1940s and early 1950s recall their time as part of a golden age of Canadian foreign policy. As Holmes had discovered on his own first day back in 1943, at the personal level, the DEA was one of the best places to work in the country. Full of bright, educated, and motivated young veterans and intellectuals, and led by an equally committed group of hard-working Canadian nationalists with a desire to play a meaningful role in the world, it was an experience not to be missed.[36]

Holmes was a particularly good mentor when it came to helping colleagues, new and old, manage some of the pricklier members of the team. Escott Reid, whose intellect was matched only by his arrogance, was one of them. A famous story is told by DEA alumni from the period during which Reid, thanks to a series of unforeseen events, was temporarily elevated to acting under-secretary of state for external affairs.[37] At the time, a member of the Far Eastern Division had a policy recommendation that he knew Reid would not like. Nevertheless, his analysis was reasonable, and he was unwilling to compromise. Not knowing what to do next, he sought advice from someone more experienced. Holmes, who quite liked Reid, knew exactly how to play him. The former Rhodes Scholar abhorred lacklustre prose and spent much of his career in the foreign service on a crusade to force officers to draft more simply and accessibly. After Holmes read the memorandum in question he told the official to have his secretary retype it, only this time to include three glaring grammatical errors, and to return to him at the end of the day. Five o'clock came and Holmes accompanied his colleague to Reid's office. When Reid noticed the first error he told the officer that he ought to have known better. When he reached the second, he grimaced. When he noticed the third, he fumed. He did not read to the end of the document, signed the memorandum in a huff, and told the two to go home. Holmes left the room wearing a slightly sheepish grin.

As for the job itself, Holmes spent much of 1949 negotiating between two sets of responsibilities. His UN duties left him in charge of a staff of about five, with much of the autumn dedicated to trips to New York and attendance at committee meetings. The rest of his time was taken up by educational and public affairs duties similar to his previous responsibilities at the CIIA. In March, he spent a week at the University of Toronto speaking to an informal international relations society and looking for new recruits. The DEA was continuing to expand rapidly and remained in desperate need of educated Canadian internationalists. He made trips to Montreal and London later that spring for similar reasons and represented the department at a CIIA meeting in the early summer. He also became an instructor at the University of the East Block, specializing in the writing of general reports. On this issue, Holmes was as much of a stickler as was his friend Reid. As one former student recalled fondly:

John Holmes descended on us at Canada's Permanent Mission to the United Nations in New York and promptly asserted that Externalites do NOT feel; they *think* such-and-such, or *believe*, or *hold the view* that, or *are of the opinion* ... John did NOT report to Ottawa that he felt that the United States would support Canada's draft; rather, he *believed* that the U.S. would. He *thought* that our draft might command a majority; although the French delegate *held the view* that we might fail ... Except to the denser among us, John Holmes' impeccable crafting on pieces of paper was infectious.[38]

At one point, the officers of the UN Division even wrote a poem, entitled "J.W.H.":

The Boss of our Division
Has certain reservations
About the use of words and files
On the United Nations

For instance, he instructs us
In writing memoranda
To use the proper English phrase,
Not slipshod propaganda.

By which I mean to tell you,
(In fact to emphasize)
That if your meaning is "inform,"
Don't dare to say "advise."

And so, if you are anxious
To become a diplomat,
Don't mutilate the language
Like a red tape bureaucrat.[39]

Officers preferred Holmes to Reid because of the former's humility and encouragement. In his University of the East Block lecture he stressed the need for commitment and hard work. Drawing inspiration from Norman Robertson, he often concluded: "You must try by all possible means to report the truth as you see it, for the foreign policy of Canada must be based on solid foundations."[40] Holmes was quite enamoured with the job, except for the trips to Lake Success for the UN meetings. He never was comfortable with the bustle of the city, nor did he like the disruptions to his routine, so he did what he could to keep his US travel to a minimum.

The attempt to confine himself to Ottawa was a complete failure. In January, Holmes was posted to New York and assigned alternate status on an interim committee on atomic energy. In February, he represented Canada at the tenth session of the Economic and Social Council and then served on the delegation to the meeting of the seventh session of the UN

Trusteeship Council. All the while, he was gathering all too many leave credits and continuing to pay rent on his apartment in Sandy Hill, a flat that he very much enjoyed sharing with junior colleagues H. Basil Robinson and John Watkins. Holmes spent much of the spring negotiating his way out of a trip to Geneva, using his month-long sick leave from the previous fall as evidence of what the stress of his UN responsibilities could do to him. In this case, he was a victim of his own success. He made himself so valuable as a Canadian representative at the UN that it became difficult to assign him to anything else. Still a relatively new officer, and not yet forty, John Holmes had already become an indispensable force within the East Block. His influence was felt at the policy level, where his memoranda were treated with the utmost consideration. He was known, according to a former colleague, as "a man with a quick, highly creative mind whom everyone liked and respected."[41] His impact was also felt diplomatically, where his range of international contacts was virtually unmatched for someone with less than seven years of experience in the public service. Perhaps most important, he was looked upon by the increasing numbers of new recruits as a father figure: a role model for every Canadian foreign service officer. He enjoyed all three aspects of the job, even if his overwhelming responsibilities at times became a physical burden. That too, however, was set to change after Under-secretary Arnold Heeney promised to grant him three weeks off in July. Much to his surprise, things would turn out quite differently.

4

John Holmes' Golden Age

The early 1950s are typically considered among the golden years of Canada's national history.[1] A booming economy, a stable government, a people united in their opposition to communism, and an exceptionally talented diplomatic corps allowed the country to make a disproportionate contribution to world affairs. Not coincidentally, the period beginning in the summer of 1950 through to the end of 1956 encompassed John Holmes' greatest professional years. Already a rising star in the Department of External Affairs, he was about to become a genuine leader, commanding no less respect than his original mentors. The decade, however, had a difficult beginning. Holmes' experience during the early part of Canada's first combat mission since the Second World War was his worst in the department to that point.[2]

On 25 June 1950, with moral, if not also military, support from China and the Soviet Union, Kim Il-sung, the communist leader of North Korea, ordered his troops across the 38th parallel in an attempt to take over the nationalist regime of the Western-backed Syngman Rhee in the South. It was a Sunday, and most senior Canadian officials were either at the cottage or away on business. Ottawa had sensed the danger of the situation in Korea – the country had been divided since the Second World War and neither side was pleased with the arrangement – but since US secretary of state Dean Acheson had recently stated publicly that South Korea was not within the United States' sphere of influence, no one had thought that an immediate response from Canada would be necessary.

Holmes, who was in New York at the time as Canada's acting permanent representative to the UN, learned of the attack on the radio. He was also surprised to discover that the Security Council would be meeting immediately to discuss it. Shortly after the government in Ottawa collected itself, he received instructions from the East Block to travel to an old factory at Lake Success, just outside of New York City, to observe the great power discussion. Led by US president Harry Truman, a committed internationalist who had strong personal feelings about the negative role that the League of Nations had played in the breakdown of the international order in 1939, the United States had decided that the communist invasion was a legitimate threat not only to Western Cold War interests but also to the credibility of the global organization that had been created to ensure that the crisis of the Second World War would never be repeated.[3] The American representatives therefore quickly moved a Security Council resolution condemning North Korea's aggression and demanding its immediate withdrawal from the South. Since the Soviet Union was boycotting the deliberations to protest the United States' unwillingness to recognize communist China, it took no more than two days for the council to authorize a US-led UN force to intervene in the conflict and drive Kim Il-sung's army back to the 38th parallel.[4]

Although shocked by the extent of the American commitment, Ottawa expressed its support and made plans to contribute troops of its own. As Lester Pearson explained in a letter to the Canadian missions, "If the strategic consequences of the loss of Korea would not be serious, the moral consequences would be grave in the extreme. A state which had been created by the United Nations would have been destroyed by naked aggression. And other countries, particularly in South and South-East Asia, which are open to communist attacks would be disheartened and demoralized."[5] Over 22,000 soldiers eventually participated in the Korean War on behalf of the St. Laurent government.

Their success was not immediate, but by the end of September 1950, the North Koreans were in retreat. The American general in charge of the mission, Douglas MacArthur, whose bold decision to land behind enemy lines had reversed Western fortunes, saw an opportunity to take over the entire North and democratize Korea once and for all. Crossing the 38th parallel, however, would have run counter to the original UN mandate and risked provoking the neighbouring Chinese. Now back in Ottawa, Holmes was angered and disappointed. Provoking the Chinese was a strategic military error, and MacArthur's attempts to manipulate the UN to suit his own ambitions could have a permanent impact on the organization's reputation. He was equally unimpressed by the US-inspired Uniting for Peace resolution, which empowered the UN General Assembly to deal with military issues when a Security Council that once again included the Soviet Union proved unable to agree. The resolution undermined the authority of the council and violated the fundamental spirit of the organization.[6] Holmes tried to express his concerns through a DEA liaison committee, which he hoped could coordinate strategy between Ottawa and New York, but the pressure of the situation on the individuals involved made that impossible. His hesitations were not a priority for a government that was busy explaining to its Western allies why its military support for the mission in the early days had been relatively meagre.

The Chinese did enter the war, and the Americans introduced a resolution declaring China an aggressor, an action that could have expanded the conflict across Asia. Holmes, who opposed the strategy but also recognized the importance of maintaining Western unity, argued that Canada should abstain. Back in New York to manage the crisis personally while Prime Minister St. Laurent negotiated with the British and non-aligned Indians at a Commonwealth conference in London, Lester Pearson agreed that the Americans' antagonism of the Chinese was a mistake, but he thought it impossible not to support Canada's greatest ally in the midst of the first significant military conflict of the Cold War. In February 1951, even though he had spoken out against American actions in committee, Pearson voted in favour of the resolution at the General Assembly. Within about a month, Holmes' position seems to have been vindicated. The Chinese responded aggressively, causing UN forces to retreat.

In late March 1951, as he returned to New York as acting permanent representative to the UN in place of Gerry Riddell (who had died tragically of a heart attack), Holmes drafted a memorandum on the relationship between Canada, the United States, and the UN that was particularly critical of the United States' unpredictability, its lack of self-discipline in foreign policy rhetoric and action, and its insistence on informing, rather than consulting, its allies in the midst of what was supposed to be a multilateral initiative. Canadians, however conservative, were "more interested in practical resolutions than in declarations," he argued. "We are also, I hope, less under the hypnotic influence of our own slogans." He concluded with greater balance, noting that provoking the United States unnecessarily was helpful to no one, but his message was clear: when the Americans were in error, and particularly when their policies risked the credibility of the UN, it was in Canada's best interest to make its objections heard.[7] Just over two weeks later, Pearson took some of his advice to heart in a speech that declared that the days of "easy and automatic political relations between Canada and the United States" were officially over.[8]

In spite of this statement and General MacArthur's unceremonious dismissal by President Truman, Holmes' frustration did not subside. In a private note to Escott Reid, he described the United States as "intolerable" and lamented "the extent to which the whole United Nations [had] been Americanized over the last twelve months."[9] His frustration hardly abated through the rest of the year as US representatives attempted to manage international negotiations over relief and reconstruction.[10] After the conflict ended, Pearson asked Holmes to summarize the Korean situation for memoirs that he planned to write during his retirement. Although Holmes typically would have acted immediately, this time he struggled and delayed. His loyalty to Pearson and his commitment to harmonious relations within the Department of External Affairs largely prevented him from describing what he believed had truly happened.[11]

Exactly why John Holmes ended up where he did next is unclear. The National Defence College (NDC) had been established in Kingston in 1948 as part of a conscious attempt to educate and train Canadian officers at home instead of in Great Britain. Its more specific goal, in Holmes' own words, was "to establish closer understanding and closer working relations between the civilian and armed services. If anything, the purpose was to make the military more aware of the facts of national and international life." There were no formal courses, no exams, and the officers who attended did not receive degrees when they completed their year. The teaching was by members of the DEA and NDC seconded to the college for up to two years. The students worked in syndicates and learned by discussing and assessing case studies of hypothetical international situations. They also toured some of the more important military bases around the world, where they were lectured to by prominent experts.[12]

Holmes was first notified of the possibility of his placement at NDC by the under-secretary for external affairs, Arnold Heeney, yet another Rhodes Scholar who excelled as a Canadian diplomat. He then had a less than enthusiastic discussion about the potential opportunity with his old advisor, Marcel Cadieux. Shortly after their original talk, for reasons that he never revealed explicitly, he changed his mind. "My brain is growing fat," he wrote to Cadieux, "and I think this might be a chance to develop a little cerebral muscle for a change."[13] At the time, he was noticeably frustrated with the state of his department. His university friend, Herbert Norman, was being hounded by radical anti-communists in the United States for alleged disloyalty, and Holmes was unimpressed with the way that Heeney and others were handling relations with the RCMP.[14] The under-secretary's team had done a good job of reorganizing a department that had never fully recovered administratively from Lester Pearson's entrance into politics, but Heeney's inability, or unwillingness, to convey the message to the rest of the staff that he would stand by his officials and protect them from the wrath of US senator Joseph McCarthy's propaganda machine and "an American public which [had] inherited from its ancestors in Salem superstitions about those who consort with the devil," was having a profoundly negative effect on morale.[15] The witch-hunt targeted the old Institute of Pacific Relations, of which Holmes had been an active member, and this worried him. (The IPR was eventually vindicated.) There was the policy in Korea with which he had not agreed, leaving him somewhat at odds with Pearson at a time when his two other greatest mentors and career boosters, Hume Wrong and Norman Robertson, were inaccessible. Finally, thanks to a combination of circumstances beyond his control and his dedication to his job, he had accumulated close to 150 days of unused vacation time and was in desperate need of a change of pace.[16]

It is possible that Holmes chose to go to NDC because it was a chance to get away and, indeed, to recharge in a much less intense atmosphere. In Kingston, he could read, learn, and think in a way that had not been possible in the hectic circumstances of diplomatic life in Ottawa and New York. Moreover, as is stated in the official departmental release, his wide national and international experience as well as his advanced academic training made him a logical choice for the position.[17] On the other hand, some – both back then and upon reflection many years later – found it strange that a shining star in the Department of External Affairs, one who was almost certainly destined, at the rate at which his career had been progressing, to become under-secretary in the future, seems to have been taken off the fast-track. A number of former colleagues have admitted that they had always viewed a secondment to NDC as a demotion and were shocked to learn that Holmes was ever there.[18] Others have suggested that the appointment of both Holmes and Doug LePan – two men who later left the department under awkward circumstances – in the midst of increasing McCarthyism in the United States was nothing but consistent with the way that the department had dealt with the Herbert Norman controversy. It is possible that Holmes' views on the Korean War had caused some discomfort among his superiors; Hume Wrong was far more sympathetic to the American case than was Pearson and would have been particularly disappointed with Holmes' analysis of the situation. There is also no doubt that he was tired and not at his best throughout the spring and summer of 1951.

Although the reasons behind the secondment will probably never be clear, the results of the change of scenery were excellent. Holmes spent part of July on a well-deserved holiday and the rest of it in Kingston for orientation. He returned to the department in August but spent two additional weeks on annual leave while he was there. He was fresh and relaxed when he arrived at the NDC barracks to take up residence in September.

It did not take long for him to fit in. He knew and liked LePan and soon befriended a number of Canadian servicemen as well as others on exchange from the United States and Great Britain. He enjoyed this rare opportunity to observe the military lifestyle first-hand, and the slower pace was good for his health. He became a teacher once again, an experience that he had missed, and his students were largely motivated and focused. "This is a rejuvenating experience," he wrote to Terry MacDermot after four months:

> There is something adolescent about Service life that has its attractions when one is aging and balding and growing crusty. I haven't heard dirty jokes for so long ... There are better things about the military which Morley put his finger on when he said one of the things he liked about them was that they were very polite. This quality I was inclined to write off along with their fascination for dress until I realized how much I liked living with people with a code. For whatever reason there is a kind of self-discipline which [makes their lives] pleasant and unprecarious ... They are very tolerant about us and can be won over to friendliness by great care in not flaunting one's intellectual wares.[19]

He also enjoyed the travelling that came with his new job. During the winter of 1951-52 the student body crossed the Canadian North, beginning in the far west and stopping in Whitehorse, Yellowknife, Churchill, and a number of other cities and towns before touring Quebec and the northeastern United States. Holmes gained a new appreciation for the Canadian tundra and its impact on his country's national security and identity. He also met officers from the air force who impressed him greatly. Hearing about some of the bureaucratic struggles at home – it was during this period that an unhappy Norman Robertson was arranging his own return to London – made him even more grateful to be away.[20]

He arrived back in Kingston in teaching mode and led a four-week course on communism and the Soviet Union before heading off again, this time for a two-month tour across the Atlantic. Everyone stopped in London for two weeks, where the British Ministry of Defence treated the group to a series of lectures by its most senior personnel and select cabinet ministers. The course then split into two, with half staying in Europe and the rest, including Holmes, flying to North Africa, and then the Near and Middle East. Throughout their travels, they alternated between hotels and messes. At times, they were billeted by local officers.

A four-day stopover in Jordan was particularly memorable. On the road to Amman, the group's vehicles were delayed when a small Chevrolet came to a halt in front of them. Out of the car strode the newly crowned King Talal I bin Abdullah. The monarch, who, during his brief reign, revitalized the Jordanian Constitution and improved relations with neighbouring Egypt and Saudi Arabia, greeted the tour warmly. The next day, four of the tour leaders, including Holmes, ate lunch at the royal palace.[21] In Iraq, Holmes stayed in a beautiful hotel near Lake Habbaniya, on the west bank of the Euphrates. There he drank orange squash, a gift of the Ministry of Defence. On Bahrain Island, he bunked with the American vice-president of the Bahrain Petroleum Company in a fully air-conditioned seashore cottage. The Asian experience was culturally revealing, even if discussions of defence and foreign policy were never more than surface level. On the whole, the Arab community and its leaders made an excellent impression, leaving Holmes sympathetic to their view of the state of Middle Eastern politics. "The Arabs are no more interested than the French in being liberated by the Western Powers," he wrote. "We ought to show a little more imagination than we too often do in assuming that the neutrality of these countries is due entirely to their blindness to the real nature of communism. It is neither wise nor honest of us to demand that the Iraqis and their neighbours stand up and be counted if all we plan to use their countries for is scorched earth." The trip did not include a stop in Israel.

Holmes' reflections on the transition from Asia to Africa demonstrate the strong Anglo-Saxon influences that shaped his sympathetic attitude towards what he sometimes called the right kind of imperialism. "Many of the Europeans," he wrote (perhaps ironically) of his guides, "seemed to have something approaching a real affection for the Africans, not, of course, an affection for equals, as they are not equals, but for pleasant children." Holmes had a well-meaning but at times paternalistic view of developing societies. "One impression I gained from this journey," he explained in his report on the trip, "was the continuing need of the British in the Middle East and of course in Africa. We saw little of the Americans, except for their training missions in Turkey and their oil men in Bahrain." Nevertheless, the British were not perfect, and Holmes abhorred the arrogance that was often exhibited by the soldiers towards the colonists. There was a disturbing, "apparently inextinguishable tendency of British soldiers of almost all ranks to treat them as wogs, people who must on no account be kicked or otherwise maltreated but who are not expected to have feelings like white men." The experience evoked feelings similar to those he had dealt with in Germany with C.D. Howe.[22]

Stops in Kenya, Libya, and Sudan focused primarily on military issues and were of less interest. Sudan, however, left him with a great story. The landing was unplanned as the plane carrying the group ran out of fuel. Disappointed, the travellers had expected to wait for hours for another plane to pick them up; instead, a Sudanese government representative gathered inmates from the local prison and brought them to the replacement aircraft by tractor. From there, they attached a giant rope to the original plane and pulled it all the way to Khartoum.

Back trouble, a concern throughout the rest of his life, kept Holmes from travelling with the group that summer, and he spent much of June in physiotherapy. As the department contemplated his next placement, he grew comfortable in his residence at Fort Frontenac and offered to stay longer. Now one of the veterans at the college, he took the lead in the winter of 1952-53 in entertaining the increased number of international students who had arrived from India, Pakistan, Australia, France, Belgium, Norway, Italy, and Turkey. He also went to great lengths to care for the families of the Canadian officers. When the men went off on the next tour, he and two colleagues threw a party for all of the soldiers' wives who lived in the Kingston area. It was a huge success and, in later years, was remembered fondly as "Operation Harem." Shortly after, with his physical condition improving, he rejoined the European part of the 1953 tour for stops in Germany and Austria.[23]

As his second academic year at the college was coming to a close, Holmes reflected on his time at NDC with nothing but fond memories. "I have never belonged to such a good community," he wrote, "and I can hardly bear the thought of leaving it. The way the officers not only of NDC but also of the Staff College have accepted me and made me feel one of them is something I shall never forget. They have their foibles and limitations, but they are a breed of gentlemen in the best sense of the word. They have taught me a good deal I needed to know about restraint and self-discipline and some of the virtues I brashly thought were outmoded. And they have incidentally revived in me the art of enjoying myself."[24]

In Ottawa, his superiors could not decide where to place him next. It was a difficult process, complicated by personnel changes in the capital. Arnold Heeney was sent to Paris as Canada's ambassador to the North Atlantic Treaty Organization (NATO) in 1952, and his replacement, Dana Wilgress, who never wanted the job, almost immediately began to negotiate his own departure. The idea was to bring Hume Wrong back from Washington to fill a position that had been owed to him for years. Wrong, however, was in poor health and, therefore, arranged for a three-month leave of absence before agreeing to assume his duties in the fall of 1953. The deputy under-secretary, Charles Ritchie, was placed in charge on a temporary basis. In the midst of all of this change, Joseph Stalin died, the UN welcomed a new secretary-general, the two sides in the Korean War reached an armistice, and the Liberals under St. Laurent were re-elected.

It is hardly surprising that plans for Holmes took time to straighten themselves out. While Wilgress was still in charge, the thinking had been that Holmes and LePan could go to Washington to work under Hume Wrong in the same political and economic roles that they had fulfilled in London under Norman Robertson. By June, however, with Wilgress preparing to leave and Wrong no longer planning to remain in the United States, the situation changed, a letter announcing the move to Washington was withdrawn, and Holmes was told to prepare to return to Ottawa, where his experience and calm hand would be helpful during the under-secretary's absence and thereafter.[25]

Hume Wrong, who saw Holmes' arrival as good news amid the stresses of the new position, arranged to have him promoted to assistant under-secretary and proposed that he rise from FSO 6 to FSO 8, a level that most officers did not achieve until they had served fifteen, or even twenty, years (Holmes had been employed for just ten). Administrative complications meant that he only reached FSO 7, but he remained ranked significantly higher than peers who had entered the service at the same time. The release announcing his promotion was glowing. Through his work both in the department and abroad over the last ten years he had become "a credit, not only to himself, but also to the Department and the Government as a whole." He was "a man of rare ability and integrity, who has rendered, and continues to render, inestimable value to the Department."[26]

On 4 September 1953 Holmes moved back to Ottawa and settled into a downtown apartment on Cartier Street. He was officially promoted the following month and, thus, entered into what was his "Golden Age" as a Canadian diplomat.[27] He was the assistant under-secretary of state for external affairs responsible for the UN, the Far East, and Commonwealth Affairs – basically the old Political Division and more. Later, the Historical Research and Reports Division was added to his portfolio. His office was in the southeast corridor of the second floor of the East Block, known affectionately as Killers' Row, the home of all of the senior staff.[28] He received a salary of $8,000 (increased the following year to $9,000) and a terminable allowance of $3,000, making him among the best compensated officers in Ottawa. He was looked upon as a leader by his peers and had begun to develop an international reputation for his sharp thinking, clear writing, and dedication to his job and country.

He worked with Hume Wrong for only two weeks in November 1953. The senior diplomat's poor health worsened during his leave, and his return to the office hastened his physical decline. Wrong's heart eventually failed, and in January 1954 the department suffered the loss of the man whom noted historian Jack Granatstein later called "the ablest diplomat the Canadian service had produced."[29] Holmes drafted Lester Pearson's published dedication to Wrong; he knew that all of Canada would suffer because yet another of its greatest diplomats had, at fifty-nine, worked himself to a premature death.[30]

Ironically, it was not long before morale in the DEA improved. After years of under-secretaries who did not enjoy their duties, the forty-one-year-old Jules Léger evoked memories of an earlier Norman Robertson when he accepted the position ahead of a number of men senior to him and then succeeded brilliantly. Educated in Quebec and France, he had been a journalist before his recruitment into the civil service by Mackenzie King. Having become Canada's youngest ambassador ever the year before, he had no problem establishing his credibility. Léger had a close relationship with Lester Pearson and an excellent rapport with his colleagues. Departmental officers were more upbeat than they had been in years, and senior members of the DEA found themselves included in what were known as daily "prayer meetings" with the minister. For Holmes, these sessions typically continued at professional baseball games. When he and Pearson were in New York together, they frequented Yankee Stadium. During the games, Pearson often discussed the strategy of both managers. It was a way of relaxing that made him a more flexible thinker when he returned to UN headquarters, and it gave him a sense of where his ideas were taking him in advance of the formal discussions of policy.[31]

Although he was certainly not the only assistant-under-secretary, nor was he the most senior, Holmes' outstanding rapport with his younger colleagues made him the one they looked up to the most. He encouraged them to send him their observations while away on postings, and he always responded in detail. He was known not just to approve memoranda written by new officers but also to leave short personal notes on the best ones, letting the drafters know that their work and thinking were appreciated.

His humility was legendary. When one new recruit to the DEA prepared to move to Ottawa for the first time in late 1953, he did not know where to turn for advice on accommodation. In England at the time, he contacted the one person he knew who had lived there: H. Basil Robinson. Robinson recommended that he write his old roommate, John Holmes. The recruit, who went on to become under-secretary, took the advice and received a polite and thorough letter back, which included a clipping from the local paper highlighting a particular establishment that was already home to a number of young foreign service officers. When James (Si) Taylor later realized that he had asked one of the most senior members of the department for housing suggestions, he was embarrassed, but he had no reason to be. Holmes understood this type of support as part of his mentoring role. He also shared professional banter and jokes with anyone, regardless of rank or age.[32]

Others recall how supportive Holmes was both to them and to their families. His get-togethers at the home he later rented in Sandy Hill were legendary. He had become skilled at Ukrainian dancing in Moscow and happily displayed his abilities after a drink or two. He had a wide-ranging music collection and loved to quote song and theatre (although his singing voice, recalls his niece, Ann Skinner, left much to be desired). His ability to make people feel at ease brought him respect that travelled with him long after he had retired from the DEA. And he did not focus exclusively on the officers. Just as they had been at NDC, most Sundays were spent taking the wives and families of colleagues abroad for lunch. They found that he was not only great company, but also exceptional with the children. He spoke to them about what they were learning in school, and had the ability to make them feel that whatever it was that interested them was important.

Another time, during a trip through Beirut, Holmes helped a junior officer in his twenties through an awkward dilemma. A Lebanese Canadian was in the hospital with a badly infected foot. The injury was life-threatening, and the patient could not afford to pay for the treatment. He was a despicable man who had already been convicted of arson in Canada, and there were fears of another violent response if he did not receive medical care quickly. The officer's superior, the chargé d'affaires, was ill, leaving the junior to decide whether he should authorize payment. If he said yes he would have to justify his decision to an Ottawa bureaucracy composed entirely of senior officials. If he did not, the man would almost certainly die. Holmes' advice was straightforward: life came first, no matter what. This firm statement was the encouragement that Michael Shenstone needed, and it left him with the confidence necessary to make the right decision.

As for the foreign policy that he would help develop, Holmes explained to the Canadian Army Staff College that it was based on six principles. First, "Canada First but not Canada Alone" meant that, in order to promote Canadian interests, the country had to be willing to help preserve the peace on other continents. Second, the economy's relatively disproportionate reliance on foreign markets created a vital interest in maintaining open trade routes, stable international financial organizations and institutions, and civil relations with any potential economic partners. Third, foreign policy could not be hostile to fundamental American interests: weakening the United States would hurt Canada strategically. Fourth, at the same time, maintaining a counterweight to American domination by propagating continued positive relations with the United Kingdom and the rest of the Commonwealth was crucial to national independence. Fifth, external affairs could not divide the country along ethnic lines; the conscription crises of the past could never be forgotten. Finally, the Canadian approach to global politics had to recognize both the potential and the limitations of a medium-sized power. "It doesn't mean, of course, that we just sit in the back row and look holy – or commit that unfortunate Canadian error of telling other people that they should just follow our lead and learn perfect peace," he said. "There is, in fact, a role which we can play and which we have played with some success. It is the role of the responsible member of a world community willing to provide his good offices if they can be used – as a mediator or a moderator or just as a thinker-up of practical solutions ... In the long run we haven't got much but our moral influence in a hard world, and if we have [sic] too many people off they aren't going to listen to us."[33] This was one of the first articulations of Canada's place in the world that Canadians and international students of world affairs came to expect from Holmes as he evolved into one of the most sought-after commentators on foreign policy of his era.

Holmes' attitude might well explain his continued frustration with the United States (this and the fact that particularly virulent Americans had taken to accusing Mike Pearson of being a communist). He believed that Canada had erred in following the United States and refusing to recognize communist China. He was also unimpressed by the recently elected President Eisenhower's "new look."[34] The doctrine of massive retaliation, announced by Secretary of State John Foster Dulles in a speech to the Council on Foreign Relations on 12 January 1954, meant that traditional military forces had become too expensive to maintain and that, as a result, enemies of the West had to be made aware that future threats would be met by an overwhelming preponderance of nuclear force. Because it was crucial to keep the United States involved in world affairs and on good terms with Canada, Holmes conceded in early 1954 that his country had little choice but to accept the new attitude and dedicate itself to ensuring that Western enemies understood the implications of war with the US in the clearest terms possible.[35]

Active participation in the Geneva conference scheduled for April 1954 to resolve the unfinished business of the Korean War was one way of pursuing this agenda. After a brief stop for a shocking NATO meeting in France – the chairman, French foreign minister Georges Bidault, was apparently drunk during most of the discussions[36] – Holmes travelled to Switzerland to join Secretary of State for External Affairs Pearson and the rest of the Canadian delegation. The meetings, which essentially restored the status quo between North Korea and South Korea, were dominated by one of Holmes' favourite politicians, Anthony Eden. Eden combined charm, an air of Britishness, and a respect for Pearson's opinions. Once his superior returned to Ottawa, leaving Holmes in charge of the now three-person Canadian delegation, he consulted with Eden regularly.[37]

Canada's impact was minor, although at one point it did play the interpreter role, literally, that Holmes took so seriously. At the closing session on the Korean issue, the Belgian foreign minister, Paul-Henri Spaak, was preparing to respond on behalf of the Western powers to comments made by his Chinese equivalent, Chou En-lai. Because translation at the time was consecutive and Spaak was expected to answer immediately, Holmes recruited colleague Chester Ronning – fluent in Chinese – to sit beside him and translate. After Ronning finished a thought, Holmes quickly turned his head the other way and passed along the information to Spaak in French. If there was ever a case of Canada acting as genuine go-between on the world stage, this was it.[38] The problems in Korea were never resolved, and the territory remained divided between the communists in the north and the nationalists in the south, but the stalemate ultimately held and Canada continued to withdraw its troops.

Discussions about the war between France and the communist Vietnamese led by Ho Chi Minh followed. Indochina, which included Vietnam, Laos, and Cambodia, had been a part of the French colonial system since the 1880s. France's difficulties during the Second World War allowed the Viet Minh to take control of North Vietnam. By 1950, they had been at war with France for close to four years with support from the Chinese. Even with US assistance, the French struggled, and by 1954 they were on the verge of complete defeat. At the time, the Canadian representatives – including Holmes – knew so little about Indochina that they had to purchase a map of the region from the Quai d'Orsay in France when the meetings began.[39] Clearly, this part of the world was of little interest, and Holmes had been overseas for almost four months. He therefore asked for and was granted permission to leave Geneva at the end of the initial conversations. By 12 July 1954 he was back in Canada, having landed in Halifax for a brief vacation.

In his absence, a basic armistice was achieved. Vietnam was divided into a communist North and a Western-backed South, and Laos and Cambodia were recognized by all of the relevant parties as independent states. Members of the conference volunteered Canada to serve with India and Poland on a series of three international commissions on supervision and control (ICSCs). The ICSCs were meant to support the ceasefire by supervising the free flow of refugees across the territories as well as a planned unification election in Vietnam. Although the Canadian government had not been properly consulted, and there were strong doubts among Holmes and his colleagues as to whether elections to unify Vietnam would ever be held, there was little option but to agree to serve. Its allies were depending on it, Canada had relatively good relations with the Indians, and the opportunity to act as a bridge-builder throughout the period of the ceasefire was enticing. What is more, if Canada had said no, it would have risked re-igniting the conflict and perhaps even expanding it. In Holmes' own words, his government's moral obligation "was honestly and objectively to do the best we could with our impossible assignment and use whatever influence we had to the fulfilment of the hope, even though it might have been a vain hope, that if the two parts of the country could settle down and tackle their economic problems, some day reconciliation might be possible."[40]

Over the next six weeks, what became known as the "Indochina octopus" overwhelmed the DEA.[41] And although Holmes saw his salary rise again, the additional money hardly compensated for the headaches that accompanied his responsibility for the file. He did try to make light of his circumstances. "Stop Hanoi-ing me" and "Let Saigons be Saigons" became his two favourite puns. More seriously, between October 1954 and March 1955, the situation in Vietnam, which included supervising the movement of close to 800,000 refugees, consumed virtually all of his time. He became one of the principal drafters of government statements on the issue and the ultimate coordinator of Canadian policy.

The challenges were never-ending. At the departmental level, senior officers would not travel to Southeast Asia, making it hard to recruit an acceptable team. The United States, presumably Canada's greatest ally, continued to refuse to recognize China, an action that Holmes believed contributed to the tension throughout the continent. American officials also tended to ignore foreign policy recommendations that did not come directly from their own government, and, as had been the case in Korea, they preferred to inform rather than consult. Finally, while the Canadians were making a genuine attempt at impartiality, the Poles echoed the Soviet position on every issue. This made the situation almost untenable. Canada could not disagree with the United States publicly out of fear of encouraging Polish intransigence. At the same time, any failure to denounce Western breaches of the armistice compromised Ottawa's credibility as an impartial mediator.[42]

Holmes almost got a respite in the spring when Norman Robertson requested that he be transferred to London and appointed deputy high commissioner, but Pearson decided to send him on what was called an inspection trip instead.[43] On 1 April 1955 Holmes departed for Indochina. On his way, he stopped in Paris to attend a North Atlantic Council meeting and in New Delhi to nurture the relationship with India. In Hanoi, he experienced first-hand the force of a Cold War turning hot. Like almost every foreign service officer posted to Vietnam, Holmes left the country more strongly anti-communist than he was when he entered. After about a week on the ground he wrote to his family, "now I am behind the Iron Curtain again [and] it seems more sinister than it did in Moscow."[44] Visits to cities spread out across the country and to nearby Laos and Cambodia did nothing to change his mind. He finished the Indochina portion of his travels with four days in Saigon, meeting personally with South Vietnam's leader, Ngo Dinh Diem, and later with the American ambassador. There was a formal dinner in his honour, and he visited the refugee camps in Bien Hoa. After a return trip that included stops in New Delhi, Paris, and London, he landed in Montreal on 23 June and quickly made his way home to Ottawa.

In his report to Pearson, Holmes expressed mixed feelings. The control commissions had been largely effective in their first year. Their most important task – maintaining the peace – had been achieved. For the time being, full-scale war had been averted. But the Canadians on the ground were growing frustrated. It was difficult to appreciate that the lack of progress in achieving a long-term resolution of the conflict was compatible with any measure of success, and it was hard to feel useful without any specific accomplishments to point to as evidence of progress. "We must keep our eyes steadily fixed on the fact that our real contribution in Indochina cannot be judged primarily by our success on any specific items of the agenda," he maintained: "The real contribution is our being there." His comments, later referred to by one analyst as "the classic rationale for remaining on the Indochina commissions," were considered valuable enough to be distributed across Ottawa and Hanoi.[45] Then, before he could re-acclimatize to life in Ottawa, he was sent to Washington to present his country's case to an increasingly troublesome US State Department.

The Americans were in a difficult position. With France no longer able to support the South Vietnamese against the Viet Minh, it was up to the United States to step in or to allow the communists to take over the country, if not the region. The government in Washington supported the Geneva agreements in principle – they were an effective and inexpensive way of maintaining what was then a relatively peaceful status quo – but refused to accept some of their implications. For example, the Americans were convinced that if Vietnam were to hold unification elections, the communists would win. They hoped, therefore, to delay any vote, even though that meant compromising the spirit of the original agreement. For a while this approach seemed possible because the United States never signed the Geneva pact.[46]

How Canada should respond was unclear. Criticizing the Americans was hardly in the national interest, but permitting them to damage the credibility of the agreements, and of the control commissions, was of no help either. The alternative, allowing the United States to delegitimize the agreements, would hasten their dissolution and enable the dispirited Canadian diplomatic corps to return home; however, the mission would be deemed a failure. Holmes concluded that the decision was not Canada's to make. No matter how much it wanted to, it could not abandon the commissions while they were still contributing to the maintenance of peace, nor could it fulfil its role on those commissions with complete integrity since it would have to continue to protect the Western side. After the Indochina situation reignited into war, Holmes reflected: "In my view, and I think this may be typically Canadian, the evil in Vietnam was neither the North Vietnamese nor the Americans but the war itself." It was not the disagreement per se but, rather, the failure to agree to disagree that was the real crisis.[47]

Holmes returned to Ottawa at the end of August having taken just five days' leave all year. Although his peers often wondered in amazement where he found the time to think and write clearly, the answer was simple: he rarely left the office.[48] He then learned that he would be accompanying Pearson to the Soviet Union in October. The visit was part of an effort to improve understanding and to increase trade between the two countries, and it followed the reception of nine Russian agricultural experts in Canada. As one of the few senior officers who spoke any Russian, as well as one of the most trusted of Pearson's potential colleagues, Holmes was an obvious choice.

The Soviet Union in which he arrived was profoundly different from the one he had left eight years earlier. As part of a ministerial entourage, he came by plane and was chauffeured around the country by limousine. Instead of the embassy, he and the associate deputy minister of trade and commerce, Mitchell Sharp, stayed in six-room suites in the Sovietskaya Hotel and were treated to extravagant meals and amenities. A highlight for Holmes was watching Sofia Golovkina and Maya Plisetskaya perform in *Don Quixote*. Seeing Plisetskaya, a twelve-year veteran of the professional stage, would have been particularly memorable since anti-Semitism in Russia prevented her from touring outside of the country until 1956.

It is difficult to judge what role Holmes played because Pearson's description of the trip (in his diary and his memoirs) all but leaves him out. It is clear, however, that Holmes was personally involved in two of the significant discussions with the Canadian delegation's host, Foreign Minister Molotov, and that he and old friend George Ignatieff were useful to Pearson in managing the Canadian media members who had joined the group, including an ambitious CBC correspondent and future Quebec premier – René Lévesque.

Holmes' own comments on the trip suggest that he took three lessons from it. First, the Soviet government differentiated between Canada and the United States. Communist officials expressed strong discomfort with the United States and its policies throughout the visit but never suggested that those criticisms applied to Canada. In fact, they spoke repeatedly of the possibility that the government in Ottawa might act as an interpreter between the two sides. Second, the emergence of Nikita Khrushchev as first secretary of the Communist Party in September 1953 was a mixed development. The new regime was more sensible than its Stalin-led predecessor and did appear interested in reducing the intensity of the Cold War, but that also made it more attractive to the non-aligned states that the countries of the West were hoping to recruit to their side. Finally, any hope for an improvement in the state of the Cold War had to be cautious. As much as the Khrushchev regime had tried to portray itself as more inviting, there was no doubt that its eventual goal remained the triumph of communism over capitalism, and no amount of diplomacy was going to change that view in the immediate future. At the same time as Khrushchev promoted greater dialogue and trade with the West, for example, he also created the Warsaw Treaty Organization (the Warsaw Pact) to rival NATO and repealed treaties of alliance with Britain and France.[49]

There was room for meaningful negotiation on smaller issues. One area in which the Canadians could play a significant role was membership in the United Nations. In April 1955, twenty-nine Asian and African states, the majority of which were newly independent, met in Indonesia to commiserate over their treatment by the great powers and to plot strategies to mobilize their opposition to colonialism. One of the most significant problems was their inability to acquire standing at the UN. Because of the Cold War, the permanent members of the Security Council, all of whom had veto power over new admissions, had reached an impasse: the Western representatives refused to admit communist satellites, while the Soviets vetoed real and potential NATO allies. By 1955, the tenth anniversary of the founding of the world body, the West had used its majority at the General Assembly to exclude seven states and the Soviets had vetoed fourteen others. Led publicly by Paul Martin, the minister of health and welfare who served in Pearson's place when the secretary of state for external affairs was unavailable to chair Canada's UN delegation to the General Assembly, Canada took the lead. Before he left for Moscow, Holmes appears to have drafted a proposal that was reminiscent of the way that the United States had admitted new members to the Union before the Civil War.[50] The organization would agree to take an equal number of communist and capitalist states at the same time. The idea was tabled at the tenth session of the General Assembly in 1955. According to Holmes' own recollection:

Life in New York was hectic not so much because of the amount of work as because of the emotional temperature. The Chairman was astride his white horse and you know what that means. When I first started drafting statements and telegrams for him about our proposal for admission of 18 new members I could merely say that it would be a good thing for the United Nations. Within a matter of weeks, it had become the one thing which would save the United Nations and by the time I left it had become the most important event in exactly 1,955 years.[51]

In spite of repeated warnings from the DEA counselling caution, and attempted bullying by his American colleagues, Martin pushed Canada to the forefront of the new member debate, working tirelessly to use his country's international reputation and his own determination to break the impasse. For Holmes, this was a turning point in both Canadian and UN history. The middle and lesser powers basically forced the great to admit sixteen new members, at least eight of which one power or another would not have wanted, creating the precedent that led the organization towards a membership policy of universality. Canada established itself as an expert international conciliator, capable of reaching difficult compromises that would be accepted by all of the great powers. Holmes later called his role in the event his "greatest contribution to the UN."[52] It was proof for him, as he liked to say later in life, that nice guys didn't always finish last.

While it might explain why he was soon officially promoted, most historians would disagree with the suggestion that the negotiations that resulted in the expansion of the UN's general membership by more than 25 percent marked the pinnacle of Holmes' diplomatic career. Less than a year later, the stakes for Canada were much higher. The Suez Canal was so crucial to British trading interests in the Far East that London had maintained defence forces in the area for much of the first half of the twentieth century. By 1956 those soldiers had left, thanks in part to an agreement with Egyptian president Gamal Abdel Nasser to keep the area freely accessible. When the withdrawal of US (and British) economic support for another Egyptian project led Nasser to nationalize the canal that July, the British panicked. Prime Minister Anthony Eden made a secret agreement with the French and Israelis to retake the area by force. Israel attacked Egypt pre-emptively, and France and Britain intervened to protect the integrity of the Suez region. The strategy, which was little more than old-fashioned imperialism, enraged the United States, India, and the Soviet Union, threatening the future of NATO, of the Commonwealth, and of the UN as well.

On 30 October 1956, when Holmes was informed by the Canadians stationed in New York that the Soviet representative to the Security Council was alleging that Israel had invaded the Gaza Strip and that Britain and France had announced that they would be taking over the canal region temporarily, he thought it was a joke. Nevertheless, he arrived at Pearson's office to find the minister receiving confirmation of the intervention from London. The next day, Pearson and Holmes completed arrangements to fly to New York. The idea of an emergency UN police force had been percolating for months, if not years, but on the plane on 1 November it was Holmes who, on a napkin, sketched out the first draft of what soon became the United Nations Emergency Force (UNEF). A short delay on the landing strip made the pair slightly late for an emergency session of the General Assembly that afternoon. Before they took their seats, Pearson instructed two of his most senior advisors in New York, Geoff Murray and Bert MacKay, to begin to float the idea of a UN peacekeeping force among the delegates.

As the young aides worked the corridors, the United States put a resolution to the assembly condemning British and French aggression. Thinking quickly, Pearson abstained and then sought permission to explain his action. His speech, which officially introduced the idea of a UN intervention force organized by the secretary-general, was drafted for him largely by John Holmes. US secretary of state John Foster Dulles spoke in support of the idea and urged the Canadians to return with a concrete proposal as quickly as possible.

Holmes and Pearson left the assembly well after 4:00 AM, bumping into actor Marlon Brando, whom they overheard explaining that he, like so many others, could not stay away from the excitement. A few hours later, they met with UN secretary-general Dag Hammarskjöld for an early lunch. Hammarskjöld was frustrated and thought that there was little chance that a proposal for a peacekeeping force would ever be accepted, particularly by the Israelis. Nevertheless, he did not reject the idea outright. Over the next two days, in consultation with the American representative to the UN, Henry Cabot Lodge, and a number of others, Pearson's team compiled a draft resolution. During that period, Holmes served as the primary intermediary between the authors of the forthcoming proposal and the British and French representatives, who had made themselves discreetly available. His years at the UN had made him one of the most trusted officials at the assembly.

Colleagues recall how it was largely Holmes' mediatory and diplomatic abilities, along with his drafting skills, that made Pearson's ultimate success possible. This is not to take away from the accomplishments of Lester Pearson – his sound strategic thinking, outstanding rapport with the most senior members of the major delegations, and reputation for getting things done at the UN were crucial – but he was not acting on his own. Along with Murray, MacKay, Marshall Crowe, John Hadwen, and others, John Holmes was an indispensable part of the Canadian team that brought a temporary ceasefire to the conflict in the Middle East. And after all sides accepted the Canadian proposal for a UN peacekeeping force, again it was Holmes who was instrumental in convincing the Egyptians to allow the Canadian military, which still wore British uniforms and therefore evoked in Colonel Nasser images of great power imperialism, to participate.[53]

The Suez story is told differently today in large part because John Holmes wanted it that way.[54] There are three possible reasons. The first is that, by this point, he had been overwhelmed by Pearson's diplomatic abilities and, in his own modesty, seems to have at least temporarily convinced himself that his minister could have succeeded on his own. In a letter to close friend and colleague Saul Rae, then working at the US embassy, just days after the final details of the crisis had been completed, he explained: "I think looking back that my best contribution was a couple of very good jokes in the early hours of the morning which I can't remember now. I should feel more ashamed of this performance if it were not for the realization that the Minister was operating beyond our comprehension and really had no need of advice."[55] Second, Wendell Holmes died before the final negotiations to include Canadians in the UN force had been concluded, and son John later told Pearson that his guilt over having "had to run out on the Delegation when they were hard-pressed"[56] might well have affected his assessment of his own role.

Finally, like Pearson, Holmes was never fully satisfied with the way that the crisis was ultimately resolved. He had envisioned a stronger force, one that could not have been held hostage by President Nasser. Just as important, he felt that matters such as the Suez crisis should have been handled by the Security Council. In this case, the British and French had vetoed council action and the General Assembly had reverted to the controversial Uniting for Peace resolution to take over jurisdiction. That the assembly was able to solve the problem indicated a power shift from the elite to the masses. For Holmes, this was cause for concern. The members of the larger body were less predictable and, indeed, less disciplined than the great powers. Moreover, Canada's allies could no longer dominate the assembly as they had in the UN's early days. The West had lost its "power to command an automatic majority whenever we crack the whip," he wrote prophetically to the under-secretary, Jules Léger, and this did not bode well for Canadian interests in the future.[57]

Looking back, as was often the case, Holmes' modesty and cautiousness prevented him from accepting what had really happened. Canada had made a difference, and it would not have done so without him.

5

Descending through the
Diefenbaker Era

The resolution of the Suez crisis was the most significant foreign policy event of the early postwar era for Canada and for John Holmes. Its positive impact was obvious: Lester Pearson's Nobel Prize brought the country incomparable prestige. The concept of peacekeeping became a defining component of Canada's international identity, and respect for Ottawa's diplomatic team reached a high point.[1] The negatives were less clear at the time but equally important. Suez marked the end of the consensus that had characterized the relatively non-partisan approach to foreign policy – unified by a national commitment to oppose the spread of communism – that had been adopted by the Canadian government since the Cold War began. For the first time in well over a decade, the rhetoric of anti-Americanism re-entered the national lexicon and gradually began to impede rational discussions of the way ahead. This took place during what analyst Trevor Lloyd has called "the beginning of a natural and probably unavoidable decline in Canada's influence on world affairs."[2] The creation of the European Economic Community in March 1957 symbolically marked Europe's return to the world stage as a notable force. Ottawa had to adapt to remain a significant global actor in the future, and it struggled to do so.

John Holmes had also reached the pinnacle of his diplomatic career in 1956. By the end of the year, he had become the third highest paid member of the East Block, behind just the deputy under-secretary and the under-secretary himself.[3] He had been promoted so quickly that his rank now exceeded that of Herbert Norman (who had joined four years earlier); George Ignatieff (three years his senior); Marcel Cadieux (two years); Bob Ford, whom he had replaced at a lower level in the Soviet Union; and Arnold Smith, yet another Rhodes Scholar who had joined the Department of External Affairs during the war. His contribution to the resolution of the Suez crisis had won him international accolades in diplomatic circles, and his prestige both at home and abroad could not have been higher. "I can see him now," wrote one former colleague: "Walking down the corridors of the UN delegates' lounge in 1957 ... Holmes was dressed in a sporty, checked brown suit, and his face was bright and ruddy as he loped through the corridors with his own special stride. Delegates and others, black and white, jumped up to shake his hand, banter, have a word, exchange information, give a compliment, touch his sleeve, or whatever. He was the prince of the UN, as well known and popular as the great Lester himself."[4]

He was, according to a young American diplomat who at that point had not even met him, a "legendary figure in the world of diplomatic reportage." An Australian peer called him "the best senior Foreign Office man I have ever come across anywhere, and, at the same time, a modest, sensitive, civilized human being."[5]

Tragically, it was the death of Wendell Holmes, rather than any of this acclaim, that was most indicative of what was to come. The combination of the passing of his father and his overwhelming duties at the UN reminded Holmes of his mentor and colleague, the late Gerry Riddell. In the winter of 1956-57, he spearheaded a campaign within the DEA to establish a bursary in Riddell's memory at the University of Toronto.[6]

A few months later, in April 1957, Herbert Norman committed suicide by jumping off the rooftop of a nine-story building in Egypt. Norman, who had played a significant role on the African side during the Suez crisis, took his own life when pressure from the US Senate's subcommittee on internal security to admit his communist past became too much to bear. Holmes was shattered, and he spent a great deal of the next few weeks comforting Irene Norman and her children.[7]

Louis St. Laurent was next. Although he did not die, during the 1956-57 period he was not himself. Suffering from bouts of apparent depression, family difficulties, and simple old age, he hardly led his government through much of its final years. Perhaps because of the prime minister's unpredictability, the relationship between the Liberal Party (and the Canadian diplomats who served it) and the national media also collapsed. As historian Patrick Brennan has explained, "This deterioration both led to and was the result of the ascendancy of a new approach to political journalism which repudiated the special relationship as too civilized and not responsible enough and replaced it with unvarnished adversarialism."[8] For a public servant like John Holmes, who had excelled in front of the podium at press conferences, this was another difficult and disappointing adjustment. It also meant additional responsibilities. As the government struggled to communicate its message effectively, the civil service was called upon to work harder to support it.[9]

Finally, there was the demise of the Liberal Party. For fourteen years, Holmes had served just two political masters, and for most of the last decade only one. Louis St. Laurent, along with his external affairs minister, Lester Pearson, shared his ideals. They knew and trusted him, and they had the experience necessary to promote Canadian interests abroad in a way that made the people of the country proud. Pearson in particular was, in Holmes' own words, "a very special kind of person to work for. He was one of us."[10] Such could not be said about Canada's new Conservative prime minister. Nevertheless, although Holmes later complained bitterly to family and friends about Mr. John George Diefenbaker, his original impressions of the Chief (as he was sometimes called) when he took office in June 1957 were not negative. In fact, at the prime ministerial level, Holmes was accepting of his new boss. St. Laurent had lost his way personally, the Liberals had been in power for too long (twenty-two years), change often sparked much needed innovation, and, as the leader of the government, Diefenbaker was always decent and, indeed, receptive to Holmes and his ideas.

As secretary of state for external affairs, however, Diefenbaker was a problem. The Chief had no real international experience and was naturally distrustful. He referred to the civil servants in the DEA as "Pearsonalities," believing, not entirely incorrectly, that they were inherently sympathetic to Liberal Mike Pearson's ideas and ideals. He was also too unsophisticated to realize that, since these Pearsonalities had been largely trained by Norman Robertson, their first loyalty was to their country, and they would therefore serve the Conservatives with equal dedication if simply given the chance. Under Diefenbaker, they were rarely allowed that opportunity.[11]

After the Liberals' defeat, most of the East Block had hoped that the Conservative Member of Parliament, Roland "Rollie" Michener, a former Rhodes Scholar and close friend of Lester Pearson, might be appointed as their minister. With Diefenbaker in charge that was never an option. Michener had supported Donald Fleming at the 1956 Conservative leadership convention and was therefore not among the prime minister's trusted colleagues. When Stanley Knowles of the Cooperative Commonwealth Federation declined an offer to be speaker of the house, the prime minister asked Michener, and he accepted.[12] As for the external affairs portfolio, the Chief initially took it on personally, bringing with him nothing but inexperience and suspicion. "I don't think Diefenbaker had a clear understanding of international and military affairs," Holmes later recalled. And he was too busy with the rest of his job to give foreign policy the attention that it required.[13]

This would have been disconcerting at any time, but in the summer of 1957 it was particularly difficult. As a new minister with minimal international experience, Diefenbaker faced a steep learning curve, and the infrastructure necessary to support him was lacking.[14] The combination of Bert MacKay's retirement, Herbert Norman's death, and an unfilled vacancy at the rank of deputy under-secretary left the DEA desperately under-staffed at the senior level. Among those experienced officers who remained, many, like Norman Robertson and Arnold Heeney, had recently changed posts. One step below, at the assistant under-secretary level, Holmes was the only official to have served in his position consistently over the previous eighteen months. Diefenbaker's hands-on approach to his new portfolio aggravated the situation. Since he did not trust the majority of his civil servants, a select few – including Holmes – found themselves called upon to dedicate an unusual amount of time to briefing him on the issues of the day.

The Chief recognized that he was burdensome and was, in fact, quite polite to those upon whom he relied for advice, but the ease with which he dealt with the people he trusted could not compensate for the additional work he imposed upon them. Just five days after the Conservative victory, Holmes wrote Charles Ritchie in despair: "The possibility of a holiday for longer than a week-end seems remote indeed. This is at a time when I feel even more worn out and depressed than most of the inhabitants of the East Block." The change of regime meant "an awful lot more work, longer memoranda, more explanations and a period of frustration. If you have any words of wisdom," he added, "don't forget that I am in constant need of guidance."[15] Holmes had only recently lost his father. He wanted to spend more time in London with his mother and had the leave accrued to do so. That he could not take a vacation was extremely upsetting. Norman's suicide only made things worse. Add to that the new government, and he was close to breaking – and it showed in his behaviour.

It was during this period that he had one of his most embarrassing experiences as a Canadian public servant. The DEA's francophones had traditionally pronounced his last name as "Ol-mess," and a few of his anglophone colleagues would tease him occasionally by mimicking them.

Holmes found the humour irritating, and by the late 1950s had grown quite impatient with it. Around this time he received a phone call asking for Mr. Ol-mess and he snapped at the speaker. A moment later he was stunned to learn that he had just offended a French-speaking official who had been attempting to make arrangements to present his credentials to the new government.

As often happens in these instances, when things could not get any more difficult, they did. Jules Léger was having a distressing summer. He was in the process of losing both of his elderly parents to illness and was away from the office for a number of extended periods. The group in Ottawa was already under-staffed, and the new prime minister was not sympathetic.[16] Ron Macdonnell, the associate under-secretary who would have typically substituted for Léger, was out of the country covering for Norman in Cairo, so the role of acting under-secretary of state for external affairs fell to Holmes at a most inopportune time. To complicate matters, a situation soon arose of which he had little knowledge, even less experience, and, thanks to other staffing changes, no one to turn to for advice.

The negotiation of a defence cooperation agreement with the United States had begun under the previous Liberal regime and was all but complete when the Conservatives arrived. The only thing missing, it seemed, was a briefing to the new government, the relevant additional consultations, and final approval. Holmes had never been responsible for the Defence Liaison Division, and, typically, if anything potentially controversial had come up, he would have been briefed by its chief representative. But there were personnel changes under way, and Paul Tremblay, who was set to take over, had not yet been updated himself. The Department of National Defence, which had the lead on this project, was hardly helpful. It figured that its work was already done and had little patience for interference or even questions that might have caused delays. As a result, with the East Block in a state of confusion and no one able or willing to set it right, the DEA was largely, although not entirely, ignored in the final stages of the negotiations to create the North American Air Defence Command (NORAD). In some ways, this should not have mattered. Members of the East Block did not oppose greater collaboration with the United States; rather, as they later argued, most believed there should have been more discussion – for example, with the yet to be constituted Cabinet Defence Committee – before the arrangement was approved.

In typical accounts of the founding of NORAD, John Diefenbaker has been condemned, sometimes quite viciously, for allowing his new minister of national defence, George Pearkes, and the chairman of the Chiefs of Staff

Committee, Charles Foulkes, to bully him into approving the agreement without proper consideration.[17] While this interpretation is not incorrect, the prime minister does not deserve all of the blame. Diefenbaker was not wrong to take Pearkes and Foulkes seriously. Nor must he be faulted for not thinking to consult his officers in external affairs right away. He was informed, legitimately, by his military advisors that, throughout 1956 and early 1957, the East Block had been kept up to date in the negotiations to create NORAD. Diefenbaker would have had a better sense of the file if it had been on the parliamentary agenda, but Parliament was not in session. A well-placed question from the press corps might also have encouraged the prime minister to proceed more cautiously, but the media were not aware of the NORAD negotiations.

Diefenbaker's real failure was in creating a working environment in which his foreign policy officials lacked the resources to do their jobs effectively. The day that Canada and the United States formally announced that they had come to an agreement, Holmes wrote to Norman Robertson, now Canadian ambassador in Washington, in despair:

> this is a terribly hot seat and the sooner I can retreat from it the happier I shall be. It seems to me that by giving in to the impassioned pleas of our colleagues overseas (saving your reverence) we have allowed the establishment here to become so gravely depleted that we are just not able to cope with this emergency. During one of the most difficult times in the Department when policies have to be extremely carefully considered and laboriously explained, there are only three people in the Under-Secretarial row, John Watkins, Marcel and I. This is at a time when Heads of Divisions and other important people are on holidays which makes a pretty dangerous situation. It is not the fact that people go on holidays that makes us unhappy because they absolutely must do so if they are not all going to crawl into hospital with Doug [LePan]. However, I do think that the policy of exporting all our brains and leaving weaker links behind can produce disaster in an emergency. I expect myself to make the hospital by about the 1st of September if not earlier.[18]

Clearly, then, Diefenbaker had left the residents of the East Block in an awkward position, one that he failed to remedy even after the NORAD situation had ended. There were an unusual number of unfilled secretarial positions in the DEA throughout the Chief's time in office.

Nevertheless, acting or not, Holmes was the under-secretary in 1957, and his unwillingness to confront his minister on the need for greater consultation on the proposed defence agreement right away reflected a weakness of leadership. He seemed to fear a direct confrontation, and his inability to overcome his aversion prevented him from defending the interests of his department and of Canadians. Hours before the NORAD announcement was made, Holmes was approached by Paul Tremblay and Jim McCardle. McCardle was a member of the Defence Liaison (1) Division, secretary to the Canadian section of the Permanent Joint Board on Defence, and the only foreign service official with any real knowledge of the agreement. He and Tremblay reported that the Department of National Defence had convinced the prime minister to go ahead without any additional consultation. Holmes should have gone directly to Diefenbaker with his concerns; instead, he took the more cautious approach of seeking out Foulkes and was immediately blown off. As the acting under-secretary reflected less than three weeks later, "firm hands have been needed at prows or ploughs." In the discussions that resulted in NORAD, his hands were not firm enough.[19]

He was more forceful when it came to the importance of the UN to Canadian interests and to world order, but in the first year of the Diefenbaker era, there was little he could do to prevent its decline. The expansion of the membership had created unexpected difficulties for the Western allies. By 1957, the newly decolonized Asian and African members of the organization could secure sufficient votes to defeat Western resolutions that were not to their liking. This meant delays in dealing with some of the start-up problems incurred by the UN Emergency Force in the Middle East, where the so-called non-aligned were increasing Western sympathy towards Jerusalem by insisting that Israel withdraw from the Gaza Strip and the Gulf of Aqaba without assurances that its future security would be maintained. Additional debates and accusatory resolutions criticizing, among others, the French over alleged imperialism in Algeria and South Africa over its policy of apartheid added to the antagonism that pervaded the organization. By 1957, a struggle for influence was being waged at the expense of the UN's credibility. Soviet officials portrayed themselves as the enemies of colonialism and courted the newly independent African and Asian states in an attempt to turn them against the United States and its allies. As the communists and their new partners manipulated the results of a series of votes at the General Assembly, members of the Western alliance began to question the UN's value. Moreover, even with general agreement that the nuclearization of the international community was a sign of trouble, the campaign for disarmament, long a concern of Holmes, was uninspiring.[20]

As one of his country's most fervent supporters of the world organization, Holmes took it upon himself to write, and also deliver, a series of national and international speeches on the UN's global importance. Just as the Canadian delegation had stressed in 1945, he was adamant that any UN remained better than none at all. He urged his colleagues at home and abroad to accept that resolutions of the General Assembly, no matter how disturbing, could not obligate states to change their policies. If passing such motions, regardless of how foolish or offensive, seemed to empower the newer members of the organization, then the West would have to learn greater tolerance and simply ignore the policy implications. And if the Soviets wanted to exploit the non-aligned, it was up to the West to work harder to develop sympathetic relationships with countries in Africa, Asia, South America, and Eastern Europe. This did not mean succumbing to their every demand but, rather, listening to what they had to say with an open mind.[21]

On the Middle East itself, Holmes was concerned that the West was extending too far to protect Israel from its Arab neighbours, who had never accepted the UN's decision about its borders and who remained bitter about their loss in what became known as Israel's war of independence. The Americans in particular seemed obsessed with maintaining a dominant influence in the area to defend against a Soviet invasion. "Now seems to be the time for Western countries to cut their losses and to settle not for victory but for the avoidance of defeat," he wrote in late 1957. "The alternative to letting the Middle East become a Soviet dominated area is no longer that of having it as a Western dominated area. The only hope is that it might become genuinely neutral." He advocated support for a united Arab world, one that would feel sufficiently confident and independent so as not to need to attach itself to any great power. "It may well be argued that a united Arab world presents a greater threat to Israel, and this is probably one reason that the West, perhaps unconsciously, has opposed Arab unity," he conceded. But a confident and united Arab community in the Middle East would be better able to negotiate a permanent settlement with Israel than could the unstable collection of states and governments that currently existed.[22]

Holmes was involved in the negotiations that resulted in the creation of the 1958 UN Observation Group in Lebanon (UNOGIL), a contingent of 591, including over seventy Canadians, that was meant to protect the country from Egyptian and Syrian arms smugglers seeking to overthrow the government. But when American marines landed in Lebanon and British troops arrived in Jordan not much later to deal with a revolt against Western influence in neighbouring Iraq, the East-West divide in the Middle East only grew deeper.[23] Over time, Holmes came to believe that the ultimate solution involved the withdrawal of the Anglo-American contingent and the imposition, instead, of a series of control commissions similar to those in Indochina. However, his ideas never gained real acceptance, and his hope devolved into disillusionment.[24]

Things were hardly better at the Commonwealth. For years, Holmes had idealized the old British organization and its role in world affairs. It was a legitimate bridge between the conflicting forces in the Cold War, he told colleague Alfred Pick in 1951. Moreover, within it, Canada had a special contribution to make. This was especially true in the case of India, which looked upon Canada as a close ally.[25] Under Diefenbaker, that enviable relationship began to unravel. Although the new prime minister had presented himself to the Canadian people as a proud supporter of the Commonwealth, his commitment was weaker than his supporters expected. He was uncomfortable with the idea of non-alignment in the Cold War, and India's unwillingness to stand up against communism baffled him.[26] When the Chief appointed former University of Toronto president Dr. Sidney Smith as his new secretary of state for external affairs in September 1957, maintaining positive relations with India hardly appeared on his list of priorities.

To a diplomat still heavily involved with the Indochina file (and therefore in constant negotiations with both Indian and Polish representatives), the decision to neglect the government in New Delhi was disappointing. Holmes objected to a proposal to diminish Canada's military presence in the region and urged the government to send only its highest-ranking representatives to a planned Commonwealth conference on foreign aid in October 1957.[27] The problems inherent within India's approach to external relations were undeniable: the government's condemnation of British colonialism while it turned a blind eye not only to the policies of its neighbours but also to its own attempts to dominate the non-aligned movement was disconcerting. Its claim to a policy of neutrality in the Cold War was also at times less sincere than it was politically convenient.[28] But even if India did seem to forgive Eastern atrocities more willingly than it pardoned Western indiscretions, as a democracy, it was still a more reliable power than communist China, and the extension of its influence in Asia better protected Canadian interests than the most obvious alternative. There were, therefore, good reasons to tolerate Prime Minister Nehru's inconsistencies and Foreign Minister Krishna Menon's anti-American rhetoric. Nonetheless, under the Diefenbaker Conservatives, disputes between those who believed in treating India more sympathetically and those who would not forgive the Indians for their position in the Cold War were allowed to fester, and Canada's commitment to the Commonwealth as a whole suffered.[29]

In the midst of these disappointments, a third pillar of Canadian foreign policy, the North Atlantic Treaty Organization, struggled to recover from the divisive effects of the Suez debate. An aggressive American campaign to increase the alliance's nuclear capabilities was a cause of additional tension. Member states, particularly the French, faced mounting trouble at home (and in Algeria), and they were beginning to doubt NATO's viability. While some argued that it was time for members of the organization to put aside their differences and find common ground to protect against the disintegration of the alliance altogether, Holmes' view was more nuanced. Unity was certainly important – it represented a show of strength against the Soviet menace – but it was not an end in and of itself. British and French behaviour at Suez proved that there would be times when Canada's allies would make mistakes. Blind support for their actions in such cases would do more harm than good. "We must try to remember," he advised his government in late 1957, "that NATO is only one of several associations which are important to us." Membership implied "an obligation to seek an agreement with other members and to oppose them with special reluctance," but there was a difference between special reluctance and giving one's allies a blank cheque. In his typical, pragmatic way, he concluded, "If the [North Atlantic] Council is going to create the impression required by present circumstances, then it should give a low priority to unity declarations and give its earnest attention to the policies on which it might be united."[30]

According to Holmes, it could not come together in support of the aggressive expansionism being promoted by US secretary of state John Foster Dulles. NATO was meant to be limited in its aspirations, not the first step towards a worldwide union of Western-friendly security organizations. Such a development would make the vast majority of Asians and Africans uncomfortable and risk driving them into the arms of the Soviets. Here was Holmes trying to act as a mediatory voice in foreign relations, but under Diefenbaker no one was listening.[31]

By the end of 1957, the prime minister had begun to take pride in announcing just how little stock he put in the advice of his civil servants. A junior colleague of Holmes, Peyton Lyon, was asked to prepare a few words for the Chief to deliver in Bonn, Germany. When Diefenbaker began his talk, he boasted of the care that went into the crafting of his speeches by his advisors in the Department of External Affairs. He then added that he nevertheless paid no attention to the prepared material. The young official was crushed, and he sent a copy of his text to the East Block for reassurance. When Holmes compared what Diefenbaker had said to what Lyon had written, he preferred the latter. Making reference to the prime minister's attempt to disassociate himself from his civil servants, he wrote back, "Thank God, we're exonerated." While this statement was made partly in jest, and partly to support a younger colleague, the sentiment, as it became more common throughout the DEA, caused significant harm to departmental morale.

In 1958, Diefenbaker's personal liaison between the Prime Minister's Office and the DEA, Holmes' close friend Basil Robinson, lectured to the new recruits recently admitted to the University of the East Block. Back in August 1957, Robert Bryce, the secretary to the Cabinet, had arranged to have the former Rhodes Scholar act as a buffer between the Chief and the alleged Pearsonalities, so it was expected that the young officers would seize the opportunity to inquire about the truth behind rumours of Diefenbaker's disparaging attitude towards them. "What does the prime minister really think of us?" someone asked. While the ever-diplomatic Robinson considered his answer, a noontime gun sounded. The resultant laughter decreased the obvious tension, but only temporarily. It is hardly surprising that so many civil servants retired or changed postings during Diefenbaker's first years in power.

Holmes released his personal frustration in a letter to a new officer about prospects in the East Block. "I wish I could give some clear indication of what is in store for you," he wrote to Peter Campbell:

All movements and appointments in the service since last summer have been quite incalculable. The long delay in making appointments slowed down the machinery and the effects are being felt on all levels. I have had several schemes for you which I thought would suitably make use of your talents and which you would find attractive. The timetables, however, constantly get unstuck. When one or two people who are supposed to move at a certain time don't move, the effects are far-reaching. I know that such uncertainty about your future makes things very difficult for you. If it is any comfort let me assure you that there are a great many of us in exactly the same position. One of the many unattractive aspects of rising in the service is that postings, which for junior officers can be fairly regular and routine, become increasingly difficult to plan and calculate as you reach the stage where there are fewer openings and where the coincidence of openings is much less determinable.[32]

Holmes was tired, and, during the spring and summer of 1958, he was hardly himself. At the first UN Law of the Sea conference he dismissed an idea from an ambitious junior civil servant, Allan Gotlieb, with a one-word note: "No." Admittedly, the meetings had been frustrating: the Canadian delegation maintained that its proposed formula to codify international law on the control of territorial seas had received the backing of its major allies only to find itself abandoned shortly after the formal discussions began. Even worse, by the end of the conference no proposal had received the two-thirds support necessary to create new regulations. Still, Holmes' response to this enthusiastic young officer was hardly consistent with his typically open and supportive approach to new recruits. Although he re-embraced his mentorship role fairly quickly, the effect on Gotlieb was long-lasting.[33]

During this same period, Holmes' policy recommendations with regard to the Cold War became inconsistent. He appeared to maintain his standard view that it would be better to negotiate with the East than fight, but he also wondered whether, considering the Soviets' intransigence on nuclear disarmament, it was equally appropriate to act radically. In a single memorandum on US foreign policy he defended John Foster Dulles as a Canadian ally and well-intentioned strategist, and then called his policies "shoddy," "cowardly," and even "lunatic."[34] His unreliability might explain why his perceptive April 1958 assessment of the contributions that his country could make through "a judicious habit of mind, an honesty of approach to problems, and a recognition that issues are complex and there are usually two sides to them" was never distributed. Admittedly, most officers would not have expected their every word to reach the highest levels of the country, but when John Holmes' thinking was ignored, something was wrong.[35]

There was, thankfully, a respite. In the summer of 1958 a group of twenty-two new probationary foreign service officers entered the East Block; among them was Arthur Kroeger. Holmes took him and his future wife Gay under his wing, and they soon developed a strong friendship, which helped him survive the difficult period that lay ahead. Holmes had become a mentor again.

In better spirits, and with a new salary of $14,000, that September he accompanied the prime minister to Montreal for a Commonwealth trade and economic conference. Before the meetings, Holmes had been involved in discussions to establish what has since become known as the Commonwealth Scholarship Program. The combination of Sidney Smith, a former university president, and John Holmes, a tireless proponent of both the Commonwealth and of education, resulted in a commitment from the Canadian government to fund one hundred elite international graduate scholarships to be held within the former empire. They were not exact replications of the Rhodes Scholarship, in part because they were restricted to Commonwealth members, but it was hoped that they would carry a similar amount of prestige.

Dialogue at the conference itself was positive but non-committal. The evening before the delegates were scheduled to leave, Holmes and Sir Henry Lintott, the permanent secretary to the Commonwealth Office in the United Kingdom, departed early to draft a concluding communiqué. Holmes was adamant that the plan not be forgotten, and over dinner he negotiated its inclusion within the text of the joint statement. The next day, the members of the conference committed their governments to establishing a Commonwealth scholarship program. Not long after Holmes left the foreign service in 1960, the plan became a reality.[36]

For a while it appeared that this positive momentum might help solve another long-standing international problem. Even in the late 1950s, as the situation in the DEA and for Holmes personally seemed to be deteriorating, when foreign representatives hoped to begin a dialogue with Canada, they generally approached John Holmes first. As colleague Charles Ritchie said, he was on good terms with everyone, "the more exotic the better. Indo-Chinese princes, Polish communists, Indian intellectuals – all [ate] out of his hand."[37] Just before he left for the Commonwealth conference, Holmes had been in contact with a former member of the Polish Legation in Ottawa, Adam Zurowski. Like Holmes, Zurowski was a problem-solver, and his problem was the location of a selection of more than eighty pieces of art from sixteenth- through eighteenth-century Poland, the value of which, both in monetary terms and by way of their emotional importance, was said to be comparable to that of the British crown jewels.[38]

In 1939, the Polish government transferred the treasures through Romania into France in anticipation of a German attack. When the French army faltered, they were redirected to the Dominion Experimental Farm in Ottawa. Once the war ended and the communists in power in Poland requested the return of the treasures, the old exiled government – which continued to lay claim to the artwork – arranged to have everything hidden. The majority of the treasures eventually ended up in Quebec. Quebec's staunch anti-communist and controversial premier, Maurice Duplessis, kept them locked in a vault at the provincial museum, away from the grasp of the federal government and the RCMP, both of which sought to maintain positive relations with Poland. In spite of requests from the communist government to have the treasures repatriated, and in spite, or perhaps because, of the federal government's desire to cooperate with a regime that it had long since recognized, Duplessis refused to release them. Ottawa therefore had little choice but to maintain that the situation was out of its control. Poland recalled its ambassador and relations between the two governments deteriorated. Over the next decade, the Poles campaigned aggressively to reacquire the treasures and even brought their case to the United Nations, but the governing Liberals could do nothing to change Duplessis' position.

Holmes saw Zurowski's contact as an opening for renewed dialogue. When he arrived in New York for the UN General Assembly meetings that winter, he met with his old friend Manfred Lachs, a doctorate-holding war veteran who was then legal advisor to Poland's Ministry of Foreign Affairs. Lachs proposed a solution that, on its surface, should have been universally appealing: the case could be submitted to the International Court of Justice (ICJ) for arbitration. The communist government in Poland was comfortable with the idea because it felt confident that it would win. Diefenbaker should have been pleased because he was a strong supporter of the ICJ and resolving the dispute there would enhance its credibility. Holmes and the members of his department were satisfied because they foresaw the ending of the controversy as a means of improving relations with a partner on the control commissions in Indochina; moreover, Canada's intransigence had become embarrassing on the world stage. Finally, even Duplessis should not have complained because he had often claimed that he would be willing to return the treasures if a proper court instructed him to do so. Nevertheless, the proposal died when the prime minister – whose popularity had decreased notably when he acted decisively in cancelling the Avro Arrow – refused to commit to the process. Duplessis died in 1959. Two years later, with Holmes working quietly in the background, the treasures were finally returned.[39]

Holmes' frustration with the Polish treasures discussions was typical of his experience all winter. Exhausting late night sessions with Sidney Smith to develop a text on nuclear disarmament were largely wasted when the international debate for which they had been preparing resulted in the creation of a powerless commission with little hope of ever meeting. Holmes clashed openly with Krishna Menon over India's outspoken condemnation of Western actions on the world stage and corresponding refusal to criticize Soviet policy. He was disgusted with a lack of progress on the establishment of a protocol on the peaceful use of outer space. Once again, it seemed, the two superpowers were acting unreasonably and refusing to cooperate. Even worse, he found Canada's international mediatory role muted by the unwillingness of any of the great powers to compromise on even the most insignificant of issues and by the immature, if not childish, approach of the newly decolonized Asian and African states towards meaningful international negotiations and discussions.[40] Not much later, Charles Ritchie called the thirteenth session of the UN General Assembly "disagreeable, disturbing, and unproductive ... Intransigence rather than moderation, propaganda rather than constructive action seemed to be the order of the day."[41]

Holmes let his frustrations get the best of him over a long-standing sore spot: the place of China in the international community. His belief in the urgent need to recognize the communist government never subsided, and, at the end of October 1958, it appeared that Prime Minister Diefenbaker might have begun to agree. The Chief was a strong supporter of the UN, and in his first meeting with Secretary-General Dag Hammarskjöld, he was apparently convinced that the international community was growing more willing to accept the communist regime's legitimacy.[42] The following month, Holmes wrote a letter to Norman Robertson (who had only recently returned from Washington to take over once again as undersecretary of state for external affairs) that betrayed the tact and political awareness that had characterized his typically superior diplomatic conduct throughout his career. Instead of providing observations and analysis, he implied that the civil service should consciously seek to initiate government policy. He expressed his conviction that Canada had become the key player in facilitating the entrance of the Peking government into the United Nations. He was virtually certain that the prime minister supported recognition and looked forward to moving the process along as quickly as possible. "We have always," he wrote, "been in favour of recognizing and seating the Peking government although our attitude really has been more negative. We have been conscious of the illogical nature of the US policy but never entirely certain in our minds what the alternative should be." It was time to take the final step. "I may be misjudging trends in Ottawa," he added, "but if I am not, then I presume that in a very short time, we may have to put forward some concrete suggestions to the Government." The first move "might be an impetuous public declaration of intention."[43] Holmes recommended that the under-secretary of state for external affairs find a way to soften the United States to the new Canadian position.

Robertson did not respond positively. As much as he too had been frustrated by the arrival of the Diefenbaker regime, it was not the civil service's job to promote a political agenda; rather, its duty was to serve the government. The following week, Holmes composed a convoluted apology for having gone too far:

> The impression which you would probably gain from my letter was that I was urging the initiation on the part of the Department of steps leading towards a change in our China policy and that I was somewhat impatient to get on with this. In fact, what I had in mind was rather that the Department should use the brake rather than the accelerator. Perhaps I was misreading the signs and trends but it is my impression that it might be the Government rather than the Department which would be pressing for a change. If I am misreading the signs, then my letter lacks a principal point. What I have been afraid of most of all was that, for various reasons, some of the Government might make declarations which would have to be implemented. What I am advocating is that, if there are intentions of this kind, they should be given very serious consideration with a view to planning a cautious preparation and a feeling of the ground before talking out loud.[44]

No matter how he tried to frame it, Holmes had in fact violated his duty to remain detached from politics and suggested that the DEA, and not the government, take the lead. As he admitted in another letter, his professional lapse was the result of his having become "intolerably stale." All the years without a real holiday, along with the constant increases in responsibility and growing frustration with Diefenbaker's approach to foreign policy, had taken their toll.[45] Robertson was in no position to sanction his senior assistant under-secretary: Canada was in the midst of its second term on the Security Council, and his expertise was desperately needed in New York. But it did not take a formal reprimand for Holmes to know that it might be time to think seriously about a career change, or at least some significant time away.

He did return to Ottawa in the new year, and over the next six months he grew increasingly closer to Escott Reid, now representing Canada in Germany. They shared an obsession with the decline in the writing skills of the new officers, and, although this was true much more of Reid than it was of Holmes, both were beginning to annoy some of their colleagues with their ambitious and assertive views on Canada's proper role in the world. Holmes recognized (even if Reid did not) that the international environment had changed and that Canada no longer commanded the same position in the global hierarchy as it had in the immediate aftermath of the Second World War; nevertheless, both were adamant that their country maintained a degree of influence that would enable it, if the leadership acted appropriately, to build bridges between the developing and developed worlds. Canada remained capable of exercising leadership on issues that were of primary concern to the non-great powers.[46] Although Reid's utopianism rarely wavered, and because of this he never gained the complete respect of his colleagues in the East Block, for Holmes, such unduly optimistic thinking was uncharacteristic. He had been trained by realists like Hume Wrong and Norman Robertson, and he had learned from Lester Pearson that, while idealism certainly had a place, its main role was in promoting government policy at home, not in shaping strategic thinking.

It is ironic, then, that the period during which he was at his most senior level in the DEA, and during which he likely had his greatest impact on the outlook and spirit of the next generation of Canadian diplomats (nearly all of whom remember him with awe and admiration), John Holmes also appears to have been less influential as an interpreter and advisor on Canadian foreign policy. Once Diefenbaker became prime minister, Holmes was overwhelmed by administrative responsibilities for which he was unprepared. As 1957 became 1958, his views on the Middle East were ignored both by his government and Canada's Western allies. His concerns about his country's relations with India resonated with Escott Reid, but that point alone suggests that the impact on government policy was limited. His call for a less aggressive attitude towards the prosecution of the Cold War was not heeded. Negotiations over the Law of the Sea were unsuccessful, as was his effort to promote nuclear disarmament. He had a significant impact on the Commonwealth Scholarship Program and the Polish Treasures issue, but neither had a notable effect at the strategic level. And at the end of 1958 he was directly rebuked for his efforts to steer the Canadian government towards the recognition of communist China. Even on Vietnam, where his calls for balanced judgment on the international commissions were well received for so long, his influence was waning.[47] It is no wonder that he and Escott Reid became so close. In the late 1950s, they found themselves in nearly identical professional situations. Both had risen to significant positions within the DEA only to find the organization headed in a direction that left them uncomfortable and out of place. Both struggled personally and professionally to reconcile their unyielding commitments to their country with their increasing frustration with the direction of their government. Neither was particularly successful.

By the fall of 1959 it was clear that John Holmes needed a change. Considering what a negative experience his brief period as under-secretary had been, perhaps it was time to become an ambassador. Alternatively, it might have been more appropriate to pursue a position outside of the civil service that would allow him to be closer to his mother and his nieces. Or maybe he just needed an extended vacation. One will never know what path he would have chosen because, for reasons largely beyond his control, the final decision was made for him.

6

Ruin and Recovery

The trouble that led to John Holmes' departure from the Department of External Affairs had an innocuous beginning. In 1945, the existence of Soviet spy rings on Canadian soil, which had been exposed by Igor Gouzenko, caused security issues to become a federal priority. The following year, a royal commission made a series of recommendations to modernize the national intelligence apparatus. One suggestion was that Ottawa create a security panel to ensure that communist spies would not succeed in stealing state secrets.[1] It was a reasonable idea in theory, but over time the panel developed into something much different than was originally intended, and its efforts contributed to one of the blackest marks on Canada's diplomatic history.

While the federal government must accept much of the blame for what followed, the international context is important. In 1947, the Truman administration in the United States instituted intense security checks and began to require a loyalty oath from all current and potential members of its public service. The Americans did not just target communists, fascists, and Nazis, they also investigated other "subversive" elements in society, including homosexuals. Similarly, in Canada, in March 1948, Cabinet Directive 4 called on the Royal Canadian Mounted Police to perform security clearances on all current and potential government employees in sensitive positions. The RCMP was instructed to brief the security panel on its findings as was necessary. Within about a year, the Mounties had developed a colour-coded reporting system. If comments on an employee reached the security panel in white, it meant that the person was reliable.

Yellow indicated evidence of an occasional criminal or moral lapse that could have an impact on an individual's long-term prospects for promotion to the highest levels. A pink form denoted conclusive evidence of disloyalty that could not be ignored. It was expected that such persons would be dismissed immediately.[2] Disloyalty, or subversion, could entail anything from joining a banned political organization to stealing government secrets to engaging in homosexual relations (homosexuality was a crime in Canada until 1969). As Prime Minister Louis St. Laurent himself would say in the House of Commons, "Reasons for the transfer or removal of government employees because of unreliability include not only indications of communist or fascist activities or associations, but also indications of weakness of personality or character or habits, and circumstances that render a person susceptible to pressure or blackmail, or unintentional indiscretions."[3]

These comments help explain Cabinet Directive 24 of 1952, which differentiated between failures of loyalty and reliability in the public service. Whereas disloyalty included actions such as being a member of a banned political party, "Unreliability, from a security standpoint, referred to 'defects' of character that might lead an employee to be indiscreet, dishonest or vulnerable to blackmail."[4] As investigative reporter John Sawatksy has explained, after the Gouzenko affair, it became increasingly difficult for Moscow to recruit spies through appeals to their ideological sympathies. Western governments were paying too close attention to anyone suspected of having communist inclinations. Instead, the Soviets targeted civil servants whom they believed would be susceptible to manipulation because of personal indiscretions. In the 1950s, the public stigma across North America against same-sex relationships was strong. Homosexuals – considered by many to have a psychological disorder or a treatable disease – were therefore particularly vulnerable. Reports from Australia and the United States confirming the Soviet interest in Western officers' sexual preferences, going so far as to describe the specific techniques used by Moscow's intelligence agents to compromise homosexuals, only made matters worse. By 1955, the RCMP's Security and Intelligence Directorate had begun a nation-wide investigation of homosexuality in the Canadian government. Reports were sent to the security sub-panel, a body that had been established in 1953 and consisted of senior officials from external affairs, national defence, defence production, citizenship and immigration, and the RCMP. The sub-panel reported to the full security panel, after which the relevant deputy minister or under-secretary was tasked with taking appropriate action.[5]

Although the RCMP could have looked into a number of personal vulnerabilities, it targeted homosexuality disproportionately. It appears that the
Mounties shared the views of the US Central Intelligence Agency's director,
Admiral Roscoe Hillenkoetter, who said in 1950: "the moral pervert is a
security risk of so serious a nature that he must be weeded out of government employment wherever he is found. Failure to do this can only result
in placing a weapon in the hands of our enemies."[6] The irony is that, by
increasing the stigma at home, government agencies brought attention to
these individuals' vulnerability and added to the perceived security risk.
The more Canadian homosexuals had to lose by admitting their sexual
preference, the more appealing they became to the Soviets as targets, and
the more pressure they came under to conspire against their country.

Where Canada differed from the United States was in its approach to
dealing with suspects. The Americans used a public process that ignored
the impact of unsubstantiated charges of "character weakness" on a person's
public reputation but that allowed recourse for appeal if any accused felt
unfairly treated. In Canada, moderates inside the civil service recognized
that the public and professional humiliation that would likely follow an
individual's exposure could mean the end of any future employment prospects and the destruction of family relationships; they therefore preferred
to deal with suspects covertly. This too, however, had its dark side, often
resulting in dismissals from the civil service without reasonable explanation
or any opportunity for reconsideration.[7]

John Diefenbaker was a champion of civil liberties (partly on account
of the racial taunts he had experienced over his Germanic-sounding last
name during the First World War). As prime minister, he was uncomfortable with the indiscriminate way in which the idea of character weakness
was being used to justify dismissals from the public service. His secretary
to the Cabinet, R.B. Bryce, felt similarly, and it was not long after the
Conservatives' election victory that the new prime minister called on the
security panel to re-examine its approach to unreliability with the aim
of liberalizing the government's response. The panel initiated a research
study to see if distinctions could be made between homosexuals who were
security threats and those who were not. Until the project was completed,
however, it cracked down even harder by empowering RCMP investigators
to search for so-called sexual deviants in all government departments. By
1960, the RCMP claimed to have confirmed 156 cases of homosexuality,
117 of which resulted in releases, resignations, or transfers. One hundred
and sixty-eight alleged cases were pending, and there were 139 additional
unconfirmed suspects.[8]

Since officials in the DEA had access to more state secrets than al-most any other unit in government, they came under scrutiny. To add to the stress of the investigations, 1959 – perhaps the worst year of the crackdown – witnessed significant changeover on Killers' Row. Assistant Under-Secretary W.D. Matthews died in March; the next month, Doug LePan resigned; Ron Macdonnell departed about four weeks later. And these were just the most notable. In all, twenty-seven secretarial positions became or remained vacant. During the Diefenbaker era, these changes could hardly have been seen as suspicious (although LePan later did re-veal that he was a homosexual), and the vast majority of foreign service officers were not aware of exactly what was happening (unless they were being personally investigated). Still, between the resignations and other unexpected departures, there was something out of the ordinary taking place. As for Diefenbaker, his personal concern with those who were be-ing investigated was sincere and was recounted discreetly to his liaison with the DEA, Basil Robinson. The prime minister also had a soft spot for John Holmes, whom he understood had become a suspect by 1959. Nevertheless, the Chief had other priorities to consider, and he left the security issue in the hands of his senior civil servants.

As for Holmes himself, the situation seems to have come as a shock. Although the evidence is purely anecdotal, it is reasonably clear that he had a brief affair with a Russian man while posted in the Soviet Union in late 1947 or early 1948. Letters home during these dreary winter months referred to his loneliness in Moscow, and such feelings likely led to a secretive meeting. Like every unmarried male foreign service officer who served in the East, Holmes must have received a specific briefing before he arrived to help him detect Soviet agents who were well trained in seducing him both intellectually and physically in order to exploit any personal weaknesses. Furthermore, his department never would have sent him to Moscow if officials there had suspected that he might be vulnerable to compromise.[9] (Ironically, much later it was revealed that his two succes-sors were confirmed homosexuals, and at least one of them was probably compromised.) One might assume, then, that even though there is evidence that Holmes was indeed targeted by the Soviet secret police – they would have suspected homosexuality either because he was single or because of other information not in the public record – his affair was not with a Soviet agent assigned to discredit him.

A letter to Terry MacDermot three years later makes it clear that, given their training and their commitment to their country, Holmes did not believe that any Canadian officials on duty overseas would have fallen into the Soviet trap. Speaking about his friend and successor in Moscow, John Watkins, he wrote:

> Sometimes I wondered if it was the Soviet Union he went to … He has seriously put me to wondering if we have all been wrong about the impossibility of mingling. He got to know quite a number of "intellectuals" and even talked with them on the telephone. At one time I wondered if they were trying to frame him, and John and I explored this possibility thoroughly. (John is such a good explorer; he has no preconceived views to stop him.) Now I feel quite sure that he was seeing people who, because they were a little ingenuous or careless or too old to care or privileged, wanted very badly to talk to him … The Americans would be horrified if they knew what he was up to, and would be free of all doubts as to the reasons for what went on.[10]

The letter illustrates that Holmes was fully aware of the Soviets' attempts to compromise Western diplomats. His comfort in discussing this idea with MacDermot suggests that he did not believe that he had anything to worry about personally. He also seems confident that Watkins, a former housemate in Ottawa, was in the same position. In this case, he was only partly right. Watkins was a homosexual, and he did become close with Soviet agents. There is no conclusive evidence, however, that Canadian security was ever compromised as a result of his conversations. Tragically, Watkins died of a heart attack in the midst of an RCMP investigation into his past in 1964. Holmes was one of the last people to speak with him, and he testified at an inquiry into the suspicious nature of his death.[11] When later asked about his testimony, he said very little.

Holmes' oblivion, naïveté, or, more cynically, his striking ability to hide his own past reveals how successful he was in compartmentalizing the various aspects of his life. It was as if his own sexual experience in Moscow had never happened. This approach was, and continued to be, his way of dealing with relationships over the next thirty years. No matter whether it was a homosexual affair in the Soviet Union in the 1940s or a fifteen-year sexual relationship with a widow who lived in his apartment building in the 1970s and 1980s, his private life was his business, and he preferred to mislead, or even lie, rather than reveal. Perhaps this was a product of years of secrecy that began in Moscow or earlier, or maybe he felt that his commitment to his work and family, along with his hectic travel schedule, did not leave him time to manage a serious, committed relationship. Whatever the reason, this aspect of John Holmes' life was unfortunate. In 1987 he revealed to a new, yet very close, friend that in seventy-seven years he had never experienced true love.[12] For a man who gave so much to so many, this is the real tragedy.

Holmes learned that he was on the RCMP's interrogation list in the summer of 1959, shortly after the security panel reaffirmed its commitment to seeking out and removing homosexuals from positions that involved access to classified government materials.[13] Already tired and depressed, when he finally realized that what, for him, had been a purely private incident – one that had neither interfered with his work as an official nor put anyone in his country at risk – was now a matter of national security, he started to fall apart.

At the beginning, he internalized his pain. Always thinking of his family responsibilities first, he wrote dozens of letters to old friends and contacts, seeking, what appeared to them as quite innocently, new work. Holmes spared no one in this search. Robin Humphreys, who had not heard from him since he had left London for Ottawa in 1947, received a letter asking him to look into university positions in the United Kingdom. Holmes contacted members of the Rockefeller Foundation in the United States, based on an old association from his CIIA days, to see if they had anything available. He inquired about a teaching position in history at the University of Western Ontario, only to learn that his former department was not interested. There was also talk of spending an extended period in Geneva supported by the Carnegie Corporation.

Where he seems to have received the warmest immediate response was at the University of British Columbia (UBC). His old friend and colleague, Fred Soward, had long since left the DEA and was now the department chair in history as well as the associate dean of graduate studies. Not knowing Holmes' real reasons for writing, Soward was initially surprised at the opportunity to bring one of the most notable civil servants of his generation to UBC. Although Holmes' original letter cannot be found, based on Soward's reply it appears that, in it, the now almost seventeen-year veteran of Canadian diplomacy lamented the state of uneasiness that had overtaken the DEA since Prime Minister Diefenbaker had come to power. That, and the fact that Holmes was tired of the unrelenting pace of diplomatic life, meant that it was a good time to leave. Never having completed his PhD, he was not confident in his academic qualifications, and he therefore sought Soward's advice about either going back to school or applying immediately for a permanent teaching position.

Soward answered that a post would not be hard to obtain but that Holmes would be giving up a lot (salary, pension) to do so. Why not take a leave of absence first to try out academic life before leaving the civil service for good? Still, the UBC professor and administrator could not forsake his own interests so easily. Having consulted discreetly with UBC president Larry Mackenzie, he made Holmes an unofficial offer of a temporary or permanent position in international relations with a salary of $12,000 per year. About a month later, Holmes submitted a formal job application and received a more detailed, if still casual, contract that specified a teaching load of a third-year course on international organization and a joint honours/graduate-level seminar on Canadian foreign policy.[14]

Never one to be comfortable with a life-changing decision, now that he had a concrete option, Holmes sent out another round of letters. Doug LePan, who might have had a better sense than most of what the real problem was, spoke positively about his post-retirement experience at Queen's University and encouraged Holmes to leave the East Block. John Watkins, who, ironically, for the rest of his life remained unaware of the reasons for Holmes' departure, was much less supportive of an entrance into the academic world. Watkins thought that what Holmes really needed was time away from Diefenbaker's Ottawa and that a plum diplomatic posting might solve his problems. Jules Léger regretted that he had been so difficult to reach since his parents had taken ill and sympathized with Holmes' desire to move on. Providing yet another perspective, he thought that a sabbatical year was a perfect compromise that would allow the senior civil servant to experience academic life without sacrificing the security of his current position.[15]

It might very well have been the combination of the reality of the UBC offer and the wide-ranging and contradictory advice that he received afterwards that led to Holmes' complete breakdown. Being forced to give up the personal and professional security of his current position without having served enough years to qualify for much of a pension, acknowledging the fact that his new job would be far away from his family in British Columbia, and contemplating the decrease in salary that would come with the move to Vancouver might have been too much. Perhaps the added stresses compounded feelings of exhaustion and frustration that had been building almost uninterrupted over the last three years. In a letter to Chester Ronning, then in India, less than two months before he finally left the East Block, Holmes lamented:

> We are constantly sent, and all too often sent by telegram, far more information than we can conceivably absorb or need to know. The result is that our baskets and our minds are clogged and we can't do any useful work.

There is such a deluge of paper in the office that messages from Saigon, for example, wait six days before they can be delivered to us. Much of the reporting is very good, but there is so little related to our functions as instruments of Canadian policy. It seems to me also that we are confusing our role with that of journalists. We do want to know what is happening in countries like Iraq or the Belgian Congo, but we don't have to be kept up to date every 48 hours.

I've been crying like this for the past six years – like a voice in the wilderness.[16]

The RCMP interrogation compounded his problems. The interview took place in the dark of night, most likely in November 1959. (The exact date cannot be confirmed because the files are restricted and the few who were there and are still alive are not talking.) Norman Robertson, who as under-secretary of state for external affairs was ultimately responsible for security matters within his department, arranged all of the conversations in the evenings so members of the East Block would not know who had been questioned. Holmes was driven to RCMP headquarters by John Starnes, the head of Defence Liaison (2) Division, the unit responsible for security and intelligence. Starnes had first met him during his posting in London in the early to mid-1940s, and the two were friends. The experience of transporting a clearly terrified close colleague to what could only have been the most mortifying of experiences, and indeed the entire period of what has since become known as the purges, was so upsetting for Starnes that he called the chapter in his memoirs that dealt with them "A Rotten, Stinking, Depressing Job."[17]

In some ways, Holmes need not have been so afraid. Even if the RCMP had suspected him of wrong-doing, he could not have been dismissed outright. Unless he had been caught in a homosexual act, or admitted to having compromised state secrets, Norman Robertson would have had no grounds to remove him. What Robertson could have done, and indeed would have done, however, was deny him the high-level security clearance that Holmes needed to do his job.

There can be no doubt that the under-secretary was extremely disturbed by the entire situation. Not knowing much about homosexuality, he had discreetly purchased a book on the subject, which he hid in the back of a bookshelf at home, away from the prying eyes and hands of young daughter Judith, the voracious reader. In October, almost certainly before the RCMP interrogation, Robertson spoke out at a meeting of the security panel, making reference to an individual who could only have been John Holmes. As the minutes reflect: "The Under-Secretary of State for External Affairs stated that he recognized the risk in employing homosexuals in sensitive positions, but felt that the report under study exaggerated the risk. It was his view that the assessment of an individual for a position of trust involved a mixture of considerations, and pointed out that a weakness such as homosexuality might exist in an individual of great discretion and with a brilliant capacity for public service. In many cases, he said, the security dangers of the sexual propensity might well be neutralized by other aspects of the person's character."[18]

When the panel, led by aggressive and dogmatic members of the RCMP and the Department of National Defence, roundly dismissed his plea for flexibility, Robertson resigned himself to doing his duty: if, after questioning, Holmes did not agree to leave the service voluntarily, he had to take action against him.

Robertson began making inquiries to help Holmes find work outside of the public service. And while a call to Robert Bowie of Harvard's Center for International Affairs did not quite work out, and Holmes chose to ignore an offer secured by Professor Humphreys and Gerald Graham to take on a fellowship managed by Ken Robinson at the Institute of Commonwealth Studies in London, there was an attractive fellowship opportunity through Duke University's Commonwealth Studies Program. Shortly after, arrangements were made to allow Holmes to spend a few months there collecting himself if he so chose.

December 1959 was a most difficult month for John Holmes. He had a cryptic and uncomfortable conversation with Basil Robinson about his great many female friends. He visited a doctor who ordered him to take sick leave because of stress and exhaustion. He kept all of this from the younger officers in the DEA, none of whom seems to have suspected that he was about to resign, let alone why (Holmes' commitment to his job and to his mentorship role with the East Block remained beyond reproach to the very end).[19] And on the evening of Sunday 13 December, he sat down with Norman Robertson one final time to discuss his future. Once again meeting secretly, to avoid suspicion, the two agreed that it would be best for Holmes to begin his sick leave the following day and to stay away for at least two months.

Officially, he could have returned to work, but the decision for him to resign and go to Duke had already been made. It was clear that he was no longer welcome in the civil service. Nothing makes this more obvious than his decision to reject a job offer from Canada's high commissioner to the United Kingdom, George Drew, that was made just days before the final decision had been formalized. The position was exactly what Watkins had prescribed – a chance to leave Ottawa and work in one of Holmes' favourite cities. It entailed challenges and responsibilities but would not have been overwhelming. Drew, moreover, thought the world of John Holmes. But rather than even asking for more time to consider the proposal, Holmes simply said no, blaming his "present jibbering state" for his inability to commit.[20]

The next day he disappeared from the East Block without saying good-bye. In the United Kingdom, George Ignatieff, who wondered why Holmes had been so distant, received a letter from Assistant Under-secretary Marcel Cadieux explaining that their friend had not been sleeping and was unwell. He was therefore returning indefinitely to London, Ontario, to spend time with his family and was non-committal about his future. Two days later, Holmes drafted a rather misleading note to parliamentary secretary Wally Nesbitt: "I am sorry that I have had to run away before having a chance to see you," he wrote. "As you may have heard, the doctor ordered me off on a rest cure with a certain degree of urgency. It may be that I shall spend some time in the Ontario Hospital at Woodstock, but at the present time I am hoping to avoid complete decay with a change of scene ... I look forward to seeing you in several months' time when I am returned to health and Ottawa."[21] It was the first of many largely successful efforts to frame his departure as anything but a forced resignation.

Holmes moved in temporarily with his mother and one of his aunts, never explaining what had caused his breakdown. Over the next six weeks, he slept, worked for Lester Pearson, and travelled. Holmes' assistance on an essay Pearson had written entitled "The Normal Processes of Diplomacy as an Instrument of Peaceful Relations among Nations," for which he received $2,000, is intriguing.[22] One of John Diefenbaker's greatest fears when he took office was that his civil servants were so loyal to Pearson that they would conspire to support him behind his back. And while this is not exactly what Holmes was doing, it was still improper for a civil servant on the government payroll to accept a contract from the leader of the Opposition. The explanation in this case is simple. Pearson was one of the few who knew the truth about his friend's sick leave. John Diefenbaker had felt it necessary to inform the Liberal Party head of what was taking place. Since Pearson was aware that Holmes was not returning to the public service, he likely did not see any conflict of interest in his request. Moreover, the agreement served both of them well. Holmes never felt financially secure and was facing an uncertain future, and Pearson's reputation benefited from the superior writing of his younger colleague.

The travel was to visit trusted friends who did not ask difficult questions. Holmes spent time around Christmas with Basil Robinson and his family, bringing joy to the children through the attention he gave to the goings-on in their lives and the boxes of chocolate that he brought with him. Holmes went to New York to see the ubiquitous Charles Ritchie and made stops at the Rockefeller Center and Carnegie Foundation to inquire about employment opportunities. Once again, however, the story he told to prospective employers was misleading. He did not confirm that he was retiring from the foreign service, suggesting instead that Lester Pearson himself had strongly advised him to think seriously about what he would be giving up if he did. He also refused to explain the nature of his sick leave.[23] Predictably, the meetings did not yield anything.

While Holmes was away, events were taking place in Toronto that, in retrospect, seem serendipitous. On 19 January 1960, the CIIA's president – the new title for what had been called national secretary in Holmes' day – Edgar McInnis, yet another old friend, informed the National Executive Committee that he planned to retire within the year. That day, the executive struck a subcommittee made up of the chair of the CIIA, Douglas Gibson, the honorary solicitor, Peter Wright, and the head of public education, Burton Taylor (B.T.) Richardson, to consider a successor. Before they went any further, Gibson spoke with Alexander Brady, a professor at the University of Toronto and a prominent CIIA member. Brady, whose relationship with Holmes dated back to his first term with the institute, drafted a personal letter asking if he might be interested in the job. The two of them later spoke in Toronto over lunch just days before Holmes left for Duke. According to a letter that he sent to his mother, Holmes was non-committal about the potential opportunity. "I told him I would think about it," he wrote, "but said that, if I left the DEA, I would really prefer something quieter and more academic." The CIIA job was prestigious, and the salary was generous, but he was concerned that it would be too strenuous. "It nearly killed me when I was much younger," he claimed. "I think it would be better for me to keep my mind on something free of administrative head-aches."[24]

These words were consistent with the way that Holmes dealt with most of his life-changing decisions. His unwillingness to embrace the UBC position immediately, his refusal to go to Harvard, and his decision not to accept the fellowship at the Institute of Commonwealth Studies at the University of London demonstrated that an academic post was not his greatest priority: a job that kept him close to his family and that paid competitively was what he really sought. Returning to his alma mater would have been ideal, but the history department at Western was not interested, so work at the CIIA in Toronto was as good an offer as he could expect. Since, in spite of what Holmes might have said to friends and family, returning to the DEA was not an option, there is no reason to believe that his decision to rejoin the CIIA was not made at that lunch in January, even if he might not have admitted so much right then.[25]

Themselves unaware of the CIIA offer, Norman Robertson and Terry MacDermot made certain that Holmes would be as financially secure as possible until he accepted permanent employment. His sick leave was extended a month to 18 March, allowing him to receive extra pay from Ottawa while he assumed the position of Commonwealth scholar in residence at Duke. Holmes was then allowed to take two weeks of annual leave, extending his stay on the payroll until 6 April. When he finally did resign, he was paid a retirement gratuity equivalent to about three months salary.[26]

During this time, Holmes was settling in quite happily in Durham, North Carolina. George Glazebrook, who had replaced him in the East Block, knew the people in charge of the Commonwealth Center personally. On behalf of Norman Robertson, he explained to the staff at Duke that Holmes was not to be challenged too heavily. The new fellow therefore had no specific teaching responsibilities and no research obligations. "I have been a bit uneasy as to what I could do to earn my pay," he wrote his mother, "but they made it clear that they like to have visiting people here to talk to staff and students and be around for discussion. That suits me fine."[27] He continued to suffer from short fits of depression, but within days of his arrival he was developing a reputation for collegiality and thoughtfulness that left his new associates speaking wistfully about him when he moved back to Canada in late May.

Duke was an exciting place in 1960, and although the courses in British imperial relations and Canadian external relations that Holmes often visited were enjoyable by all accounts, what was taking place outside of the classroom was more fascinating. The United States was a country divided by race, and the conflict was playing itself out in North Carolina. Segregation was still rampant, but change and revolution were in the air. During Holmes' time in Durham, Duke students campaigned to force a major department store to serve the black members of the community at its whites-only lunch counters. There were also strikes and protests against the university's racist admissions policy. The campaign was a success. The following year, under new president J. Deryl Hart, Duke University declared that graduate and professional students would be admitted based on their ability, regardless of race, colour, or creed. In 1962, the policy was extended to include undergraduate students. Holmes, who could not fathom the purpose of separating people while they were eating in any case, found it all quite intriguing.[28]

Academically, his term at Duke was taken up with two tasks. He spent some time attempting to revise an article he had drafted in 1939 for the *Canadian Historical Review* on Canadian attitudes towards the US Civil War, and he prepared a lecture on Canadian foreign policy for the university's Trinity Historical Society. The first project was largely unsuccessful and confirmed for Holmes that completing his PhD was no longer a worthwhile pursuit. Twenty years away from his research had left him so out of touch that he would have had to start over, and, at age forty-nine, he had neither the time nor the energy to do so.

In contrast, the speech was a professional milestone. "Principles and Practices of Canadian Foreign Policy: The Role of a Middle Power" was typical Holmes, drawn from a combination of deep thinking and personal experience inside and outside of the civil service. It was also a basic summary of many of the ideas that he would put forward to students, reporters, and government officials over the next quarter century. Unlike Americans, he claimed, "Canadians tend to be less absolutist in their attitudes. They incline to the view that international problems are more likely to be dissolved than solved." Canadian diplomats wanted to contribute and to be helpful. They faced the challenge of satisfying an urge to promote national sovereignty with the need to act responsibly as a member of NATO and of the international community as a whole. Canada was more useful to the world, and to the West, when it made its own foreign policy decisions instead of aligning itself automatically with the United States. "We have to work hard to keep shiny our reputation as an objective, if not a neutral party," he said. "This means keeping a rein on our language, giving parties to a dispute the impression that we listen to their case, and making it clear that we can, when we want, differ from our major allies and do not belong to any bloc."[29] This was his mentor Lester Pearson's vision, with a touch of Hume Wrong and Holmes' 1944 speech for Mackenzie King mixed in. It was also the public announcement of the Holmes middle power doctrine, an approach to foreign policy that still dominates the discourse in Canada. Holmes was establishing himself as his country's new voice on external relations.

In Toronto, the CIIA finalized the appointment of its next president. On 15 March, the search committee unanimously recommended that Mr. John Holmes replace Edgar McInnis as of approximately June 1960. McInnis' retirement officially began on 1 July, but he was paid a small monthly salary to stay on as a consultant for the rest of the calendar year. In response to a request from the DEA, the announcement of the decision was delayed until the formal arrangements for Holmes' retirement had been completed.[30] The next week, Holmes submitted his official resignation to Norman Robertson. His letter was a token both of his professionalism and of his commitment to framing the terms of his departure in a way that suited him and his family. "For me it will mean a return to an institution with which I was associated before joining the Department and in the world of which I have maintained a continuing interest," he wrote:

> It presents, I believe, a challenging opportunity for service in the field of international affairs complementary to the world of the Department of External Affairs. As you are aware, there are also reasons of health and family obligations which have affected my decision to take an appointment in Toronto.
>
> I hope you understand, nevertheless, the deep regret I feel on leaving a service to which I owe so much in rich experience and in the friendship of a remarkable company of men and women. It is reassuring on departing to realize that there are so many of this company brilliantly qualified to carry on the work in which I was engaged. I was proud to be a member of the company, and I shall watch with confidence and pride the growing strength of the Department.[31]

Norman Robertson accepted the resignation with what he described as "the greatest regret, both personal and professional."[32] It should not have had to happen this way. In Holmes' personnel file, the final line of his career report reads: "Reason for Leaving: Resigned to accept employment outside of Government Service."[33] It is astounding how a statement that is technically so accurate can be so far from the truth.

Reactions to Holmes' departure, both before and after it became official, were heart-felt. Most expressed hope that he would return to the DEA. Marcel Cadieux was head-hunted himself, by his alma mater, the University of Montreal. In spite of his own frustration, he decided to remain in the East Block in anticipation of a quality appointment abroad. Nevertheless, he understood Holmes' decision. How the department would recover from the loss of its conscience, however, he did not know. A young officer in

Vienna, Klaus Goldschlag, felt the same way. Fred Soward saw the CIIA as a temporary respite before an eventual move into the university system. It was the right position, he thought, one that would expand Holmes' contact base and allow him to write. John Watkins' response was similar: "It closes no doors," he observed, "either academic or for that matter diplomatic ... It seems to me, too, that you should be able to bring your knowledge and common sense to bear on instrumental questions more effectively than in a university chair of international relations."[34]

Members of the media who had always been enamoured with Holmes' collegiality, his wit, and his uncanny ability to provide articulate capsule summaries of complicated issues – he was the master of the sound bite before the sound bite existed, a colleague once said – were equally supportive. The highly regarded Blair Fraser of *Maclean's*, himself a member of the CIIA, looked forward to having Holmes in Canada more consistently. I. Norman Smith of the *Ottawa Journal* also sent his best wishes. Nevertheless, both journalists were angered that the East Block was losing so many talented officials. Smith used his position as editor of his widely read and largely Conservative paper to print a lengthy editorial detailing external affairs' most recent loss. He called it "John Holmes' Voice." His sentiment was sufficiently indicative of the feelings of the vast majority of influential figures in Ottawa and across the country at the time as to merit repetition in detail:

> Mr. Holmes had become a craftsman in policy and in diplomacy, a man acquainted with the bricks of international issues and with a first-hand idea of what is possible and what is not. His way was to try to speak the other man's language both in fact and in the figurative sense. At the UN or in some foreign capital one would find him in his leisure walking or dining or going to the theatre with people from the opposing camps or from the vast motley of neutral grey. He did this not only to try to persuade others to his thinking, but to reassure himself of the rightness of his own case and its feasibility. He was, in short, the kind of career diplomat that Canada has been proud of in the last several decades ...
>
> However our regret at Mr. Holmes' departure must be lessened by the fact that as head of the Institute he is able to continue his service to Canada in the field of his special knowledge. Indeed, as head of the Institute he may be even more influential, his knowledge and conviction no longer restrained by the inhibitions of an official in a department which must labour in quiet.
>
> The *Journal* hopes that Mr. Holmes will do two things: (1) avoid letting his mind and time be squandered among the demanding shallows of

administration and minor engagements, (2) avoid letting his own modesty dissuade him from speaking up and out to the country and to his old Department when he feels something should be said. If he will do these things his appointment is public gain. We have little enough informed discussion on international affairs; the addition of Mr. Holmes' voice could be a considerable national asset, as doubtless the Department realized when it consented .to the Institute's pressing for his services.[35]

The article explicitly called on Holmes to fulfil a need in Canada for a new national voice: an interpreter of Canada to Canadians and of Canadians to the world. It was also prescient: John Holmes was an outstanding civil servant, but he was never the "man of influence" that Jack Granatstein called Norman Robertson, nor did he even have the power of Hume Wrong or Lester Pearson. His greatest impact as a member of the East Block involved his cultivation of the collective spirit and commitment of the DEA to the national good. His leadership and mentorship were his legacy. Only later, after he had left the public service, did he make the greatest public impact on Canada and Canadians more generally. It was in 1960, free of the constraints of government life, that John Holmes began to cultivate the voice to which Smith had referred.

There was only one error in the *Ottawa Journal*'s editorial. The DEA did not release John Holmes from duty out of recognition of his value to the Canadian intellectual community. This was, however, a good story, and Holmes did not mind borrowing from it as he began to shape public memories of how and why he left the East Block.

The way that Holmes explained his departure varied depending on his audience. He told the head of the DEA's Personnel Division that the CIIA presidency kept him close to family, that it allowed him to continue to do the travelling that he enjoyed and to participate in the conduct of international affairs without the stresses of his old position in Ottawa. He never wanted to be an ambassador, he claimed, and he was neither unsatisfied with Prime Minister Diefenbaker nor with the conditions within his department. "I hope you will point out that my reasons were personal and had much to do with family obligations and my disinclination to inhabit embassies," he deliberately wrote to one of the biggest gossips in the department. He said similar things to Escott Reid, but he also expressed regret for having deserted the East Block in a time of need. Over fifteen years later, in an interview with journalist Peter Stursberg, he again denied that the Diefenbaker regime had anything to do with his leaving. Family responsibilities, and specifically difficulties in coping with the death of his father, explained his decision to resign. He told the same story to scholar David Dilks in 1985. He had never wanted to be under-secretary of state for external affairs, and obligations at home called him back to the CIIA.[36]

The explanation was not so much untrue as it was misleading. John Holmes did not resign from the foreign service to accept a job with the Canadian Institute of International Affairs. When his sick leave began, Edgar McInnis had not yet announced his intention to retire, so there was no position available. Holmes had no plans for his future when he left because he did not control his moment of departure. Nor was the CIIA his first choice. That would almost certainly have been the University of Western Ontario. Holmes was thinking of his family when he made the decision to resign but not quite in the way that his words suggest. It was, rather, the embarrassment that he imagined some of his relatives would have felt over his impropriety that concerned him most. Holmes was teased throughout his life for being single. His mother often asked him when he planned to get married. Forcing her to witness his mental breakdown was unfair enough.

Although he respected John Diefenbaker at a number of levels, there can also be no denying that John Holmes' life in the East Block after the Conservatives' electoral victory in 1957 was miserable. He was overworked and frustrated. And while only some of this was the fault of the governing party, among his close friends, he did not shy away from criticizing the new regime. Finally, it is also true that Holmes kept in touch with the CIIA throughout his time in the DEA and never ruled out an eventual return, but among his countless letters from late 1959 seeking advice on future employment, not one appears to have been addressed to a member of the National Executive in Toronto.

The purges of the civil service continued largely unabated until 1963 in spite of Norman Robertson's attempts to moderate. In June 1960, the DEA's under-secretary of state criticized the RCMP for attempting to exploit some of the most vulnerable individuals under its investigation without concrete evidence that they had compromised national security. Robertson's most pressing concern was that the Mounties had begun to recruit lesbians and gay men who were not members of the public service, probe them for information, and then open investigations of government officials based exclusively on hearsay and speculation. The chair of the Civil Service Commission, Samuel Hughes, supported him, but largely to no avail.[37]

In June 1963, Robertson expressed regret over what he called "some painful separations for reasons of security."[38] By then, changes were finally under way as John Diefenbaker's orders to make the system fairer were slowly implemented. In December 1963, with Lester Pearson leading the country as Liberal prime minister, the Cabinet issued directive number 35, "Security in the Public Service of Canada." The new policy allowed that, in particular cases, if the risk were justified, members of the public service who might be deemed unreliable because of weakness of character could still be retained and allowed access to classified information.[39] The RCMP fought the decision but to no avail. Nor did it mean anything to John Holmes, who had long since compartmentalized that part of his life and begun afresh.

The story of the purges largely disappeared until journalist Dean Beeby of the Canadian Press published two newspaper articles in 1992 that used access to previously restricted government documents to reveal the massive RCMP witch-hunt of homosexuals that had taken place some thirty-five years earlier. In his second report, Beeby quoted former Mountie William Kelly, who identified John Holmes as one of the individuals who had been forced out of the DEA. Two days later, Prime Minister Brian Mulroney called the occurrence "one of the greatest outrages and violations of fundamental human liberty that one would have seen for an extended period of time" and ordered a more rigorous investigation.[40] Holmes was not alive to hear this, nor would he have necessarily wanted to be. Like Norman Robertson, he understood that national security was critical and that sometimes difficult decisions had to be made to protect the country. Always a diplomat and a gentleman, Holmes would have likely preferred that the whole incident be kept private. He believed in history and the accuracy of the historical record but not to the extent that it hurt people unnecessarily. He would have seen little good in what might have come from the story of his expulsion. And he was able and willing to make the best of his situation, just like his British neighbours had during the bombings of 1944 and 1945. Nevertheless, if he had only known how sympathetic his progressive family would have been had they been told the truth, perhaps he would have reacted differently.

7

Headfirst into the CIIA

I n 1960, the Canadian Institute of International Affairs was the most prominent non-governmental organization in the country dedicated to promoting awareness of Canada's role in the world and stimulating debate over future directions in Canadian foreign policy. Under Edgar McInnis' leadership in the late 1950s, the CIIA had managed to expand its influence, increasing the circulation of the *Behind the Headlines* series that Holmes had founded to between 3,500 and 4,500 copies per issue (the journal of the Canadian Historical Association had a circulation in the hundreds) and the number of study kits sold to discussion groups nationwide to over one thousand. The library, which now occupied most of the ground floor of the main building at 230 Bloor Street West, had been enlarged in 1954. While still understaffed, it remained the premier locale for the study of Canadian external relations. Admittedly, this in itself was not a grand achievement; the University of Toronto's Robarts Library was not completed until 1973, and the place of Canada in the world was hardly being taught in universities. But the scholarship needed somewhere to grow, and at the time, the CIIA was it. The institute's financial situation was not ideal, but it had been improving. In all, John Holmes was returning to an organization with a strong history and excellent potential.[1]

The day-to-day workings of the national office at what was called Edgar J. Tarr House depended on the powerful and determined Edna Neal. During Holmes' years as president, it was routine to hear him say, "If that's what Edna wants then we'll do it that way ... I don't want to upset

Edna." Things that were done "Edna's way" tended to work; change was unlikely without a good reason. The women who joined and later replaced Neal over the next number of years were outstanding. Exceptionally intelligent, thoughtful, and loyal to a fault, they laboured tirelessly to keep the organization afloat. Their pay was pathetic, and overtime was part of the job, but it hardly seemed to matter. They were dedicated to the CIIA and to John Holmes. The building at 230 Bloor Street West also housed the University of Toronto's Bob Spencer, a historian, and James Eayrs, a political scientist. They edited the *International Journal*, the premier academic publication in Canada on foreign policy, founded by the CIIA in 1946. As professors, they formed a link between the academic community and the institute that Holmes sought to exploit.

Membership in the CIIA was dominated by anglophones, generally elderly upper- and upper-middle-class professionals and former diplomats whose political views tended towards conservative. A sponsor was required to join. The women's committee was active, and its leadership complained that the institute's policy of separating the sexes was out of date. They were right, but it took time for the old boys' network to evolve. In an organization sustained largely by volunteers and old money, change was not effected quickly. Another challenge in the 1960s was how to respond to the increasingly prominent role of the media in the coverage of external affairs in Canada. Fifteen years after the end of the Second World War, in a society that was growing smaller thanks to advances in communication technology, the CIIA's niche as the host of exclusive and confidential briefings by respected international officials was becoming tenuous. Funding was always a concern, as was the relationship between the Department of External Affairs and the general public. Ever since John Diefenbaker had all but muzzled his civil servants, the situation had been deteriorating. Many in the CIIA, and Holmes in particular, felt that the institute had a role to play in bridging the gap. Finally, the lack of francophone involvement remained an issue, one that had concerned Holmes during his previous tenure as well. All of these challenges were faced, and most were at least partly overcome, as the years went by.

First, though, Holmes had to refamiliarize himself with Toronto and with the CIIA. He arrived in the spring of 1960 after a brief detour through Chicago for a conference on world tensions. His invitation had likely been coordinated discreetly by Lester Pearson, who was hoping that his former colleague would ghost-write a book for him based on the meeting's themes. Holmes was delighted with the extra money (Pearson paid him another $2,000) and always enjoyed the opportunity to work with one of his mentors. He was also comfortable keeping the project secret to avoid any appearance of impropriety: the CIIA took great pride in being a non-partisan organization. Nevertheless, he had mixed feelings about the conference itself. "Having been so close to responsibility for some years," he wrote to his mother, "I find it hard to accept some of the easy generalizations these professional conference people make about peace and disarmament."[2]

Holmes never considered himself a true academic. They were "touchy and difficult and very suspicious of outsiders,"[3] caught up in theory and big ideas, and detached from the cold realities of world affairs. Brilliant and crucial to the policy process, sure, but too many of them became comfortable in the ivory towers of academe and ended up with an inflated sense of self-importance. Holmes saw himself as a hybrid: part practitioner, part scholar, part teacher, part public intellectual. Comfortable in all of these worlds, he positioned himself as a helpful analyst, one who brought a combination of personal experience and deep thinking to policy debates on Canada's future. He sought to shape the CIIA and its membership in the same image.

Officially, he began his new job exactly three weeks after his fiftieth birthday. His office, where he could usually be found when he was in town, was not in Tarr House but across a courtyard in a pleasant look-ing three-story brick building. The CIIA did not have enough room for everyone in its home location (which it owned), so Holmes and one or two others were housed in space rented from Baxter Publishing next door on the second floor. This provided protection for the president from some of the tediousness of office administration, but it also left him alone during times when it would have been nice to have people around – like on his first day. He arrived nervous and without a real sense of how he would be spending his time. Within hours, however, his future role as public representative of all that was Canadian became starkly clear.

Sitting quietly at his desk, Holmes received a phone call from Joseph Johnson, president of the Carnegie Endowment for International Peace in New York and one of the many people with whom he had spoken during his stopover with Charles Ritchie in January. Johnson was organizing a fellowship program for foreign service officials from newly independent countries and was hoping that Holmes might lend his expertise.[4] His ex-perience would benefit those in charge of selecting the fellows themselves and also those responsible for designing the training curriculum. As became routine during those first few years, he said yes immediately. In August he spent three days in New York in committee meetings, rekindling a relationship with the Carnegie Corporation that was critical to the CIIA's future prosperity.

It was also important to Holmes personally. Fewer than two years later, a recommendation from another Carnegie employee led to a trip to Jamaica to teach the government there about the intricacies of diplomacy. The country had just achieved independence by leaving the federation of the West Indies, and its leading political figures had limited international experience. They turned to North America for assistance, and the people at Carnegie thought of Canada's John Holmes. He agreed to go, and he gave a series of well-received lectures to the fifteen participants. When he returned, he lobbied his own government on their behalf. "These really are people who can become among our closest friends in a rather chilly world, and who could, with the right guidance, play the kind of effective role in UN diplomacy that the Irish and the New Zealanders or the Tunisians have managed," he told George Glazebrook. Ottawa did not send a high commissioner to Kingston, but in May Holmes learned that his former department planned to provide financial assistance to the newly independent government. Already, he was making a difference.[5]

Endless travel was a pattern in Holmes' life that did not end when he left the foreign service; being president of the CIIA, he quickly learned, required a lot of it.[6] Even before he officially assumed his duties in July, he embraced his role as the public face of the organization. On 10 June 1960, he drove to Kingston to attend the opening of the CIIA's annual study conference. At the time, the meetings took place in conjunction with the Conference of Learned Societies, an issue that later frustrated historians and political scientists who struggled to attend the institute's events and those from their own disciplinary associations.[7] Along with attending academic panels and presentations during the day, Holmes met with the CIIA's National Council. As president designate, he was also seated at the head table at the Royal Military College that evening for the annual dinner. After another full day of sessions on the twelfth, it was back to Toronto for a meeting of the CIIA's journal advisory committee on the thirteenth. Two days later there was a National Executive Committee meeting that stretched from the late afternoon into the early evening.

The pace never slowed down. In the fall, Holmes was involved in coordinating the dissolution of the controversial international council of the Institute of Pacific Relations. Some of its functions, such as the publication of *Pacific Affairs*, were taken on by the University of British Columbia's

new Department of Asian Studies, and Holmes agreed to join the advisory
committee to the journal to ensure continuity.[8]

To his international and organizational duties he added the role of public commentator. Since he had always been comfortable with the media,
it seemed natural that the Public Affairs Department of the Canadian
Broadcasting Corporation approached him in early August in an effort to
promote greater collaboration between the CBC and the CIIA. He took
on the responsibilities personally and gave his first radio commentary
on disarmament that month on a program called *Midweek Review*. "You
have no idea what a terrifying experience it is for a well conditioned civil
servant to express an opinion out loud,"[9] he wrote to Escott Reid. But he
enjoyed the work and accepted more of it as time went on.

In October, he commented on Nikita Khrushchev's memorable explosion of the previous month in New York. Captured live on television, the
inflammatory leader of the Soviet Union pounded on his desk twice to
demonstrate his frustration with the UN's recent intervention in the (formerly Belgian) Congo. To Khrushchev, it was not a peacekeeping mission
but, rather, a colonial invasion pushed through the world organization
by irresponsible and imperialistic Western powers in a blatant attempt to
forward their own interests at the expense of international security and
stability. He accused Secretary-General Dag Hammarskjöld of complicity
in the intervention and demanded that he resign.[10]

While many thought that Khrushchev was out to destroy the organization through his disruptive tactics, Holmes' analysis was more nuanced.
For one, the Soviet leader's analysis was reasonable. Belgium had granted
its former colony independence at the end of June, and within less than
two weeks a mutiny by the army had created virtual anarchy across the
country. In response, the government in Brussels violated the Congolese's
newly acquired sovereignty by deploying paratroopers to protect its 100,000
citizen residents. After the UN dispatched peacekeepers to restore stability,
the Soviets accused the organization of taking sides. Khrushchev's support
for the rebels, Holmes argued, was meant to counteract what he perceived
to be Western domination at the UN. The recent influx of still non-aligned
former colonies provided him with an opportunity to alter a balance of
power that had been tilted against the USSR since 1945. Western nations
who hoped to see the UN survive had to accept that they could no longer
win every vote at the General Assembly.[11] It was an argument Holmes had
made as a diplomat five years earlier (and indeed throughout the later
1950s), one that praised the UN as a cooperative institution and viewed

multilateral negotiation as an ideal form of conflict management. For Holmes, it was the war that counted, not the battles, and it was therefore acceptable to lose an occasional vote for the sake of greater international harmony. This approach to world affairs, what one analyst has termed an "advocacy of balance and moderation,"[12] became, for many, the essence of what defined Canada's foreign policy during the Cold War.

With John Holmes at the helm of the CIIA, the Canadian people received a clearly articulated view of their country and its place in the world. Canada, through Holmes' eyes, was a calm, moderate power. A firm supporter of the Western side in the battle against communism, it was nonetheless able to act reasonably, and rationally, in its international dealings. The new president was also conscious of spreading his message through every medium at his disposal, be it interaction with powerful world figures in the political and non-governmental communities, meetings of the CIIA membership, popular media like the CBC, or academic writing. He published the rough text of his CBC talk in the *Canadian Forum* – Canada's oldest political magazine, known nationwide in spite of its relatively limited circulation – and then drafted an explanation, and indeed defence, of the Congo mission in the *International Journal* that winter.[13]

By holding most of his business meetings at or near Tarr House, Holmes increased the use of the CIIA library by 70 percent in his first year, making the institute's main floor a hub for students and leading foreign policy thinkers. He also advocated creating opportunities for younger scholars by expanding the Contemporary Affairs publication series. As he explained to the national research committee, he envisioned a collection of more specialized, yet accessible, studies of aspects of Canadian foreign policy published by promising junior academics and printed in paperback to increase circulation.[14] The next generation always mattered to Holmes. At the end of November, he made a brief trip to the US military academy at West Point to attend the annual meeting of the Student Council on United States Affairs, later using the contacts that he acquired during his visit to secure invitations for two Canadian students to attend the event yearly in the future, with all of the arrangements coordinated by the CIIA.

By the end of 1960, Holmes was comfortable in his job. When the new year began, it was time to take charge and make the CIIA his own. He did so at two levels. First, he provided the organizational leadership and vision necessary to allow the CIIA to flourish as a globally recognized think tank. Second, he became a personal force in the development and discussion of Canadian foreign policy at home and around the world.

Holmes returned to the CIIA with concerns that had never been resolved to his satisfaction during his time as national secretary. The institute was a pan-Canadian organization, but most of its activities outside
of the headquarters were coordinated by local branches. The success of
the branches was uneven, and the demands and complaints coming from
them tended to monopolize the time of the Toronto office. "In a number
of the branches ... the members undoubtedly believe that the Institute
exists entirely for the purpose of sending speakers to talk to them," he had
lamented to historian Arthur Lower in 1943. "So long as they feel this way
there will not be any very conscious interest on the part of their members
in organizing thought within the branch."[15]

In January 1961, the president headed west on a fact-finding tour, visiting
as many branches as he could along the way. What he found was troubling.
The membership was well intentioned but also old and tired. Attendance
at too many meetings was abysmal, and a number of local offices lacked
leaders with the enthusiasm necessary to reinvigorate what was becoming a
stale organization. "In this country we seem to have a few able people who
are tied up doing too many things," he complained to Joseph Johnson of
the Carnegie Endowment for International Peace. It was time for a new
way of thinking and a new way of conducting CIIA business.[16]

The National Council met that June. For the first time since Holmes
had arrived a year earlier, there could be absolutely no question as to who
was in charge. He began by proposing a more open approach to official
discussions. After outlining some of the main challenges facing the CIIA,
he welcomed comments and criticism. He anticipated a more interactive
meeting than usual, one that would make the members feel that they were
a part of the CIIA's future.

After that warm beginning, Holmes conducted himself autocratically.
While a number of the branches were performing adequately, some were
not, and providing services to those that were not properly taking advantage
of them was taxing the national office. Perhaps, he suggested, branches
should be required to meet minimum membership and attendance standards to qualify for support. In terms of that support, top priority was to
be given to soliciting good speakers. Considering his own contacts, Holmes
was confident that the process of obtaining guests would be significantly
improved the following year.

The concept of membership also had to be reconsidered. Holmes had
been disappointed to learn that a number of distinguished Canadians quit
the CIIA when their schedules made it too difficult for them to commit to
participating regularly in branch activities. Perhaps, then, there could be

two types of members: those who were active in all aspects of the organization, and those who lent their names and prestige to the institute, provided strategic advice when they could, and promoted the CIIA through their connections across the country and abroad.

The institute also had to improve the effectiveness of its publications program. Young scholars needed more support in their efforts to publish their PhD dissertations and first books. The organization required a more focused research agenda, perhaps with an emphasis on middle-power peacekeeping initiatives. And Canadian researchers depended on what was still unreliable access to government archives. Negotiations with the relevant people in the Historical Division of the DEA would help in this case. Finally, the public education program needed to be redesigned.[17]

By the time that he was finished, the framework for the discussion had been set, and Holmes had begun to shape the future of the CIIA. He focused on two issues: development assistance in Africa and strategic studies. The former responded to growing popular concern with the state of what was then called the Third World; the latter was meant to fill a glaring gap in the Canadian academic literature. It was, in short, the typical Holmesian strategy of mixing the popular with the professional. To begin, he envisioned a conference of former aid workers who could share their experiences of working in Africa with interested Canadians and current officials in Ottawa. "I am particularly anxious that this should not be viewed as a pressure group conference or in any sense a gathering to criticize past or present Government policy," he told the director general of the government's External Aid Office, Herb Moran. "The conference would, rather, be based on the belief that it would be useful for all concerned to pool experiences and examine the very complex problems of assistance abroad."[18]

At the same time, he worked with Senator Donald Cameron, a long-time active supporter of adult education, to solicit backing for a national conference on strategic studies in the broadest sense. "Attention would be devoted to continental defence, NATO, and also to problems of arms control, disarmament, the use of international forces," he proposed to the chairs of the CIIA's regional branches. "It would, in other words, be concerned as much with what is usually called foreign policy as strict military matters."[19] Once again it was typical Holmes: a broad, inclusive definition focused primarily on politics and weaker on the economic side. It was also part of a larger plan to find external funding to establish a Canadian institute for strategic studies.

Such projects required a strong staff to support them, so Holmes convinced the CIIA executive to create a pension program for the largely female contingent that kept the institute on its feet. They also required an informed public, so he commissioned journalist and friend Bob Reford to compile a monthly report on Canadian external relations that would be distributed by the CIIA. Reford's work was objective, accessible, and completed on time. It caught the attention of the Canadian press and of departments of education across the country.[20]

The CIIA's visibility increased, and with it Holmes' personal influence also grew. He spent close to half of February 1961 in Japan. Officially, he was there as a guest of the Japanese Institute of International Affairs, but it is doubtful that another CIIA president would have been invited. While overseas he travelled with an interpreter and met with representatives from the foreign ministry as well as with major leaders from all of the political parties. He lectured on Canadian foreign policy towards the Far East (one of his old DEA responsibilities) at the International House of Japan and gave another talk to the Japanese Broadcasting Corporation. He also spoke to staff and students at universities in Tokyo and Kobe and collected souvenirs for his many nephews and nieces who looked forward to the stamps on his postcards from all over the world.

When he returned to Canada, he gave the expected report to the National Executive but was more candid in a private letter that he sent to Secretary of State for External Affairs Howard Green. He noted, for example, that Canada's immigration policy – which privileged white Americans and Europeans – was a source of humiliation for many of his hosts, especially since the Canadian government seemed to treat other east Asian countries more favourably that it did the Japanese. He also spoke positively about prospects for improved relations with Japan in the future.[21]

Even though he had left the civil service, and in spite of the awkward circumstances surrounding his departure, Holmes' loyalty to his country never faltered. Reporting back to his old department on his experiences and observations became routine, and he continued to advise officials and practitioners of all political inclinations throughout his career.

Holmes was so active on Canada's behalf on the world stage that many outside of the country considered him an associate member of the East Block. This was most evident in early 1961 when Secretary-General Hammarskjöld asked him to come to New York to discuss the situation in the Congo. In the aftermath of Khrushchev's outburst, the country was dealing with four separate claimants to governmental authority. The UN's attempts to restore calm had failed, and Hammarskjöld believed that personal diplomacy was the only hope. Having worked so well with Holmes in 1956, it was only natural to ask for his help once again. He did so through his under-secretary and special representative on the Congo Crisis, Andrew Cordier.

As Holmes explained to Norman Robertson, he had misgivings about representing the UN in Stanleyville.[22] He came from Canada, Belgium's NATO ally, and he was white, just like the former colonizers. Privately, he also appeared concerned over whether external affairs would grant him the security clearances necessary to go. Nevertheless, his respect for the UN secretary-general was so great that he could not decline. Fortunately for him, at the last moment, the staff in New York decided that it would be better for Hammarskjöld to go himself. Whether it was because of the colour of Holmes' skin, an intervention from Ottawa, or something else remains unclear. One can be certain, however, that the outcome was fortunate for him. Later that same year Hammarskjöld died in a plane crash on his way to Rhodesia (now Zimbabwe) to visit with one of the major disputants. This was the second time in Holmes' life that a plane that could have been carrying him had not reached its destination.[23]

With responsibility for the situation in the Congo no longer an issue, Holmes was free to accept more of the personal offers that began to come his way. One of the first was from the exclusive Bilderberg Group, an ultra elite collection of policy practitioners and businesspeople from across North America and Europe who had been congregating annually since 1954 to discuss issues of mutual interest and concern. Meetings were by invitation only, and participants had to agree not to reveal what was said inside. In 1961, the group – which normally held its events in Europe – met in St. Castin, Quebec, and the CIIA was asked to assist organizationally. Holmes reported being overwhelmed by the distinguished people around him, but his invitation to attend made it clear that the Western elite already considered him to be one their own.[24]

The new CIIA president was never one to become overly comfortable in any single, intellectual environment. For every Bilderberg, there was also a speech at the Lawrence Park Home and School Association, a guest lecture to the United Nations Club at the University of Toronto, or a voluntary contribution to a local United Nations Educational, Scientific, and Cultural Organization meeting. In March, Holmes spoke on Canadian foreign policy at Northern Secondary School as part of a Toronto Board of Education Saturday morning international relations series. In May, he returned to Pickering College to discuss communism in Asia. July saw him in Sackville, New Brunswick, serving as the principal speaker at Mt. Allison University's United Nations seminar for high school students (in this case he cancelled a scheduled appearance at Colgate University in New

York City to appear).[25] He lectured to members of the Toronto Christian Movement when they asked him to, and to a current events club in the city that was interested in his views on internationalism.

He also cultivated his academic reputation. Holmes had two distinct areas of interest, both of which were drawn from his diplomatic experiences. The first was examining Canada's place in the world, specifically as what he liked to call a middle power. It was a fitting term in the early 1960s, a time when so many newly decolonized countries were finding their way in a world that had a clearly defined elite but no real means of distinguishing between the rest of the international community. In such an environment, Canada, an established yet still non-great power, which, thanks to a series of changes at the international level (the economic recovery of the European community) and domestic political decisions (a focus on social as opposed to defence expenditures), was fast losing the standing it had gained in the immediate postwar period, faced numerous questions both from within and from its allies about its rightful place in the evolving global order.[26]

Holmes declined a request from Harvest House Limited Publishers to produce a book about past and future directions in Canadian foreign policy, but this did not stop him from writing shorter pieces on the subject. At the thirtieth annual Couchiching Conference, an event that the CIIA, along with the Canadian Institute on Public Affairs, organized on the lakeshore north of Toronto, he revised a lecture on the politics of independence. Calling for greater objectivity and rationality in global political decision making, he portrayed Canada as having a limited, albeit potentially effective and crucial, role in the Cold War and international relations more generally. Its small size and proximity to the United States made it hard to be heard at times, but this could also work to the national advantage. Since the Soviet Union hardly took Canada seriously, Canadians had more freedom than their great power allies to take chances and lead multilateral initiatives through organizations such as the UN. The key for Ottawa was to relax its fear of being taken advantage of by its more powerful friends and to channel its energies into areas where its mediatory skills could be helpful. Holmes dismissed the argument recently published by the journalist James Minifie, and championed by the far left, which claimed that Canada had to be neutral in the Cold War to make a difference. It did, and should, take sides in the conflict. A reputation for impartiality and an independent decision-making ability enabled it to support the West while at the same time working to reduce great power tensions.[27]

"What we have to do," he wrote in a paper that was later published in the prominent American periodical *Foreign Affairs*, "is find a reasonably consistent philosophy for working in harmony with a neighbor, ally and partner on a basis of mutual independence in which equality is not possible." At the same time, he added, "If a country is to establish a reputation qualifying it to perform the duties of a middle power it must demonstrate that it is objective enough and strong-minded enough to differ, if necessary, with its great-power allies" without, of course, disagreeing simply to satisfy a petty need to express independence.[28] In all of his commentary, he remained optimistic. In one of his best essays of this early period, he wrote in the University of Toronto's *Commerce Journal*:

> The pessimist is one who believes that nothing is possible without a near-perfect system of world justice with unquestionable powers of enforcement. This being impossible, he is without hope. But he has no historic sense. He fails to see the world as it is, a whirling mass of peoples and states of various shapes and sizes and in various stages of political and economic development, quite incapable of fitting themselves for a long time into any rigid system of world order but willing in a rough way to combine together to improve their lot and escape destruction ... It is the conflicting interests of peoples rather than the skilfulness of leaders which present the basic problems.[29]

He was less hopeful when it came to the Commonwealth's future prospects. The early 1960s was a difficult time for loyalists like John Holmes. Although the organization had survived a near break over the Suez crisis in 1956, it was unclear how it would withstand the divisions caused by the apartheid regime in South Africa. The 1950s witnessed the aggressive separation of races throughout the country under the dominance of the white minority. Public criticism of the undemocratic and discriminatory approach of the government abounded; even British prime minister Harold Macmillan – whose instincts were to preserve the UK-South Africa economic relationship – condemned apartheid. Shortly after London's intervention, a protest by blacks in the South African town of Sharpeville met with a violent response from government authorities, resulting in at least fifty deaths and hundreds of injuries. International criticism over what became known as the Sharpeville Massacre caused South Africa to turn even more inward. Not long after, the state voted to withdraw from the British Empire and become a republic.[30]

Leaving the empire was a private matter; renouncing membership in the Commonwealth, however, affected Canada. As a rule, members that

declared themselves republics had to reapply for admission: India was
the most prominent example of a state that had done so successfully. Readmission required the unanimous approval of the membership, something
that was typically granted without much difficulty. The South African
situation was exceptional. The recently decolonized members of the organization threatened to reject the governing National Party's application
if it did not end its policies of racial segregation and discrimination. Most
of the predominantly white member-states, led by Great Britain, were
uncomfortable with this confrontational approach. The Commonwealth,
they felt, was not designed to interfere with the internal business of its
members.

Canada was caught in the middle. Conservative elements within the
government and the DEA hesitated at the prospect of turning a former
ally into a pariah state. Others, including Prime Minister Diefenbaker,
did not believe that their country should associate itself sympathetically
with the racist policies of the apartheid regime. When the South African
government realized that its application for readmission would not be
accepted unanimously, it chose not to apply at all, effectively ending the
crisis for all but those who were asked to comment on the result, like the
CIIA president.[31]

While Holmes was unimpressed with the regime in South Africa, he
saw more at stake in the debate than just Commonwealth membership.
First, there was the future of the organization itself. As he wrote with deep
regret in May 1961, "There isn't much left in the Commonwealth except an
idea, and its health depends on the vigour, freshness, and aptness of that
idea." The tradition that members refrain from interfering in the inner
workings of their fellow states was old and stale. At the same time, no state
was perfect, and those who condemned the South African regime had to
be careful of what they wished for. Although he did not say so specifically, based on his experience in Japan, he might well have been referring
to Canada's immigration policy. Nevertheless, racial equality was one of
those new ideas that kept the Commonwealth fresh and alive. Choosing
the old principles over the new weakened the organization's chances for
survival. The decision to exclude a government that legislated apartheid
was therefore the right one.[32]

The implications for Canada were not so clear-cut. Britain was using
the decision on South Africa to help justify its conscious withdrawal from
the Commonwealth while it contemplated joining an economic union
with much of Western Europe. In response, pundits in Ottawa suggested
that Canada join the Organization of American States, a move that would

tie it more tightly to the countries of the western hemisphere. Holmes had never supported this idea as a civil servant in the East Block, and his feelings did not change once he left. Canada still had historical ties to the British Empire, and its commitment of foreign aid to Africa through the Colombo Plan was no less valuable than any new investments in Latin America might have become. Moreover, Ottawa had only so many development assistance dollars. Spreading them too thinly would lessen their impact.[33]

Holmes was disturbed by the international trend towards greater formalized regionalism. What had made the Commonwealth so great, in his eyes, was its voluntary nature. States were not bound to any common policy or economic approach, and decisions were made by consensus rather than by majority vote. Membership, therefore, did not conflict with active participation in the broader international system. In fact, it encouraged it: "The Commonwealth association must be regarded as complementary," he wrote in the prestigious *International Organization* in early 1962. "Its unique strength is that it has sought to promote unity by enlarging understanding rather than to induce unity by imposing constitutional straight jackets." He concluded with a warning: "We are in danger of losing sight of the fact that the promotion of unity within regions does not serve the cause of world order if it exaggerates disunity between regions."[34] He summarized his thoughts in a brief note to Escott Reid: "I find myself more and more drifting into a kind of philosophical anarchism. I am sure peace is better preserved by a multiplicity of alliances and inter-related associations. God save us from the new absolutism in Europe."[35]

His candour and forthrightness with Reid was not as evident in public. Fewer than two years into his term as CIIA president Holmes received a friendly, yet firm, rebuke from a prominent long-time member of the CIIA. J.M. Macdonnell had just returned from Boston, where he and Holmes had attended a conference on Canadian-American relations. "First of all, I wish to scold you," read the note. "I wish to protest in the strongest manner the way you persistently efface yourself and I find that I am not the only one who has this feeling – to see you sitting in the very back row gave me no pleasure. Seriously, in the interest of the Institute, you must try to develop at least a tincture of regard for your own position."[36]

The criticism was only somewhat reasonable. It is true that Holmes had been accustomed to, as he liked to say, carrying the bags of the real policy makers when he had worked under Lester Pearson, Norman Robertson, and Hume Wrong. And indeed, as CIIA president, asserting his authority while representing the institute abroad was important. But sitting in the back, speaking only when called upon at conferences, deliberately understating his case when he judged it appropriate – all actions that helped define the Holmesian style as time went on – were, as one analyst has rightly concluded, tactical moves as well.[37] John Holmes was a master of reducing expectations. He understood how harmful failure could be not only to politicians but also to committed people of any sort, and he recognized what a difference even the smallest of victories could make to their patience and enthusiasm. It was not for him to dominate discussions. He was there to learn as much as anyone else. When he finally did choose to intervene, his prior silence amplified his impact.

Nevertheless, if the membership wanted Holmes' leadership to be more visible, then it would be. The period between the middle of 1962 and the end of 1964 marked one of the most aggressive and exhausting periods that he spent in what was fast becoming his joint role of president of the CIIA and Canadian ambassador to the world. The changes began with a state of the union-like address at the first meeting of the institute's National Council in June 1962 at McMaster University. It took place in the midst of the annual CIIA study conference, this time focused on defence and disarmament. Speaking to his audience with an air of increasing authority, Holmes highlighted three priority issues that would drive planning over the next two years: funding for the research program, outreach to potential new members, and collaboration with interested parties on conferences and similar initiatives to elevate the level of discussion of Canadian foreign policy at home and abroad.[38]

The future of the research program depended on the size of its budget, and it was the job of the president to solicit financial support. The Ford Foundation was a good place to start. The not-for-profit organization had been created in 1936 to promote internationalist causes that celebrated democracy, freedom, and social justice. Its board was interested in Holmes, and in the CIIA's work, and members had suggested in confidence that a well-drafted, comprehensive funding application might well be looked upon favourably. After consulting extensively with former colleagues Norman Robertson and Bob Bryce, Holmes submitted a five-year, US$200,000 research proposal centred on four themes: the impact of modern weapons on contemporary international relations, the evolving role and nature of the Atlantic community, the contributions of the non-great powers to world affairs, and the implications of recent trends in economic regionalism.[39]

A John Holmes proposal was difficult to reject and rarely caused a granting agency undue grief. By 1968, Ford Foundation money had supported the publication of eighteen books, twenty reports, and a new research secretary, Jone Schoeffel.[40] The funds also provided the CIIA with leverage to obtain additional grants from other sources, such as $3,000 per year from the Canada Council to pay for the cost of importing distinguished speakers from overseas. Even more important, since the Ford money was the major driver of the CIIA's research agenda, and since Holmes made sure to integrate government representatives into the new projects as often as possible, it largely framed debates about Canadian foreign policy across the country for the next five years. Under Holmes, the CIIA became a national player in guiding public policy discussions.[41]

With the grant secured, Holmes spent much of the winter and early spring of 1963 travelling the country in search of ideas for projects that the CIIA could fund. His schedule was hectic, and flying in primitive airplanes was physically taxing. He recalled his experience in one of his many letters to his mother: "Lecturing every evening, seeing people, visiting universities and preparing the extra talks I have had to give to students and other groups has kept me tied up until I fall asleep." But he loved the people and believed in what he was doing, so even after doctors forced him into a steel brace to protect an aching back, he continued, at times even dictating letters to Schoeffel while lying on the floor of his apartment, his head resting only somewhat comfortably on his copy of the *Columbia Encyclopedia*.[42]

The pain might have affected his travel schedule, but it had no noticeable impact on his drive and determination. As had been the case in the East Block, much of this was directed towards educating younger people. The lack of international relations scholarship in Canada was undeniable, and Holmes realized that the few senior researchers in the field were called upon by organizations like the CIIA so often that many hesitated to participate in new initiatives. The solution, it seemed, was closer contact with students at the universities and mentorship of some of the more promising leaders of the next generation. Under Holmes' direction, the institute collaborated with the University of Toronto to present an affordable (twenty-five-dollars) series of twenty lectures on foreign policy through the university's extension department. The first talk attracted over two hundred people.[43]

The CIIA president also never hesitated to use contacts he had developed in the academic and diplomatic worlds to bring promising graduate students into the national dialogue. Holmes was a prominent member of the selection committee of the esteemed Newton Rowell Fellowship, which funded UBC law graduate Frank Iacobucci's graduate studies in international law at Cambridge in the early 1960s. After practising briefly in New York, Iacobucci joined the Faculty of Law at the University of Toronto. He later left to join the public service and rose to the rank of deputy minister of justice and deputy attorney general for Canada, all the while keeping in touch with Holmes through the occasional lunch and yearly Christmas notes, and never forgetting how Holmes' advocacy had secured him the award that so changed his life. Iacobucci was appointed to the Supreme Court of Canada three years after Holmes' death and served for thirteen years before retiring in 2004.

In 1963, a young MA candidate at McGill, Maureen Appel (Molot), who went on to become one of the foremost analysts of Canadian foreign economic policy of her generation, was first hired as a research assistant thanks to a recommendation from John Holmes. That same year, Christopher Dagg, a Queen's graduate student, received the CIIA's inaugural research fellowship to complete a study on Canada's participation in the international commissions on control and supervision in Indochina. In this case, the project was less successful.

The following year, Harald von Riekhoff, a talented recent Yale PhD graduate was gently coerced into moving to Ottawa to assume what was likely the first postdoctoral fellowship in strategic studies in Canada. In convincing von Riekhoff to make Carleton University's Department of Political Science his academic home, Holmes promised him the unique opportunity to play a leadership role in turning Canada into an international centre for high-quality scholarship in strategic and defence studies. He did everything he could to keep that pledge. Research for von Riekhoff's path-breaking study of the NATO alliance was financed largely by the Ford grant. Holmes wrote countless letters of introduction to allow him access to restricted documents and high-level individuals in Washington, Paris, London, and Germany. The mere mention of the name John Holmes seemed to open doors, and the results of the fellowship were excellent for everyone involved. Like Molot, von Riekhoff later served as director of the soon to be established Norman Paterson School of International Affairs, the leading graduate institute for the study of global politics in Canada.[44]

One did not have to aspire to an academic career to make Holmes take notice. In January 1964 he was in Winnipeg lecturing on Commonwealth affairs at a conference organized by the University of Manitoba. As he often did when he visited university towns, he agreed to speak to a group of interested students outside of the meeting. His talk took place at the historic Marlborough Hotel, home of the famous Skyview Ballroom. The weather, as is typical of a Winnipeg winter, was unforgiving, and the crowd was smaller than anticipated. This suited Holmes as he preferred to speak in a more intimate setting. He spent the evening making the students feel important by listening and responding sincerely to their thoughts and ideas on Canada and its place in the world.

In the audience that night was first-year undergraduate Thomas Axworthy, later principal secretary to Prime Minister Pierre Trudeau. Axworthy was amazed by the whitish-haired, well-dressed former diplomat who had a twinkle in his eye when he spoke. He was witty, pleasant, and exuberant. When he joined a number of audience members afterwards for a drink, the students ordered draught beer, but he chose red wine. Elegant and dignified, thought Axworthy – just what a diplomat was supposed to be. Perhaps because he was an active Pearsonian Liberal in a town of Diefenbaker Conservatives, he and Holmes became almost immediate friends. For the next twenty years, Holmes offered him career advice and the two spoke candidly about political affairs.

Attracting and developing a new core of informed Canadian nationalists did not detract from the CIIA's efforts to take full advantage of the expertise that was already available. Over time, Holmes' recipe for success at conferences became clear: Find a supportive host institution; engage and nurture an effective conference organizer; ally or coordinate with other interested bodies that could provide financial assistance; choose a relevant, topical theme that was sure to attract a wide audience; solicit relevant and significant speakers from government, the public service, and the academic world to add to the event's prestige and make it easier to fundraise; whenever possible, travel to the conference site a few weeks in advance to ensure that everything was in order; attend in person but never dominate the discussions (instead, spend most of the time listening, cultivating relationships, and supporting others); report back to all of the relevant constituents, being certain to promote any tangible output that arose from the event; and, finally, never complain publicly if anything goes wrong. When one former colleague reflected on the CIIA president's skill at event coordination, he recalled with pleasure the exclusive invitation he and his wife had received to share in late evening drinks in Holmes' cabin during one conference and, more seriously, the host's effective use of what he termed "strategic silences as well as timely understatement."[45] Vincent Massey taught Holmes about the social graces of diplomacy, and Lester Pearson added lessons in charm and negotiation. The combination resulted in a series of CIIA successes.

One of the most notable was the launch of a seminar on international development for adults in Banff, Alberta. It began as a proposed collaboration between the province's United Nations Association and the CIIA.

Holmes had to campaign to convince the institute to provide support, arguing that it would be an opportunity for serious discussion among the policy elite and a vast improvement over the disappointing open meetings on foreign aid that had dominated the previous year. It was not that he opposed these larger gatherings; rather, he felt that a mix of the popular with the professional was crucial. The CIIA contributed $2,000 from its Ford grant, and, by all accounts, Banff was a great success. Close to fifty of the brightest political minds in Canada came away so pleased with the level of discussion – and with the experience in Alberta more generally – that the conference became an annual event.[46]

Over the next two years, the CIIA collaborated with the World Peace Foundation in Boston, the University of New Brunswick, the American Assembly at Columbia University, the University of British Columbia, and the Institute for Strategic Studies in London, England. The president was personally involved each time, liaising with relevant planners from the co-sponsors, consulting on or drafting conference agendas, discussing possible outlets for publication, and recruiting the participants. If a conference organizer struggled, as one did at the University of Western Ontario in 1962, it was not unusual for Holmes to step in personally and assume most of the planning responsibilities until the event was back on schedule. It was exhausting work, but it created an international reputation for the CIIA that was crucial to its continuing success.[47]

Although, in just a few years, John Holmes expanded the CIIA's membership (to over 2,500), its budget, and its ambitions, not everything ran smoothly. His personal touch could not always mask his old-school elitism, and this did not go over smoothly with the occasional office worker as well as with some of the bolder, more rebellious young members of the institute who could not fathom the need for invitation-only events and restrictive meeting rules.[48] His energy also far exceeded his budget. In 1963, the CIIA accumulated a $16,000 deficit. It attributed the problem to rising costs at the *International Journal*, over-spending on new initiatives, and a shortfall in the annual fundraising campaign. With the Ford grant yielding just $40,000 per year, the deficit, if not managed, could have become serious. At the time, however, the National Executive was too caught up in the excitement of Holmes' achievements to pay much attention. As the minutes of one meeting noted, "it was the consensus of opinion that the Institute was in a dynamic stage with many new projects and increased activity and that the budgetary deficit should not be a reason for retrenchment."[49]

A 1964 grant of $50,000 from the McConnell Foundation was a mixed blessing. For the moment, the CIIA's financial advisors could breathe more easily. But as a one-time contribution, it was less than helpful strategically because it inspired false hope. The institute was not conducting itself in a financially tenable manner. Too reliant on unpredictable external support to meet its contractual obligations, and too ambitious for its own long-term good, it became reliant on its president's abilities and reputation. With Holmes at the helm, this was fine, but if, or when, he left, trouble and uncertainty were sure to follow.

Nonetheless, for the time being, John Holmes was riding a wave of what was, for a Canadian commentator on world affairs, unprecedented popularity. As a speaker, he was in demand more than ever before, and as a foreign policy generalist, there were no limits to the topics of his lectures and writing. For the most basic requests, he developed a stock presentation on the history of Canadian foreign policy since the Second World War. Drawn mostly from personal experience, his assessment emphasized the familiar and reflected his largely positive experience in the DEA. Still, he rarely allowed himself to be carried away by his own idealism. "Canada strove after 1945 to play an active role in the United Nations for sound and conscientious reasons," he told the American Historical Association in December 1962. "In the foreign policies of democracies, however, there is always an element of calculation as well as conscience, and neither the cynic nor the idealist is ever right in absolute judgement on motives ... The zeal with which a distinct foreign policy was pursued was not unrelated to the constant compulsion Canadians felt to preserve and assert their identity." Canadian behaviour on the world stage was fairly consistent after the departure of Mackenzie King. The transition from Liberal to Conservative governments had a limited impact on the overall direction of foreign policy. "In the record since 1945," he concluded with optimistic caution, "there are some grounds at least for satisfaction and encouragement for those who believe that powers of middle size have the capacity, if they wish to use it wisely, to contribute to the international community as sovereign entities."[50]

He repeated this speech, modified in various ways, over the next eighteen months. Seven hundred members of the League of Women Voters heard it in Boston at the Massachusetts Institute of Technology. Others read a summary in the *International Journal*. His insistence on the use of the phrase "middle power" in place of the proposed "minor power" in the title of an article for the *Atlantic Monthly* was intended to make the same point, as did a speech entitled "What the World Expects of Canada" that he delivered to the Hamilton Canadian Club.[51]

The majority of his lectures and essays on issues in Canadian foreign policy during this period drew on familiar themes. Holmes had not stopped worrying about what he called "the new dogmatism about regionalism." As he explained to Australia's ambassador to the Hague, Sir Walter Crocker, the desire of much of the international community, led by the nations of Europe, to split off into geographical groupings was "nonsense as a development of the century in which communications have made it regionally unnecessary. The trouble with the movement for European union," he added, "is not that it is intrinsically wrong but that its dedicated supporters are pushing this idea to illogical extremes."[52] In contrast, the Commonwealth remained a model of international organization. Non-confrontational, tolerant of difference, and civilized in conduct, it was just as important to the future of world order as were the more militant blocks designed to maintain the balance of power in the Cold War.

Even though, or perhaps because, his message clashed with the general public's support for regional associations, Holmes preached it whenever he could. Whether it was through the CBC, at a Progressive Conservative Association conference in New Brunswick, in the noted British periodical *The Round Table*, in *The Times* of London, at the Royal Commonwealth Society, or in front of an entirely European audience at a conference in Bellagio, Italy, he spoke positively and optimistically about the Commonwealth and its future. At its core, it was the international organization that most reminded him of Canada. Its ability to accommodate a variety of member states was no different from his own country's growing embrace of a culturally diverse national population. Its ability to resolve problems by consensus and without violence mirrored Ottawa's historic success in managing relations with its allies through compromise and negotiation. In speeches to sympathetic audiences, Holmes occasionally admitted that its British traditions reflected much of what he felt was best in a civilized society. It pained him to watch the Commonwealth fade into obscurity, particularly when its decline was fuelled as much by apathy and neglect as it was by its decreasing relevance to world politics. He did what he could to slow its decline.[53]

To his American colleagues he told another story. The early years of Holmes' term as CIIA president were bitter ones for the Canada-US relationship. In 1962, the combination of a weakened economy and a series of controversial political decisions reduced popular support for the

Diefenbaker Conservatives. That June, they only barely returned a minority government. The Chief found himself backed into a political corner: criticism of his handling of the economy and of foreign policy abounded. As he had throughout his career, he fought back by appealing to Canadians' anti-Americanism. This time, however, there was an element of desperation in his approach. Diefenbaker was used to being Canada's most popular politician. He had won the country's largest majority ever in 1958 thanks largely to his intense, booming speeches and his natural passion, both of which were effectively conveyed through his piercing, penetrating blue eyes. Four years later, to his dismay, the Canadian public had fallen for a young, handsome American president, John F. Kennedy – a man whom Diefenbaker neither liked nor understood – and the sixty-seven-year-old struggled to respond effectively.[54]

This became clear during the Cuban Missile Crisis. When the United States discovered that the Soviet Union was transporting missiles into Cuba on 16 October 1962, the world moved as close as it ever had to a full-scale nuclear war. Six days later, Kennedy announced a naval blockade, or quarantine, around the island to prevent the communists from delivering additional war matériel. The American president acted largely on his own, but then, just before going on national television to announce the blockade, he solicited vocal support from his major NATO allies. Faced with photographic evidence of the Soviets' actions, only Ottawa hesitated. Diefenbaker was furious that Canada, America's NORAD partner, had not been consulted on a security issue that affected both countries, and he sought independent confirmation of the US findings. Influenced undoubtedly by his personal animosity towards Kennedy, for two days he also refused to synchronize Canada's NORAD forces with those of their US colleagues. The prime minister must have thought that the electorate would applaud him for refusing to be pushed around by the brazen American president. He was wrong. The public sensed the immediate security threat and supported Kennedy, causing Diefenbaker's standing in the polls to decline further.[55]

In the middle of the crisis, with Soviet ships fast approaching the American blockade, John Holmes was in Ohio, giving a lecture at Bowling Green University entitled "Are Canadians Really Friends of the United States?" His answer, he insisted in spite of the political machinations taking place around him, was "Yes, a thousand times yes." The speech was again typical Holmes, and it drew heavily from the ideas he had first expressed in his MA thesis. He reminded the audience that the peaceful state of the Canadian-American relationship was unnatural, that the inequality inherent in any relationship between two countries so disparate in size and power was bound to make things complicated, and that only with patience and level-headedness could the countries overcome their difficulties.[56]

Two weeks later, long after the Soviets had turned their ships around and the crisis had passed, Holmes spoke at the University of Windsor. His daring, balanced analysis of how both countries had dealt with the situation was enlightening. "There is a good case to be made that Washington might have allowed its allies more voice in shaping its Cuba policy before committing them to the consequences of a dangerous unilateral act," he began: "There is a good case in logic also for the argument that the final decision should have been made jointly. I think we shall do better, however, not to worry over the logic but to recognize that ultimate decisions are going to be unilateral for a long time to come ... If we want to have some influence on events we must not be obsessed with the illusion that this can be expressed in a veto on US decisions."

He went on to add that, regardless of the legitimacy of the Canadian response, its impact had "left something to be desired. Too many of us have given the impression that we were differing with the Americans out of prejudice and perversity rather than conviction."[57] As much as Holmes was dismayed by Washington's unilateralist attitude during the international crisis, he recognized that Canada's dependence on the United States both economically and militarily meant that it could not expect to be treated as an equal. He advocated professionalism, consistency, and the development of realistic expectations to counter the venomous and unhelpful anti-Americanism that tended to emerge whenever US policy disappointed Canadians. "We cannot deny the obligation to assist in United States defence and we must not consider it in itself unreasonable," he wrote in the *Toronto Star*: "It is part of the price we pay to maintain the international cover under which we can fulfil a national destiny more significant than guarding our real estate."[58] He repeated this message to the Canadian Council of Churches, to the American Assembly at Columbia, and in the widely read American periodical *Foreign Affairs*.[59]

Holmes' reputation for sagacity and eloquence continued to spread. As an American colleague noted after one of his earliest performances, "I was struck by how effective Holmes was in conveying the depth of Canadian feeling on a given issue, always without anger, but with a quiet intensity that made a far deeper impression than louder voices on both sides."[60] Perhaps because he lacked the confidence to recognize how established he had become, he accepted as many offers to speak as he could handle, even when they caused him to venture outside his areas of expertise. This was one of the few mistakes of his early years as CIIA president.

Requests to comment on the North Atlantic Treaty were perhaps the best example. Holmes was not an expert in strategic studies, nor had he worked on the NATO file in the DEA. His thinking on the future of the organization was shallow, a mixture of his general analysis of Canadian foreign policy and observations on the alliance itself that he had borrowed from Escott Reid. In his lectures on NATO, his favourite statement – one he repeated on the CBC and in print for at least eighteen months – was that the Atlantic community was what he (and Reid) called a spiritual idea. Its role was the defence of Western civilization in the broadest sense and, as such, it defied categorization. The organization was at its worst when it refused to assess the conduct of its own members sufficiently critically. "There are things worse than disunity," he often said, "and sometimes diversity strengthens the diplomatic arm of the West."[61] It was the Holmesian way of preaching tolerance of French idiosyncrasies and of American inclinations towards unilateralism without the typical accompanying analysis of the political implications.

Holmes was rarely criticized for his less rigorous commentaries because his delivery was so effortless and his conclusions so intrinsically reasonable. He was perceived as an intelligent, authoritative analyst, but no one is capable of speaking meaningfully on the entire global foreign policy agenda. Because he was so gracious and so eloquent, it was difficult to notice that on topics that extended beyond his areas of expertise, he occasionally said very little.

Conversely, there could be no questioning his authority on such subjects as United Nations peacekeeping. When Lester Pearson returned the Liberals to power in 1963, Canadians across the country assumed that Canada would re-emerge as a significant international actor. Holmes provided a more sombre analysis for the CBC. He criticized the general public for making incessant demands on the government to repeat the Suez experience through dramatic, well-documented leadership initiatives at the international level. "The pressure to put a made-in-Canada label on our activities in the UN is self-defeating," he argued, "for the best work of a middle power is achieved in combination with others ... Insofar as Canada has achieved a reputation in world politics it has been as a country using its particular advantages in the interest of the world community not for the projection of its own image. We have a delegation well fitted to make a worthy contribution, but we shall have to take a good deal of this on faith because it is by nature discreet. We ought not to judge their success by the number of headlines they achieve."[62]

This approach – lowering expectations, appreciating the little things, and having faith in the United Nations – was part of the Holmesian prescription that caught on more slowly. Peacekeeping arrangements, he said at a conference in Oxford hosted by the Institute for Strategic Studies, "are fashioned in moments of pressure and desperation, their mandates obscure because of haze or the need to fuzz the hard issues, and they are always improvised."[63] The public was enthralled by the middle power idea and the recognition that came with it. It was less enamoured with the harsh realities of Canada's limitations both at the UN and in the world at large. On such issues John Holmes was certainly listened to, but he was not always heard.

He was rarely heard pronouncing on government policy, and this provides yet another reason why he appealed to so many different segments of the Canadian population. Holmes opined on Canada, on the Commonwealth, on the United Nations, but rarely on elected representatives in Ottawa and their personal initiatives. As he explained to one former colleague who chided him for keeping his political views too much to himself, he refused to engage in partisanship in part because he found it inappropriate for civil servants to criticize administrations under which they served without good reason and also because it was his duty as CIIA president to behave consistently with the organization's mandate of political neutrality.[64] This explanation may not have been true, but it was convenient. Staying above the political fray suited John Holmes. It gained him respect from members of the public and the government and allowed him to develop his reputation as a helpful commentator and an astute analyst among a broad cross-section of Canadians.

Holmes had a remarkable ability to speak critically while leaving his listeners feeling exempt from his concerns. One might consider, for example, his views on recognizing communist China. His diplomatic experience demonstrates that he was in favour, but when he spoke to the CBC on the issue in early 1964 he was less definitive. First, he said, "The United States has got itself in a position in which the inevitable recognition of Peking and acceptance in the UN by a majority of nations will be a moral defeat, but even if the United States has been foolish in her policy we Canadians can't afford in our own interest to let her power and authority sag." Later in the same segment, however, he noted: "A change of policy on Canada's part towards China, if tactfully and unprovocatively explained, could in some way help the Americans over the hurdle."[65] Listeners on either side of this argument could easily emerge confident that John Holmes agreed with them.

There was a drawback to this approach. Because Holmes was so pleasing, he was rarely challenged. Never comfortable as the ultimate arbiter or decision maker when he was a civil servant, he often used his position as president of the CIIA as a justification for not reaching specific conclusions on some of the hard policy choices that practitioners faced.[66] This was disappointing, particularly since he was a well-connected man of significant influence.

After just two years, Holmes' ideas were, in the words of John Watkins, "getting around pretty far"[67] in official Canadian foreign policy circles. Once again, in 1962, Lester Pearson arranged for him to attend a conference in Bahia, Brazil, on world tensions. As had been his experience in 1960, he was hardly impressed with the pre-written, platitude-filled speeches, but the chance to be with Pearson, to travel through Lima and Mexico City, and to holiday briefly in Rio de Janeiro made the excursion worthwhile.

Invitations from international practitioners were also forthcoming. In 1963, he was asked to fly to Barbados to train a number of their aspiring diplomats along with others from British Guiana, Trinidad and Tobago, and Jamaica. It was a UN operation, which Holmes framed in a letter to Arthur Campbell of the Commonwealth Division as an opportunity for the Canadian government to add to its diplomatic understanding of the region.[68] Holmes demonstrated repeatedly that his dismissal from external affairs had no impact on his loyalty to the state or on his view of himself as a servant of his country. When he was abroad, he acted as if he was the voice not only of the CIIA but also of the interests of Canadians more widely, and the responsibility that he felt ensured that he represented his country with dignity and integrity.

The experience in Barbados was a satisfying one. The week-long course began at the Extra Mural Centre at the University of the West Indies at 9:00 AM and ran for three hours each morning. There was a brief afternoon session, and participants then met in the sitting room of the Aquatic Club in the evenings for more free-ranging, informal discussions. Holmes' lectures covered the meaning of diplomacy, the role of the lesser powers in international negotiations, the organization of a foreign service, and the importance of confidentiality, the duties of an ambassador while abroad, diplomatic protocol, and consular work. They were written in plain language and portrayed the profession as a noble duty. Diplomacy in the 1960s, he explained, "is a craft, a technical skill, an art – a great and honourable profession, more important now than it ever was. In diplomacy there is a need both for idealism and scepticism, above all a sense of proportion because the most important quality is objectivity." Diplomats were not crusaders. They had to accept situations for what they were, use history as their guide, and "practice the art of the possible."[69] It was a Canadian approach to the foreign service that left many of the more significant officials in the West Indies enamoured with John Holmes and with his country more generally. They also emerged with a view of Canadians as a generous people, since Holmes donated 20 percent of his honorarium to the University of the West Indies' library.

A few months later, he was off to Australia, presumably to build a relationship with the Australian Institute of International Affairs but also to report to Ottawa on his views of one of Canada's long-time allies. Still convinced that his country's Commonwealth ties were essential, he advised the DEA that Canada had best take Australia more seriously as a diplomatic partner, especially since the new view of security in the Antipodes, which stressed the centrality of the United States, was very close to Canada's.[70]

That same year he undertook, again tangentially on behalf of the Canadian government, a meeting with two communist Chinese reporters who were visiting Toronto. It was a memorable experience. The restaurant the group had chosen was unlicensed and the reporters wanted to drink, so Holmes negotiated an arrangement in which a bottle of Scotch was delivered to the table in a paper bag and placed at his feet. Canadian journalist Fred Nossal, who had arranged the event, played the role of bartender throughout the night, pouring drinks off the floor. Holmes reported that there was interest in developing stronger relations with Canada but that it was contingent on a change in his government's policy of recognizing Taiwan. China claimed jurisdiction over Taiwan, and Ottawa's refusal to cut ties insulted Beijing's sensibilities. Holmes' sympathies for the Chinese position came through in his insistence that that they were far more moderate than the Soviets, or even the Americans, in their approach to the Cold War. Still, perhaps recalling his experience in the East Block, he never advocated recognition directly.[71]

After so many unofficial missions, in November 1964, Secretary of State for External Affairs Paul Martin sought to formalize Holmes' ad hoc connection to the DEA (without, of course, readmitting him). For over ten years, the government in London had been trying to grant British Guiana independence without allowing communist sympathizers within the leading People's Progressive Party (PPP) to take over. The PPP's political success kept the British from leaving completely. London saw an opening after riots and protests that began in 1962 stretched into 1964. The British imposed supervised elections, and Canada was asked to appoint two individuals to a Commonwealth observation group. Along with Liberal Party member William Parker, Martin asked Holmes to go, noting that he would technically receive his appointment from Britain's colonial secretary, that he would be paid for by the host government, and that he would not be representing Canada officially. The CIIA president was delighted to accept, even though he eventually found the vast majority of his fellow observers – two men from Ghana, two from India, two from Malta, one from Nigeria, two from Trinidad, and A.G.R. Butler from Great Britain – to be "a collection of prima donnas" as they travelled together to hear speeches in wooden shacks in remote villages and navigated through jungles to inspect polling stations.

When it came time to write the final report, thanks largely to his growing international reputation, the colonial secretary asked Holmes to lead the working group that would negotiate the wording. He declined, recognizing that acceptance would imply that he was a British appointee. Moreover, as chair his material contributions would have been limited. Instead, he offered to lead the first meeting until an alternative chair was elected, and then he proceeded to draft the report virtually on his own. The majority of his colleagues endorsed his proposed text, and the commission was able to disband fairly quickly. A coalition government that was more friendly to Britain soon wrestled power from the angered and ungracious former PPP premier, Dr. Cheddi Jagan, and Guiana's independence was granted in May 1966.

For Holmes, the experience reconfirmed the value of the Commonwealth. "We did all have similar attitudes towards elections," he reported back to the DEA: "In spite of the varying natures of democratic practice in our countries, there was a consensus on what constituted fair and free elections, and the conclusion that these had been fair and free was in the end quite inescapable." It was an adventure that he would not have missed.[72]

In the midst of these varied experiences, between 1962 and 1964 Holmes also found time to give a number of guest lectures at the National Defence College in Kingston; to speak multiple times to the Canadian Forces Staff College in Toronto; to lecture to the professional development program of the Engineering Institute of Canada – a group of twenty engineers from all phases of industry who met weekly to discuss current events relevant to their discipline; to join the History Advisory Group for the Toronto Public Library Board; to join a committee on the teaching of international affairs in universities (and to attend, on its behalf, a meeting of the National Conference of Canadian Universities and Colleges in Quebec); to participate in a conference of directors of institutes of international studies at the Johns Hopkins University; to provide interviews to the British and Australian press; to contribute to a Quaker conference for diplomats in Portland, Ontario; to speak to the University of Toronto's Students' Administrative Council's annual conference on the changing face of English Canada; to attend parts of Toronto's Faculty of Law's conference on the Supreme Court and Canadian federalism; and to be elected to the Senate of the newly established Brock University.

Throughout his first five years at the CIIA, Holmes was ubiquitous. President, mentor, adviser, commentator, diplomat – there was almost nothing he would not do to promote the institute and the broader interests of his country. His dedication, intelligence, and good nature developed for him a personal reputation that was virtually unsurpassed in Canada and around the diplomatic world. In 1964, Holmes had become so much a public figure, and was so well liked, that it was common for Canadians travelling abroad in government roles to hear the words, "Oh, you're from Canada. Do you know my friend John Holmes? How is he?" He had certainly found the right job, and Canada was lucky to have him as a leading voice, even if the next few years were significantly more complicated.

An early picture of the Holmes children. Helen (Buzz) is on the far left and John is second from right. They are standing next to twins Elizabeth and Isobel (living family members unable to determine who is who in this photo). *Nancy Skinner Papers*

A young Holmes dressed more formally, with his three sisters and an unknown girl. *Nancy Skinner Papers*

Wendell Holmes and his four
children. *Nancy Skinner Papers*

As a child and a young man,
John Holmes took a serious
interest in theatre. This photo
was taken while he was a student
at the University of Western
Ontario in the late 1920s. *Nancy
Skinner Papers*

In 1939, John Holmes was a
PhD candidate at the University
of London. *Holmes Papers, Box
P1560, photo 010*

Acting Permanent Canadian
Representative to the United
Nations John Holmes presents
Trygve Lie, Secretary General
of the United Nations, with
Canada's $8 million contribution
to the United Nations Relief and
Rehabilitation Programs in Korea
and Palestine, 5 April 1951. *Holmes
Papers, Box P1560, photo 0148.
United Nations No. UN33501*

Left to right: His Excellency, Mr. U On Sein, Ambassador Extraordinary and Plenipotentiary to Burma, Major-General (retired) Georges Vanier, Governor General of Canada, and John Holmes, 9 October 1959. Sein is presenting his credentials. *National Film Board No. 90509 / Holmes Papers, Box P1560, photo 028*

Commonwealth Education Conference, Oxford, United Kingdom, August 1959. Holmes is in the back row, third from the left. *B.J. Harris, No. A-605-2 / Holmes Papers, Box P1560, photo 0168*

Holmes with Arnold Heeney (date unknown). *Holmes Papers, Box P1560, photo 0178*

Holmes at the CIIA Library, 230 Bloor Street West, Toronto, 1960. *Gilbert A. Milne / Holmes Papers, Box P1560, photo 022*

Left to right: John Holmes, Felipe Herrera (Chile), and Hans A. Havemann (Federal Republic of Germany) at the 5th session of the United Nations Institute for Training and Research's Board of Trustees, 29 March 1967. *United Nations No. 98369 / Holmes Papers, Box P1560, photo 0154*

Holmes at work at the CIIA, Wellesley Street Office, 1973. *Holmes Papers, Box P1560, photo 023*

Accepting an Honorary LLD at the University of Waterloo's Convocation ceremony, 1976. *Maurice Green, University of Waterloo Central Photographics / Holmes Papers, Box P1560, photo 0196*

Presentation at Anglo-Canadian Conference, Brotherton Library, University of Leeds, United Kingdom, October 1979. Holmes is third from the left. *Photograph by Edward A. Winpenny, Otley, UK, ©1979 / Holmes Papers, Box P1560, photo 0193*

John Holmes in front of the main grounds of Trinity College, University of Toronto, 1980. *Holmes Papers, Box P1560, photo 008*

8

A Diplomat in Action

For Canadians who had come of age in the 1930s and 1940s – when surviving the Depression and a world war was simply what had to be done – the 1960s must have been unsettling. At its most basic level, the decade was a period of unprecedented affluence and, after the Cuban Missile Crisis, relative peace. Vocal members of the postwar baby boom became teenagers and rejected the conservatism of their parents in favour of a radical approach to politics and community. They were adventurous, unpredictable, and spoke their minds without the typical caution of their elders. Their passion and enthusiasm excited John Holmes but also made him uncomfortable. His anxiety was compounded by the tremendous physical pain he experienced upon his return to Toronto after spending the Christmas of 1964 in London with his family; the condition of his back had left him with no choice but to use a cane. Nor did it help that the radicalism of the 1960s propelled the international system into a period of profound uncertainty, much of which had a direct impact on Canadian foreign policy. Finally, there was his job at the Canadian Institute of International Affairs. After nearly five years of saying yes to nearly every request, and responding personally to the complaints of every member, Holmes was tired, and he began to say no.[1] He was also wanted, and, at age fifty-four, he knew that the opportunities that were presenting themselves outside of the institute would not last indefinitely.

His first public appearance of 1965 was on CBC Radio's *Weekend Review*. The UN General Assembly was to begin its annual meetings the following week, and the organization was in disarray. The Soviet Union refused to pay its peacekeeping dues, Indonesia prepared to announce its withdrawal from the organization, and the United States threatened to deny voting rights to nations that were in arrears of their financial obligations (as was permitted by the charter). Instead of debating its future prospects, commentators around the world spent the winter arguing over how quickly the UN would collapse.

At a time when their prized institution was in danger of failing, Canadians needed a calm voice, and they turned to John Holmes. His response to the controversies combined brutal realism with an equally strong sense of hope: "It is not time for panic," he declared. "Let's keep our eye on essentials. The UN can continue without Indonesia, it can also continue without a more satisfactory means of paying for its peacekeeping missions. It is not bankrupt; it is simply unable to pay for the expensive kinds of forces it has called into being in the latest decade of its existence." He never denied that the end might be near, but he added that it was too soon for the international community, and for Canadians, to give up.[2]

He was right, but the future of the UN should have been the least of his concerns in 1965. Closer to home, Lester Pearson was having unexpected difficulties managing foreign policy as prime minister. It appeared to an increasing number in Canada that his mediatory approach to conflict management, the one that he had passed on to Holmes and to so many of his colleagues, was unsuited to modern times. Canadians were looking inwards in the 1960s, re-examining such issues as official bilingualism, women's rights, and, most important for Holmes, Canada's role in the world. In this context, a new generation of vocal nationalists was emerging. These baby boomers were proponents of a brand of Canadianism that emphasized independence from the United States and perhaps even neutrality in world affairs. As they entered university, they used their newfound platform to denounce what they perceived as the increasing Americanization of Canada and the failure of their overly timid and out of touch government to stop it. To them, in the words of one leader of the movement, "self awareness was at a remarkable low among Canadian intellectuals as we moved through the decade from colony to hibernation."[3]

Although they were initially most concerned with dramatic increases in foreign direct investment and the resultant loss of national control of Canadian industries, before long their criticisms carried over into the security realm. When the United States launched Operation Rolling Thunder – a series of air attacks on North Vietnam – in February 1965, India and Poland, two members of the (now eleven-year-old) International Commission on Supervision and Control condemned its actions as a violation of the Geneva agreements. Canada issued a dissenting report criticizing both sides. For the young nationalists, this was further evidence of compromised independence and Canada's decline from major international player to gutless servant of American interests.

It is clear from Holmes' experience in the foreign service that he was hardly a blind supporter of US foreign policy; in the case of Vietnam, he went so far as to say that the president of the United States "may have, foolishly, and contrary to the views we expressed to him, got himself into an appalling mess" for which Canada bore no responsibility. Nevertheless, he reminded a CBC audience, the United States was Canada's "champion, on whose strength and prestige our own security depends." It was therefore in the Pearson government's best interests to work with the US government to help it get out of Indochina. Simplistic condemnations did no one any good.[4]

The nationalists' attack on the Canadian tradition of soft-spokenness, balanced analysis, and non-confrontational negotiation in its relations with Washington disturbed Holmes. In Hamilton in early 1965 he declared in frustration, "I think we Canadians are too much pre-occupied with the United States ... We ought to get used to seeing ourselves not as a failed great power improperly appreciated by our larger neighbours and cousins but rather as a middleweight performer in a world ring crowded with other middleweights and lightweights with whom we form varying combinations in good causes." Two weeks later, in Montreal, he added, "we serve best and are liked best when we are responsible and sensible, inventive and tolerant, because we do not want to be a great power but are content to fulfil a function that is unique and essential but modest and appropriate ... I find it hard to see any effective alternatives to our traditional style."[5]

He also found the increasingly radical calls for neutrality in world affairs and unilateral disarmament off-putting. As great as they sounded in theory, based on his years in the foreign service, he could not see them promoting Canadian interests. Peace was maintained by the balance of nuclear forces on both sides. Everyone wanted to see an end to these weapons of mass destruction, but those advocating change had to be certain that their proposed alternatives would actually work. Instead of acting alone, the real solution, as he had suggested while dealing with the issue at the UN in the 1950s, was devising proposals that all of the established nuclear powers could accept, and doing so gradually. The most significant danger to world peace in the nuclear context had little to do with Canada's attitude towards disarmament; rather, it was a breakdown in communication among the major players that could lead to "a panic rush to arms much more dangerous than the relatively purposeful kind of arms programme which we have now achieved after some years of experience and emotional discipline."[6]

He was bothered even more by the way the critics took the United States' role and responsibilities as leader of the Western alliance for granted. It was not easy being a superpower, he liked to remind his audiences. And while the United States had made a number of significant errors in judgment of late, one had to keep in mind the enormous strains and pressures that it faced as the guardian of the security of the free world. Canadians had no right to flaunt their alleged moral superiority. Being a middle power was a much easier job than was being a global leader.

The war of ideas between the more traditionally minded current and former members of the Canadian diplomatic establishment and the new nationalists intensified with the release of *Canada and the United States: Principles for Partnership* in July 1965. The document was the outcome of an eighteen-month bilateral investigation by two well-respected former ambassadors, American Livingston Merchant and Holmes' former colleague Arnold Heeney. The two had been asked by President Lyndon Johnson and Prime Minister Pearson to explain why the Canadian-American relationship no longer seemed as stable as it once had been and to provide a prescription to fix it. Their report was expected to help restore the positive tone that had been so evident during the King-Roosevelt era.

Merchant and Heeney concluded that, in the case of bilateral disputes, both countries would be better served if they negotiated resolutions "in private, through diplomatic channels."[7] This was the "quiet diplomacy" that Holmes had practised so effectively at the United Nations and throughout his career as a civil servant. It was also utterly inflammatory and indeed offensive to the new Canadian nationalists. To them, the old generation was suggesting that Canada received favourable treatment in the United States only when it spoke politely and acted modestly. This was insulting to a country that had a right, if not a duty, to assert itself and its values forcefully on the world stage. The Merchant-Heeney Report became a symbol of everything that was wrong with the Canadian political and diplomatic establishment, a proverbial dart board at which they hurled their criticisms. Anyone associated with it came under spoken attack from what one analyst light-heartedly called the "angry young men."[8]

Holmes' response to the study was, as usual, nuanced. He fully agreed with the views of his friends and colleagues, but he was distressed by all of the publicity. "What they have to say is exceedingly sensible," he remarked to one associate, "but I think it was foolish ever to ask anybody to set it down." To another, he wrote, "it is the sort of thing which one just can't say out loud." Since the radicals would never accept that diplomacy worked – one nationalist soon condemned "the bankruptcy of this approach to world affairs,"[9] – trumpeting such an approach to foreign policy could only inflame them further. Their anger was destructive for Canada, and for the Canadian government, especially since they would eventually realize the errors of their ways and accept the general recommendations for what they were. "It is because Canadian Civil Servants have, on the whole, been such good Civil Servants that they are inevitably impatient with those who don't just want to let everything be managed nicely and sensibly and rationally," he concluded.[10]

There can be no denying that Holmes believed that his former colleagues were among the world's best. There is also a sense of elitism in his comments that is a product of his time in the East Block and perhaps of his upbringing in a loyalist household. But unlike many of his peers, Holmes was conscious of his own prejudices.[11] That is likely why the majority of the nationalists tolerated him. That summer, for example, he was enlisted to help organize part of University of Toronto philosophy professor Charles Hanly's teach-in entitled "Revolution and Response."

The program attracted over five thousand participants to Varsity Arena. There were lectures on a number of revolutionary movements, but the largest crowd gathered for the discussion of Vietnam. Perhaps because of his position as CIIA president, Holmes chose not to be officially recognized in the program. Nonetheless, he was consulted regularly by the panel chairs for assistance in soliciting reputable speakers to participate. "Instead of just gathering a collection of people to denounce American policy," he wrote excitedly to a colleague in California, "they are trying to get spokesmen from all points of view, including the American." Holmes thought the experience successful in welcoming the various perspectives. He was less pleased with members of a well-organized, disruptive, and bossy left-wing claque that attempted, unsuccessfully, to prevent a US official from presenting Washington's position on the conflict. Obnoxious behaviour never impressed him, nor did he believe that it was effective in doing anything other than polarizing issues even further.[12]

Serious, impassioned, rational debate was something different. At the same summer's Banff Conference on Canada's role as a middle power, he got just that. Three years after its original inception, the gathering had grown in size and stature. With sponsorship money from the national office and two regional branches of the CIIA, the United Nations Association in Canada, and the University of Alberta, the conference attracted an impressive list of speakers. Holmes, of course, was present, as was Arnold Heeney. Even Prime Minister Pearson made an appearance. Overall attendance reached well over one hundred, almost triple the forty that came in 1962.

After an introductory talk by the noted political journalist Blair Fraser, Holmes formally opened the discussions with a lecture on the future of what he called "middlepowermanship." In an effort to keep the dialogue constructive, he noted that the purpose of the conference was "to find out not only what Canadian foreign policy should not be, but also what it should be." He went on to explore a term that was, for him, ambiguous: "The more one tries to define middlepowermanship," he began, "the more difficult and perhaps pretentious it appears to do so at all." Nevertheless, the world needed the middle powers, including Canada, to play helpful and constructive roles in the future. How could his country make its greatest contribution? The answer was through the approach advocated in *Principles for Partnership*: "If our conception is to be realistic, adapted to our size and the shape we are in, it seems to me that it is bound to be complex in nature, sensitive to equilibrium and opportunity and, for the most part, discreet."[13]

A few days later, a more confrontational Arnold Heeney took the argument further. The most inflammatory line in his presentation attacked the new nationalists directly: "If our objective is merely, or even chiefly, to convince the world – and perhaps ourselves – that we are independent of the United States, then of course we are relieved of the restraints of common sense and good behavior and can give full play to our emotions. The lid is off." Heeney ended his speech with a quotation from none other than John Holmes. "Canada's capacity to influence United States' policy," he said, "is Canada's principal diplomatic asset."[14] It was, to many members of the audience, a call to arms, a pitting of the old, gentlemanly diplomatic establishment against an overwhelming naïve new generation of passionate youthful thinkers.[15]

The response to Heeney's presentation was what Holmes described to one friend as a revolt against the very idea of middlepowermanship and the allegedly antiquated notion of quiet diplomacy. His personal verdict was mixed. "I don't go with the kids all the way," he admitted, "but I do think we have to take into consideration their impatience and stop behaving quite so much like mandarins." Communication between the East Block and the Canadian public had broken down, and Holmes' former colleagues were seen as arrogant, stuck in their ways, and out of touch. Regardless of whether the foreign policy they advocated was appropriate, the disconnect was problematic. As a former civil servant and as president of the CIIA, Holmes felt personally obligated to help solve it.[16]

The solution began with making peace with the most vocal critic at Banff, Lloyd Axworthy (Tom's brother). Axworthy was a passionate, articulate academic and political activist who opposed the United States' conduct during the Vietnam War. Less than a week after the conference ended, Holmes wrote the Princeton-educated University of Manitoba professor personally:

> I have been concerned for some time about the impatience of much of the public in general and of our younger people in particular with our terribly sensible foreign policy. The trouble is that I share this impatience but I can't see how we can accomplish very much by abandoning the more discreet role. At any rate, I do see the paradox. After last week, you will notice that I am very defensive. I find myself constantly wanting to grab people by their grey sweaters and assure them that I am not an old fogey. I liked very much your contributions to the discussion and in particular your comment in the final panel ... I also liked what Jim Arnett said afterwards about not making too much of the gap between Marthas and Mars, but then of course I am by temperament and experience a gap closer.

Holmes went on to praise Axworthy for his thoughtfulness and courage. Anointing him a "licensed critic," he encouraged the promising academic to continue to speak his mind. Included in his letter was a draft of a chapter on Canadian nationalism that Holmes was contributing to a collection being edited by University of Toronto scholar Peter Russell. In what could only have been interpreted as a flattering request by any young scholar, Holmes asked Axworthy, technically a more junior colleague, for his feedback.[17]

Three weeks later, Axworthy replied in detail. His comments revealed an inner conflict. Axworthy was fairly certain that Canadian foreign policy could be improved, but he was also aware that he had no evidence to demonstrate conclusively that a more forthright approach to diplomacy would necessarily do so. What he wanted, he told Holmes, was greater public debate about the difficult issues of war and peace, about Vietnam, and about nuclear disarmament. He aimed to replace the restrictive influence of the business establishment in the policy process. And he sought to help fashion a Canadian foreign policy that ensured continued independence from the United States:

People need to have some coherent set of ideals and principles to attach themselves to, something which they can believe in. Our present actions may have solid worth to them, but they appear grey and oh so solid. We can both improve our own sense of independence, become more of a value to other nations, especially lesser ones, and even reinforce our own basic national interest if we present our foreign policy in terms of well defined principles and pursue it with a more creative outlook. You are right, in stating that it is too easy to seek out black and white issues – and that often they are just not that way. But, on the other hand, it would be a mistake to assume too much ambiguity when there is the opportunity for real choices …

There is no doubt in my mind that Canada does have an important role to play. But there is the need for generating a sense of nationalism that should be shared by the whole population and that can give this role the push it needs. Perhaps the course of "internationalism" can be our form of nationalism.[18]

Holmes was impressed. Not only did he incorporate some of Axworthy's comments into his text almost verbatim but, two years later, he also recommended to Foreign Minister Paul Martin that he recruit the young scholar as a speechwriter. "One reason I would like him to have this experience is that I think he is one of the coming leaders in this country," he explained. He was rebellious, "but his criticism was a great deal better disciplined and based on much better comprehension of reality than most of the academic protestors."[19] Holmes was right on all counts. Thirty years later, the always controversial Axworthy became the boldest and most noteworthy Canadian foreign minister since Martin himself.

Axworthy was not the only one in line for a change in occupation. At fifty-five, John Holmes understood that his opportunity to leave the CIIA was narrowing, and after five years at the institute, he was open to something new. The first official sign was an innocent-looking request to change his title. He had never believed that the term "president" accurately described what he did at the CIIA, but it took half a decade to build the confidence to express his discomfort. He had two interrelated concerns. First, none of his colleagues at similar institutes was called president; they were all directors. Second, in these same associations the presidency was an honorary position, equivalent to the chair of the CIIA's National Council. Holmes felt miscast, and he had also found it necessary to explain to his colleagues (and perhaps also to potential future employers) that his job as president was a legitimate one.[20] His council was sympathetic, but it decided to fold the change into a broader series of policy adjustments that it was set to explore through a special committee.

At the same time as Holmes was coming to view his position at the CIIA more critically, a series of offers of employment arrived. In 1963, the chair of the Department of Political Science at the University of Western Ontario, Henry Mayo, began urging him to retire from the CIIA for a better-paying and less taxing teaching position. The idea was interesting, but Holmes was uncomfortable leaving the institute so quickly after obtaining the Ford grant. The president of the University of Toronto, Claude Bissell, was more cautious, but in early 1965 he, too, sought to lure Holmes away. Hart House, the hub of intellectual life at the university, was in need of a new warden. The job was prestigious but less intensive than work at the CIIA. It also provided a better salary than did Holmes' current position. Still, he eventually refused to let his name stand. He owed the CIIA, he explained, and if he were to leave, he would be most interested in an academic-type opportunity in international relations. Next, a generous gift from Senator Norman Paterson enabled Carleton University to open a school of international affairs. Old friend Bert MacKay was already committed, and Harald von Riekhoff was almost certainly going to be recruited as well. The directorship was open and Holmes was a leading candidate. Again, though, he could not say yes. The more attractive the offer, the more his ever-present caution appeared to tie him to the CIIA.[21]

The overwhelming evidence that his services were wanted did give him the courage to make demands of the CIIA that he would not have made when he first arrived. Over the next year, Holmes and Arnold Heeney, who, among his many duties, chaired the National Council and sat on its executive, candidly discussed the future of the institute and John Holmes' role within it. In Holmes' view, the expansion of the scope and reach of the CIIA's activities had made his position untenable. Essentially, he had two multifaceted jobs: one was primarily organizational, coordinating between the various branches and supporting their individual programming aims while serving as an institutional figurehead at relevant national and international gatherings; the other was academic, promoting and developing a national research and publications program that integrated the work of the universities, the civil service, and the government to enrich the study of international relations across the country in a distinctly Canadian way. The first job called for a director general, the second for a director of studies. Holmes said that he would do either but was more interested in the latter.[22]

He and Heeney did not initially discuss the cost of the proposed changes – which involved hiring another relatively senior staff member – but they should have. The CIIA was still struggling financially, largely because the branches were no longer able to support the general operating budget through their yearly fundraising campaigns. In the first four months of 1965 alone, donations decreased by almost 60 percent compared to the year before, and the institute's honorary treasurer mused about drawing from the reserve funds to make up the deficit.[23]

In the midst of the difficulties, another offer arrived. Robert Clark, an economist at the University of British Columbia who also served in the Office of Academic Planning, insisted on taking Holmes to lunch while he was in Toronto in the middle of May. The topic of the conversation was not made explicit in their subsequent correspondence, but the history of UBC suggests that Clark had a particular job in mind for the CIIA president. The university was in the midst of an economic boom spurred by increased governmental and unprecedented philanthropic support. After the sudden and unexpected death of Kaspar Neagle, the recently appointed dean of arts, it found itself in desperate need of an acclaimed academic to direct what it foresaw as dramatic expansion at both the undergraduate and graduate levels. Thanks to his relationship with Fred Soward, Holmes knew UBC well, and its future prospects were outstanding. Nevertheless, he appears to have refused to be considered for the deanship. This time, he claimed that he lacked the necessary experience to do the job. And while he did not say so explicitly, it was also unlikely that he would have accepted any opportunity that would have forced him to move so far away from his mother and sisters.[24]

The following month, the special committee tasked with studying the future of the CIIA issued its preliminary report. Its findings were consistent with the president's proposals. The CIIA needed more staff, more money, and separate directors of what it called research and public education. Recognizing that the scope of the plan was immense, the committee also recommended that the CIIA define public education in elitist terms. "The Institute has not the organization or the means to carry on a programme of mass public education," it declared: "Communication with the general public is a proper function of news media and educational institutions and the role of the Institute is to furnish material to these established organizations."[25]

This approach was not universally well received. Henry Langford, president of Eastern and Chartered Trust Company and chair of the National Executive, was the most vocal critic of what he interpreted as a disturbing trend. The CIIA was becoming too academic and, with its continued insistence on closed-session meetings, too much a servant of the federal government.[26] The conflict between Langford and Holmes, while always couched in civil terms, escalated, with the latter making a spirited defence of the CIIA's improved relationship with the Department of External Affairs at a National Council meeting that December. There was closer collaboration than there had been before his arrival, Holmes conceded readily, but no member of the government or of the civil service exercised any influence over what the institute did or did not publish.[27]

That same month, as his frustration with the CIIA increased, Holmes received his most tempting offer yet. In 1964, before the Paterson School was established in Ottawa, Holmes had initiated a dialogue with the University of Toronto in the hope of founding a centre for international studies. Canada lagged behind some of its allies in this area, and with the CIIA's activities expanding so rapidly, and the university's leadership role in the academic system already established, Toronto seemed to be ideal for such a project.

President Bissell reacted positively. Less than two weeks later, he asked the dean of graduate studies, Ernest Sirluck, to investigate the possibilities in greater detail. Sirluck enlisted Holmes to join his exploratory committee. Over the next year, the group determined that the best way forward was to follow the Harvard model: the university planned to create what was called a coordinating centre (as opposed to a teaching one). Rather than offering classes, the centre would serve as a national meeting place for scholars and promising graduate students interested in international studies. At the end of 1965, Bissell asked Holmes to leave the CIIA to become its first director.[28]

The implications of the request reached beyond John Holmes. One of the financial options that the CIIA had been exploring to reduce costs involved selling Tarr House. Since the proposed new centre would undoubtedly be in close contact with the CIIA, it made sense to relocate as close to the university as possible. In the spirit of mutual cooperation, the administrative team at Toronto was willing to entertain an arrangement in which the CIIA leased a university building and sublet the space that it did not need to the new centre for international studies. Alternatively, the institute could consider acquiring space in the research library (which was set to be built in the centre of campus) or in the new arts and sciences hall (which was planned for nearby).

On 3 January 1966, Holmes wrote a private note to his executive that, in its own delicate Holmesian way, was an ultimatum. He could no longer

continue to fulfil both his research and his public education duties. He
was tired of the day-to-day rigours of the CIIA and preferred to confine
himself to academic work. He needed a sabbatical to do more of his own
reading and writing. And if the CIIA leadership did not believe that his
current job required two people, he was happy to step down and be replaced
by someone more energetic. He demanded a prompt decision because he
had received a tempting offer from the University of Toronto that he was
seriously considering. Moreover, there was a short window to acquire the
services of the secretary of the Canadian Institute on Public Affairs (later
the Couchiching Institute), Gordon Hawkins, and if Holmes did stay,
he would advocate Hawkins as a partial replacement. He concluded with
what was for him a clear threat: "In spite of the material rewards of this
and other posts I have been offered, I value this freedom of the CIIA and
especially the happy association with its officers and Council. I feel also
a personal attachment to the Institute and a responsibility for its present
programme. However, I do have to look to the future. So does the Institute,
and I am not at all sure that my inclinations and limitations being what
they are, it is in its best interests that I continue as director."[29]

Once again the executive divided. Langford thought that Holmes should
accept the university's offer. He was less interested in having a director
with academic inclinations and was more concerned about the sorry state
of the branches and the role of the CIIA in educating the wider Canadian
public. The rest of the group, led vocally by Peter Wright, the man most
assumed would eventually succeed Langford as chair, argued that most
of the CIIA's successes over the previous five years could be attributed
directly to John Holmes and that it was the duty of the executive to do
everything in its power to keep him from leaving. If that meant allowing
him to acquire an affiliation with the University of Toronto, so be it.
What was most important was that he continue to draw his salary from
the CIIA and owe his allegiance exclusively to it. Arnold Heeney sided
with Wright, and the executive drew up three plans to accommodate the
president. They all included a 20 percent increase in salary (to $18,000)
and the recruitment of Gordon Hawkins.[30]

Anecdotal evidence suggests that Holmes was then presented with
another employment opportunity, this time with a UN agency. Now
contemplating offers from Carleton, Western, Toronto, and the UN, he
seemed to be in complete control. When Dean Sirluck promised to match
any salary proposal that might have tempted Holmes to leave Toronto, and
to counter any offer made by the CIIA, his position became even stronger.

If the CIIA had a chance, Langford would have to go. After a private inter-vention from Heeney on 21 February 1966, Langford announced that he planned to step down as chair. Holmes wrote him politely, thanking him for his service and regretting his resignation, but a private letter to Heeney demonstrated that he was quite pleased. Peter Wright became the new chair, and the executive moved quickly to keep Holmes from resigning.[31]

The University of Toronto preferred that he cut all ties with the institute. The CIIA was open to any arrangement that would keep him at Edgar Tarr House. As was always the case in these instances, Holmes struggled to come to a decision. What he wanted was the best of both worlds: an affiliation with the university that did not include serious administrative responsibilities and a continued relationship with the CIIA that demanded less and paid more. The strength of his bargaining position made both achievable. Holmes implied to Sirluck that leaving the CIIA was not an option. As a result, it was not possible for him to become director of the new program. He much preferred the idea of serving as a committee member and perhaps joining the faculty as a part-time professor. The administra-tion at Toronto decided that any connection to John Holmes was better than none. Professor Cranford Pratt of the Department of Political Science became the inaugural chair of the International Studies Programme, and Holmes accepted the chairship of its committee on international relations. He was offered $2,000 to serve on the committee and another $3,000 to teach, all of which was paid to the CIIA (to increase his salary there and thus augment his pension). Since Arnold Heeney had been made aware of the entire negotiation process, it was easy for Holmes to return to the institute with all of his demands met. He received permission to take his sabbatical, he was named director general (even though his duties were those of his proposed director of studies), and the board hired Gordon Hawkins to take over the administrative and organizational work that had occupied so much of his time since he arrived in 1960.

Holmes was delighted. Before the arrangements were finalized, he drafted a lengthy note to Pratt outlining his vision for the new academic program. Progress in the study of international relations required more graduate students and more interdisciplinary cooperation among the faculty. Stronger relationships with the DEA could also provide greater resources and research opportunities. The program could develop a seminar series that would bring in noted experts to speak to interested professors and exceptional students. Most important, the centre had to hire note-worthy academics to enhance its national and international reputation.

He had the highly regarded Oran Young in mind, but the offer eventually fell through, as did Holmes' contributions to his committee. A medical condition (nervous dermatitis), along with his other responsibilities, precluded him from adding much to the centre over the next two years. The university did not seem disappointed. It had finally secured John Holmes, and its reputation benefited from his presence, however limited.[32]

Holmes' time outside of his day-to-day duties at the CIIA was divided among three main priorities, all of which expanded the reach and influence of his voice in Canadian and world affairs: his academic work, a subtle but entirely important and active contribution to the public policy process at the political level, and a similarly influential yet under-appreciated role in public education both in Canada and abroad. Academically, he remained concerned with the ongoing worldwide trend towards greater regionalism. In Italy, at a European-American colloquium on relations between the developing world and the nations of the Atlantic, he warned his audience against the oft-proposed strategy of uniting – in the UN and outside of it – to confront the growing "Third World" bloc. Regional units created global conflicts, he argued. They could hardly help improve the lot of the fast-expanding developing world. He also continued his campaign against Canadian participation in the Organization of American States (OAS). If there was one region to which Canada did not "naturally belong," he said to the American Historical Association, it was "the so-called Western Hemisphere." Moreover, the UN was best suited to promote international security, not the US-dominated OAS.[33]

He used these ideas as a basis for his ongoing efforts to resuscitate the all but forgotten Commonwealth. Caught up in a conflict over the discriminatory and internationally condemned regime of Prime Minister Ian Smith in Rhodesia, the organization appeared to be near its end. In a September 1966 article for the journal *Optima*, Holmes responded by celebrating the body's noble intent. The Commonwealth was "a force for good," ahead of its time in terms of its tolerance of difference and engagement of countries from a diversity of racial and ethnic backgrounds. The relationships among its members were critical to the long-term development of effective foreign aid programs worldwide, and its non-military nature was an example for other subinternational organizations to follow. For Canada in particular, it was a counterweight to the United States and a gateway to the countries of the developing world.[34]

His clear understanding of the Commonwealth contrasted with his questioning of the meaning of middle power: "If I have fuzzed the issue as to who is a middle power and why," he told an American audience, "I have done so deliberately. It is not a fixed category, and it is hard to say exactly what the term means. It comes perhaps more easily as a term of historical assessment than as a prescription for the foreign policy of a state. It can sound pretentious or obvious ... Nevertheless, without some definition of its status, both to limit its pretensions and realize its opportunities, smaller countries are likely to flounder ineffectually or turn nasty."[35] In this somewhat amorphous role, Canadians had a duty to behave like model international citizens: "We are more influential when we act as responsible partners than when we act as carping critics," he wrote in a paper directed at a left-leaning French-Canadian audience. "I do not argue that this is an ideal situation, but we do not live in an ideal world and we should hesitate to abandon an advantage we have because it seems wrong in the abstract." Canada's most significant contribution to NATO, for example, was calming the tensions between De Gaulle's France – which had recently threatened to withdraw from the organization completely – and the equally obstinate United States.[36]

More than any other commentator of his generation, John Holmes solidified Canada's image as a middle power at home and abroad. But at a personal level, he was never wholly satisfied with its implications. Being a middle power denied Canadians the opportunity to strive to be a greater force on the world stage. Holmes envisioned a future in which an exploding global population would lead to increased demands for food and agricultural products worldwide. Canada, with its geographical vastness, and its abundance of natural resources, was well positioned to capitalize and develop disproportionate influence over the next generation of leading global actors. Similarly, he wrote to a colleague in 1967, "it has seemed to me that fresh water might prove to be the essential element which will redress the balance of this continent ... If California is too dry for civilization then Californians can move to Canada, or at any rate industry should develop where the water is and attract population." If his country increased its population fast enough, it could eventually grow more powerful than the rest of its middle power allies. Until then, however, as much as he was uncomfortable with the term, it seemed to be the only way to keep Canadians from being "afflicted either by illusions of grandeur or inferiority complexes." Middle powers were responsible and respectable. He would therefore continue to publish and talk about them and their roles around the world, at least until he could propose a more fulfilling description.[37]

He augmented his writing and speaking with concrete contributions to the national policy process. In fact, from his conduct in the mid-1960s, it appears that the longer he spent outside of the public service, the more influence he had within it. Holmes maintained a direct and candid link with Secretary of State for External Affairs Paul Martin, and he was not beyond making personnel recommendations. Paul Junior was an excellent writer with the necessary skills to excel in the diplomatic world, Holmes wrote in the summer of 1965. The next year, he offered to arrange a visit between Martin and Henry Kissinger, using the CIIA as a cover. The institute had served in a similar role when Vu Van Thai, an economist working for the South Vietnamese government, visited Ottawa not much earlier. In 1967, he advocated increased federal support for the United Nations Association in Canada.[38]

When American congressman Stanley Tupper spearheaded an initiative to improve Canadian-American relations in 1965, he entered into a more intense dialogue with Holmes than he did with government officials in Ottawa. The CIIA's director general was also in regular touch with Marcel Cadieux when the latter served as under-secretary of state for external affairs in the mid-1960s, using him as a contact point to recruit foreign service officers to attend and participate in institute functions. He was supportive of his former colleagues who accepted post-retirement positions at the CBC, offering whatever assistance he could to increase the network's coverage of international relations. He agreed to appear before the Senate Steering Committee on External Relations in 1966. For close to a decade it was also Holmes' voice that volunteers heard in their final briefing session before travelling abroad on behalf of Canadian University Services Overseas. And he happily accepted an invitation in 1967 to join the Board of Trustees of the UN Institute for Training and Research (UNITAR).[39]

His productive relationship with the government and the East Block enabled him to play a crucial role in an international assembly on nuclear weapons in the summer of 1966. Although it was an initiative driven largely by the American Assembly with funding from the Carnegie Endowment for International Peace, it was Holmes, acting on behalf of the CIIA, who brought together leading political and academic experts from twenty countries, including Egypt, Israel, India, Pakistan, the United States, and even the Soviet Union, for four days at the Guild Inn in Scarborough. Using a tactic that recalled the Suez crisis, the Americans thought that the Soviets would be more receptive to an invitation from Holmes' CIIA than one from Washington. They were right. The talks were constructive, and there are clear links between the results of the discussions and the Nuclear

Non-proliferation Treaty that was opened for international signature at the United Nations almost exactly two years later.[40]

With Lester Pearson in the Prime Minister's Office, Holmes – and through him the CIIA – had unprecedented access to the highest levels of government. He could reach Pearson personally when he was in Ottawa, and the prime minister promoted the CIIA while entertaining.[41] Holmes also drafted speeches for Minister of Trade and Commerce Robin Winters. When he finally began his long promised three-month sabbatical in October 1966, he travelled to Eastern Europe, where he attended a number of conferences and reported faithfully to the DEA.

Inasmuch as such briefings benefited the governing party, it would be unfair to suggest that Holmes was partisan. He had a great deal of respect, for example, for one Dalton Camp, chairman of the Progressive Conservative Party and the man largely responsible for the removal of John Diefenbaker from his leadership post. Before Camp left for a trip to France, Holmes wrote to his friends in government, in the media, and in the academic community, encouraging them all to meet and speak openly with "this serious and thoughtful citizen." It was this perceived impartiality that made him the liaison between the University of Toronto and his old department when Cranford Pratt arranged to invite Tanzanian president Julius Nyerere to speak. To bring a head of state to Canada without including a formal meeting in Ottawa was awkward, and the university was in no position to set the prime minister's schedule. If it wanted Nyerere, it had to devise a creative solution. Holmes suggested that the invitation be framed in the context of one of the Tanzanian's other roles – chancellor of the University of East Asia. The visit was promoted as evidence of the close relationship between two institutes for higher education. It was a strategic compromise, illustrating the CIIA president's skill as a peacemaker.[42]

Not much later, that same ability precluded him from signing a press release authored by three former colleagues calling on the United States to declare an unconditional ceasefire in North Vietnam. It was not that Holmes disagreed with the sentiment but, rather, that he feared that expressing his personal opinion might compromise his mediatory function. What he preached for Canada he practised himself: quiet diplomacy was almost always his approach of choice.[43]

As comfortable as he was mixing with the Canadian elite, and as loyal as he was to the CIIA's exclusive approach to public education, Holmes spent significant personal time interacting with general audiences. In 1965 he accepted an invitation from a future prime minister, Joe Clark, to speak at the Canadian Political Youth Council. Later that same year he spent three days at the University of Manitoba discussing Canadian foreign policy with the student body. Another time he accepted a request from Doug LePan, then principal of University College in Toronto, to give the keynote address at a scholars' dinner, recognizing the college's best and brightest. He almost never refused an invitation to speak at a Canadian high school and delivered an outstanding address to York Central in February 1966. The next year he served as moderator for the York University School of Business' Seminar on International Trade and Development and spoke at the UN Association's Inter-provincial Seminar for high school students in Montreal. That same year the Graduate School of International Studies at the University of Denver reproduced one of his essays for its thirty-sixth annual high school conference.[44]

Adult learners were equally important. In one shocking, aggressive speech to the same United Nations Association in Canada that he had advocated so strongly to Paul Martin, he issued a staunch admonition: "There are too many half-baked truths which pass for wisdom and confuse the issues, and I hear too many of them at meetings of the élite – including the UNA [United Nations Association] and the CIIA. Nothing gets in the way of constructive thought more stubbornly than the utterly inane idea, for example, that we would have peace if only the desire for peace of the common man were not frustrated by politicians or diplomats, or the Kremlin and the Pentagon! It is the natural bellicosity of the common man that is at the root of our trouble." He later added that the best Canadian foreign policy would be one informed by an educated general public. If, however, the public did not engage itself first, Canadians might "have to accept the unattractive proposition that international affairs are now too difficult, too complex, and too technical for the average man and have to be left to the experts." These comments were Holmes at his most essential: a mixture of idealism, realism, frustration, hope, enthusiasm, and, above all, a commitment to Canada and its future.[45]

It was this commitment that made him so sympathetic to requests from the Canadian military. By 1966 he had become a regular visitor at the Staff College, and in 1967 he accepted an invitation from the commandant of the National Defence College, Air Vice-Marshall F.S. Carpenter, to increase the ties between NDC and the academic community. Holmes played an active role in rewriting the college's curriculum, in soliciting new guest lecturers from across the country, and in commenting on final course projects submitted by the officers.[46]

Finally, in 1966 John Holmes became a professional journalist. In May, Lou Fleming of the *LA Times*' UN Bureau approached him about writing for the paper. That summer, he received an official invitation to develop a series of articles on current affairs from a non-American perspective. He focused his distinctly Canadian columns on hemispheric and global matters. His first, "A Canadian Viewpoint: Vietnam is Your War, Not Ours," outlined the long-standing policy dilemma facing the superpower government: America wanted its allies' support but refused to permit them influence over security strategy. As Holmes had been saying since Hume Wrong first articulated the functional principle, there was "a perspective which the United States must try to understand. It involves a political principle which the Americans themselves have long held dear: the relationship between taxation and representation, between the obligation to carry out a policy and the responsibility for making policy." It was not fair, he wrote, "to expect allies to fight and have no voice."[47]

There was nothing new in his commentaries. He spoke out against regionalism, in favour of the UN, and in support of a more flexible approach to the NATO alliance. Still, the articles were important. Reprinted widely across the United States, they served as yet another indicator of how John Holmes was fast becoming what one colleague later called "Mr. Canada." His pragmatic, largely non-confrontational yet still critical approach to world politics – a generally traditional, conservative style based on his upbringing and his experiences in the foreign service – was increasingly understood worldwide as the "Canadian" view. In this way, he cemented his country's reputation as a rational, sensible, and respectable middle power in the national and international psyches, leaving behind a popular image of Canada that persevered for generations.

9

1967: A Year of Transition

"Tonight we let the world know ... that this is Canada's year in history,"[1] Prime Minister Pearson announced on 31 December 1966. Nineteen sixty-seven had been anticipated by students of Canadian history and politics for close to a decade. Ever since Pearson accepted his Nobel Peace Prize ten years earlier, Canadians had watched their country's status in the world steadily decline. Europe was a major world player, the Commonwealth was hardly the force it once was, and the international community was no longer as dependent on Canadian goodwill and support as it had been in the immediate aftermath of the Second World War. What is more, ever since the long-standing consensus on the direction of foreign policy among the general public was shattered by the Conservatives' insistence that the Liberal government had abandoned Great Britain during the debate over Suez, the country had been divided internally about its future role as a global player.

Canadians were looking for a way back, a means of restoring the sense of pride in their international contributions that had been so strong in the 1940s and 1950s. The new nationalists argued that it was time to rethink their country's global purpose, to do away with old alliances and start afresh as a neutral, moral heavyweight. Others were more cautious, if unrealistic, in hoping that the momentum that would inevitably build up during the celebrations of the one hundredth anniversary of Confederation, along with the opportunity to host the World's Fair in Montreal, could restore some of that former glory. Escott Reid captured both sentiments in an article for a commemorative edition of the CIIA's *International Journal*. "There was a golden age in Canadian foreign policy," he wrote, "a period where, because of a peculiar and temporary set of circumstances, we in Canada, became, on certain issues of world affairs, one of an inner group of three countries which moulded the shape of the future." Moving forward into the country's second century, he saw a chance that it could do so again.[2]

John Holmes was more measured in public than his good friend, but he, too, was optimistic. "Canada," he said at one point, "had been in a tiresomely depressing state, but now the almost embarrassing naïve enthusiasm of people I know makes me think that may be a thing of the past."[3] In a year-end article for the *LA Times*, written in the aftermath of the success of Expo '67, he proclaimed, "Canadians are winding up their Centennial year more confidently than they began it … What has changed is suddenly this summer Canadians found that their attachment to the Canadian idea was deeper than they had realized."[4] If he was correct, it was in no small part because of his own writing and speaking. In 1967 Canada, John Holmes was everywhere. He accepted $1,200 to write a journalistic piece on his country's international role for *Century* magazine, the first official Canadian publication of the year. He was included in a Toronto Dominion Bank series called *Your Canada*, which became so popular during the centennial celebrations that over 700,000 copies were printed for high school and university students nationwide. His name could be found in a well-received collection of essays published under the title of *The Decisive Year*. And his speaking and academic engagements remained overwhelming.[5]

For Holmes, the passing of 1967 also marked the culmination of a number of major projects that shaped his country in the years to come. Perhaps the most significant was the creation of the Parliamentary Centre in Ottawa. The institution was the brainchild of Peter Dobell, yet another Oxford-educated foreign service official. During the Diefenbaker era, Dobell had shared many of his colleagues' frustrations over the direction of the DEA. When Howard Green became the new secretary of state for external affairs, his ignorance of the portfolio reminded Dobell all too clearly of a disturbing trend at the political level in Ottawa: members of Parliament had limited to no understanding of the world outside of Canada's borders. Rather than resigning in frustration, he decided to effect change. Action, however, required credibility, and Dobell was thirty-one when Green replaced the late Sidney Smith in 1959. He spent most of the next nine years establishing his profile and reputation in the East Block as one of the DEA's more thoughtful members. All the while, he devised a plan to leave the civil service and create an organization that would be tasked with educating MPs on international matters.

Dobell had been a member of the CIIA since 1952, so approaching Holmes about his idea was natural. Conversations in the summers of 1961 and 1962 convinced the institute's president that, rather than establishing a stand-alone centre, it might be better to consider a parliamentary branch of the CIIA in Ottawa. With this idea in mind, in 1963 Dobell accelerated his discussions with trusted civil servants and politicians to gauge their support. The governing Liberals, led by Mitchell Sharp, a former mandarin turned MP, reacted favourably. There were concerns, however, about whether John Diefenbaker would believe that both Dobell and the CIIA were non-partisan. Having Sharp – a prime example of the Chief's Pearsonalities theory – as a leading supporter was less than helpful.

While Dobell continued his quiet but determined campaign, Holmes remained cautious. He did meet with Sharp and Arnold Heeney to express his support for the project on behalf of both himself and the CIIA, but underneath he was less confident. A well-managed Ottawa office with strong links to MPs would have been an excellent addition for the CIIA, but the timing was not ideal. Holmes and his meagre staff were overwhelmed with responsibilities, and it was hardly the perfect moment for what he called "empire building." There was also a debate within the CIIA over whether the new structure should be considered another branch or a genuinely national office. Holmes, who was comfortable in Toronto and had already rejected better offers to leave, had low expectations. Others, like Peter Wright, thought that it might make sense to move the CIIA's central office to bilingual Ottawa, closer to the heart of the government. Bob Reford's monthly reports were already being produced there, and research for the Ford Foundation grant, particularly that which included interaction with national defence and external affairs, took place in the capital as well. There were added costs – moving, staffing, and inevitable unexpected expenses – but the benefits to the CIIA's profile might have made them worth it.[6]

Holmes first presented the various alternatives to the National Council in December 1964. The discussion was moved to a subcommittee, where he sensed that support for a full-fledged Ottawa office was strong. He therefore put little effort into the issue for the next couple of years. This did not stop Dobell, who continued to lobby feverishly. By 1967, his plans had overtaken those of the CIIA. There was going to be a centre in Ottawa, and he was going to manage it. CIIA involvement would be appreciated, but the project was no longer dependent on it. Dobell, related by marriage to the prominent Matthews family of Toronto (which has more recently produced a provincial premier and a federal cabinet minister), was a capable fundraiser. Having established his professional credibility through five years with the Canadian mission at the UN and three more with NATO, he had already begun to lay out the details of his resignation from the East Block.

It was in this context that Holmes returned to the project with renewed zeal. Having achieved for himself greater power at the CIIA over the previous two years, he could now be confident in his ability to keep his own office in Toronto while at the same time helping Dobell make his vision a reality. In January 1967, he lobbied Prime Minister Pearson, Heeney, and a number of others in support of the proposed parliamentary centre. What once again became a joint Dobell-Holmes initiative saw an autonomous, non-partisan body in Ottawa linked to the CIIA in two ways. The institute would name two members to the centre's six-person advisory board, and it would also appoint Dobell head of a new Ottawa branch. The cost, as Holmes noted in a memorandum that March, would not be excessive. The CIIA would contribute $12,000 on an annual basis, and this would cover about one-quarter of Dobell's anticipated expenses. It would also pay for him to attend relevant conferences and meetings and allow members of his staff to join the CIIA's group health insurance and pension plans. If necessary, the institute would also advance limited funds to help with start-up costs. The relationship was to be reviewed every five years, but Dobell's specific ties to the head office in Toronto would be re-examined at the end of year one to ensure that the expectations placed upon him were manageable and that both partners were satisfied with the arrangement.

The next challenge focused on personalities. One of the few people who did not yet know of the plan was the under-secretary of state for external affairs, Marcel Cadieux. Holmes' long-time friend admired Dobell's work and viewed him as an integral member of the East Block; he would not want to see him leave. He also would be less than excited about learning that the CIIA had played a role in engineering his departure. Holmes had remained on excellent terms with Cadieux since his retirement in 1960, and at the president's urging, the institute published a short book on diplomacy that Holmes had encouraged his former officemate to write in 1962. It also sponsored a translation into English the following year.[7] In return, Cadieux had been particularly helpful in making his staff available for CIIA events and improving the overall tenor of the relationship between his department and the broader Canadian public. Holmes therefore worked closely and carefully with both Heeney and Pearson to ensure that the under-secretary's feelings were not hurt. The negotiations were successful, and a reluctant Cadieux promised the project his full support. After a meeting of the National Council at Carleton, the CIIA's National Executive formally endorsed Holmes' proposal on 5 December 1967.[8]

Years later, with the centre well established, Dobell sent Holmes a Christmas card:

> If I had known how many obstacles had to be overcome, would I have started? I hope I would have, but I can now see how lucky I have been to begin with a Parliament and with Ministers who care about the problems where I hope I have something to offer.
>
> But above all else, there must be an idea, and – aside from all the support you have given me and the Centre in the years since – I am grateful to you for helping me to work out the concepts on which the Centre is based. I often feel jaded when I hear people referred to as being creative; but I know from personal experience that my thoughts might never have worked out satisfactorily without your help. Thank you, wise teacher.[9]

The end of this story is typical of John Holmes' experience in the post-East Block period. In helping to create another successful venue to educate Canadians on world affairs, he had demonstrated his incomparable skills of making his friends and colleagues feel like they had his complete support, all the while ensuring that his personal interests were well looked after. Had Holmes not been director general, the CIIA's head office might well have made the logical move to Ottawa – a move that would have benefited the institute in the long term by increasing its access to both the government and to relevant non-governmental organizations headquartered there. In addition, by sharing space with the centre, the CIIA would have reduced its overwhelming and still growing operational expenses. (Then again, without Holmes there would not have been such a strong centre in the first place. And if it had not succeeded, the institute would have found itself homeless.)

The CIIA did have a home in 1967, and it was supposed to be open to all Canadians. The truth, though, was that the majority in the institute spoke English. The inclusion of French Canada, and particularly of Quebec, in the foreign policy process had been an ongoing concern of Holmes' since his days as a student at the University of London. At the time he had written: "What must be remembered is that the very large French minority in Canada has full constitutional rights and that one of those rights is that of having its own opinion on the conduct of foreign affairs, that whether or not we like those opinions they must be given full consideration not only for the sake of their wisdom but because of the fact that they are the opinions of a section of the country."[10]

In elite discussions of foreign policy in Canada, that was rarely the case. Part of the problem was a language barrier, which explains why Holmes was so adamant that the CIIA sponsor the translation of Cadieux's book on diplomacy. Another challenge was the lack of involvement of French Canadians in the public dialogue. In this case the CIIA's record was disappointing. For a long time it maintained a Quebec branch, but that group consisted largely of English-speakers from Montreal who were unwelcoming to interested newcomers. Even it had suspended operations by the early 1960s, leaving no national forum within which distinctly French-Canadian views could be heard.

Holmes began thinking about this seriously in 1962, when he proposed to a colleague that, instead of attempting to resuscitate the old branch, the CIIA might help organize what he called "a separate but closely affiliated" organization with the freedom to pursue similar goals on its own terms.[11] Later that year he wrote a young Pierre Elliott Trudeau, inviting the part-time university professor to participate in this new venture and to undertake a CIIA-sponsored speaking tour focused on changing French-Canadian attitudes towards foreign policy. The invitation, which appears to have been declined, was followed by an unofficial recruitment drive of French-speaking academics to write papers as part of the Ford Foundation project, along with institutional commitments to prepare bilingual documents for the annual conference and to solicit prominent French Canadians to participate.[12]

Until the Banff meeting of 1965, Holmes was unsuccessful. In attendance that weekend, however, was Paul Painchaud of Collège Brébeuf in Montreal. A francophone academic with energy and interest in Canadian foreign policy, he made an ideal target for Holmes' campaign. When he learned that Painchaud would be coming to Banff, Holmes invited him to join his panel and offer a ten-minute prepared response to his opening comments. By all accounts, Painchaud's performance was excellent, and it led to a conversation about whether Quebeckers were welcome in the CIIA and how he might become more personally involved. He and Holmes seemed to agree that a separate but affiliated French-speaking institute was the logical and most inclusive way to move forward.[13]

The following year Painchaud accepted a position in international relations at the Laval University, providing him with the stability necessary to advance the plan. Early on, it took the form of a relationship between the CIIA and the university. By the spring of 1967, with Painchaud's encouragement and support, Holmes and Jacques Parizeau, one of the brightest and boldest of the French-Canadian nationalists (and a future premier), had arranged for Quebec City to host a joint Canadian-American meeting of the World Peace Foundation focused on the world economy. Although the conference was not as successful as Holmes had hoped, it solidified the relationship with Painchaud (and his colleagues). That December, Painchaud became the CIIA's "directeur pour le Québec."

By the end of 1967, Holmes had brought French and English Canadians together. After Painchaud organized one of the most successful conferences in the CIIA's history (on Canada, Quebec, and defence policy) in 1968, the director general wrote to a board member: "I may sound over enthusiastic but this looks like the fulfilment of a dream I have had for a long time." The great unifier in Canadian foreign policy was successful once again. The CIIA, still an influential voice in public affairs, had become more representative of the country at large.[14]

After a frustrating beginning, Holmes also achieved success with his first published book.[15] He had begun thinking about putting together an edited volume of his essays in the fall of 1964, but his schedule and the controversies at the CIIA left the project on hold for much of the next two years. He remained committed, though, and turned down at least two requests to pursue new studies on Canadian foreign policy and the future of the Commonwealth in the meantime. At the prodding of Peyton Lyon, chair of Carleton's Department of Political Science; James Eayrs; and the already well-established historian Ramsay Cook, Holmes returned to work on his collection in 1967. By the end of the year, Bert MacKay, now representing a committee of the Institute of Canadian Studies, had promised to include the book in the Carleton Library series. McClelland and Stewart was the official publisher.

The title, *The Better Part of Valour: Essays on Canadian Diplomacy*, was drawn from Act 5, Scene 4 of William Shakespeare's *Henry IV*, Part 1. It was the famed Sir John Falstaff, the cowardly knight, who said, "Discretion is the better part of valour," a phrase that Holmes used ironically to emphasize the importance of calmness and caution in world affairs. "We need heroic ideas and heroic deeds in both domestic and foreign policy," he wrote in his introduction, "but they are best left to engineers and politicians. The diplomat's primary responsibility is to 'cool it.' ...

to negotiate the adjustment and ease the pain of it." He went on: "Discretion in diplomacy is not incompatible with boldness of initiative in foreign policy or even with dramatic moves in international politics. The discretion is in the calculation of the issues at stake and the forces which can be mustered. Above all it lies in the recognition of contradiction and the acceptance of paradox."[16] This last phrase was forever to be associated with John Holmes.

The book that followed was a testament to his cautious brand of realistic optimism, one that combined Falstaff's hilarity with the bitter edge of an analyst who had lived through a depression and two world wars. Thoughtful and witty, it was a best-of package of articles and speeches that had already been individually well received by the Canadian and international publics. There was nothing particularly new in the book, save a delightful introduction, but it drew together Holmes' thinking in a way that nothing before it had. Considering the dearth of quality writing on Canadian foreign policy at the time, it was also desperately needed. Holmes dedicated the collection to Hume Wrong and Norman Robertson, his original mentors and inspiration. On Wrong, he later wrote, "no man did more than he to sculpt an identifiable Canadian foreign policy."[17] Robertson, he reflected shortly after his death in 1968, was "the greatest mandarin of them all." He strove, as did Holmes in this book, "to save us from ourselves, to channel our good intentions away from moral posturing into activities that could and did alleviate the lot of humanity."[18] Twenty essays followed, divided into the seven most significant themes he had considered in public since rejoining the CIIA in 1960: Canadian foreign policy, international organization, the Commonwealth, the Atlantic community, the United States, the Pacific, and the western hemisphere.

The publishing process was less rewarding, and it remained incomplete until 1971. The book was edited by research assistant Sally Wismer in early 1968, but unexpected delays kept it from being released until 1970. A complete lack of marketing by McClelland and Stewart in the early period meant that, by the end of June of that year, Holmes had sold just six hundred copies. The problem, it appears, was financial. The company was put up for sale in early 1971. To reduce costs, no copies of *The Better Part of Valour* were sent to potential reviewers until after a provincial bailout and private fundraising efforts restored the organization's economic solvency. The additional year made Holmes' essays even older than they had been when he had first submitted them, and this hardly encouraged reviewers to evaluate the collection. Nonetheless, thanks to the scope of his reputation by 1975, sales of *The Better Part of Valour* approached five thousand.

Looking back at his old writings in Canada's centennial year left Holmes with feelings of nostalgia, a longing for the good old days that seemed to have been lost during the controversies of the 1960s. He was frustrated by some of the new scholarship on Canadian foreign policy, writing that accused the mandarins of being too cautious and too willing to sell out Canada to American interests. He feared that in their efforts to reposition Canada on the world stage, the generation of young nationalists was losing sight of what made the country great. The balance for which Lester Pearson was so famous – the ability to satisfy competing interests, be they national or international – was essential to any Canadian success abroad.[19] The solution, he felt, was to present the public with the real history, in the words of those who were there. And what better place to start than with Lester Pearson?

In late 1967, he spoke with Geoffrey Pearson about his father's memoirs. Lester Pearson was approaching seventy, less than fully healthy, and set to retire from politics. Holmes insisted that he publish an account of his experiences before he became too old to do so effectively. The prime minister needed help, and his former right hand had lots of ideas. After a conversation in February 1968, Holmes drafted a proposal for a Pearson Foundation: a centre for the study of Canada in world affairs located in Ottawa, ideally at Carleton University. The centre could eventually take over some of the CIIA's expanding responsibilities and would be financed through a fundraising campaign spearheaded by the institute. Pearson would be the titular head of the foundation, and his budget would provide for the secretarial, travel, and research help he needed to complete his memoirs in a timely manner. Although Holmes later maintained that certain members of the CIIA advocated constructive involvement in the Pearson memoir project while he preferred "to remain on the sidelines and be helpful if needed," his claim is inconsistent with the documentary record. He himself took charge of the campaign, and it was only because of the more cautious response of the institute, an organization that had enough trouble raising funds for its own activities, that the foundation project never went forward.[20]

Over the next four years, until Pearson's death in 1972, John Holmes was one of the most active players in the production of the Pearson memoirs. It was he who first suggested that the retired prime minister begin what became a three-volume collection with the period during which he was employed as a civil servant in the DEA; this would guarantee that this most crucial story was covered effectively. It was also Holmes upon whom Pearson called to help determine which of the hundreds of speaking and research invitations he had begun receiving (once word of his retirement became public) would be accepted. Holmes was the one who urged that a young historian be hired to help Pearson with his research and writing, and he was crucial to the success of a $15,000 grant application to the Donner Foundation to hire Alex Inglis and John Munro to play that role. He had been, in his own words, almost "fanatical on the necessity for Canadian public servants to put down their record."

It makes sense that Holmes also turned the mirror on himself. As he later lamented to a former colleague in the public service, their experiences within the policy process remained relevant, and contemporary academics seemed to ignore them: "I wouldn't suggest for a moment that the universities of this country ought to be staffed by policy-makers but there ought to be some place where they are exploited," he wrote.[21]

A return to the classroom was something he had considered since his arrival back at the CIIA. Indeed, in many ways, he had never stopped being a teacher. Throughout his public life, teaching meant more than just lectures and seminars. Mentorship, actively supporting younger scholars and policy makers as they developed into the future leaders of Canadian society, was just as important. This became his approach to graduate supervision, but he had made a conscious decision to begin serving as a mentor and role model well before that.

Meeting John Holmes, the gracious middle-aged man with the bushy eyebrows, the avuncular expression, and the twinkle in his eye, was certainly not a necessary step to career success in the academic world, but in the 1960s it never seemed to hurt. French-Canadian Albert Legault became acquainted with him at a conference on the situation in the Congo in Geneva in 1964. Legault noted that the former Belgian colony was five times the size of France, implying perhaps that any form of UN intervention would be difficult to sustain. Holmes – the self-proclaimed "anglosaxophone" – responded by reminding the audience that it was also just about the same size as Quebec. There followed a typically Holmesian discussion of the importance of international cooperation and multilateralism more generally. Legault was impressed by Holmes' quick thinking and his respectful way of dealing with differences of opinion. The two stayed in touch after that, and, privately, Holmes spoke highly of his new friend to Queen's University. Not long after, Legault – who went on to an impressive academic career himself – was hired by Queen's, becoming the first professor there to offer a course in strategic studies. Not much later, Holmes' influence helped to bring the acclaimed scholar Nils Ørvik to Kingston to establish a full-fledged centre for strategic studies.

Within months of returning from Geneva, Holmes became friendly with a former Rhodes Scholar named Denis Stairs. Stairs had returned to Canada in 1964 to pursue a doctorate in political science under James Eayrs and was planning to focus on Canadian foreign policy. He quickly gravitated to the CIIA, which seemed to be the hub of academic thinking about such issues in Toronto. There he met Holmes, who was immediately impressed by him. They kept in contact, and when Stairs began to think about a dissertation topic, he looked to Holmes for advice. In their conversation, they considered the history of Canadian diplomacy during the Korean War. Less than five years later, Professor Stairs completed one of the seminal works of Canadian external relations scholarship, coining the phrase "the diplomacy of constraint" to describe the government in Ottawa's approach to relations with the United States during the war. Based largely on interviews that were often made possible by Holmes' connections, Stairs' thesis, and later his book, suggested that, as a smaller power in the early Cold War, Canada was hardly positioned to have an impact on Soviet foreign policy. Where it made its mark was in constraining the Americans from pursuing policies that might have escalated the conflict. It did so largely by encouraging the US government to forsake unilateralism and to work through the United Nations.[22]

Brian Tomlin was another emerging academic superstar in political science in the 1960s. Then a PhD candidate at York, his thesis advisor recommended that he attend an inter-university consortium on international relations to meet some of the leaders in the field. Shy, and at the time more interested in quantitative theory than in Holmes' narrative approach to the study of Canadian diplomacy and foreign policy, Tomlin was somewhat sceptical about the meeting. He went, though, and Holmes – who was hosting the event – took it upon himself to introduce him to everyone there. Young people needed encouragement, he explained, and they deserved the opportunity to land on their feet. Like so many of those who were mentored by Holmes, Tomlin has had a first-rate academic career. And, later on, he indeed did become a scholar of Canada's place in the world, authoring an award-winning narrative history of the Canada-US free trade negotiations.[23]

Holmes did not have to be physically present to make a difference in a young academic's future. When Charles Pentland moved to Kingston to begin an illustrious career in political science and international relations at Queen's University, he knew who John Holmes was but not much more. Nevertheless, after he published a brief but poignant article in the *Queen's Quarterly* about the question of independence in Canadian foreign policy,

Holmes scribbled a note of congratulations.[24] He had liked the piece and hoped to discuss it with Pentland the next time he came to Toronto. The meeting occurred, and the two kept in touch intermittently. Later, when Pentland – now an established scholar – co-edited the *International Journal* in the 1980s, it was the seventy-something Holmes to whom he often turned if there was a troublesome manuscript that needed a second opinion.

Holmes met Paul Evans, now one of Canada's foremost experts on relations with China, under similar circumstances. Evans was working on a biography of John King Fairbank, a leading US scholar on East Asia, when Holmes initiated a series of conversations about China and US foreign policy.[25] He was interested in Evans' approach to studying a living person and in his research methods more generally. He left a profound impression on Evans, who was overwhelmed by the attention that John Holmes was willing to devote to a relatively junior scholar.

Gerald Wright met Holmes by setting up an appointment at Edgar Tarr House. He was seeking advice on graduate study in foreign policy, and the CIIA's director general appeared to know everyone in the field. As tended to happen whenever Holmes met interested students, the two got along and Wright soon found himself invited to a conference at Niagara-on-the-Lake, serving as note-taker while Lester Pearson addressed the audience. It was a weekend that he never forgot. Wright eventually settled on Johns Hopkins University and later returned to Canada to work at the Donner Foundation. After he had officially cut back his duties at the CIIA, Holmes offered him the position of director general, but Wright declined. He went on to a successful career in business and politics, lunching with Holmes when he visited Toronto and even attending the occasional public lecture.

Political affiliation meant little to John Holmes, especially when it came to mentoring promising young Canadians. Wright worked for Conservative Brian Mulroney in the 1980s, but Holmes also endorsed Liberal Charles Caccia's first political candidacy and contributed money to a young Bob Rae's campaign to represent Ontario's provincial New Democratic Party. Of all of the political players whose lives he touched, future Liberal cabinet minister Robert Kaplan probably has the fondest memories. On the way home from a conference in Mexico in 1967 Holmes found him in great pain, having broken his leg in a traffic accident. The fifty-seven-year old used his connections (friend Saul Rae was then the Canadian ambassador) to arrange for a wheelchair and then pushed Kaplan around as he gathered his luggage and boarded the plane home. A call after he arrived back ensured that everything was all right. It was an act of kindness that colleague John Sokol – who travelled with him to Mexico – still recalled twenty-five years later.[26]

Holmes inspired similar feelings of gratitude and admiration in the formal classroom setting, where he soon re-emerged. He would have happily transitioned back to the academic world at Western in 1960, but the administration there was not interested. His next teaching venture came in 1962, when he signed a contract with the University of Toronto to serve as a special lecturer in political science while James Eayrs was on research leave in Uganda.

At the time, there were few, if any, scholars in Toronto who had been formally trained to teach international relations. This was an awkward situation for Holmes, who had felt uncomfortable around the co-editor of the *International Journal* when he had become CIIA president in 1960. International relations, and the Canadian side in particular, literally belonged to Eayrs. He had recently published the first comprehensive analysis of the Canadian foreign policy process and was widely respected as a historian, political scientist, and public intellectual. As one analyst later reflected, "not everyone could be expected to agree with Eayrs' views, which were as pungent as they were critical, but none could fail to take them into account."[27] For all of Holmes' prestige and acclamation, at the university level he was the upstart, and he admitted this to Eayrs one of the first times that they met. It felt wrong to infringe on someone else's area of expertise, and Holmes took on his classes with trepidation.

His experience as a lecturer was revealing. In a letter to Eayrs at the end of his first month he wrote:

> This is a brief note to reassure you that I have been fulfilling my obligations to appear before your classes at the appointed times. The results have been educational for me, at any rate, I hold the teaching profession in still greater awe. By the third attempt I was feeling somewhat more at home but am still terribly disconcerted by children taking notes on what I am saying ...
>
> ... I started out trying to be a professor, and flopped rather badly. Since then I have decided that I can perhaps put across more by raconteuring. My principles are slipping and I shall probably end up exploiting the "Dag and I" theme. In justification of the historical approach, I keep telling them that they can understand the United Nations only by considering the implications of its responses to challenges ...
>
> I am quite honestly not very well satisfied with my performance, and I know that the class has been somewhat bewildered. However, I remain very grateful to you for the experience.[28]

At this point in his life, Holmes was not best suited to instructing first-year students. As a teacher he was less comfortable as a conveyer of information than he was as a facilitator of discussion. While he was an engaging lecturer, his expertise was in the small group seminar. The letter also shows that his philosophy of teaching international relations was grounded in his value of history. An understanding of the past was what social scientists might call his methodological framework. Theory might well have been interesting to theorists, but Holmes never used it as a learning tool.

Finally, his modesty is apparent. Holmes' performance was good enough to lead the University of Toronto to offer him a $5,000 contract to act as a special lecturer in political science for the 1962-63 academic year.[29] His responsibilities at the CIIA precluded him from accepting; however, they did not prevent Carleton's dean, James Gibson, from promising him a similar position in 1967 if the Ford grant was not renewed. But Toronto was home, and Holmes did not want to leave. When, in 1966, the University of Toronto offered to make him a professor in addition to maintaining his work with the International Studies Programme, he thought about it seriously. Full-time teaching was out of the question, and Holmes preferred a graduate-level seminar to any undergraduate lecturing. For the U of T this was not a problem; the university had almost doubled its graduate enrolment between 1963 and 1966. As it continued to expand, faculty with Holmes' reputation and expertise were aggressively solicited. Holmes' other concern was psychological. Accepting the offer would mean officially becoming a member of the so-called academic community. "Professors get me down with their jealousies and their intellectual intolerance," he told a friend at Harvard, who presumably – as a former civil servant – was an exception to the rule.[30]

This distaste for the so-called ivory tower remained an issue for John Holmes throughout the rest of his life. Remarks about the privileged class whose year-long sabbaticals, four-month summers, and generous salaries and allowances made their jobs almost too easy can be found throughout his personal correspondence. Moreover, the academics' lack of professional experience and their obsession with theory left too many of them out of touch with reality. As a result, when they did attempt to comment on contemporary foreign policy issues, their ideas generally tended to be either utopian or simply stupid. Add to that their sense of moral superiority, and Holmes' instinctive reaction was one of disdain.

His attitude was hardly fair. Unlike many of his University of Toronto professor colleagues, Holmes was paid – often generously – for the increasing number of articles he wrote and speeches he gave from the 1960s on. And although it was always a working holiday, in his later years he spent two months every summer at the family cottage (it was originally his sister Isobel's and he later purchased it from her), far away from the chaos of the CIIA offices in Toronto. When he initially came to the U of T, he was provided with a comfortable salary to do limited work chairing a committee of the International Studies Programme. As for the role of theory, he rarely differentiated between those who used it effectively as a tool to improve understanding and those who hid behind it as an excuse to avoid empirical research. John Holmes could rarely be called petty, but in his diatribes against the academic profession he often portrayed himself as part of the neglected and downtrodden. This was not the case. He lived a comfortable upper-middle-class life; and, while he worked hard, he enjoyed much of the flexibility of his academic colleagues without (what he would have found to be) the burdensome commitments to undergraduate lecturing and university administration.

Because he compartmentalized, Holmes' views of university professors never affected his commitment to his own teaching or to his students. He also admired more academics than he sometimes let on. It was only a select few, generally political scientists and economists wedded to theory and intolerant of ideas that contradicted their own, who truly annoyed him. As he made clear in his personal correspondence, even though he joined the Department of Political Economy he never considered himself a social scientist. In a letter to a former East Block colleague in the summer of 1967, he wrote ironically, "After all these frustrated years, I am now 'Visiting Professor of Political Science' – a curious title for an old historian who never took a course in political science in his life."[31]

In September 1967, he began teaching POL 2203: Canadian Foreign Policy because he was viewed, in part thanks to his relationship with the International Studies Programme, as a specialist in international affairs. When he accepted the offer, he was uncertain about how to approach his assignment. Knowing that, with neither a PhD nor any formal training in the social sciences, his strength and credibility came from his practical experience as a diplomat, he focused on the idea of foreign policy making. Specifically, he sought to expose his students to the conflicting options and considerations that practitioners faced before reaching a decision. To do so, he began with a series of introductory lectures to set the historical context and explain the bureaucratic and political structures in Ottawa. From there, the students analyzed, assessed, and evaluated case studies of specific foreign policy decisions made by the Canadian government since the early 1950s. The case study method, now used regularly in business schools, medical schools, and indeed political science programs, was innovative in the 1960s and unheard of in the arts programs at the U of T. It was effective, and many of Holmes' students who went on to teaching careers borrowed from his practices.

That summer he wrote the four introductory lectures. Some years, he delivered them orally; in others, he distributed them to his students in advance as a stimulus for discussion. Regardless, they read just as he spoke, capturing his effortless approach to understanding Canada's place in the world. The first essay began with a quotation from Heinrich Brüning, the former German chancellor who fled his country during the rise of the Nazis:

> I think the greatest hindrance to constructive political action in the last thirty years has been the influence on final decisions of experts, especially experts obsessed with the belief that their own generation has gained a vantage point unprecedented in history. No quality is more important in a political leader than awareness of the accumulated wisdom and experience handed down not only in written documents but also by word of mouth from generation to generation in practical diplomatic, administrative and legislative work ... The more we work with mass statistics and large schemes the more we are in danger of neglecting the dignity and value of the human individual and losing sight of life as a whole.[32]

It was an apt summary of Holmes' approach to academic study: history mattered and so did people – the idea that foreign policy could be understood by simply reading books written by so-called experts was foolish. Moreover, as he said in the first paragraph of his general introduction, "although challenges to Canadian foreign policy are constantly changing, they are also endemic and cyclical, and historical perspective is essential to a comprehension of present dilemmas."[33]

Within the rest of the text were kernels of Holmesian insight. "Foreign policy is essentially making the best of circumstances," he wrote in lecture one, "The Era of Confederation." "Relations with the antagonist tend to be relatively simple; the problem is to cajole or bully one's allies into putting up a united front," he added at the end.[34] He did not hesitate to criticize Canadian governments for their past actions. In lecture two, "Canada in the Age of Imperialism: 1870-1918," he rejected the idea that national attitudes towards the concept of empire were much different from those of Canada's British and American allies. The distinction was that, for Canadians:

Theirs was a particularly ambivalent imperialism. Canadians found glory and
stature, not to mention trade and protection, by sharing in British imperialism. Although their survival depended on resistance to American imperialism, Canadians have shared much of the ideology, the sense of mission, the
belief in the peculiar virtue of North American life and institutions, and its
message for mankind. Specifically, Canadian imperialism is rarely identified
as such because it lacked, of course, the power to intimidate other peoples.
Not quite consciously, however, Canadians have known how to borrow ad
hoc the intimidation provided by the two greatest empires and the powerful Anglo-Saxon culture in which they can enfold themselves if necessary.[35]

The more contemporary lectures were not as strong. Influenced too
much by Holmes' personal experiences, they justified Canadian foreign
policy as much as they explained it. "The Second World War and After"
served to instil in his students the belief that there indeed had been a
golden age in the history of external relations. "Perhaps the principal reason
why Canadians were listened to more than might have been expected in
the creation of postwar institutions was the high quality of the Canadian
officials and their constructive contributions as well as their mediatory
inclinations," he observed. In this final story, Lester Pearson emerged as
a hero: "His extraordinary personal qualities and the relatively detached
position of Canada from imbroglios in distant places led Canada into a
decade of intermediary activities which set a mark on the Canadian image
and on Canadian foreign policy to this day. The pattern was incremental,
success breeding a reputation which led to further obligation, rather than
calculated."[36] Holmes' own public comments, along with much of the
historical research undertaken since the 1970s, have demonstrated that
Canadians were far less selfless than he let on.[37] In Holmesian terms, however, teaching foreign policy in Canada also meant teaching citizenship,
and a critical pride in national achievements was important. It is hardly a
wonder that the next generation of scholars grew up believing so strongly
in the golden years. Their mentor, the man who gave the history of their
country's external relations a global voice, had taught them to do so.

In retrospect, Holmes' first class in 1967-68 was a historian's dream.
Organized so late as to miss inclusion in the U of T calendar, it was one
of the first year-long graduate-level courses in Canadian foreign policy offered in Canada. It included at least two students who went on to reputable
academic careers in political science but who approached Canadian foreign
policy from opposing perspectives: defence specialist Dan Middlemiss and
new nationalist Daniel Drache. It was initially so popular that it had to

be moved from its original classroom to a location in the Royal Ontario Museum (Holmes later held his classes at the CIIA). And it took place during the most radical of times at the U of T. That November, the university experienced its first significant disruptive event: students objected to the recruitment efforts of Dow Chemical Corporation. The company was known to produce the napalm used by the Americans in Vietnam, and the non-violent protest was eventually successful in ending on-campus interviews.[38]

Holmes' seminars in that first year were an exercise in judicious mediation. Some members of the class doted upon his every word and were entirely comfortable with his vision of Canadian foreign policy. Others disagreed adamantly, challenging both him and their fellow students each week. It was what a seminar was supposed to be: the grey-haired, gentlemanly professor with the ruddy complexion and the tweed jacket introducing the topic of the week, listening intently to student presentations, moderating the discussion of the case study to ensure that all sides were heard and no feelings were hurt, and providing concluding thoughts. If the discussion generated consensus, Holmes did not hesitate to play the devil's advocate, but otherwise he was content to let the dialogue flow naturally.

Those who disagreed with their teacher enjoyed the course because Holmes was unflappable, polite, and interested in their opinions. Although he was never close with students like Drache, largely because he had so little in common with them, this did not mean that he did not provide his fullest support and encouragement. His detractors also appreciated the organized chaos that encouraged a sincere free flow of ideas without ever allowing the discussion to get too far off track. What Holmes would not accept were disrespectful comments and personal attacks. Apart from that, every idea was welcomed, so long as it could be supported by evidence.

Some weeks, instead of, or as a supplement to, a student presentation, he invited a guest – an old colleague who had been directly involved in the case of the day – to discuss his experiences, demonstrating to the class the differences between what had actually happened and what was later written down. Other weeks, the readings were drawn from yet-to-be-published manuscripts that his friends had asked him to read, or hard-to-get government documents that he obtained through his various contacts in Ottawa.

His reach and influence across the country, along with his caring and nurturing attitude towards the next generation, made him an ideal mentor. He secured research grants, arranged interviews, and read and responded to draft essays quickly and thoughtfully. For Middlemiss, who later became his first PhD student, there was a paid research assignment and access to prominent Canadians and Americans for insights into the Defence Production Sharing Agreement. For Michael Tucker, who first met Holmes in 1968, there were job opportunities and letters of reference. Professor Holmes never stopped thinking about his students, putting in good words about their work with his colleagues, and, later on in their careers, using their books and articles in his courses.

At the same time, however, he was not a pushover, nor did he teach in order to make new friends. He had high standards, serious expectations, and demanded good writing. Without the latter, he liked to say, his students would be subjected to textual harassment. He cared, and he was generous with his time (and indeed with his grades), but he was also firm. He often learned about his students' personal lives because they felt comfortable speaking with him, but he did not gossip and did not allow personal feelings to affect his teaching.

When Fen Hampson, whose father had known Holmes in the foreign service, attempted to take the graduate seminar in Canadian foreign policy as an undergraduate, Holmes did not refuse. But his decision was based on the younger Hampson's intelligence, not on his connections. Holmes later wrote one of the letters of reference that landed him in the PhD program at Harvard. He would have been proud to learn that Hampson, like von Riekhoff, Tomlin, and Molot, eventually became director of the Paterson School.

Looking back, 1967 was a turning point. "It was a golden year," reflected one of Canada's greatest storytellers, Pierre Berton. "A year in which we let off steam like school boys whooping and hollering at term's end. We all thought big that year."[39] John Holmes' experience confirmed it. It was a time of great successes and new beginnings, an opportunity to start a new career as a professor in a country in the midst of virtually unprecedented transformation. The transition from leading force at the CIIA to one of Canada's great university teachers had begun.

10

Breaking Free from the Institute

Canadians emerged from the success of Expo '67 as a confident people. Many, John Holmes prominent among them, sensed real change in the air and looked forward to it with optimism and excitement. Whether they were unreasonable in their expectations is debatable, but there is no question that, for Holmes in particular, the post-1967 era had its lows as well as its highs. Internationally, the Vietnam War continued amidst increasingly aggressive displays of protest and radical anti-Americanism. In Quebec, musings about separation crept into the mainstream provincial dialogue. In Toronto, while the situation appeared to be better than ever at the CIIA, the organization faced a budgetary crisis. And culturally, the explosion of Trudeaumania in early 1968 brought with it challenges as well as opportunities. It was only in the area of teaching that, at least for Holmes, the late 1960s and early 1970s marked a period of genuine and unconditional exhilaration.

He had been experiencing tremendous personal success since arriving at the CIIA, but, unbeknownst to many, the institute was struggling in 1968. Pride in his achievements might account for why his former staff overlook some of the difficulties and still remember the period as a glorious time. Indeed, there is no denying the positive energy that surrounded Edgar Tarr House during what many still recall as the John Holmes era. And there was good reason for the enthusiasm: the development of the library, the commitment of the staff, and the ever-increasing profile of the director general all served as evidence of a golden period. But underneath there were serious problems. The CIIA's financial situation was deteriorating.

The membership was aging, and the organization was having difficulties bridging the generational divide and replacing its older supporters. Finally, the director general – the glue that held everything and everyone together – was doing his utmost to divest himself of any obvious responsibility for the organization's future. The CIIA was saved in large part because he was not wholly successful.

John Holmes could never completely pull away from the CIIA. He was too emotionally invested. Even with the Parliamentary Centre under control, for example, and the Quebec link firmly established, there was unfinished business with the library, a project that had been close to his heart for over twenty years. In July 1965, Holmes' former colleague and Canadian representative in the United States, Thomas Stone, died in Paris. At the time, he had been co-chair of the CIIA branch in New York. Recognizing his passion for the institute, his wife Emily and daughter Ellen instructed well-wishers to direct contributions in his memory to Edgar Tarr House. When generous cheques began to arrive, Holmes suggested that the money be used to build up what would be called the Thomas A. Stone collection in Canadian foreign policy. In 1968, the CIIA convinced designer Allan Fleming, most famous for his creation of the CN trademark, to create a plaque to honour the still-growing new holdings. Holmes paid for it himself.[1]

The strong ties between Holmes and his predominantly female staff at the CIIA were reinforced by a series of memorable parties. There was drinking, although never too much – Holmes' nephews, the Beer boys, often served as the bartenders – and after one or two, the director general recited poetry and classic British literature. Thanks to the conversations at the parties and around the office, he could refer to members of their families by name. He also asked for and took their advice seriously. Most of the women were over-qualified, and Holmes knew it. If the CIIA could not pay them well enough, then he could at least make them feel comfortable and appreciated.

It did not hurt that he had a charming way with women and a surprising boldness that sometimes went along with it. One nephew recalls how Holmes flattered his francophone girlfriend and future wife at their first meeting by speaking to her in French all night during a party dominated by anglophones. Another case involved the visit of Empress Farah (Diba) Pahlavi of Iran in the late 1960s. A number of prominent Canadians, Holmes among them, were invited to meet her. When he was introduced, he bowed from the waist, as per traditional protocol. The empress asked whether he had ever been to Iran, and he answered that he had not but that his suit had. Suddenly, the crowd stood still, not sure what he had meant. He waited for a moment, revelling in the anticipation, and then explained. During one of his recent trips to Geneva, his luggage had been lost. Six months later, his briefcase, along with his suit, was returned to him in Toronto with a note saying that it had been held in the Teheran airport. Holmes grinned, and expressed his gratitude to the empress for her country's willingness to release it. Even Farah Pahlavi herself could not help but smile.

It seemed to his many admirers during this period that Holmes could do no wrong, and his public achievements made it easy to think so. In 1969 he was forced to decline his first offer of an honorary degree because he had committed to an assignment in Geneva for the Carnegie Endowment for International Peace. At almost the same time he learned that he had been nominated to receive the Medal of Service of the Order of Canada. In just its third year, the award was already one of the most significant national distinctions a Canadian could receive. The staff at the CIIA were ecstatic and threw him a party at the home of Marion Magee, the associate editor of the *International Journal*. When Holmes arrived, he was presented with a medal made of an old tin can lid and inscribed with the letters "SM," the title that he could now list after his name (although he rarely did). It came on a tacky chain that he was encouraged to wear for the rest of the evening. Beaming with pride, he did. Three years later, when the Order of Canada was restructured into its current three levels (companion, officer, and member), Holmes returned his SM insignia to Government House and accepted the officer's OC in its place.[2]

The national recognition brought with it unprecedented exposure for the CIIA. There seemed to be no end to the external funding available to support institute initiatives. In 1968, the Ford Foundation provided $80,000 to promote the study of China. The Department of External Affairs awarded another $4,000 to investigate the degree of expertise in international relations available within the Canadian university system.[3] The money directed towards strategic studies was even more generous.

The process to obtain the latter grant began with discussions between Holmes and members of the Canadian Forces College, the national hub of military education for intermediate and senior-level personnel in 1967. The directing staff envisioned a government-sponsored institute of strategic studies to support their curriculum and thought that Holmes was the right person to bring the idea to fruition. In some ways, they chose correctly. The CIIA's leader had recently become a director of the Institute for Strategic Studies in the United Kingdom. He believed passionately that

Canada was losing its ability to contribute to international discussions at the strategic level because its universities were failing to teach the nation's youth about the relationship between defence and foreign policy.[4] He had already accepted a request from the Department of National Defence to join a selection committee to award professorships in the area. And he was open to doing more. The CIIA, however, with its own financial concerns, dwindling membership, and only limited expertise in the area, was hardly the best venue from which to pursue the idea.

Holmes' enthusiasm got the best of him. Don Rickerd, a long-time CIIA member, and Gerald Wright, a former Holmes protégé, were in charge of the Donner Foundation, an organization that had recently decided to dedicate its impressive resources to funding public policy projects. After hearing about Holmes' interest in strategic studies, Rickerd made it clear that the foundation would welcome an ambitious application to establish a full-fledged institute. The CIIA's director general rationalized his decision to push forward in a letter to Arnold Heeney: "I would not, myself, at this moment, have picked strategic studies [as an area] for us to expand. However, there is a way not to look at gift horses. If we could, in this way, get on our staff a first-class scholar whose competence embraces strategic and other aspects of foreign policy we would greatly strengthen our establishment. He would probably have to sit on the roof but we can't allow real estate to curb our good endeavours."[5]

This was, in retrospect, a poor decision. The CIIA lacked the physical and intellectual infrastructure to support the establishment of a new institute, and its leadership failed to dedicate the energy necessary to mobilize the resources to change this. As a result, the three-year, $200,000 grant that did arrive in the summer of 1969 spawned a mediocre program in strategic studies that failed to fill the existing void in any meaningful way.[6] Seven years later, Brigadier General George G. Bell and a number of former and current CIIA members founded the Canadian Institute for Strategic Studies, the body that the Donner money should have created.

When they looked back on Holmes' career at the CIIA in 1977, Peter Dobell and graduate student Robert Willmot captured one of the great paradoxes of his time as director general: he was so highly regarded in Canada and abroad that "funding organizations almost volunteered support." Unfortunately, the money caused the CIIA to expand in ways that were unsustainable.[7] Holmes understood the problems with foundation grants. As he explained to Lester Pearson, they were temporary infusions of capital that obligated an organization to increase its permanent level of income in order to sustain the resulting infrastructure once the start-up funds had expired.[8] But instead of doing so, the CIIA continued to spend. The success of the Painchaud experiment in Quebec, for example, had its price. To maintain the momentum the CIIA had to divert more of its budget to French-language activities than it had anticipated. These measures were not profitable, especially in the early years. The CIIA's increasing international respectability had also resulted in an overwhelming and eventually burdensome number of requests for information and commentary from the media, the academic and policy communities, and even the general public. The Toronto office in particular needed more people, on a permanent basis, even though much of its new funding was short-term and non-renewable.

In 1970, the CIIA ran a deficit of close to $70,000. Projections for the following year anticipated another loss of close to $50,000. Holmes reacted defensively. The minutes of a National Executive Committee meeting make this abundantly clear:

> Mr. Holmes pointed out that the deficit situation the Institute found itself in should not be attributed to a lack of foresight by the Executive. In his early years with the Institute the philosophy had been that it was best to have a slightly unbalanced budget. However this had been to some extent replaced in the past few years by the theory that in the interest of growth the Institute should use its large reserve funds. On this basis the Executive had authorized an expansionist programme. However, the prevailing attitude had changed when the expected deficits had occurred.[9]

His temperament was understandable at a personal level. He was, after all, careful with his own budget (except perhaps for one out-of-character purchase of a white Jaguar automobile) and took the principle of financial accountability seriously.

The response to the budgetary situation was not justifiable as a comment from the leader of the CIIA. The decision to expand so aggressively had been Holmes' more than it had been anyone else's. Throughout his years as president and then as director general the executive largely did his bidding. Holmes' great weakness as head of the CIIA was his inability to accept that its success largely depended upon his personal commitment; no one could replace him. When he cut back his involvement without, at the same time, setting out to reduce the expectations of the membership correspondingly, the organization began to unravel.

What is more, even as he distanced himself, Holmes never seemed ready to let go completely, and this made innovation difficult. The role of the CIIA in public education was a prime example. A journalist and proud institute member, John Harbron had been demanding that the executive change its ways since at least 1966. As chair of the public education committee, he grew frustrated with his group's diminishing role. The study kits for which the committee held primary responsibility were discontinued in 1964, and most of the group's other duties were gradually taken over by the full-time staff. Harbron thought that his unit could evolve to help make the CIIA's activities more "public." This meant doing away with closed meetings.[10] The old guard claimed that the rules of non-disclosure encouraged participants to be frank and candid, but these restrictions, responded Harbron (and others), merely served the interests of select government bureaucrats. The CIIA emphasized views from Ottawa too much as it was, he claimed, and opening the meetings might encourage greater independent thinking and policy pronouncements. This was the type of approach that might attract the next generation to the CIIA. Harbron was in a position to know: there were five hundred students in the political science classes that he had been teaching at the University of Toronto, and the CIIA could not claim a single member among them. Discouraged that nothing was being done to stop this trend from continuing, in the fall of 1967, in frustration, he resigned his chairship.

Harbron was a maverick, and his inflammatory comments and outbursts at CIIA meetings were hard for some to take, but many shared his sentiment. Don Rickerd recalls that part of the impetus for the strategic studies grant was a hope that the CIIA would use the money to expand its membership base. Comments from staff at the Ford Foundation and from some of the leading female members of the CIIA also focused on the need for the organization to reach out more actively and more effectively to Canadian youth.[11]

Holmes' response to the suggestions and criticism reflected his typical caution and restraint, an approach that worked well at the diplomatic level but was not suited to reinventing a languishing institution. He oversaw sincere, albeit poorly thought out efforts to involve Toronto youth leaders in the organization of a national conference, and he entertained talk of other initiatives in the future. But on the idea of taking public positions on foreign policy, something that he knew the younger generation wanted, there was no change. "Professors and teachers and members of the Institute can take stands," he argued, "but I think our work of public education would be gravely hampered if we as an institution were identified with certain schools of thought."[12] Later, after a scathing public outburst from Harbron, and while suffering from a relapse of a form of dermatitis that caused him significant discomfort, Holmes responded with less tact: "It is not of course very easy to deal with an approach to the Institute which relegates me to the ash can, because, of course, according to your theories, I am a hopeless relic of my associations with the root of all evil which is Ottawa." Conceding that the CIIA would have to evolve, he went on to argue, "We are not the CBC and are not the publishers of newspapers. It is not our function to reach the masses directly; that's yours … Our duty … is also to try to extract and make available information, to try to know what the Government is doing and also to try to know what other governments are doing. We cannot divorce ourselves from the people in the know."[13]

But it was more than that. At the CIIA, even though he was withdrawing, Holmes could not help but express his discomfort with radical change. Although he did nothing to interfere with them directly, he was never a strong supporter of the national and international briefing tours that Alex Langford began to organize in 1962. Even as they became one of the CIIA's significant successes in the late 1960s, he did little to promote them. And although he regretted the closure of the New York branch of the CIIA in 1968, as he explained to Guy Smith, the Canadian consul general there, he was "inclined to accept the New York situation somewhat philosophically."[14] The successes elsewhere, he seemed to think, such as the large foundation grants, more than made up for what had been a noble experiment. In reality, though, they did not. As short-term awards they only added to the pressure on the CIIA's long-range future.

What was most frustrating to those like Harbron and Langford who wanted to revitalize the CIIA was that Holmes recognized the problem, and knew that significant change was required, but refused to take a leadership role in devising a comprehensive solution. Finally, in 1969, after a brief sabbatical, he began to address some of the concerns through the revitalized national research committee. A decision was made to move the CIIA towards a greater emphasis on policy as opposed to purely academic projects. Holmes provided the committee with a summary of the major gaps in the literature on Canadian external relations, and the research group reoriented its work towards filling some of the most significant holes. He also supported the move to transform the committee into an advisory board no longer responsible for research itself but, instead, for matching interested scholars with relevant projects. Last, the institute attempted to decrease the expectations placed upon it by the outside community. It was time, Holmes admitted, to think strategically about how best to use the CIIA's limited research funds.[15]

His lack of timely initiative in the later 1960s was born at least in part of personal frustration. It had taken years to free himself of extensive responsibilities at the CIIA, and now it seemed that the organization needed him more than ever. He had tried, for example, to leave the coordination of the 1968 Banff conference to Gordon Hawkins. This might have worked, had Hawkins' liaison in Banff, J. King Gordon, not been disengaging from the process as well. Even worse, King Gordon wanted to deal only with John Holmes. Not surprisingly, the event was disappointing, and the series never regained its former stature.[16]

In March 1968, for the second time, John Holmes threatened to leave the CIIA. In a letter to the chair of the National Executive, Peter Wright, he outlined four conditions for his staying. First, he asked to be released from all executive and administrative responsibilities. Second, he wanted more time for his own teaching and personal research. Third, he needed the institute's support for his attendance at a greater number of national and international meetings. Finally, he had to be given more flexibility in accepting some of the myriad external offers and opportunities that continued to come his way. He proposed that he assume a supervisory role at the CIIA and that Hawkins be assigned a new executive assistant to compensate. Wright agreed, apparently without conditions.[17]

Nevertheless, the chairman's views of Holmes' freedom were different from his own. Shortly after accepting his demands, Wright advised him to pass on an opportunity to be considered for an appointment to the CBC board of directors. Holmes was furious but stood down. In a frank letter to Arnold Heeney he explained that he could not justify creating a disturbance immediately after Wright had just gone so far to meet his every need.[18] He was less willing to compromise on an offer from the Carnegie Endowment. The executive had been pressing him to participate in an international study on mediation for close to a year, and he requested leave from the CIIA at half-pay so that he could spend the summer of 1969 in Geneva. Once again, Wright hesitated, feeling that the offer for Holmes to act as organizer-rapporteur was beneath him. A note to Heeney afterwards was revealing:

I have been considerably shaken ... by Peter's ... unexpected opposition. It has confirmed my fear that Peter's idea of my responsibilities and my own are pretty far apart, and that is disconcerting. Frankly, I thought he would welcome this as a chance for me to do the kind of thing I thought I was supposed to do – and do it at someone else's expense. However, he implied that officers of the Institute ... would be upset at my being away when I should be here in Canada promoting the Institute. It isn't exactly what I had concluded was to be my role when I rejected a *couple* of academic jobs with four month summers in order to stay.[19]

The sabbatical became a deal breaker, and Holmes was allowed to go.

It was for the best. In addition to producing a report on the study, he spent part of his time away taking his niece, Nancy Skinner, through Switzerland, France, and Italy, recounting to her the history of each country as they travelled. This appears to have helped him achieve a degree of personal peace. About four months later, he returned to Toronto recharged, having accepted that he would never break free from his CIIA commitments and become a scholar in the traditional sense. The article that he later wrote for the *International Journal* about his experience abroad was as much about his personal situation as it was a study on mediation and the future of the United Nations: "We have reached either the end of the age of idealism or the end of the age of illusion," he observed: "Unless we resign ourselves to chaos, we have to decide that it is the latter." For John Holmes that meant accepting that the benefits he gained from his affiliation with the CIIA came at a price. So long as he was involved with the institute, he had to accept the inevitable administrative headaches.[20]

It was fitting that he came to this realization when he did. In January 1971, Gordon Hawkins suddenly resigned to take up a position at Dalhousie University. The Toronto office, which had only recently found him an assistant to reduce his workload, was unprepared. Holmes stepped in at the executive level while Evan Gill of the National Advisory Committee (and a former diplomat) spent the spring of 1971 at Edgar Tarr House assisting with financial and administrative matters. The Ottawa office lent assistant Julian Payne, British academic Colin Gray took over direction of the strategic studies program, and Richard Pouliot took responsibility for liaising with the Painchaud group in Quebec. In his director general's report for 1970-71, Holmes noted that the CIIA could no longer be everything to everyone, that cuts would have to be made, and that the years of expansion were over. Consolidation, he claimed optimistically, was healthy in an organization that had grown so quickly, and it was time to place the CIIA back on sound financial footing.[21] As for Hawkins' replacement, it would not be John Holmes; instead, he wanted, and succeeded in recruiting, Bob Reford that fall. Although the man who personified the CIIA did not abandon it in its greatest time of need, he was not willing to return to his former position.

John Holmes was moving on to other things, one of which became his life's work as a scholar: a comprehensive history of Canadian diplomacy during the so-called golden age. The process began in late 1968 when he contemplated taking responsibility for the 1971-73 volume of the Canada in World Affairs series – a set of books that chronicled the most significant recent developments in Canadian foreign policy.[22] The CIIA was struggling to ensure that writers completed their assigned manuscripts in a timely manner, and his assumption of an authorship would have helped. By 1969, however, thanks in part to prodding from his friends, he was less certain. Escott Reid urged him to write something more challenging. Rather than merely reporting on recent events, Reid proposed that the director general develop a book on the major problems in foreign policy facing Canadians in the 1970s.[23]

Since it was the past that excited him most, Holmes transformed Reid's idea into a study of Canadian foreign policy during his years at the DEA. He proposed to call it "Principles and Practice of Canadian Foreign Policy" and promised that, while the book would look to the future, its principal aim would be to assess and evaluate the methods and purpose of foreign policy making in Canada from the 1940s through the 1960s. He sent a summary of his idea to the Humanities and Social Sciences Division of the Canada Council and asked for a senior research scholarship of $15,000 per year over three years to complete it. The application was reviewed and then accepted. He almost immediately received a $7,700 tax-exempt Killam award (worth closer to $11,000 in total) and a $4,000 research account. The grant was renewable for two additional years, pending reports of acceptable progress.[24]

The fellowship justified a further reduction in his CIIA commitments, and Holmes initially suggested that, in exchange for giving up his other duties, he might take responsibility for the institute's research agenda. Everything else was supposed to be left to his anointed successor. When Hawkins left for Nova Scotia, Holmes stopped his research. Ironically, this had a positive impact on the scope of the project. The break helped him realize that completing the study would take more time than he had anticipated, and he therefore eliminated any discussion of specific contemporary foreign policy issues from his analysis; instead, he told the Killam program, he planned to focus on historical trends and underlying national principles as they manifested themselves from the Second World War onwards.[25]

Hawkins' departure also had an impact on Holmes' career outside of the CIIA. In part because of the additional burdens he now faced, he leaned more heavily on Gayle Fraser, a woman whom he had hired in January 1968 and then added to his Killam research team in 1970. From that point forward, Fraser was the most important source of support to Holmes' public life. She was a perfect fit, having grown up in his hometown with the same basic sensibilities as the Holmes family. She had been a close high school friend of his niece, Ann Skinner, and therefore first knew Mr. Holmes, as did all of Skinner's friends, as Uncle John. After graduation, she and Skinner travelled to England where the latter eventually worked at the British Council and the former at the *Economist*, thanks in part to John Holmes' letter of introduction to staff member Andrew Boyd. When he visited London, Holmes made sure to treat both women to dinner, listen intently to their ideas, and make them laugh. Later, when Fraser was hired on at the CIIA, she had to remind herself not to call him Uncle John. She remained an admirer for the next twenty years, forever loyal and exceptionally giving of herself and her time.

Technically, Fraser's primary allegiance should have been to the CIIA. Over the years, however, while she served it with distinction, it became clear that John Holmes came first. She coped admirably with his desire to avoid confrontation, so often manifested by his habitual disappearances when it came time to deal with a serious conflict. It was that Norman Robertson approach to conflict management, the creative delay, that could drive her to complete frustration. She typed his letters, keeping drafts of every one, organized his calendar – juggling student appointments, CIIA commitments, and his countless speaking engagements – and served as his editor. Most important, in spite of being over-qualified and underpaid, she never left. Without her, he could not have accomplished as much as he did both inside of the CIIA and as a commentator at large.

Beyond the CIIA, the early years of the Holmes-Fraser era took place in the context of emotional debates over the Vietnam War. By 1968, public opinion in Canada and in the United States had shifted significantly. Opposition to the war had gained momentum. With this change came renewed and even stronger calls from the new nationalists for Canada to abandon its obligations to the Western alliance and pursue a foreign policy based on a commitment to global humanitarianism and a renunciation of violence as a means of conflict management.[26] To some, this was academic code for opposing the United States publicly and aggressively at every opportunity. To Holmes, such an approach was still not helpful. It was also ironic, he liked to remind audiences, that Canadians manifested their frustrations with the war as anti-Americanism. In doing so, rather than expressing independence, they merely echoed the sentiments of the majority of those whom they were criticizing.

In a speech that he gave twice in early 1968, he warned:

> It is particularly important for Canadians and others who profit from a peaceful world to judge this American system in all its aspects ... We must not judge the American system by its follies alone ... American idealism transformed into what Walter Lippmann calls globalism can go terribly astray, but we would be losers if it was replaced by cynicism and isolationism. The compelling reason to end the fighting in Vietnam is to prevent American power from discrediting itself. In their dismay over this wretched war, Canadians, Europeans and many Americans are losing their sense of proportion, ignoring the indispensability of American power and productivity in any calculations for a happier world.

Holmes was unimpressed by Canadians who called their MPs hypocrites for opposing the war in public while still allowing the United States to purchase war supplies from Canada under the long-standing and legally binding Defence Production Sharing Agreement. He reminded those who thought that Canada should rededicate itself exclusively to the UN that peacekeeping, while noble, was also easy. "It costs us relatively little," he said, "abets our diplomacy, gives our armed forces one function on which there is general agreement, and raises few domestic problems." The Americans might be too aggressive, they might use inappropriate tactics, but at least they felt a sense of international responsibility and were willing to sacrifice. "We don't much like the Pax Americana as a way of keeping the peace," he added: "Not many Americans, who pay for it with treasure and blood, like it either. Nevertheless Pax means peace, and we can advance from one kind of peace to a better kind more surely than we can move forward from chaos." There was no question that the United States had to reorient itself and its foreign policy, but its errors would not be remedied by moralistic finger pointing.[27]

All of this was not to suggest that Holmes had lost his faith in Canada. In fact, he was a stronger nationalist than ever. "I am for maximum co-operation of the Canadian government with the United States government in foreign policy if and when they agree," he told a Canadian-American relations seminar at the University of Windsor, "and I hope they agree much more than they disagree, but I do not want to see the Canadian government tied to any automatic formula of collaboration." Rather, he

rejected calls for independence as naïve and parochial.[28] The new nationalist demand took away from what he saw as an opportunity for Canada
to expand its influence on the world stage. The Cold War had entered a
phase of relative calm. Both great powers had lost their moral authority,
leaving space for the smaller states to play a role so long as they did not
overreach. To Holmes, this made collaborative work – *with or without* the
United States, and ideally within the framework of the United Nations –
more inviting than ever.[29]

Although few would have thought so instinctively, this approach
to foreign policy was remarkably consistent with that of Canada's new
prime minister, Pierre Elliott Trudeau. Trudeau rode a wave of youthful
popularity to victory at the Liberal Party convention to replace the aging
Lester Pearson in early 1968. Neither the most experienced nor the most
accomplished of the leadership hopefuls, he was by far the most inspiring.
He believed in change, indeed radical change, and nowhere was this more
evident than in his vision of Canada's role in the world. "No more helpful fixers" was his slogan: Canadians had spent too much time doing the
world's handiwork and had to focus much more on their own interests.
Under his watch, he promised, it would.[30]

Holmes shared with the prime minister the belief that Canada had a duty
to play a significant role in the world. Both of them saw the thawing of the
Cold War as an opportunity. Both maintained that it was time to rethink
and re-evaluate Canada's international commitments with the goal of re-
aligning them to reflect the country's national interests. Trudeau was more
sympathetic to the new nationalists than was Holmes, but – admittedly for
different reasons – both understood that pragmatism dictated policy in the
end. Trudeau accepted this because he was a politician, Holmes because
of his experience as a practitioner. As for the prime minister's seemingly
deliberate attack on Pearsonian internationalism, it did not bother Holmes
at all. "Between ourselves," he wrote to a colleague privately, "I have always
assumed that comment from on high about helpful fixing was, insofar as it
was a criticism, directed not at Pearsonian but at Martinian policy. Being
helpful when it is the natural, sensible and in fact unavoidable thing to
do ... is I think in the Pearsonian tradition. This is quite different from
the rhetorical attachment to middlepowerism and the glorification of a
Canadian role as an end in itself."[31]

Trudeau and Holmes had a history. Holmes had called on him to speak
at CIIA events in the past and thought highly of his ability and potential.
In 1966, when Joseph Johnson, president of the Carnegie Endowment for
International Peace, asked him to recommend members of the Canadian

government who might be well suited to attend a conference in Peru, he thought of Trudeau, describing him as "one of the ablest Federalists in Quebec [and] one of the promising young people in political life."[32] Holmes was excited by Trudeau's energy and wrote to a senior Quebec Liberal just days after the leadership convention: "With his ability to cut through the clichés in which we have become entangled he could stimulate a grand debate across the country. The New Left and old Right I am afraid are polarizing the argument over a lot of utterly false issues like quiet diplomacy ... We need scope. I am greatly excited by the prospects of a new look in foreign policy even though I may be associated with the ancien régime."[33]

A week later, Holmes described Trudeau's new approach in the *LA Times*. On his foreign policy he wrote: "A fresh look at Canada's place in the world is to be welcomed, even though the room for maneuver is limited."[34]

In a book written long after his retirement, Canada's fifteenth prime minister described Holmes as "the most highly regarded of all Canadian foreign policy practitioners." He later added, "His grace, wisdom, sense of humour, and sense of 'Canadianism' made him one of the most admired and most loved members of the foreign-policy community in Canada and elsewhere."[35] Anecdotal evidence suggests that Trudeau consulted with Holmes before agreeing to contest the Liberal leadership and spoke to him in detail about his plan to re-examine the premises of Canadian foreign policy just weeks before the 1968 election. Later, he recommended that Holmes represent the federal government in conversations with Nigerian general Yakubu Gowon in an effort to mediate the civil war (his foreign policy advisor, Ivan Head, was eventually chosen instead).[36]

Shortly after Trudeau called on Secretary of State for External Affairs Mitchell Sharp to begin a foreign and defence policy review, with the prime minister's approval, Sharp asked Holmes to gather and coordinate input from interested non-governmental organizations. On 28 September 1968, historians Peter Waite and Lewis Hertzman, political scientists Hugh Thorburn and Donald Smiley, and Geoff Andrew from the Association of Universities and Colleges of Canada met with the minister and his under-secretary in Ottawa. The government's intention was that the meeting widen the scope of its consultations to include the academic community in the foreign policy dialogue. Doing so, however, required a degree of confidentiality from those involved. The academics, who had long complained about being left out of the process, were concerned about the suggested limitations to their academic freedom.

Holmes served as the peacemaker. Notes from the meeting explain that he was "inclined to 'agree with both sides.'" He knew that the academics would refuse to be publicly committed to a partisan plan. Nevertheless, he noted, "it was possible to have a good discussion without *secret* information. It was perhaps at the level of confidential material that a serious exchange could take place, off the record, with a profitable confrontation of differing views. There had to be personal contact." Sharp was welcoming in his response. He was adamant that the government do a better job of including the academic community in the policy process and looked forward to more serious debate. Holmes, in exchange, promised to help improve the relationships between the government, Canadian historians and political scientists, and the non-governmental world.[37]

A meeting was arranged for Hull, Quebec, in early January. (By then, in the *Montreal Star* journalist Peter C. Newman had broken the story of the academics' involvement, drawing Holmes' ire over accusations that the CIIA's director general had become a government agent.) The three days of talks dealt with the future of Canada's involvement in NATO. It was a profitable experience, in which the left-leaning academics seemed to acknowledge the value of the organization – even if they still questioned the need for Canada to belong – while the more conservative government elites admitted that major changes to their approach to Europe were required. In a moment of particular elation, Holmes wrote to Canada's representative to the North Atlantic Council, Ross Campbell: "I think I shall coin a new motto: those who drink together think together."[38]

The following months were difficult as radicals from a variety of perspectives attempted to manipulate the debate. Most of them – regardless of their politics – blamed Holmes and the CIIA for favouring their opponents.[39] Those who supported the status quo within NATO were more convincing. Holmes had become confident that, with the thawing of the Cold War, Canada's role in the alliance had to change. The organization had originally promoted Canadian national interests because its north Atlantic scope served as a counterweight to American domination of the western hemisphere. Lately, however, Washington had managed to control NATO without regard for its allies, and Canada now had NORAD as an additional buffer. "The only reason for us to stay in at the present time is a strong belief in Europe that our disengagement would set off tremors. That is a good enough reason for me," he wrote to an American colleague, "but perhaps we ought to start disengaging gently so that we can cease to be a domino in the game." He added:

Canada doesn't really belong in NATO because it isn't really wanted ... I used to get annoyed at the way in which we were disregarded in all discussions of the design of NATO but I am not so any longer. I think we should recognize that it is basically a US aid to Europe scheme and that it is far better for the US to have its special relationships with European countries and for us likewise to exempt some kind of bilateral correspondence from the United States ... It is getting harder and harder to convince Canadians that our military contribution to NATO makes any sense and my concern is that we should not respond to this feeling in a way which would do harm to the alliance.[40]

Although he did not attend it, Holmes coordinated a second meeting of academics and government officials, this time focused on Latin America, in early March. At the end of the month he spent three days in Scarborough with yet another group discussing the future of Canada and the United Nations. This final session included a memorable dinner with the prime minister himself. After that, as James Eayrs put it, "any Canadian professor who doesn't think he has been consulted must have been asleep." The dialogue made Holmes more sympathetic to the views of the new nationalists. He came to see international development as both a security and a humanitarian issue, and he looked forward to a time when funds dedicated to national defence could be used as foreign aid. Still, in reallocating government money, the impact on the morale of the Canadian military could not be ignored. Funding to the armed forces, he wrote to Trudeau's advisor, Ivan Head, "cannot simply be turned on and off like a pipeline."[41] Memories of his time at NDC resonated more than fifteen years later.

When the European community criticized the prime minister's decision to reduce the number of Canadian troops stationed abroad as continentalist, isolationist, and even neutralist, Holmes came to Trudeau's defence. He reminded a British audience at the Foreign Affairs Club that Europe itself had been moving towards greater continentalism. Moreover, Canada was proposing to shift its international investments not reduce them. He was even more blunt to Canada's representative to NATO, Gordon Smith: "if Canada is faced with escalating military costs in Europe and on the continent, the instinct to see first what has to be done at home seems to me natural and sound." He then added, "It is very hard to find anyone under thirty in Canada (and most Canadians are) who has much enthusiasm for our military tie with Europe. I don't believe the school of thought which thinks that youth is bound to be right but its voice can't be ignored. You had better come home and put your ear to the ground."[42]

All of this is not to say that John Holmes was swept away by Trudeau-mania. He was critical of the prime minister's rudimentary understanding of the role of diplomacy and the civil service. Suggestions that there was no longer any need for professional diplomats and that Trudeau could learn anything of significance to international relations from the *New York Times* infuriated him. And although Holmes supported a change in the way that Canadians conceived of external relations, he objected to claims that Trudeau's approach to foreign policy would result in much that was new. "A country of our size is caught in an international game and it is very hard to change the rules," he explained to a colleague. "I am inclined to say that all we can do is shift the priorities but even this can be false. The priorities tend to be dictated by what happens."[43]

Holmes received a personal copy of 1970's *Foreign Policy for Canadians* – the Liberal white paper on foreign policy – from Under-secretary of State for External Affairs Ed Ritchie shortly after its publication. That July, he told the CBC that he respected the document for its realism, even if it contained little that was profound or ambitious. Privately, he told Ritchie that what disappointed him was the presentation. He saw no need for a formal white paper or, more specifically, for the six colour-coded and therefore supposedly more accessible pamphlets that described the results of the review. Since the final version must have been a compromise, meant to satisfy a variety of domestic and international constituencies, the ideas might have been presented through a less glamorous series of government speeches.[44] John Holmes was disgusted by attempts to politicize foreign policy. International issues were too important to be dragged through such a demeaning process.

He tried to make this clear throughout the 1969-71 period as he spoke and wrote on the subject of Canada-US relations. The most comprehensive expression of his views came in front of the House of Commons Standing Committee on External Affairs and National Defence in November 1969. The basic argument was typical Holmes: "Problems between Canada and the United States should be regarded as permanent. They will not go away when we have 'solved' them or found a formula. It is a question of 'process' rather than 'solution.' What we need are the right perspectives on the process so that we can live with the problems. In international as well as internal relations the definition of the paradox is the first step towards what is usually more the acceptance of and adjustment to a situation than its 'solution.'"[45] The message was straightforward. There were differences between Canada and the United States that were never going to change. This was a good thing, insurance against the tiresome fear among radical anti-Americans that Washington hoped to dominate the continent. The relationship was never equal, nor was it ever balanced, but that too could work in Canada's favour. For example, being ignored by Washington at the day-to-day level allowed Canadians to pursue international initiatives without the scrutiny that would have been incurred by another US ally.

In doing so, however, the government in Ottawa and practitioners worldwide had to be certain that their country was acknowledged as distinct from the United States. Nothing made John Holmes angrier than conference organizers who invited him to participate as a representative from North America. "It is very difficult," he told the director of the Institute for Strategic Studies, "to persuade Canadians to retain any real interest in Europe and one reason of course is that Europeans ... are so profoundly uninterested in us ... Atlantic conferences endlessly discuss problems of European unity but I can't remember any of them considering the unique and quite instructive problems of continental relations in North America worth even a sub-heading." "It isn't as if we are Luxembourg," he went on: "In population and resources we are after all considerably larger than all the rest of the European powers put together."[46] He so despised the rhetorical and ideologically charged fixation on the United States because it caused Canadians (among others) to ignore the world beyond North America, a place in which the opportunities for national influence were growing.

There had to be more research on multilateral institutions like the UN, he preached, and more international study of Canada and its worldwide role and responsibilities. Canadians were too introspective, too focused on the national and regional levels of foreign policy. They were failing to recognize that the greatest way to expand Ottawa's influence on the world stage was in fact to preserve American hegemony.[47] If there was to be more research on the relationship, it was time for the Americans to take the lead. As for Canadians, they had to "at last give up the illusions of being poor and undeveloped," an image that could only be possible in comparisons with the United States, "and recognize the responsibilities and the vulnerabilities of extreme affluence."[48] Speaking out against the policies of the United States was hardly global leadership; rather, it was an excuse to avoid participating more ambitiously and indeed more effectively in making hard political choices in the world at large and in the developing world in particular.

Although his work on the executive of the Canadian University Services Overseas (CUSO) and his attendance at a meeting of the Conference on Science and World Affairs (the Pugwash committee) certainly had an impact, it is hard to imagine that Holmes' university students did not stimulate his new focus and perspective on international affairs during this period. There was a progressivism in his words that seemed to reflect a degree of revitalization. In a letter to the journalist Bruce Hutchison in 1971 he wrote:

> One thing that keeps me optimistic is that for some years now I have had a graduate seminar at the University of Toronto and the students constantly reassure me of the good sense and objectivity of what I like to think is a majority. I sense a distinct turn away from the claustrophobia and xenophobia which is such a humiliating part of the national debate on foreign policy at the moment. I have always thought of myself as a good Canadian nationalist ... but much of what passes for nationalism today seems to me awfully sick. If only we could regain our national capacity to live with paradox.[49]

He committed much of the rest of his life to teaching Canadian youth to accept these paradoxes.

One of those students was another future academic star, Kim Richard Nossal. The son of one of Holmes' reporter friends, the younger Nossal first met Holmes at the age of eleven or twelve serving drinks at a dinner party held by his parents. Upon entering university, he made his way to the new CIIA board room at 30 Wellesley Street West and enrolled, as had Fen Hampson, in Holmes' graduate course in Canadian foreign policy as an undergraduate. Nossal's first paper was so good that his professor deposited it in the CIIA library. Holmes later supervised Nossal's MA thesis and his PhD dissertation on the origins of Canadian policy towards the People's Republic of China. If there ever was a graduate student who inspired awe it was Kim Nossal. He was so capable that at times Holmes thought he needed little or no supervision. In fact, when asked to reflect on his best graduate student dissertations, Holmes sometimes forgot Nossal's altogether. Nevertheless, whenever he needed to advise other students on writing and research, he pulled the Nossal thesis off a shelf in the library and said, "this is how it is supposed to be done." Holmes wrote him what was likely the strongest reference letter he ever drafted, and Professor Nossal began teaching at McMaster University before most people his age had finished their MA. Not much later, he authored what quickly became the standard political science textbook on Canadian foreign policy, full of references to John W. Holmes.

The third edition of the Nossal text, published in 1996, was dedicated to another of his professors, James Eayrs. In retrospect, Nossal's loyalty to Eayrs symbolizes the transition between two eras in the teaching of Canadian foreign policy at the University of Toronto. As Holmes was establishing himself as a professor, Eayrs was losing interest in supervising theses on Canada's external relations. Nossal therefore took Eayrs' undergraduate classes, but it was Holmes who became his graduate supervisor. Eayrs' professional withdrawal coincided with Holmes' increasing involvement with PhD students. As he said to one young man who planned to return to school to do graduate work in 1970: "Certainly, I would be delighted to welcome you whatever you decide to do but particularly if you want to work in the field of Canadian foreign policy. If you do, you may have to work under my direction because I seem to be the only person now in that field. Prof. Eayrs has too many theses to supervise and wants to get away from the Canadian emphasis."[50]

There was a bigger problem. Shortly after Holmes began teaching at the U of T, his friend Frank Walker asked him to write a weekly newspaper column on Canada and the world. Holmes was too busy, so he recommended Eayrs. The columns were well written, flashy, and extremely popular. They criticized Ottawa and the diplomatic establishment with wit and, at times it seemed, malice. While Holmes was disappointed, he did not react until an incident in the summer of 1970. Well after he left the DEA, he continued to receive private, off-the-record notes from an old friend, C.E. McGaughey (McGuff), which focused on the lighter side of the diplomatic establishment. That July, McGuff was posted as ambassador to Israel and wrote to Holmes about an incident in which the diplomatic team in Liberia was taken to task because of a mistake regarding an inscription on a tray meant as a gift for the ambassador from Sweden. It appeared that the message had been engraved on the front, and the ambassador would have preferred it on the back. It was typical of the humour that McGuff passed along and was meant to be kept private.

Holmes shared this particular note with the trusted Gordon Hawkins, and, later on, Eayrs emerged from his desk as editor of the *International Journal* at the same time as Hawkins was laughing over the incident. Shortly after, on 6 July 1970, Eayrs based one of his columns in the *Montreal Star* on the frivolities of the Canadian bureaucracy regarding what he called an aide-memoire that had been "filched from a diplomatic pouch" in Jerusalem. He argued that McGuff might well have been recalled for consultation because he should have had better things to do than comment on such absurdities. The article resulted in profound embarrassment for the DEA and for Holmes personally. He immediately wrote a long letter of apology to Under-secretary Ritchie, asking for forgiveness for his carelessness and indiscretion in allowing the letter to be passed on to Eayrs. He also insisted that McGuff had nothing to do with the incident.

There followed a letter to McGuff about Eayrs' conduct: "Because of his bias against diplomats I would never have shown this particular piece of paper to him but even if I had I could not have conceived that he would be so lacking in integrity to make this kind of use of it. Jim is brilliant but irascible and prejudiced."[51] The Holmes-Eayrs relationship recovered, at least temporarily, as Holmes the director general recognized that working with Eayrs the editor of the *International Journal* was part of his job at the CIIA; but Holmes the professor no longer trusted him with the future scholars of Canada's place in the world. He increased his own teaching responsibilities in part to fill what he now saw as a troublesome void. Thirteen years later, Eayrs crossed the line once more when he published a book on Canadian foreign policy in Indochina in which he accused the government of being complicit in a disastrous American war. "Canada's policy for Indochina converged fully with that of the United States when Ottawa finally decided that it no longer need be constrained by concern for the commissioners' judicial impartiality when giving them guidance," he wrote. On his last page, he cited Holmes – who in fact lent him his own personal photographs for the book – twice, all but blaming him for Canada's "apprenticeship in complicity." It was a scathing and unjustified indictment that was never completely forgiven.[52]

Holmes moved on nonetheless. He accepted an invitation from Marjorie Seeley, the principal of Trent University's Lady Eaton College and the widow of a former provost at Trinity College in Toronto, to spend a few days in Peterborough, Ontario, as a guest of both the college and the Department of Politics. Trent was beginning to develop an international relations program under the leadership of Margaret Doxey. Doxey was another promising academic who had come to know Holmes through his work at the CIIA and relied upon his letters of reference in her applications for graduate fellowships and then for her job at Trent itself. In fact, it was because of Holmes' commitment and dedication that Professor Doxey – soon to become a leading international expert on UN sanctions – felt compelled to write excellent letters for her students throughout her career.

The first visit to Trent in the winter of 1970 lasted five full days. Holmes participated in seminars, met individually with interested students, and ate his meals in the college dining hall. He adored his guest suite with its view of the drumlin and found the calmness and peace of the campus rejuvenating. Doxey recalls once catching him reciting Shakespeare at his window. He seemed entirely at home, comfortable in nature and with Trent's enthusiastic student body. He made his best effort to return to the campus annually over the next fifteen years, even if the visits became shorter as time went on. Eventually, Lady Eaton College made him an honorary fellow. In 1985, on behalf of the university, Doxey presented him with an honorary degree. Trent was not the only university outside of Toronto to which Holmes paid repeated visits, but it was likely his favourite, and his first trip in 1970, combined with his disillusionment with Jim Eayrs, almost certainly contributed to his decision to take up undergraduate teaching not much later.

John Holmes was evolving. As he separated himself from the tedious-ness of CIIA administration, he was able to devote more of his time to his duty, public policy, and his passion, public education. Sixty years old in 1970, his life was in many ways just beginning.

11

Freedom, Passion, and Frustration

If the late 1960s were a period of radical change in Western society, the early to mid-1970s might be seen as one of more subtle transition. In Canada, interest in the United States shifted from Vietnam to Watergate as Richard Nixon became the first US president in history to resign from office. The focus of international relations shifted from Europe to the Middle East, where an energy crisis and the establishment of the Organization of Petroleum Exporting Countries (OPEC) altered the dynamics of global politics. This change had significant implications at the United Nations, where a series of motions and resolutions condemning the State of Israel provoked controversy. It also affected Canada, whose abundant supplies of oil and gas became a source of both strength and internal friction. The prime minister in charge of leading the country during this period was in the midst of his own transition. The relegation of his government to minority status in 1972 led Pierre Trudeau to limit his political boldness in order to secure a firmer mandate. He was successful in 1974. With his ambitions tempered, he concentrated his energies on domestic issues.

It was in the midst of this relatively bland period for Canadian foreign policy that John Holmes marked his arrival as a genuinely independent national commentator on world affairs – a "professional internationalist,"[1] as he liked to call himself. Freed from the burdens of running the faltering Canadian Institute of International Affairs, he overcame the physical challenges that are almost inevitable for any man in his sixties who is carrying the workload of someone twenty years his junior and pushed ahead with his books, increased his teaching responsibilities, and allowed his classroom experience to take his research in new directions. For Holmes, the mid-1970s were an exceptional period of professional development, tarnished only by his unsettling engagement in the debate over Zionism. His attitude was disappointing but could not diminish what had become a flourishing third career in Canadian public life.

It is hardly surprising that Holmes sought to divorce himself from any hands-on involvement in the running of the CIIA after Bob Reford's arrival as the new director general. As the chair of the Executive Committee, Brian Crane, explained to the National Council at the end of 1973, even with the stability that Reford provided, the situation was verging on disastrous. Membership had dropped from 2,500 to 1,500, involvement within the branches was declining, fundraisers across the country were failing to meet their goals, relations with the academic community had stagnated, and the institute faced public criticism over the quality and relevance of its program. As damning as it seemed, Crane's report neglected to mention that the CIIA executive had also recently made a number of questionable real estate decisions and at one point nearly lost the space that housed the library.[2]

It was a depressing state of affairs, which Holmes made sure he did not hear about directly. In July 1973, he stopped attending CIIA meetings and negotiated a new position of research director. As he described it, his job was to "act as an entrepreneur or middleman, arranger, expediter, editor and all sorts of other things for research being done in the country." As Canada was to the world, so was John Holmes to the CIIA.

Holmes received a salary of $22,000, $18,000 of which was paid to the institute by his other employers to reflect his teaching responsibilities (which had recently increased). Along with the remaining $4,000 per year, the CIIA provided a $1,000 expense allowance for entertaining visitors (and potentially relieving the director general of some of the burdens of his position). Never mentioned, but most important, Holmes kept his office. The institute remained his primary point of contact with the academic and policy communities. As a result, in spite of his diminishing involvement, Canadians and others worldwide continued to associate John Holmes with the CIIA up until his death. The institute's executive wisely accepted the proposal, if only to maintain a formal association with the most prominent public voice of Canadian foreign policy in the country.[3]

Holmes did relatively little in terms of research direction but was ir-replaceable as a roaming representative. He played a significant role in

Toronto mayor David Crombie's ultimately unsuccessful efforts to locate a
campus of a United Nations University in Toronto, he represented Canada
at the International Peace Academy's Vienna Project (a training seminar
on UN and regional truce observation), and he joined the boards of the
Center for Strategic and International Studies, the Rockefeller Advisory
Group, and the Norman Paterson School of International Affairs. He also
helped develop a strong relationship between the CIIA and the newly
formed Niagara Institute, a not-for-profit organization meant to promote
effective leadership within Canadian businesses, governments, and other
relevant intellectual communities. Thanks to him, not only were there joint
CIIA-Niagara conferences but the linkages between the public service and
business leaders in Canada also improved. This was important to the man
who, freed from the limitations imposed as head of the CIIA, could position
himself comfortably as a "bureaucrat in exile." In 1979, he abandoned the
directorship to take up the more amorphous position of counsellor.[4]

As his commitments increased, he faced many of the physical challenges often associated with men in their sixties. The music that emanated
from his south Rosedale apartment grew louder as his hearing declined.
In 1972, for a number of weeks, a slipped disk in his ever-unreliable back
left him lying flat on the floor of his apartment while entertaining guests.[5]
There was a car accident in 1973, presumably not his fault but indicative
of his nervousness and irritability as a driver, along with his discomfort
with commuting long distances. When he was contacted in 1974 about
the possibility of a defection of the acclaimed Soviet ballet dancer Mikhail
Baryshnikov, he consulted another one of Ann Skinner's public school
friends and a future Liberal cabinet minister, Jim Peterson. Peterson, a tax
lawyer, quickly became an entirely capable immigration adviser. By removing himself from any active role in the process (something he might not
have done a decade earlier), Holmes missed an exciting trip that worked
its way into dancer Karen Kain's apartment; through Toronto's O'Keefe
Centre; into a getaway car containing a case of beer, two bottles of vodka,
and a box of food; and finally to a farm in Caledon East. Baryshnikov was
kept safe from Soviet interrogators, and the only impact on Holmes was
a call to his apartment from *Time* magazine when he was out of town.
Perhaps it was for the best. He did not need the stress.

Later that year, he lost a close relative. In 1975, one month after the
staff at the CIIA celebrated his sixty-fifth birthday by putting together a
book of poems and limericks that they had written (called, appropriately
enough, "Better Holmes and Gardens"), he developed rheumatoid arthritis

and spent much of the summer with his mother in London. That fall, he began receiving gold injections, which temporarily reduced the pain.

Most of the time that he spent at the CIIA was devoted to his book. Because Gordon Hawkins' departure had interfered so radically with his research progress, in January 1972 the CIIA granted Holmes a period of paid leave. Even with the sabbatical, however, it was clear that the project was in trouble. That February, under the leadership of historian Arthur Blanchette of the Department of External Affairs, the East Block offered to finance an analysis of Canadian foreign policy from 1945 through the early 1960s. The author would receive full-time research assistance and support staff as needed. An honorarium of between $20,000 and $25,000 would be provided for the first year, and additional funds were set aside in case the assignment extended into 1973.

The arrangement was tempting, but it would have meant writing a different book than the one Holmes had planned; the DEA envisioned something more academic, focused at least in part on issues about which he lacked expertise. With Peter Dobell acting as a liaison to Ottawa, Holmes refused the honorarium but accepted the research support in exchange for committing to a project on the establishment of a Canadian presence on the world stage during the first two decades of the postwar era. He planned to divide his work in two sections, the first concentrating on the 1945-57 period and the second on Diefenbaker and beyond. With this proposal in hand, he convinced his Killam sponsors to extend the expiration date of the research funds (which he had failed to exhaust over the previous three years). By April 1973, with the help of Mary Taylor and Lois Beattie, both spouses of DEA officials, and a number of members of Dobell's staff, Holmes had completed more than half of the first draft of Volume 1.[6]

That July, he contacted Ronald Ian King (known to everyone as RIK) Davidson of the University of Toronto Press. The Scottish-born Davidson, the pre-eminent academic publisher in the country, responded enthusiastically and read the six-hundred-page manuscript over the summer. In September he wrote back positively, predicting that the final product would "stand as a definitive account of what was done in the Golden Age and be the envy of other writers, other countries."[7] From Davidson, who also supported the Pearson memoirs, it was quite the compliment.

Nevertheless, there was a lot of work still to be done. John Holmes is remembered as having the rare ability to compose short articles of publishable quality in a single draft, but his experience with books was different. He began by writing down everything he knew and thought, largely without concern about logic and flow. The product was then polished through time-consuming editing and consultation with relevant peers and experts. The second draft to Davidson was revised in the fall of 1974 and arrived at his office just before Christmas. Much of the next twelve months was spent revising yet again and waiting for comments from former colleagues in external affairs and select trusted academics.

In February 1975, Holmes found himself reflecting on a statement made by Mackenzie King to the House of Commons in 1945. The prime minister was trying to convince Parliament to support the appointment of a Canadian delegation to the San Francisco Conference on International Organization. "Our contribution to the fashioning of victory has been far greater than could have been imagined six years ago," said King: "Our part in the shaping of peace may be no less urgent and no less effective." *The Shaping of Peace* was appealing, and became Holmes' new title. To it was later added *Canada and the Search for World Order*.[8] Shortly after this revelation, Holmes re-evaluated the manuscript and proposed to divide it into three volumes. The first two, now both dealing with the pre-1957 period, were at least reasonably under control. The third was eventually eliminated.

In early 1976, Davidson submitted Volume 1, focused on the creation of international institutions between 1943 and 1947, for external review. The readers were positive, but there were criticisms. For one, the writing was not personal enough. This was John Holmes' story, but there was little of him in it. Second, the footnotes were lax and unhelpful. A scholar seeking to revisit the research in this book would have a hard time doing so with the sparse information that had been provided after each note.

Holmes accepted the first criticism. Balancing his own views as a practitioner with those of a detached historian was a challenge, and he was not certain that he had yet found the right mix. There were limits, however, to how personal he was willing to make a book that was still, to him, a work of history. Eventually, he compromised by including first-person reflections in his preface and conclusion.

For the "Ayatollahs of the Faculty Club" who had concerns with his approach to referencing he had no tolerance at all. His response to Davidson released much of his frustration with academics, which had been festering for years:

As for the footnotes, I had not planned, of course, to leave them in the rough state they were in for the most part in the drafts. On the other hand, it would take me a whole summer in the archives to track them all down, list the file number, and make life easier for scholars using this as a reference book … I recognize that it would be nicer to include all the information but if this is not going to be a "reference book" then perhaps I might be excused from additional labours which would certainly postpone publication a year or more. I assume that 99 percent of the readers merely want to have a rough idea of my source and the one per cent who would be able to trace them in the archives are scholars who would not have much trouble doing so.[9]

Holmes was tired in 1976, and the project, which he now sometimes referred to tongue in cheek as "The Shipping of Peas," was taking too long. He needed a break, an opportunity to detach himself from the research so that he could look back at the manuscript with fresh eyes. Davidson told him to leave it for a year and to return to it in the summer of 1977 with the goal of reducing the length by 40 percent. When Holmes reacted negatively, his publisher responded: "At this point, I see you throwing up your arms in horror … And I can see that you'd be tempted to take it to your other publisher. Well, one can believe that temptations are the only thing to yield to, or have even more positive ideas in their favour; so should you want to do that, I can understand completely. And my regrets will be concealed under hair over a stiff upper lip."[10] The book was not publishable in its current state.

Holmes' mental and physical fatigue and frustration were understandable. In the early 1970s, when most of his contemporaries were planning their retirement, he saw his university teaching load increase dramatically. He accepted the additional responsibilities for three reasons. The first was that he sincerely enjoyed his time in the classroom. Young people inspired him, and there was no better remedy to lapses in his idealism than to participate in events such as the model UN conference for Manitoba high school students in August 1972 or the inter-university seminar week at York in 1973. The second, and most pressing, was that his primary source of income, the Killam grant, was set to expire. Since he was not willing to increase his responsibilities at the CIIA, he needed – or thought that he needed – additional employment. The final reason was a mixture of personal and professional. Between Jim Eayrs' gradual withdrawal from teaching Canadian foreign policy (and eventual move to Dalhousie University) and his discomfort with Eayrs as a teacher, Holmes concluded that someone had to take over the task of educating undergraduate Torontonians in the intricacies of Canada's external relations, and he took it upon himself to do so.

He made inquiries into teaching in nearby Hamilton at McMaster, and there was always Carleton (which formally offered him $25,000 per year if he would accept a full-time position), but by far the best proposal came from Albert Tucker, Escott Reid's successor as the principal of Glendon College in Toronto. Glendon was one of the most promising educational experiments of the 1960s. It was a satellite campus of the still new York University, whose founding president, Murray Ross, had envisioned it as a small, residential college dedicated to the liberal arts and public affairs. The campus was set within eighty-four acres of beautiful parklands in northern Toronto ("glen" means narrow valley and "don" refers to the Don River, which flows through the ravine on the lower campus). The lands had been donated to the University of Toronto by the wife of financier and philanthropist Edward R. Wood in 1959 and then passed on to York in 1961. Officially bilingual, and with a commitment to civic education in the Oxford tradition, Glendon was envisioned as a training ground for future diplomats. Its students, like its professoriate, were young and ambitious. What they lacked was the practical wisdom of a man who had lived what they were studying. Escott Reid had made his usual mark on the institution – in part inspiring and in part frustrating – and Holmes would have been familiar with Glendon when, in 1971, Tucker approached him with an offer of employment in the Department of Political Science.[11]

He began by teaching his U of T graduate-level Canadian foreign policy seminar to third- and fourth-year undergraduate students at Glendon that fall. He taught primarily in English, but he encouraged the students to speak in either language, and he responded to French comments in French. York paid the CIIA $6,000 for his efforts, $500 more than he was receiving from the U of T (he convinced Toronto to match its competitor's terms in 1972). The first year, he had sixteen students. His classes were held in the Glendon Hall manor, Edward Wood's Italian-style mansion, which was included with the property. The location set the atmosphere. There was an eatery in the basement, where many of the students, and fairly often their professor, could be found having a quick dinner before the evening class, which began at 7:00 PM. They then wandered upstairs to an old drawing room. Holmes emerged from his office, a comfortable anteroom attached to the main classroom, and put his hands together in front of him as if he was warming them up. It was a way of making his students feel at ease, as was the way he sat down in the corner in a cozy old armchair to conduct class discussions, using his now perfected case study technique. The students arranged the comfortable sofas and chairs in a circle. Looking in on the fireplace, they felt as if they were in Professor Holmes' living room. In many ways they were. Discussions in GL 428 were animated and informal. The students were idealistic, and Holmes took pleasure in nurturing their ideals.

One might have expected a significant number of Glendon students to end up in the public service, and indeed many – like Jill Sinclair, Paul Robertson, and Steve McCauley – flourished. One year Holmes had to cancel a seminar because nearly the entire class was scheduled to take the foreign service entrance exam on the same day. At least three highly successful journalists – James Daw, Chantal Hébert, and Christopher Hume – also passed through the courses and recall them fondly.

Particularly in the undergraduate setting, Holmes was a teacher who inspired students to pursue their own interests and to follow their aspirations. Never considering himself an academic, he did not feel duty-bound to pressure them to attend graduate school, nor was there a clear political message that he attempted to convey. His goal was to make the history real, to encourage his students to question previous interpretations, and to do the reading and research necessary to speak with authority.

He was both approachable and considerate. There were annual Christmas parties for which the greying and slightly stooped professor brought along a full case of beer or a few tasteful bottles of wine, and there was always an open invitation to visit him at the CIIA and use its library. Holmes was patient, confident, and balanced. His courses were among the favourites of those who walked through the doors of Glendon Hall in the 1970s.

Admittedly, through his first two years in particular, the grades in GL 428 were unusually high. As is true for most professors, marking was a burden for Holmes. He took pleasure in reading and commenting on student work, but the idea of attributing a letter or numerical score for what was meant to be a learning experience never agreed with him. The grading schemes in his syllabi were rough, and the letters he assigned for oral and written work were intuitive. As was typical of the time, there were no explicit, measurable criteria upon which the students could fall back. Nevertheless, when he was impressed – which was often at Glendon – the marks were generous. When his practices were questioned by the chair of the college of arts and sciences at the end of his second year, he defended himself by praising his students for their outstanding work: "In a good seminar, as you know, students inspire each other and I think that the high proportion of really first-class students did set standards which the others reached for. I don't suppose I can be as lucky again but I have now adjusted my expectations upwards and I trust the marks will be more in line with those of others."[12]

In accepting his first of many honorary degrees in May 1973, he said to the graduates of Lakehead University, "unawareness and acquiescence are not the qualities I note among the students to whom I am presently exposed ... I have never known such a combination of healthy scepticism, honest enquiry and intellectual integrity. My optimism ... is based on a faith that ... the universities of this province are turning out people with the qualities badly needed to run this fractious country."[13] Certainly there were years when the students were less strong than others – and in the mid-1970s he even delicately admonished one class for its behaviour towards a visitor during a session on the Vietnam War – but the experience at Glendon represented one of the greatest and fondest of his life.

He was so successful, and so popular, that when his department head, Edward Appathurai, prepared to leave for a sabbatical over the 1973-74 academic year, he asked Holmes to take over his course in international organization. Tuesdays became busier, with the new class in the morning and the old one rescheduled for the afternoon. That year, the CIIA received $12,400 from Glendon and another $6,210 from the U of T, and Professor Holmes earned it all. Since he lacked the theoretical background to teach international organization the way that Appathurai had, he spent much of the spring and summer of 1973 thinking about and then preparing a new approach to the course in consultation with academics and practitioners who worked in the field.[14]

The result became GL 426: International Organization. His aim, Holmes told a friend in Ottawa, was "to grab the interest of the students at the beginning by getting them to see that international organization is a means by which Canadians promote their national interests rather than seeing it as the failed world government in Manhattan." He dealt with the United Nations for virtually all of term one and then broader issues of policy and other multilateral institutions after the new year. Every class, or case, had a Canadian component, and the format was no different from his foreign policy course. The assigned research essay was linked to a seminar subject for which the student also provided an oral report to launch the week's discussion. Instead of a second essay, Holmes added a pair of take-home examinations. Near the beginning of the year, the students received a short list of sweeping, topical questions. Their written responses to those questions were due before the end of the each term. This was an innovation borrowed from Roger Wickwood, a former student who had recently begun teaching in Alberta. Inis Claude's classic *Swords into Plowshares* was the unofficial course textbook. It was supplemented by contemporary reports on Canada's role at the UN provided to Holmes by former civil service colleagues and in-class visits from some of those same people.[15]

By the fall of 1974, John Holmes' popularity and reputation at Glendon had soared. So many students wanted to take his course in Canadian foreign policy that he split it into two two-hour sessions, one on Wednesdays at 4:00 PM and another at 7:00 PM. Also because of demand, he agreed to admit graduate students from York's main campus. His new class swelled to over thirty, leaving him to divide it into two ninety-minute sessions on Tuesday mornings. Add to that a full seminar at the U of T on Wednesdays at 10:30 AM, and he was essentially teaching five year-long senior level courses while being paid for just three. Before Holmes could contemplate cutting back, Principal Tucker recommended that he be promoted and appointed to the equivalent of full professor, the highest standing a full-time faculty member could receive. With the title came a salary of nearly $16,000, making him the highest paid part-time faculty member on campus. Not much later, there was talk of asking Professor Holmes to stand as a candidate for president when Tucker's term ended, although it eventually became clear that he was not interested in spending his senior years in university administration.[16]

His promotion brought with it another bonus: the opportunity to employ teaching and research assistants paid for by the university. Over the next few years, he made excellent use of a number of talented young people, one of whom later taught his courses at Glendon and another of whom entered the foreign service and worked in the UN division. Both Martin Shadwick and Mark Anshan remember their mentor as an excellent employer. He was relaxed and encouraging. He gave them responsibilities – editing *The Shaping of Peace*, for example – that made them feel appreciated, and he spoke highly of them to his friends and colleagues. His assistants attended his classes and led the occasional seminar. Holmes and Anshan ate together often and shared the odd glass of sherry from a bottle stashed in his office or at his Rosedale apartment. Once Anshan was accepted to the foreign service, it was Holmes who made sure that he was quickly transferred to an ideal post at the UN. He also continued to seek out publication opportunities for his young advisees: Shadwick's first article in *International Perspectives* appeared with Holmes' encouragement.[17]

At the U of T, he found another publishing opportunity for two of his stronger graduate students, Douglas Ross and Peter Mueller, who were hired by the Defence Research Board to write a report on Canada's future role in the Pacific Rim. They worked out of the CIIA offices. The result was a five-hundred-page draft text that they called *China and Japan: Emerging Global Powers*. Holmes was impressed, and when he could not convince the University of Toronto Press to print it without major revisions, he took the manuscript to Praeger, who published it instead.[18] Mueller authored another paper for the CIIA, travelled abroad, and then began a successful consulting career while Ross continued on academically. His thesis on Canada and the international control commissions in Indochina became one of Holmes' favourite books on the history of Canadian foreign policy.[19]

Ross and Mueller studied under Professor Holmes at Trinity College, which had recruited him as a fellow around 1974 and then renamed his course POL 419/2203: Topics in Canadian Foreign Policy. The new designation allowed for a mix of graduate and undergraduate students and caused enrolment to increase. By this point, PhD candidates like Donald Story were beginning to find permanent academic positions, and Holmes' reputation as the leading and most influential supervisor of PhD dissertations in Canadian foreign policy was spreading. Soon Ross and David Taras joined the list of notable professors whose worked was shaped by John Holmes.

With the release of *Canada: A Middle-aged Power* in early 1976, it would have appeared to Holmes' students that their mentor was also continuing to produce scholarly writing at the same incredible rate that had characterized his output in the 1960s. The title of the collection of essays was fitting as it captured the soul-searching phase of Canada's international history that had been launched by Trudeau in 1968 while at the same time alluding to the sentiment expressed ironically at the beginning of the introduction: "So here we are, alas, in Canada, middle-powered, middle-class, and now middle-aged." The book contained twenty essays or speeches as well as Holmes' first convocation address, and it was organized around four subjects: the Trudeau foreign policy review, international institutions, Holmes' much-loved idea of the counterweight, and North America. The texts were chosen by Peyton Lyon's senior students at Carleton. In fact, it was Lyon who drove the entire project forward before leaving the details to Holmes and Gayle Fraser. A review of the selections reveals that a disproportionate number had originally been written for international audiences, demonstrating how Holmes' influence had grown since the publication of *The Better Part of Valour* six years earlier.

The positive and generous reviews of the new book reflected the scope of Holmes' impact. Gordon Fairweather, a Conservative MP, wrote in the *Globe and Mail*, "The John Holmes of Canada makes me glad I live here and try in a modest way to take part in the public affairs of this country.

What this participation means is that I have more opportunities than most to be in contact with John Holmes, hear his intelligent and witty lectures which seem to me to contain exactly the right mix of good sense and informed criticism and analysis of Canada's role and responsibilities in the world." Historian Jack Granatstein was equally kind, writing: "Unquestionably John Holmes is the most perspicacious writer on foreign policy in Canada. His prose flows, his knowledge is vast and deep, and he is above all a reasonable man." His old friend, Fred Soward, declared: "No practitioner of diplomacy in Canada or serious student of international affairs should be without this collection."[20]

To view *A Middle-aged Power* as evidence of Holmes' productivity as a scholar, however, is largely deceiving. Focus on *The Shaping of Peace* decreased his original scholarly output significantly in the early to mid-1970s, and what notable new work he did produce was inspired largely by his teaching and reflected his interest in re-examining Canada's place in the world and in international organizations more generally. This is not to suggest that John Holmes ever stopped writing: the twenty-one chapters in *A Middle-aged Power* are proof enough. Rather, he picked his assignments carefully and made some of his decisions based on offers of remuneration. For example, his July 1972 article on Canada and the Pacific for the Japanese quarterly *Pacific Community* was well written, convincing, and generally appealing, but it did little more than reiterate his standard arguments that the interests of lesser powers were best served on the world stage by working in groups, that neutrality for Canada was unrealistic, and that his country was a fast-growing economic world force. Holmes presumably wrote it at least in part because he was offered a $300 honorarium, money that was particularly helpful before his teaching commitments and accompanying salary increased at Glendon. He had similar motivations for accepting an offer to write for the World Book yearbook, although in this case, since he was asked to review rather than to analyze and present new ideas, and could do so without engaging in extensive research, his contributions were closer to his old standards.[21]

A partial exception to this trend was an article for a special Canadian-American relations issue of *International Organization* in 1974. Having been campaigning for greater American scholarship on the Canada-US relationship for a number of years, Holmes felt obligated to participate in an exercise that brought together scholars from both countries to do that very thing. The process began with paper proposals in 1972 followed by a conference at Harvard and then another at Carleton organized by historian David Farr. The latter meeting was not without controversy. A University of Ottawa political scientist, John Trent, wrote an open letter to all of the participants protesting the exclusion of Canadian economic nationalists from the talks, and his criticisms eventually reached the *Globe and Mail*. Holmes stood behind Farr's response that the conference was not the place for people who were stuck in their academic ways and determined to advance a political agenda. He had no time for analyses that lacked objectivity in his classroom, and he thought the same way about the work of his academic colleagues more broadly. In fact, just the year before, he had castigated the legendary Donald Creighton for his lacklustre contribution to a book honouring Canada's pre-eminent military historian Charles Stacey. He later wrote more candidly to Stacey: "His treatment for example of Canada's part in the Korean War in *Canada's First Century* would never have been accepted from an M.A. student."[22]

The article that he eventually produced for the project coordinated by the acclaimed American scholar Alfred Hero Junior included the novel observation that the greatest difference between Canadian and American interpretations of the bilateral relationship was not about its nature but, rather, about its intensity. "There is bound to be a conflict between a people who regard the relationship as critical and those who have scarcely noticed the other country," he wrote. The rest of the essay rehashed old ideas. Canada was becoming increasingly powerful as an international economic player; Canadian anti-Americanism was pathetically colonial in the way that it echoed comments made south of the border; and Canada had to avoid external perceptions of being little more than a component part of North America. As he often repeated during these years, it was "better for Canadians to be ignored than to be treated as part of a continental unit with common interests as inevitably interpreted by spokesmen in Washington."[23]

Much more interesting was his re-examination of the middle power idea, a project that was almost certainly inspired by discussions in his seminars. In 1972, Holmes began to question the concept that he had been popularizing so effectively since leaving the foreign service. In what might have been interpreted as a veiled attack on the new nationalists and radical Vietnam protestors, but was really much more than that, he wrote: "A certain moral arrogance has crept into the concept of middle power. That might is not right all would agree – but neither is weakness. Middle powers are middle powers because they are weaker, not because they are more virtuous ... they threaten no one because they are incapable of doing so." Introducing a theme that would eventually form much of the basis of *A Middle-aged Power*, he called on the states formerly known as middle powers to grow up. Like the great powers, they too had an obligation to develop a vision of the most effective global approach to international security. If they had no better alternatives than the present state of affairs, they had no business criticizing those who were making the greatest sacrifices to keep the current system stable. He made a similar case in a *Toronto Star* article the following year. "Regarding mediation as the central purpose of our foreign policy was a distortion," he claimed. "It did give us a needed sense of purpose, but this was lost when peacekeeping ceased to be a steady job."[24]

During a period of prolonged détente, the end of the Vietnam War, and renewed engagement between the United States and communist China – for which functioning multilateral institutions were viewed as contributors to the progress – Holmes implored Canadians to devote more of their time to understanding global politics. His experience planning and then teaching Ed Appathurai's course at Glendon revealed to him the dearth of domestic scholarship on international organization. This was reason for concern, particularly from the point of view of a country that took the United Nations so seriously.[25] In 1972, he discussed his ideas in speeches to the Canadian military at both the Staff College and NDC. In the fall of 1975 he presented the same thoughts to the readers of *Saturday Night* magazine and concluded with a warning: "A people so utterly dependent as Canadians on the tranquil exchange of goods and services dare not lose sight of our vital interest in a structured international community."[26] Shortly after, he published a longer essay in *International Perspectives*. There he challenged calls that, thirty years after its foundation, the UN had lost its purpose:

> A basic problem in the present debate over the UN's relevance is, as always, that people never seem to get through their heads what the United Nations is ... It is a loosely-linked network of institutions and agencies within which member states can do or not do what they can find a consensus or a majority or enough great-power agreement to carry out. It is also, of course, a Charter, a common bond to good behaviour among sovereign states, and in that sense something greater than the sum of its parts. But as the UN it cannot act, and the system is not responsible for the actions taken within its component parts. If we do not like the decisions of the Assembly, the recourse is not to abandon the institution but to seek ways of altering the majority or the majority point of view.[27]

Such sentiments brought him into conflict with members of the international Jewish community. On 10 November 1975, the United Nations adopted resolution 3379, which equated Zionism with racism. The General Assembly also endorsed an August 1975 statement by the non-aligned movement that called upon the international community to oppose Zionism, describing it as a racist and imperialist ideology. The decision was the result of cooperation between Israel's Arab neighbours and the Soviet Union, and it was evidence that, in spite of the apparent détente, Soviet antagonism towards Israel's most significant ally, the United States, had not abated. Since Moscow could not challenge US policy at the Security Council, where such actions would be met with an American veto, it moved the battle to the General Assembly, where a strategic alliance with Israel's and America's enemies gave it a majority. In response, many supporters of Israel, both in the Middle East and around the world, turned their backs on the UN. The organization did not revoke its position until 1991.

On 1 December 1975, Holmes gave a controversial speech at the Canadian Club in Toronto. In it, he condemned resolution 3379 unequivocally but then went on to explain, or some might say justify, it politically. "The supporters of the resolution said some outrageous things," he conceded, but the motion itself might never have passed if US representatives speaking in defence of Israel had conducted themselves more moderately. Later on, in speaking in favour of the contemporary world structure, he added:

> What we have in practice ... is a working system of checks and balances in the UN system. A majority in the Assembly, which as we know can be unrepresentative of the military and economic responsibilities of the membership as a whole, can pass purely declaratory resolutions, such as that on Zionism. They cannot, however, start on the dangerous road of expelling members or transforming the UN structure, because in those areas the great powers can and will use their vetoes. They cannot force us to pay immense sums of money for projects we do not approve. It is a crude system, but in present circumstances it is our best guarantee that the UN does not become in fact an instrument of a temporary majority.[28]

Holmes was sincere in his belief that his comments were meant to condemn the resolution and was furious when they were interpreted differently. In a letter to King Gordon lamenting the fact that no major newspaper covered his speech he wrote: "I don't like believing in conspiracies but in the present mood of exasperation with Zionist overkill, which I find very widespread among my friends and students, horror stories are multiplying.

The end result I fear is going to be some real anti-Semitism." He made the same argument to Canada's secretary of state for external affairs, Allan MacEachen, and to Trudeau's foreign policy advisor, Ivan Head. In response, the combative Harry Crowe, a professor of administrative studies at York University and a member of the newly formed Canadian Professors for Peace in the Middle East, said simply and in direct response to Holmes' comments, "if the United Nations should not survive it is rationalization of that kind and defense of that kind which will bear much of the responsibility."[29]

People like Crowe struck a nerve with Holmes and revealed his long-standing and at times obsessive discomfort with what he called the "hard-core Zionists." His feelings had been evident as early as 1945, when, in an unsent letter intended for Hume Wrong, he described Zionist propaganda in the United States as being "as vicious and dishonest in its vilification of British policy as anything ever produced by Zaslovsky or Goebbels." He was also quick to rationalize Canadian immigration policy during the Second World War – an approach to Jewish refugees that stood as the worst in the modern world. He argued that the anti-Semitic comments made by select Canadian officials from that period had to "be put in perspective." They were evidence of the presence of disgraceful individuals within the civil service, not of institutionalized racism. Radical Zionists, through "their political pressures and their use of the media," were alienating people like him, "the most reliable friends of jewry."[30]

Although some might suggest that Holmes had anti-Semitic inclinations, his personal and professional conduct indicates that he was intolerant of all forms of discrimination. Nevertheless, at least twice in his old age, his anger and frustration bested his judgment.[31] In April 1985, he received a request for information about the Holocaust. The letter made reference to allegations that Zionists had been deliberately exaggerating the number of Jews that were killed by the Nazis to court international sympathy. Holmes' response was sincere and well intentioned but still disturbing: "As you say, it is an academic question whether there were two or six million Jews killed by the Nazis. I suppose I have always assumed that the numbers might well be exaggerated for quite understandable reasons. The truth is so awful it seems unfortunate that some sensationalists have exploited and exaggerated. In doing so, of course, they tend to play into the hands of fanatics like Zundel. There is, of course, an increasing literature on the subject but I confess that I have not kept in touch with it."[32]

The following year, in a letter to a friend, he launched an ignorant and juvenile attack on Canada's ambassador to the United Nations, Stephen

Lewis. Lewis had just spoken out against anti-Semitism in the Soviet Union. Not only were Jewish organizations being forcibly closed across the country, but Jews were also being prevented from participating in aspects of public life and at the same time being refused permission to emigrate to Israel. "It was a rousing speech and very well delivered," Holmes wrote, "but I find myself a little uneasy about the kinds of selections which have to be made when one denounces violations of human rights. If I look over the Amnesty International reports and if I had no domestic or other political considerations, I don't think I would give the highest priority for suffering to the Jews in the Soviet Union. I think I would rather be a Jew in Leningrad than a Bahai in Teheran, a Tamil in Colombo, or an Ontarian in Calgary."[33]

Taken on its own, the comment is so thoughtless that it is shocking to think that it came from Holmes' pen. Although the legitimacy of such sentiment, even expressed privately among friends, is debatable, contextually, the recipient of the letter, Howard Palmer, was an Albertan who would have understood the latter reference as a tongue-in-cheek response to Prime Minister Trudeau's National Energy Program.[34] There can be no denying that Holmes was never active in organizations that might have been considered supporters of Israel (such as Canadian Professors for Peace in the Middle East), but nor did he ever discriminate against Jewish people either in the classroom or professionally.

In its entirety, Holmes' personal correspondence reveals an intense disdain for the politicization of foreign policy through what has been called the practice of Diaspora politics. Throughout his life, Holmes was insistent that members of ethnic minorities acted inappropriately when they attempted to use their influence as voters to bring pressure upon the Canadian government to interfere in the politics of their native lands. On this issue, the extent of his purely – or perhaps extremist – Canadian, nationalist sentiment was at its clearest. "Having all agreed that it was quite wrong for the Wasps and Orangemen to press the government into policies designed for the benefit of their mother country," he asked Peyton Lyon in 1975, "have we skidded into a position where the government cannot take a rational decision on policies ... without having to submit to the violent intimidation of one or more ethnic groups?" That he took out his frustration more on Israeli advocates than he did on others can be attributed to his disputable perception that "attitudes in the press and parliament have been considerably affected by the growing effectiveness of Zionist lobbying."[35]

Moreover, his focus on Israel and Zionism was never exclusive. Perhaps missing the irony of his own vehemence, Holmes opposed political radicalism in Canada in any form. He consistently rejected calls for Canada to boycott South Africa over its policy of apartheid. In 1980, when King Gordon criticized the CIIA for planning a study tour to Johannesburg, he wrote back in anger: "These absolutist Africans sit here in their comfortable ivy-covered halls denying the possibility of change in South Africa in exactly the same way as the comfortable Zionists hereabout cling to their bloody views of the PLO [Palestine Liberation Organization]." Years later, he explained to a colleague more rationally, "in our proper enthusiasm to get rid of apartheid we think of a miracle transformation and worry too little about the morning after ... apartheid is a very bad system but it is a system and one has to think about the nature of a system to replace it."[36] As he rationalized in a paper for *International Perspectives* in 1977, "we always need the moralist who cares for values and the pragmatist who can chart a way without doing more harm than good." John Holmes clearly placed himself in the latter category, arguing: "Moral values may be eternal, but their application in international politics must be *ad hoc*. There is no alternative to grappling with complexity, looking at both sides of every argument and the step by step consequences of each policy." Based on this premise, he suggested that there could be, and had been, positive ramifications stemming from Canada's inexcusable treatment of the Japanese during the Second World War, and from Britain's imperial policy towards India before granting its independence. He even argued that the American Civil War might not have been necessary had "fanatical abolitionism" not forced the South into a proverbial corner.[37]

This was a different, and less appealing side of John Holmes, but it was hardly inconsistent with his basic approach to world order. Having grown up in a homogenous neighbourhood with strong British roots, he remained loyal to the imperial concept of peaceful, evolutionary progress. The world was not fair – his own experience in the DEA was proof – but this did not make radical approaches to change (often championed in the United States as well as by ethnic minorities across North America in response to crises abroad) helpful or valuable. The complex nature of international society meant that real, sustainable progress took time. It was unfortunate, but likely, that, in the future, generations of certain religious and ethnic groups would suffer horribly for the benefit of others. Nevertheless, attempts to circumvent this gradual and incremental process did not work; those who tried merely made the situation worse, and longer-lasting. In doing so, they became a more serious threat to long-term international order than did the instigators of the injustice. Some might suggest that this made Holmes a pessimist, but that was not true; he was, rather, a pragmatic and generally patient optimist, one who had faith that, over time, if the proper processes were observed, the world would continue to improve.[38]

From a Canadian perspective, this made him a nationalist in the purest sense, one who believed strongly that, upon entering the country, one's loyalties had to be to one's new home state. Policy towards Israel, South Africa, or any other foreign country had to be considered in terms of the impact on Canadian national interests. Since Canada prospered in times of peace and stability, calls for radical change were ignorant, inappropriate, and unnecessary. John Holmes had faith in humanity, a faith that was renewed in the classroom. In time, if Canadians pursued their own interests with passion and integrity, he was convinced that the oppressed and unjustly disadvantaged would benefit, regardless of where they lived. This conclusion, which in its most aggressive form could be off-putting, if not blatantly offensive, was also the inspiration for his commitment to vigorously represent and educate Canadians about their place in the world well into his seventies.

12

Older and Wiser

It was difficult to be optimistic about world affairs in the late 1970s. The Chinese called 1976 the year of the curse after an earthquake near Tangshan, Hebei, killed close to 250,000 people and injured another 150,000. In 1977, political activist Steve Biko was tortured and murdered in South Africa. Conflicts in Vietnam and Lebanon resulted in significant casualties in 1978, and the Iranian Revolution of 1979 led to the kidnapping of fifty-three Americans that November. New leadership in the United Kingdom and the United States accused their predecessors of administering bloated and ineffective regimes and put their faith in individuals being freed to pursue their own interests through lower taxes. Canada, meanwhile, continued to focus on itself as its economy suffered as a result of inflation caused by rising oil prices and unemployment.

Considering the extent of his involvement in international politics, it is ironic that this period benefited John Holmes professionally. Canadians sought a wise, stable voice to inform them about the state of the world, and the international community needed to hear from a Canadian who could inspire hope and faith in world order. Holmes was now a senior citizen, and his age and experience informed his teaching as well as his cogent analysis of external affairs. His reputation as one of the wisest minds in Canada and international politics continued to spread, and he remained inspired to serve his country. Throughout the later 1970s, he wrote and rewrote the second volume of his magnum opus, *The Shaping of Peace*. He dabbled in the political mayhem that marked the temporary end of nearly seventeen years of uninterrupted Liberal rule. He played a leading role in the establishment and early success of the University of Toronto's Centre for International Studies (CIS). And he even accepted an offer to spend four months as a visiting professor in the United Kingdom.

Things were not all good. Holmes could not completely escape the challenges brought on by the advance of time. He lost his mother in February 1977, and it shook him terribly. His sister Helen (Buzz) – the one with whom he felt the strongest connection – died five years later, making his family situation even more difficult. His eyesight began to decline. After purchasing his sister Isobel's cottage, he adjusted his exercise routine to accommodate a body that was less sturdy than it used to be. Napping became a regular part of his day outside of the academic terms. Life was slower by necessity, and by the close of the decade there was evidence that Holmes was beginning to wind down the most active part of his public career. Nonetheless, that end was still only just beginning, and all the while accolades for his work as Canada's unofficial ambassador to the world continued to accumulate as he relished his third career as his country's premier foreign policy educator.

Understanding Canada's role in the world was challenging in the late 1970s. External affairs under Prime Minister Trudeau were in a state of managed chaos. New initiatives such as the much-flaunted Third Option, an approach to international trade that attempted to reduce Canadian dependence on the American economy by expanding contacts with Europe and Japan, were proving more difficult to achieve than the government had hoped. Canada's global reach seemed to be diminishing, and critics, like journalist Sandra Gwyn, were sullen and pessimistic. "We are pulling down the blinds between ourselves and the world," she wrote in frustration. Canada's youth in particular had become utterly self-absorbed and ignorant of the world around them. Pointing to the decline of public engagement in world affairs, she predicted a further sharp decrease in her country's international influence.[1]

Analyzing the situation through the lens of history, Professor Holmes disagreed. In a convocation address first delivered to the students of the University of Waterloo, he presented a more optimistic alternative: "If students of the 'seventies are without convictions I think it is because they realize better than their predecessors that life is complex, that truth and morality are beset by paradox, and convictions do not come casually … Having wearied of the certainties, on the Right and the Left, today's graduates are better equipped to inject a determined pragmatism into the national and international debate." "What we need now," he later added, "are fewer proclamations of doom and gloom and more good ideas, solutions, formulas that work, some positive thinking. We need a revival of national spirit, a healthy nationalism based on a more confident assessment of our enormous heritage."[2]

Holmes' optimism came from his experience in the classroom. He continued to be awed by his students' abilities to grasp the complexities of international relations and discuss them reasonably and collegially. Even as he grew older, the thrill he gained from teaching and his success therein made the idea of formal retirement seem far away. In 1977, when he was elected to the Royal Society of Canada, the country's most senior and distinguished scholarly body, the sixty-seven-year-old concluded with pride that his legacy as an educator of young people was his crowning professional achievement.[3]

He continued to build that legacy but at a more deliberate pace. The experience at Glendon was the first to come to an end. York University support staff marked the beginning of the 1978 academic year with a strike that divided faculty allegiances. Some joined the picket lines while others, Professor Holmes included, kept teaching. "The students have paid for my services," he wrote to Mark Anshan, now at the Canadian embassy in Sweden. They continued to come to class and his loyalty was to them. Nevertheless, he wondered whether he could still handle the burdens of two universities. The work stoppage reinforced his inclination to refocus his efforts on graduate studies at the University of Toronto. When he learned that budget cuts at Glendon might cause his courses to be cancelled if he retired, he delayed the inevitable – but only temporarily. In 1979, he sub-contracted much of his obligations to Clarence Redekop, one of his PhD graduates without a permanent position. He did the same thing with the Canadian foreign policy seminar in 1980 while returning responsibility for the class in international organization to Ed Appathurai. With the trusted Martin Shadwick now in firm control of the foreign policy course, he left Glendon officially in the summer of 1981.

As was typical of his approach to change, Holmes never severed his ties completely. He kept informed, for example, of the annual winner of the John Holmes Prize (formerly known as the Glendon Prize in International Relations), an award that recognized the successful completion of the for-eign service exam. And as late as 1987 he wrote the university to advocate the establishment of international relations as an autonomous field of study.[4]

At his other teaching job a new phase had begun. An ambitious and accomplished young scholar who had been working at the University of

British Columbia, John Kirton, joined the faculty of the U of T in 1977, and he and Holmes agreed to teach POL 419/2203 together. It was the beginning of a slow reduction in responsibilities that made sense for a man in his late sixties. Kirton's professional inclinations were more theoretical than were Holmes,' but the junior academic was also gracious and respectful. Although he had not used the case study approach before, he proposed that the course retain its basic structure and themes, suggesting only minor modifications that might enable the students to take advantage of his expertise in international trade. The partnership was successful, and in the spring of 1978 the first group to complete the Holmes-Kirton experience presented their professors with large congratulatory cookies. Holmes' cookie recognized his outstanding work as teacher and mentor. Kirton's said "Rookie of the Year." The partnership lasted for a number of years, with the elder John gradually relinquishing the more taxing administrative duties to his more youthful colleague.

During this period, Holmes' students, new and old, expressed their appreciation of his commitment and dedication in ways that he could never have expected. Professor Holmes was notoriously inattentive when it came to the upkeep of his Toronto apartment. His refrigerator was usually empty because he ate out so often, and he never painted. One weekend, while he was away on business, on the initiative of Michel Charrier (a member of the Department of National Defence who had been seconded to the CIIA), a band of graduate students and their loyal "co-conspirator," Gayle Fraser, infiltrated his home (Fraser had a key), photographed every item on every wall, cleared them all out, and went to work. With just a single experienced painter among them the project took longer than anticipated. At one point, after using a rented steam machine to remove wallpaper from one of the walls, the students watched in horror as chunks of plaster fell to the floor. After patching the wall, they moved on to the bedroom, only to find that the bed had three legs: the last corner was supported by a pile of books. As might have been expected in a room of Holmes graduate students, there ensued a friendly competition to determine whose scholarship Professor Holmes might use for such a purpose.

When the job was finally finished, Holmes' apartment looked fresh and new. Every piece of art, every honorary college hood (always displayed prominently to encourage his nephews and nieces to pursue higher education), every book, and every classical record was returned to its rightful position. When the professor returned, in his own typical style he did not immediately notice the changes. Moments later, however, as he toured his home, he became so flattered that he invited his students back for a party that lasted late into the night. Many were worried that the nearly seventy-year-old man would be exhausted, but he reassured one and all that he was simply delighted to be able to thank them for such a thoughtful display of gratitude.

Shortly after, Holmes received the ultimate academic tribute. The gift – called a festschrift – was a collection of scholarly essays published in his honour. Kim Nossal first proposed the idea in 1977 and consulted with Donald Story and Gayle Fraser before he moved forward. In 1980 they surprised Holmes by presenting him with the appropriately titled *The Acceptance of Paradox: Essays on Canadian Diplomacy in Honour of John W. Holmes.*[5] Apart from Denis Stairs' thoughtful introduction, the book's chapters were written entirely by Holmes' PhD graduates. He was left overwhelmed. "That such a learned bunch should be publishing their own work was not unexpected," he explained, "but that it would be dedicated to the old man was more than I could have thought possible." There followed a heartfelt and emotional tribute to those who had made his professional life so fulfilling:

> Have you ever seriously thought how much I owe you? Aside from the amount of solid information I have pinched for my own books, there are all the bright ideas you set alight in the seminars, the office, or the pub. You all had the happy habit of listening to me with due respect, but not letting me get away with anything. You have refined my thinking remarkably, and made me do my home work. I realize how often limited my vision was when I first faced Dan and Clarence, two revolutionaries, and a nun in my first class in 1967! When I was later asked to "take on" the doctors – or royal commissioners – in training I did so knowing I was in a position to treat myself only to the best – and I got 'em. Towards you all I have felt somewhat avuncular and somewhat, I confess, cannibalistic. I have no right to feel proud of the quality of your studies in this book, because I recognize you as your own disparate monads, but I permit myself that senile illusion. Certainly they all have the qualities I admire: integrity, imagination, sensitivity, precision – some real nice paradoxes and no split infinitives. Even if I were a stranger to this book I would subscribe to and prescribe it. It is a first-class contribution to the study of Canadian diplomacy and damn good reading withal. Every essay is a classic case study in which you bring out the complexities as students and other readers should see them. You are all right on target, a perfect selection for the dedicatee.[6]

As yet another salute to his efforts, Holmes received the highest honour possible from Pickering College. In 1981, he was presented with the Class of 1842 award, a sort of hall of fame for individuals associated with the still venerable institution. The citation recognized his professional service, his academic achievements, and, most important for him, his exemplary contribution to education in Canada.[7]

As a role model for so many young scholars and a perennially concerned Canadian, Holmes felt obligated to maintain his own research productivity, and he certainly did so as the 1970s came to a close. Apart from the occasional effort to revisit the future of the Commonwealth, however, he rarely ventured beyond his staple themes: the Canada-US relationship, the United Nations, and international organization more generally. In all of his published work between 1976 and early 1980 only two pieces stand out as noteworthy, and both appeared in 1978. The first was a magazine article entitled "Moscow under Stalin." The quasi-memoir of Holmes' experience as chargé d'affaires in the Soviet Union in 1947-48 marked a new direction in his public writing. It was not so much analytical as it was reflective, meant to convey to contemporary readers the ideas going through the minds of Canadian officials and their political masters during the early Cold War.[8]

"Moscow under Stalin" was a direct response to a wave of revisionist academic scholarship that dominated first the American and then the Canadian historical landscape in the 1970s. Looking back on the disaster that was Vietnam, US revisionists proposed, with various levels of success, that US belligerence in the 1960s was evidence of a national culture of imperialism that had pervaded the country since at least the 1940s. The Cold War, they claimed, had not been caused by Soviet aggression; rather, the United States was to blame. Washington exploited a fearful public by exaggerating the extent of the threat from Moscow to justify its unilateral and militant policies during the early postwar era. The most radical revisionists implied a conspiracy reaching as high as the upper echelons of the federal government – a secret strategy devised to promote American economic domination over the rest of the world – while the more reasonable merely suggested that the Soviet dictator, Joseph Stalin, need not shoulder all of the blame for a conflict that had come far too close to igniting a third world war.[9]

A select number of Canadian historians used the thinking behind these arguments as a basis for re-examining their own government's attitude towards the Cold War. Without the benefit of documentary evidence – which for security reasons had yet to be released – they speculated that officials in Ottawa, led by Lester Pearson himself, might have fallen under the American imperialist spell in the 1940s, accepted the exaggerated Soviet threat, and then propagated that sense of fear and need for an aggressive response across the country.[10] Such accusations infuriated Holmes, who took them as assaults on his character and on that of his friends. Pieces like "Moscow under Stalin" were the first of many quasi-historical reflections meant to solidify the official record, re-establish the sincere and noble intent of Canada's public servants and politicians, and reveal from a personal perspective the independent reluctance that characterized their conclusion that the Soviet Union was a menace and an enemy. "Diplomats have been blamed of late for jaundiced reporting, for wilfully inventing a monster," he wrote. "If they were jaundiced, it was … from revulsion against the brutalities of the regime to its own people and to its neighbours." There had been diplomatic miscalculations, but analyses from Moscow were flawed because of the isolation imposed on foreign officials by Stalin's brutal and autocratic regime. There was hardly any interaction with everyday Muscovites, for example, because Canadian officials understood what the regime might do to Soviet citizens who were too close with the enemy.[11]

Holmes' second great publication of the period was his keynote address at the CIIA's fiftieth anniversary banquet in June 1978. Still recalled fondly by many of those in attendance, and later rebroadcast by the CBC because it had been so well received, the jubilee featured Holmes at his witty best. Through a judicious mix of humour, modesty, and self-deprecation, he praised the CIIA for its progressive impact on the level of international awareness in Canada and abroad. As for those who predicted its eventual demise, he countered: "I feel about the CIIA as I do about the United Nations. Everyone criticizes it, but the day after it evaporated we would be hard at work re-creating it." He celebrated the institute's focus on education as opposed to advocacy, its emphasis on possible solutions instead of public criticism, and its ability to maintain its integrity as an organization in spite of recent challenges. By noting that contemporary national heroes tended to make their contributions to negotiations behind the scenes, he refuted the suggestion that the alleged deterioration of the CIIA was symptomatic of a decline in Canada's place in the world. This sort of work was thankless, but that did not take away from its importance: one did not have to be on television to make a difference. He concluded with a touch of Holmesian wisdom: "There are issues in the world in which we are wiser not to meddle. There are some on which we have done badly and many on which we have done brilliantly. In our comment and criticism on foreign policy what is needed is discrimination and precision, complaints and recommendations which governments can take seriously because they are viable."[12] Although he was no longer an active player in institute politics, he continued to keep in close touch with the CIIA, largely through his maintenance of an office on the premises, for the rest of his life.

Holmes devoted much of his original thinking to *The Shaping of Peace*. After spending nearly a year away from Volume 1 of the manuscript, he returned to it in the summer of 1977 and completed what he thought were the final revisions. When the reviewers solicited by the University of Toronto Press recommended publication, publisher RIK Davidson sent their comments to the Social Science Federation of Canada, the government-sponsored research organization that subsidized the production of scholarly works. With the financial support assured, Holmes signed his contract that November. The book finally appeared in 1979.

The Shaping of Peace was not its author's best work – Holmes later all but conceded that he was a much better essayist than he was a historian – but it was nevertheless an integral contribution to the history of Canadian external relations. The focus was on paradox and the willingness of Canadian officials in Ottawa and abroad to manage conflicting interests and ideals in helping to shape the postwar international order. The hero was Hume Wrong, the nobly intentioned pragmatist, father of Canadian functionalism, and creative thinker. Wrong and his colleagues in the Department of External Affairs were celebrated for their sincerity, professionalism, and commitment not just to Canada but to world order as a whole. If Holmes himself was optimistic, he argued at the end, it was for good reason: "A degree of optimism is essential for policy-makers," he explained, "especially those involved in the creation of a world. They do have to believe that something can be done even if the odds are against it. They, like historians, have to identify, undistracted by utopian fantasies, just how much has been accomplished and the directions in which we are moving."[13] Reviews of the book were nearly uniformly positive, praising its success in conveying a sense of the thinking taking place among the mandarinate during a crucial period of Canadian history. Sales, however, were disappointing. *The Shaping of Peace: Canada and the Search for World Order* was long, expensive, and directed at a limited, elite-level audience. Although still sought after by researchers a quarter of a century later, it was remaindered in 1982. By 1984, it had been taken out of print.

Volume 2 followed relatively closely after its predecessor. By early 1980, a 1,200-page (triple-spaced) type-written bundle was in the hands of the Social Science Federation. Based on what were once again mixed external reviews, in April the federation agreed to provide a $7,500 subsidy in exchange for a commitment from the author to shorten the manuscript without sacrificing its message or meaning. The final product was still longer than Volume 1, but it was also a better book. It responded to re-visionist charges of Canadian complicity in American imperialism by citing the uniqueness of the middle power role, and it documented the success of the East Block in recognizing and exploiting Canada's temporarily elevated international position in the early Cold War period. The "search" referred to in the book's title, the author explained, "was more for expedients than solutions, and that did not mean failure. World order would forever be a balancing act. The requirement was a world in equilibrium, even though it is in the nature of equilibrium to be non-durable."[14] Again, the reviews outshone the sales. But by now, although he was initially disturbed that his work had been almost completely ignored in the United States, Holmes was ambivalent. Completing the second volume relieved him of what had become the greatest stressor in his professional life. It went without saying that writing Volume 3 was out of the question.

Instead, he pursued new opportunities that drew on his real strengths as a pontificator on international relations and Canadian foreign policy. He served, for example, on the Rockefeller Foundation Advisory Board as a paid consultant for its international relations program, as the Can-adian inviter for the North American Council of the International Peace Academy, and then later as part of the academy's international board of directors. He became a member of the advisory committee of the Canadian International Affairs Program at the Center for Inter-American Relations in New York, of the advisory board of Trent University's international program, and of the Council of Advisors of the Canadian Centre for Arms Control and Disarmament. He travelled to Germany to represent the DEA at a conference meant to help establish a Canadian Studies program in Germany and then to London to speak on the department's behalf to the Royal Commonwealth Society. He continued to sit on the research council of the Center for Strategic and International Studies. He joined the corporation that helped establish the Lester B. Pearson College of the Pacific. And he remained active in professional military education in Toronto and Kingston.

Not one to slow down unless it was absolutely necessary, he also ac-cepted an invitation from the under-secretary of state for external affairs, Allan Gotlieb, to serve as Canada's "eminent person" on an advisory board established by the first UN special session on disarmament. The group was formed to stimulate the member states to sponsor research on arms control and to provide the secretary-general with a better understanding of the key priorities that lay ahead. Its creation came at a high point in the disarmament campaign, building upon the momentum created by the largest and most inclusive international meeting ever to address the nuclear arms race and devise a strategy to end it.

Holmes was delighted to accept an appointment that seemed to promote progress on an issue dear to him. The political results of his experience, however, were disappointing. In November 1978 he flew to New York to join three academics and twenty-three other representatives at the first set of meetings. Any optimism he might have had about the potential for the committee to make a notable impact was dashed by the uneven quality of the attendees. At first, Holmes enjoyed his time nonetheless, relishing the quiet diplomacy taking place in the corridors of the UN building. He was happy to return the following year not because he had faith in his own committee but, rather, because the trip to New York allowed him to relive some of the fondest memories from his years in the DEA, taking in the UN atmosphere with the joy of a young official.

Two years later, with no real accomplishments to show for his efforts, Holmes was less forgiving of his peers. "The Board set a new record in cancelled sessions and wasted time," he wrote to a former colleague. An inadequate chairman, a lack of new ideas, and the failure of the international community to commit seriously to disarmament became a cause of personal embarrassment. He did not return for another session, although he later grudgingly agreed to serve as a consultant to the Canadian delegation to the second UN special session on disarmament itself.[15]

Holmes remained non-partisan in his approach to world affairs, so he did not hesitate to complement his service to the Liberal government of the day with an address to a major conference held by the Progressive Conservatives at Scarborough's Guild Inn in January 1979. The Tories, in this case leader Joe Clark and MP Doug Roche specifically, were concerned that Canadians viewed the party and its approach to foreign policy outside of the national tradition. Polls suggested that the Trudeau government could fall during the next election, and Clark recognized that his team lacked the experience in international relations necessary to lead the country. Briefings by some of the nation's esteemed voices in external policy served as a first step in addressing this challenge. As for soliciting a speaker whom many Conservatives would have unfairly labelled as a partisan Liberal, this was a non-issue for the young Tory leader. He had respect for Holmes as an individual and shared his views on most international policy questions.

The speech was standard Holmes – a thoughtful and insightful analysis of the state of the country and its future possibilities. It criticized those who campaigned for national independence (typically from the United States), suggesting that theirs was an empty cry with no strategic vision behind it. "Our influence depends on the energetic affirmation of a policy of protecting and advancing our interests by collective action," Holmes explained. "Independence as an end in itself has distracted us for too long." On disarmament, he cautioned the Conservatives against "over-estimating morally egocentric gestures." Canada had divested itself of nuclear weapons, but it did not need them, and while its actions were still noble, they were not particularly impressive. Similarly, Canada had no inherent or divine ability to mediate on the world stage. It had a duty to take an active role in conflict resolution when it had the capacity to contribute, but it also had to recognize when others were better able to fulfil that critical function. He emphasized the importance of the UN to the coming decade, noting that the opening up of global society made it more relevant than ever. He concluded with his standard, timeless advice: "Sound, flexible, and effective action in furthering our interests and those of the international community" would garner greater respect than gallantry for gallantry's sake. The world stage was not a platform on which to rally national unity; rather, it was a place to make a difference, when that was possible. As he continued to repeat, foreign policy was not an issue to be politicized.[16] His words were generally well received, even if some noted that they failed to include any concrete policy recommendations.

Holmes left the conference impressed by Clark, the man many believed would be Canada's next prime minister. Intelligent, balanced, and modest, the Conservative leader showed a real willingness to listen to advice on foreign policy and avoided any pretension to being an expert in the field. To Holmes, he was undeserving of the harsh treatment he had been receiving in the media.[17] In this case, he was only partially correct. During Clark's short-lived term as prime minister, he demonstrated the signs of inexperience that held back his reputation.[18] Later, however, when Prime Minister Brian Mulroney appointed him secretary of state for external affairs in the mid-1980s, he was a leading force in the revival of many of the traditions of Pearsonian internationalism that Holmes held so dearly.

Nevertheless, if John Holmes voted Conservative in the 1979 election, and it is quite likely that he did, it was not because of an ideological commitment to Tory policies; rather, he believed that change in politics was good and that dominance by one party for too long led to complacency. For a civil servant who had benefited greatly from the stability and consistency of the St. Laurent regime of the 1940s and 1950s this might initially appear surprising, but it should not. Holmes' forward-looking attitude was drawn from the wisdom he had accumulated during his thirty-five years in public life. As he became increasingly involved as a mentor to Canadian youth, he grew to recognize the importance of fresh ideas to the national discourse.

He brought this perspective, along with memories from his life-changing experience at Trois-Pistôles in the 1930s, to a cross-country debate over a growing crisis in Quebec. In 1976, the separatist and only recently formed Parti Québécois shocked Canadians by defeating the provincial Liberals and assuming leadership of the province. The economy was struggling, and Quebeckers were angry and demanding change. Premier René Lévesque, a disillusioned former provincial cabinet minister, was convinced that French Canadians deserved more than what Canada was willing to give them and could prosper outside of the national family. He promised a referendum on what he termed sovereignty association – essentially a combination of political independence and an economic union with Canada – during his first term. His critics, both within and outside of the province, called for the country and its people to unite in opposition.[19]

Holmes responded to the situation in his address to the Royal Society in May 1979. In it, he criticized both sides. He urged the separatists to end their constant lamenting, which had begun to obscure the uniqueness of the Canadian experiment. With its openness to immigrants, its multicultural heritage, and its consistent rejection of violence as a means of conflict resolution, Canada was an outstanding success. Moreover, the unprecedented capacity of its flexible Constitution to accommodate difference and flourish while doing so made the idea of separation illogical. He added, however, that those who opposed the separatists by insisting on the importance of national unity to Canadian prosperity were equally misguided. "Harmony, not unity, is what we are designed for," he explained. "Our purpose is peace, order, and good government, not a coast-to-coast culture." The increasingly interconnected world was becoming more like Canada, and it was foolish for Canadians to respond by arguing for a form of civic nationalism that would shortly be viewed as a relic of the past. The answer to the disillusionment prevalent in Quebec was reasonable dialogue: not more nationalism, not greater patriotism, and certainly not separation. Both sides had to step back, recognize that the "so-called crisis of national unity" was hardly an issue in international terms and deal with it for what it was – part of the inevitable struggle of the evolutionary experiment of the first postmodern state. For a variety of reasons, close to 60 percent of Quebeckers agreed, and the separatists lost badly in the 1980 referendum.[20]

Just as Lévesque took power, another project began to occupy much of Holmes' time. Bob Spencer, still a co-editor of the *International Journal*, assumed responsibility for the U of T's International Studies Programme in 1976 on the condition that it immediately be renamed and reclassified as the Centre for International Studies (CIS). He and Holmes were of one view that, once it was equipped with the necessary resources, the centre could evolve to become a focal point for scholars and graduate students of international relations. Holmes solicited input to guide the transformation and then prepared a grant application for the Donner Foundation. Along with the standard commitment to hold conferences and support publications, he proposed two basic activities. The first was a series of seminars bringing together prominent academics and up-and-coming graduate students from across Ontario who shared an interest in the role of international institutions and the global framework in which they existed. The second was a study of the Canadian-American relationship through this same institutional lens.[21]

In March 1978, after detailed consultation between the CIS and the Donner Foundation's Gerald Wright, the U of T accepted a three-year, $275,000 grant.[22] Led by its director, Spencer, and its reinvigorated research director, Holmes, the CIS committed to a multidisciplinary analysis of the institutional framework shaping Canadian foreign policy. It had four themes: Canadian-American relations, Canada and the United Nations system, Canada and international security (including NATO), and new bilateral institutional links (such as those with the European community and Japan). Holmes was allocated a salary of $10,000 and access to a portion of the $10,000 budget for research assistance.[23] He spent part of the summer recruiting speakers for two sets of colloquia, one on international institutions and the other on Canadian-American relations. The former resulted in four sessions in the 1978-79 academic year while the latter resulted in six. The highlight was a summer conference recognizing the seventieth anniversary of the creation of the International Joint Commission (IJC), a binational body tasked with resolving disputes on water boundary issues but technically empowered to moderate any bilateral challenge. The proceedings became a book edited by Spencer, John Kirton, and Kim Nossal. Its introduction, penned by Holmes, captured the tone of the seminar series that he had largely established. "It would be wrong to suggest that either side regarded the IJC as a form of continental govern-ment," it began: "It promised equality without interfering with national sovereignty. Nevertheless, it was, as governments are, a provision to cope with what was now accepted to be an endless and normal conflict, the search for ways and means of dealing with contrary interests more often than for finding solutions."[24] The goal was to share ideas as much as it was to shape policy. The following year, the numbers of colloquia increased to eight and seven, and in 1980-81, the international institutions meetings were held almost every month.

Those who attended the gatherings still recall them more than a quarter of a century later. Thanks to Holmes' exceptional contacts, he was able to bring in senior politicians such as Mitchell Sharp and Donald Macdonald; veteran public servants like Allan Gotlieb, Robert Bryce, and Marcel Cadieux; world renowned scholars like John Gerald Ruggie; and even highly placed international officials such as George Davidson, a former under-secretary general at the UN. Ontario academics made the drive to Toronto from as far away as London and Kingston to spend a Friday morning (typically beginning at 11:00 AM to accommodate the commut-ers) listening to the invited guest, enjoying a sandwich lunch in the Trinity board room, and then participating in a more general discussion for a few hours in the afternoon. The quality of the dialogue was high. Specially invited local graduate students were exposed to a rich exchange of ideas and also had the chance to meet potential future mentors – like professors Margaret Doxey and Robert Cox – without having to leave Toronto.[25]

Holmes was proud of the results of the early meetings. Increasing and improving public dialogue between the academic community and policy practitioners had become, in his own words, "my principal purpose in life over the past years." To him, these colloquia ranked among his greatest achievements.[26] He attended as many as he could, playing his usual role as facilitator, mediator, and mentor to the invited graduate students. The gatherings also expanded his range of contacts by allowing him to spend more time with some of his U of T colleagues in other disciplines. His relationship with Robert Bothwell, for example, developed through a series of lunches in the Trinity dining hall. The expert in Canadian political and diplomatic history became a helpful critic of early versions of *The Shaping of Peace*.

Holmes felt secure leaving Canada to serve as visiting professor at the University of Leeds in the fall of 1979. He was first presented with the op-portunity to spend a term overseas a year earlier, but his schedule had been too hectic. Now, however, having reduced his commitments at Glendon, he accepted with pleasure. As visiting professor of Commonwealth history, he offered a ten-week course called "The Foreign Relations of a Middle Power: Canada Since the Second World War." He also agreed to give three public lectures: one to the university itself, one to the British International Studies Association at the University of Keele, and one at Canada House, as well as to participate in a colloquium on Anglo-Canadian relations. For all of this he was paid $6,000 in addition to the cost of his airfare. To cover any additional expenses, he leased his apartment, including the use of his ten-year-old Volvo sedan, to a professor from the City University of New York who was in Toronto for research purposes.

Almost immediately after he arrived in London, Holmes broke his only pair of glasses, without which he could barely see. Fortunately, a loyal official from the Canadian High Commission was able to locate an optician in the East End who fixed them quickly. That same week, he was hit – lightly – by a large truck. When he reached Leeds, he learned that he had been allotted the former vice-chancellor's spacious office as a work space. Reaching his door in the best of spirits, he was shocked to find that the room had been stripped of all of its furniture, leaving him with just a small desk and cabinet. There was no telephone and no place for his students to sit. The chaos was similar to his initial experiences in London in 1944 and Moscow in 1947. Luckily, there was an electric fireplace, a novelty that was appreciated as the weather turned cold.[27]

Ten days later, having settled in and met his students, Holmes presented the university community with the thirty-fifth annual Montagu Burton Lecture on international relations. He called it "The Changing Pattern of International Institutions." With his notes piled high on top of two lecterns to compensate for his declining vision, he argued for renewed faith in the importance and viability of world bodies and, specifically, in the United Nations. The organization would never be everything to all people, he conceded, but it was necessary because it enabled states to discipline themselves peacefully. Although its practical power was no greater than the will of its members as a collective, its approval granted a degree of international legitimacy to state activities that still mattered in the policy community. "At the risk of glibness," he explained, "one might say that the UN's role is not to rule but to set the rules," and it was crucial that the international community not give up on multilateral negotiations as the basis of maintaining a stable world order.[28]

His lecture to the members of Canada House offered the same message from a more distinctly Canadian point of view, while the talk at Keele was also similar both in its content and its reasonably optimistic sentiment. Two articles in the *Times Higher Educational Supplement* followed.[29] Upon reflection, Holmes saw his academic contribution as "a mini-crusade for more attention to what one might call a new public philosophy of the UN," a plea for a more informed, pragmatic, and indeed respectful understanding and appreciation of the role of the organization and of international institutions more generally.[30]

The period of time he spent at Leeds was precious for everyone involved. The students were enamoured; the academics, in particular the acclaimed professor of international relations who made most of the arrangements, David Dilks, cherished his company; and Holmes himself was able to write and think in a peaceful atmosphere largely unencumbered by the stresses of his responsibilities back home. He was delighted to return briefly in 1982 to celebrate the two hundredth anniversary of the British Foreign Office and accepted an invitation to serve a second term as visitor in 1985.

Leeds became his great international escape during these later years. It allowed him to share his thinking and ideas with a new audience, one that held him in the highest regard. The elderly Mr. Holmes was aging physically, and family stresses were taking an emotional toll, but the teaching and trips to Britain kept his mind young. With *The Shaping of Peace* finally complete, and the CIS apparently no longer reliant on his services, he had reason to look forward to the 1980s with optimism and enthusiasm. John Holmes, Canadian gentleman, was refreshed and reinvigorated.

13

Regrets and Renewal

"Welcome to the eighties," said Pierre Trudeau sardonically after emerging from a brief retirement to lead the Liberals to victory in the 1980 federal election. Trudeau was one of many world leaders who made a significant impression in what was clearly a new era. In Great Britain, Margaret Thatcher became the longest-serving prime minister in over 150 years, and her radical, individualistic, conservative approach to public policy reshaped British society. US president Ronald Reagan also made his most significant impact in the 1980s. Although he alienated much of the international community through his unilateralist approach to foreign policy, he restored the American public's sense of pride and played a critical role in ending the Cold War, all the while surviving an international economic downturn that began as he took office in 1981. Trudeau himself, Canada's most colourful prime minister, spent much of his fourth and final term securing his reputation as a forward-looking and aggressive contributor to the evolution of the national fabric. His legacy included a patriated Constitution and a worldwide peace initiative that was met with a mixed response. He was followed in 1984 by a Progressive Conservative, Brian Mulroney, who not only won the greatest majority in Canadian history but also – during his time in office – promised and delivered a free trade agreement with the United States.

John Holmes contemplated his own legacy as the 1980s began. Now seventy years old, when he reflected on his public impact over the previous twenty years, he struggled with his contribution to the development of a misleading understanding of the history of Canada's involvement in world affairs. His fellow citizens were overly romantic about their past, wrapped up in a vision of national selflessness and idealism that had never been real, and his own words and ideas seem to have led them in that direction. A desire to address this mistaken view of his country's national history and to reorient the public towards a more constructive dialogue on world affairs influenced his professional conduct in the early part of the decade. In fact, to some students of his writing and thinking, the John Holmes of the 1980s was a different man from the John Holmes who had presided over the CIIA. Not long before the Soviet Union embraced *glasnost* and *perestroika*, and just as Canadians revisited free trade with the United States, for the first time in over thirty years he broke from his standard approach to international relations. Holmes advocated a new concept of security that embraced forces outside of the traditional state and military-centric realms.[1]

The evolution in his thinking was never complete, but it was indicative of a man who, in spite of his unyielding optimism and faith in the dynamism of Canadian youth, had developed profound concerns about the future of the world around him.

"I recently started a war on the myths of Canadian foreign policy," Holmes wrote to Dan Middlemiss in the spring of 1980. The idea of the national middle power role was out of hand. Holmes had read and heard too much about Canada as the peaceable kingdom and bastion of unselfish idealism. He was tired of lamentations over the lost golden age. His country had never been a faultless, altruistic global player, nor had the early Trudeau era marked its fall from grace. Canada was a state that had always looked out for its own interests in the hopes of fashioning a workable, flexible international system that emphasized mediation and negotiation over brute military strength. It served as a mediator, for instance, when mediation made sense. In the 1940s and 1950s, its impact might well have been more profound, but only because of its temporarily elevated international status and the significance of the global transformation that was under way. Since then, while the government in Ottawa might have lost some of its influence within the military councils of the great powers, its impact on social and economic issues had actually increased.[2]

Holmes brought this message to the Canadian public whenever he could. In 1981, he contributed an article to *Maclean's* magazine that discussed Canada's experience as a peacekeeper: "None of the assignments has been accepted without calculation of the political and economic cost," he wrote. "Insofar as Canada has been successful in foreign policy it has been by adroitly exploiting its circumstances, neither over nor underestimating its power and influence." To a group at a 1983 CIIA conference, he played down the long-term significance of "spectacular ventures in grand diplomacy" like the Suez crisis, noting that the main thrust of Canadian power in world affairs was evident at the socio-economic level. That same year, in a book edited by his friend and colleague Nils Ørvik, he argued that Canada had been far from innocent in its historic approach to international politics. Its successful evolution from British dominion to independent global actor was the result of "a skilful exploitation of two major powers in the interest of a country without a very strong hand to play." It was a style, he wrote elsewhere, that could and should serve as a model for the decolonized nations of Africa.[3]

Nowhere was his thinking better summarized than in his second to last contribution to the *International Journal*, published in the spring of 1984. In "Most Safely in the Middle" he argued that, when it came to foreign affairs, Canadians expected both too much and too little of their political elite. It was unfair to criticize them for failing to serve as world leaders during every international crisis. Canada was not a superpower, and its diplomatic flexibility was limited by geopolitics, the national political culture, and the economy's reliance on foreign markets to maintain prosperity at home. Nevertheless, the public deserved better than the directionless debate over Canada's role in the world that echoed on Parliament Hill. What was important was action, and although Canada was not a so-called middle power by divine right or destiny, it remained well placed to perform some of the tasks typically associated with middle powers. "Is it so demeaning in a churning world to maintain our peculiar reputation for good sense, moderation, a will to see all sides of a question, and an instinct for compromise?" he asked. "Must we call that mediocrity?" It was an argument for quality over quantity: a request of the political leadership to perform what international role they could effectively rather than wasting time and resources attempting to be everything to everyone.[4]

He made a similar case in his analysis of the history of the United Nations. "The role of the United Nations in the world is shrouded with almost as much mythology as is the history of Canadian foreign policy," he explained to members of the UN Association in Canada. In both instances, unrealistic expectations were to blame. Just like Canada, the global organization was limited in its ability to effect international change on its own. It, too, required the cooperation of the most powerful states and was prone to aggressive rhetoric and pious expressions of intent that could not be sustained at the practical level. The solution was to follow the reality, as opposed to the rhetoric, of Canadian conduct in global affairs: "to accept the world as it is while seeking to change it, to do what can be done rather than abandoning a cause that is less than perfect, creating a world order from the ground up rather than from heaven down, refusing to let the best be the enemy of good and working like hell all night in a committee rather than hollering from the rostrum." The future of international relations both in Canada and abroad had to be found in calm, practical, and rational policy execution.[5]

In the early 1980s, however, Holmes' advice seemed stale. The Cold War was once again heating up, and the rhetoric from both the American and Soviet sides suggested that a third global conflict, this time involving nuclear weapons, could have been imminent. In response, for one of the first times in his adult life, even while he continued to preach evolutionary progress instinctively, John Holmes also contemplated a full-scale re-evaluation of his political philosophy. Perhaps, in an age of nuclear proliferation and environmental degradation, his calm, moderate style had become obsolete. Perhaps security as a whole had to be reconceptualized. "Having held the pragmatic idealist's position for so many years," he wrote to Canada's ambassador for disarmament, Arthur Menzies, "I confess that I find myself becoming somewhat more radicalized ... There is, I think, an argument for sober people calling out rather shrilly, 'Hold, enough!'"[6]

In a moment of frustration, he agreed to serve as a founding member of the Group of 78, an association of progressive Canadians dedicated to world peace and international security. The organization, which included close friends like Escott Reid and King Gordon, advocated an end to the threat of nuclear war, international cooperation to eliminate world poverty, and the revitalization of the United Nations as the central body tasked with the promotion of sustainable development and human rights. Holmes' flirtation with social activism peaked in 1982 when he agreed to sign a public letter demanding that Canada become a nuclear free zone, a decision that would have put Ottawa at odds with a request from Washington to test cruise missiles in the Canadian north. Not much later, he disassociated himself from the group, limiting his contribution to financial support, speeches to non-governmental organizations like the Harvey Club (a London branch of the Canadian Medical Coalition for the Prevention of Nuclear War), and academic writing that expressed sympathy for the cause. Political activism, he concluded, was not consistent with his "modest vocation as teacher and explicator." Nonetheless, even joining the Group of 78 would have been unthinkable a few years earlier.[7]

The 1980s also found Holmes participating in conferences that focused on less traditional aspects of international security. He spoke presciently at the First Global Conference on the Future, urging greater international cooperation to solve disputes over global energy policy and resources. He attended a conference organized by the Canadian Council on International Law, which recognized the foreign service for its contribution to global legal affairs. Its recent achievements in negotiations over contentious issues such as the Law of the Sea, which established guidelines for state behaviour in and around the world's oceans, were "every bit as significant as our contributions to world order of a more spectacular kind in the fifties." The meaning of world order had evolved since then: "The central purpose of the system is now the progressive definition of rules and regulations to ensure that we do not kill ourselves off by disease, famine, storm or draught." He wrote to Stephen Woollcombe of the DEA's Science, Technology, and Communications Division about the need to focus more realistically on the security implications of climate control, and he helped coordinate Canadian involvement in a meeting of the World Meteorological Organization in 1983. In a letter the following year, he added prophetically: "I too am becoming increasingly conscious of the fact that environmental security … is at least as urgent as military security."[8] By 1984, he was meeting with groups of scientists regularly, and the future of the natural environment had become a standard consideration in his global outlook. In his final years, he pressed politicians and his academic colleagues to pay more attention to scientific research and the expanding non-governmental community.[9]

This new perspective led to two uncharacteristic conclusions. The first involved Prime Minister Trudeau's 1983 world tour designed to encourage the international community to promote nuclear disarmament and Soviet-American cooperation. To many, it was a utopian adventure by an aging politician whose party was struggling in the polls, one undertaken without much real hope for success and without US support. Such a venture seemed out of touch with the realities of world affairs (where Canada had very little of the hard power that mattered). Holmes promoted it wholeheartedly nonetheless. He argued in front of American and international audiences that, while the global community hesitated to take Trudeau seriously, no leader had publicly dared to reject what he was doing. There were times, he suggested, when it was up to the non-great to remind the superpowers that they had an implicit obligation to lead the world in a progressive manner.[10]

His views on the future of NATO during this period were similarly surprising. In spite of his ongoing frustration with Canada's lack of influence,

Holmes had until recently been a strong supporter of the alliance and of his country's membership within it. By the 1980s, however, his interpretation of how to fulfil this obligation was changing. Pierre Trudeau reduced Canada's overseas contribution to NATO by half when he first arrived in office, and by the mid-1980s, in the midst of economic cutbacks to reduce a rising fiscal deficit at home, there were renewed calls to withdraw Canadian troops from Europe altogether. Holmes was sympathetic to the idea. In thinking that hearkened back to his assessment of the organization in 1957, he suggested that, between his own country's failure to plan strategically, and a trend among the NATO allies to view the organization as a two-pronged dumbbell rather than as the multilateral forum that it once had been, it made sense for Canada to shift its priorities elsewhere. Ottawa could also better defend its strategic resources if its military personnel were located closer to home.

Holmes rejected the popular argument that defence expenditures were tied directly to international influence. As he explained to Canada's chief of the defence staff, General Gerald Thériault, no amount of money could provide their country with greater power within the structure that NATO had become. In the 1980s, he wrote with regret, the alliance had evolved into little more than "something we do under pressure from the Americans for the benefit of the Europeans." Ottawa's membership remained important for symbolic reasons, but the extent of its contribution did not.[11]

This frustration over the tendency of the international community to presume that Canadian and American interests were identical in discussions of international security revealed itself one final time in 1987. That February, Holmes was approached by the renowned Harvard historian Ernest May to participate in a worldwide project designed to chronicle the nuclear era. There were four steering committees guiding the exercise: three in Europe and one in North America. Although May hoped to call the latter the Canada-US committee, the Europeans preferred the term "American." Holmes objected to the invitation and to the forty-page great power-centric project outline that came along with it. He even went so far as to suggest that Canadian academics might be more helpful to what was an obviously exclusive project if they formed their own separate working group and submitted their findings independently. His response, he explained, represented "a growing exasperation in this country with our persistent exclusion from a community which we helped found and in which we have firmly believed but which is now regarded as simply a somewhat confrontational association between an imaginary body called Europe and a far-from-imaginary body called America, which is, however, more properly called the United States." Holmes compromised after discussing the situation with his academic colleagues. A representative did attend the steering committee's discussions and reported back to a national working group that began its own study into Canada's historical role in the nuclear question.[12]

As much as he tried in these later years, John Holmes could not avoid the topic of Canadian-American relations. In early 1980, he accepted the Centre for International Studies' offer of a Bissell professorship. The honour had been established in 1972 by a group of American alumni of the U of T. (In 1983, that same group created the John Holmes Scholarship recognizing a University of Toronto international relations specialist with the highest grade point average in his or her second year of studies.) When Bob Spencer realized that he could not convince Denis Stairs to spend a year in Toronto, Holmes became his first choice. After a brief negotiation, he agreed to accept a series of stipends totalling $40,000, along with a $5,000 expense account, in exchange for a commitment to present a set of public lectures on the Canada-United States relationship and to maintain a presence on the university campus.[13]

Holmes gave his first well-attended talk in November 1980, and he spoke again in January and March 1981. A few months later, he expanded the three lectures into a five-chapter book called *Life with Uncle: The Canadian-American Relationship*. In it, he emphasized the history of conflict and cooperation that had characterized the relationship since its inception. Crises were so normal, he argued, that to call them so was to exaggerate their seriousness. What made interaction between the two countries unique was the way in which they handled their disagreements. Canadians rarely demanded genuine equality – an absurd notion considering the disparities in size and power between them and their neighbour – while the United States generally treated Canada fairly even though it did not have to. "If there is a certain theme in these essays," he concluded, "it is that life with Uncle Sam will always be strenuous but that it can be reasonably comfortable and profitable if we take it calmly and pragmatically."[14]

Although Holmes would have willingly admitted that his words had included little, if any, new thinking, they did represent a masterful summary of his moderate attitude towards the United States.[15] They also made for an excellent short book that the University of Toronto Press could market on both sides of the border, a necessity if Holmes sought publication because RIK Davidson's team was facing a serious financial challenge. The editorial decision to place a deliberately provocative cartoon-like picture of Uncle Sam pointing his finger directly at the reader on the cover – the same photograph that had been used in recruiting drives for the US military during both world wars – was therefore understandable. The resolution to do so without Holmes' knowledge or approval, however, was less respectable, and he reacted to it with horror. Two letters of dismay reached the publisher within days, and Holmes felt obliged to contact a number of his US colleagues personally to reassure them that his book was not another Canadian tirade against the evils of contemporary America.[16]

Reviewers, all Canadian, hardly noticed. The only significant criticism came from ideologues who complained that the author had been too kind to the administration in Washington. Most agreed with University of Victoria professor Walter Young, who wrote that the collection contained "enough insight, wisdom, and wit to make it one of the most significant books on Canadian-American relations since *The New Romans*."[17] Sales reflected Young's sentiment. The book sold over six thousand copies. In 1984, two of Holmes' students, Daizo Sakaruda and Yoshi Kawasaki, took it upon themselves to solicit a Japanese edition. Translated by a good friend, Dr. Kaz Okuda, and equipped with a new introduction, the volume appeared in 1985.[18]

The following year, Holmes accepted the J.B. Tyrrell Historical Medal, an award from the Royal Society of Canada recognizing a lifetime of contributions to the study of the history of Canada. Continuing to view himself as an amateur historian, he remarked: "I wonder what the real historians will think of this. The only reason I can think of for possibly deserving it is that I have helped a lot of younger scholars write some very good things on the history of Canadian foreign policy. Of that I am quite proud, and I suppose it makes me a kind of second-hand historian."[19]

Life with Uncle was popular in part because of the marked deterioration in the Canadian-American relationship that was taking place in the early 1980s. In the aftermath of the failure of the Vietnam War, radicals in Canada and around the world revelled in the perceived decline of the United States as a global superpower. Americans, led by Ronald Reagan, replied by setting aside years of reasonably cooperative relations with the United Nations and adopting a unilateralist, and indeed militaristic, approach to world affairs. Reagan's decisiveness provided a contrast to Jimmy Carter's uncertainty and propelled him to a dramatic election victory in November 1980, but the initial impact of his aggressive Cold War rhetoric on US allies was less impressive. When the Trudeau government implemented its national energy program in the early 1980s, the Canadian-American relationship worsened. The Liberal policy, which was seen to privilege central Canadians over both western Canada and American consumers by keeping domestic oil prices below market rates while charging full price abroad, was taken to task by the US media. The Foreign Investment Review Agency, designed ostensibly to limit American economic expansion north of the border, brought further controversy. *Fortune* magazine described it as part of "Trudeau's War on US Business."[20]

The situation was distressing for Holmes, whose entire conception of international affairs was being contested. For years he had spoken relentlessly about the need for Americans to pay more attention to Canada both at the academic level and in practical policy matters. Finally, the United States was considering more seriously the conduct of its ally to the north, and the results were, in his eyes, amateurish and short-sighted. The American media, he told his U of T colleague and prominent Canadian nationalist Stephen Clarkson, was employing a "scorched earth policy," a "slanderous campaign" against Canadian economic nationalism that had little regard for truth or accuracy. There was a difference, he liked to say, between resistance to the United States – which came naturally to a smaller dependent power like Canada – and genuine anti-Americanism, which was the misguided policy of a crazed few. In Holmes' view, Prime Minister Trudeau intended no harm to President Reagan or the American people; he was merely attempting to promote Canadian economic interests using the same methods as had his US colleagues when they regulated their own industries.[21]

He became even more anxious when the United States invaded Grenada, a Commonwealth country that had been a firm supporter of the Soviet Union during the Cold War. In October 1983, a coup by the deputy prime minister, along with a US-manufactured call for help from the Organization of East Caribbean States, gave the Reagan administration the justification it needed to respond unilaterally. The decision to use military force to support what the administration termed a "rescue mission" was poorly received through much of the international community, upsetting the United States' friends as much as it did its enemies. Washington's veto of a UN Security Council resolution condemning its actions added to the controversy.

Holmes was furious. In a *Toronto Star* article he wrote despondently: "The Americans are in an imperial mood. Flushed with victory over the People's Revolutionary Army of Grenada, they are not listening to others, except, in the imperial manner, to those who exalt them." In so doing, they had abdicated their role as global exemplars. Unlike many of his colleagues who simply vented anti-Americanism, however, he explained his anger. He was disgusted by the US invasion, but he was even more upset that Reagan had been so dismissive of the UN. Holmes still believed that the future stability of the world depended on its effectiveness. The American political system, too often controlled by an irrational Congress, an impatient media, and a public not yet recovered from the loss in Vietnam, wrongly demanded action first and strategy later. The process as a whole was a cause for long-term concern. "Let us find sympathy for our friend and ally burdened by a system of government designed for 18th-century gentlemen, and a world burden for which none of us can offer any answers," he concluded with regret. Nor were Washington's opponents spared his wrath. Those countries that for years had turned the UN into a forum for American-bashing had to assume some of the responsibility for Reagan's unilateralism. Simple anti-Americanism, as he had said so many times before, was no better a policy than US unilateralism. History seemed to be repeating itself, and there was little he could do to stop it.[22]

Holmes had no answers to the US dilemma in these later years. As the increasingly anti-American Liberals under their new leader, John Turner, prepared for the 1984 election, he told his friends that he hoped they would lose. They needed "a chance to learn humility" and to tone down their combative and unhelpful rhetoric. As for Brian Mulroney's Conservatives – who promised to improve relations with the United States significantly – he was hardly more impressed. Assuming responsibility for ruling the country would give the opposition "a chance to grow up," to recognize that there was more to governing than criticizing current policy. Holmes was also not confident that the Canadian-American relationship would recover because, in an attempt to curry favour, "the yahoos" in the Conservative Party could well blindly support the poorly thought out musings of Ronald Reagan. It was not a closer relationship with the United States that Canada needed, he maintained, it was a better one. These ideas were not always synonymous.[23]

As the 1980s progressed, Holmes' views on Canadian politics and the United States remained confusing and obscure. He was furious with American conduct at the UN and on the world stage in general (and the illegal sale of arms to Iran to support the US-backed Contras in Nicaragua in particular), but he was equally flustered by academics and pundits who pointed this out. They caused Washington to retreat further, and the world could not function effectively without US leadership. His October 1985 submission to the Standing Committee on External Affairs and National Defence on defence cooperation in North America was not his best work. When he attempted to summarize his views in a keynote address to the 1987 Couchiching Conference, he again left a perplexing impression.

Calling his talk "The Future of the American Empire," he used it in part to attack a series of misguided decisions that had characterized the Reagan regime: "The Americans are so damned condescending and bossy it is hard to resist the temptation to score points, to get belly laughs and feel morally superior over the hypocrisies in Central America, their two-faced postures on agricultural and other subsidies, their unshakable conviction that their culture is internationalist and ours is nationalist, and their incurable habit of seeing the world in black and white." Nevertheless, he added, the international infrastructure that he and others had worked so hard to create risked collapsing without them.[24]

In retrospect, it is hardly surprising that Holmes opposed Prime Minister Mulroney's free trade initiative (although he never admitted so publicly). He thought it was a sign of national and political desperation that would inevitably result in American domination. Canadian foreign relations were best served by multilateral accords, and bilateral dealings with a more powerful neighbour were never anything but uneven. He did not fear an increase in cultural penetration as a result of the agreement, nor did he share with most free trade opponents a vision of the end of Canadian independence. (Toronto was not in danger of being invaded again, he liked to say, as much as being programmed out of existence by an American computer.) Rather, he believed that it would not be possible for Canada to make a beneficial arrangement. Moreover, the United States was in the midst of an economic decline, and it was the wrong time for Ottawa to be attaching itself more closely to Washington. Nevertheless, even as the Conservatives staked their political future on the success of free trade, Holmes proclaimed privately that he hoped they would win the next election. Apparently, he thought that the rabid anti-Americanism emanating from the Liberal and New Democratic parties was worse for Canada than the impact of increased economic integration.[25]

Holmes' frustrations and inconsistencies were the result of old age and over-exposure. He had spent too long thinking, speaking, and writing about Canadian-American affairs, and now, in his mid-seventies, although he joked about buying a computer and joining the technological revolution, he no longer had the patience to deal with the ideological radicalism that tainted the Canadian discussions. He was tired of issues that never seemed to be resolved, a feeling that was compounded by challenges in his personal life. The death of Harry Beer, a brother-in-law with whom he was particularly close, along with the revelation that his long-time (secret) female lover had cancer made it more difficult for him to focus on a bilateral relationship that, to him, would never change. He tried to maintain his good spirits by spending more time with his nephews and nieces in Hamilton and London. Their views on world affairs, he found, were more thoughtful than were those of the so-called experts.

The experts at the U of T, for example, had all but ruined the Centre for International Studies through their petty complaints and jealousies. While Holmes had been away at Leeds, a number of U of T faculty complained loudly that the colloquia were too focused on traditional security issues and were dominated by current and former government officials. When he learned of the concerns, he resigned from his position as research director. Often defensive about his work as he grew older, he criticized the development scholars who failed to recognize that the sessions he had organized on international institutions, however elitist they might have appeared, set the framework for constructive discussion of how to eliminate the still-growing north-south political and economic divide. He later agreed to return to his duties in a less official capacity, but his commitment was never the same.[26]

The Centre for International Studies continued to offer sessions through the mid-1980s. In 1985, with Bob Spencer set to retire, the centre came up for its five-year review before the School of Graduate Studies. The results were mixed. Concerns continued to be expressed over the quantity of publications arising from the monthly meetings and the lack of engagement of the U of T community. Although the committee recommended extending the centre's funding for three years, the budget-conscious School of Graduate Studies advised that all monies be cut off. Holmes wrote President George Connell personally in an effort to reach a compromise. His argument, that the CIS provided the university with an exceptional means of fostering constructive dialogue with the policy community, was well taken. Eventually, Bill Graham, an international law professor and future Canadian minister of foreign affairs, was recruited to assume responsibility for a much reduced program. Thanks in part to the help of the CIIA (also obtained through Holmes), Graham was able to maintain at least a skeletal organization.[27]

The end of Holmes' teaching experience at the U of T was also disappointing. In the mid-1980s, John Kirton assumed full control of POL 419/2203. Shortly after, historian Robert Bothwell and economist Ian Drummond invited Holmes to join their undergraduate course in Canadian foreign policy at Trinity College. While he accepted, and enjoyed the experience, he received a meagre $3,000 stipend, the amount typically allocated for a half course. By this point, however, it was clear that the contemporary approach to postsecondary education, with its more rigorous enforcement of prescribed grading schemes and attention to administrative detail, was unsuited to his temperament. Holmes rejected a final request from the University of Western Ontario to teach a course in international organization in 1986.

He did continue to supervise PhD students, both formally and informally, but his greatest joys in the teaching environment in his final years took place elsewhere. Sitting in on a model UN conference in Toronto and returning repeatedly to Trent, Western, and Brock as a special visitor allowed him to absorb the academic atmosphere and to lend his sage advice to young minds without the strain of grades and appeals. Even in his seventies, John Holmes retained a special ability to connect with students over fifty years his junior in a way that empowered their thinking and spirits. Equally, their lively discussions could not have been more helpful to an aging yet still sharp professional Canadian internationalist.

With the CIS struggling in the mid-1980s, and his teaching situation at the U of T unclear, Holmes returned to Leeds to recharge. It was in Britain, then, that he celebrated his seventy-fifth birthday. After class, his students, led by the two Kates, known in a typically Holmesian manner as Kate and DupliKate, presented him with a homemade cake adorned with an approximation of a Canadian flag. On the weekend, he had a picnic lunch in Yorkshire with Professor Howard Palmer, his wife Tamara (also an academic), and their two young children. The Palmers were visiting from the University of Calgary, and Howard shared responsibility for Holmes' Canadian Studies course. The two professors became close, as did Holmes and the rest of the Palmer family. He regularly joined them in their car trips across Britain throughout the term. When he was not teaching or touring, Holmes completed an interview about his career with Dilks, which was intended to augment the historical record of the allegedly golden years of Canadian foreign policy. His public lecture was, predictably, a historical consideration of the United Nations, one that represented a summary of his thinking as opposed to an introduction of new ideas.[28]

When he returned, historian Norman Hillmer invited him to Ottawa to attend a fundraiser celebrating his birthday and the CIIA's recent decision to rename its library in his honour. Holmes was both flattered and embarrassed. "Becoming a monument before having been laid to rest is disconcerting," he said to Escott Reid.[29] Not much later, he reached into his desk at the institute, pulled out his trusted bottle of sherry, poured himself and a staff member a drink, and remarked on how terrible it would be if there were to be a John Holmes school with a football team. He could just envision the newspaper headline: "Pearson thumps Holmes." The library was a safer bet, he reflected with his trademark humility.

Holmes was also fortunate to find a number of other projects that kept his otherwise preoccupied spirits high. The first, which coincided nicely with his election to the World Association for International Relations, a non-profit group mandated to promote the study of foreign policy around the world, was coordinated by the ambitious founding dean of the University of Minnesota's Hubert H. Humphrey Institute of Public Affairs, Harlan Cleveland. Cleveland was one year away from retirement in 1986, and he chose to use this year to organize a global consortium of experts to "rethink international governance." Holmes, who had known Cleveland when they both worked in government, was one of twenty senior thinkers recruited into the study.[30]

The second project was the result of a January 1986 discussion between representatives of the John Sloan Dickey Center for International Understanding at Dartmouth College and the New York Office of the United Nations University. Like Holmes, the participants at the original meeting were deeply worried by the United States' non-participation in UN initiatives during the Reagan years. Their response was to strive to improve relations between academics who were studying international cooperation and the UN itself. Gene Lyons, who soon became the executive director of what would eventually be known as the Academic Council on the United Nations System (ACUNS), contacted Holmes shortly after their first discussion and asked him to join a steering committee to help recruit Canadians into the project. Although ACUNS initially hoped to attract scholars from around the world, the founders concluded that, as a start, it was best to focus on North America.

The planning team benefited from Holmes' presence almost immediately. Victor Urquidi, a former World Bank employee who had spent the last twenty years as president of the Colegio de México, joined the group as Holmes' Mexican equivalent and proposed that the organization commit itself to supporting and indeed promoting the United Nations and the UN system more generally. Others countered that such an approach detracted from the academic nature of the project and would deny the new council the reputation for objectivity that it needed in order to have a real impact. It was Holmes who acted as the mediating voice, suggesting that the council support all high-quality studies of the UN system, regardless of their conclusions. If the UN were a worthwhile institution, then proponents would have nothing to fear.

Holmes embraced the project in its entirety. He recruited support from the DEA, the Canadian Institute for International Peace and Security, the U of T, and from former colleagues and students like Margaret Doxey, Harald von Riekhoff, and Elizabeth Riddell-Dixon. In late 1987 he helped develop a questionnaire for Canadian academics and policy practitioners to evaluate their interest in and commitment to internationalism. It sought detail about their relevant scholarly publications and courses that included international content. The educational aspect excited Holmes the most – finally, it seemed, there would be others sharing ideas to help teach the next generation about global affairs and international institutions. Over ninety surveys were returned to his office at the CIIA, and he invited each respondent to join the new council. Most of them did. It was exhausting work for a man in his mid-seventies, but it was rewarding. His additional responsibilities included attendance at a summer 1987 meeting at Dartmouth, at another in Ottawa, and the organization of a provisional conference meeting of Canadian, American, and Mexican representatives in Toronto that December, during which he served as vice-chair. He was honoured later that year when Lyons asked him to give the keynote address at the organization's founding meeting, scheduled for June 1988.[31]

The two international projects were voluntary, and Holmes financed his participation in them through contract assignments with the DEA. Along with writing reports, attending conferences, participating in a significant research project on Canadian-Soviet relations, and giving speeches abroad, he was invited to chair the editorial board responsible for producing a departmental history. The project had been through a degree of turmoil – a first draft by one staff member had been met with significant criticism – and it was Holmes' job to ensure the scholarly integrity of the final result. Doing so included lobbying Secretary of State for External Affairs Joe Clark to retain the DEA's Historical Division in the face of calls for its elimination and then reading and commenting on each chapter as it was submitted for consideration. The first volume was nearly complete at the end of 1987.[32]

The DEA also recognized Holmes' lifetime contributions to Canada and its place in the world by granting him special observer status on the Canadian delegation to the UN General Assembly. In the falls of 1985, 1986, and 1987, he was one of eight distinguished citizens invited to spend close to two weeks in New York with the delegation, watching, learning, and advising as appropriate. Ottawa paid for his travel costs and his accommodation, and provided him with a modest living allowance while he was away. The trips gave a legendary internationalist the chance to say goodbye to an institution that had been so dear to him for so many years. He returned to Toronto each time with renewed faith in the future of the world order and in the Canadian diplomatic team.[33]

Of all of these professional experiences, the most memorable took place in the fall of 1987. In December 1980, Georgi Arbatov, the director of the Institute of the USA and Canada at the Academy of Sciences of the USSR, invited Holmes to spend two weeks in the Soviet Union as his guest. At the time, Holmes feared that such a visit would be frowned upon by the DEA, and even after he received reassurance, he allowed other priorities to intervene. By 1987, however, he suspected that his age and health would soon prevent him from significant travel. When Geoffrey Pearson of the Canadian Institute for International Peace and Security offered him the opportunity to accept Arbatov's old invitation, he immediately agreed. To justify his inclusion, Holmes represented the CIIA, but in reality he was being given a final chance to return to a country that he had not visited since 1955.

The Canadian delegation included a number of prominent academics and practitioners, among them Ernie Regehr of Project Ploughshares, a non-profit branch of the Council of Canadian Churches dedicated to promoting international peace; Bob Matthews, the son of a former colleague of Holmes' and a well-respected political scientist at the U of T; Bernard Wood, one of Peter Dobell's first employees at the Parliamentary Centre and now the head of the innovative North-South Institute, the first independent, non-partisan think tank in Canada devoted specifically to development issues; and Pearson himself, a former ambassador to the Soviet Union. The group met twice before the mission to become acquainted; most stayed in touch afterwards. While they were abroad, Holmes was recognized as the senior member, even if Regehr and his recent work on prospects for the end of the Cold War attracted most of the Soviets' attention.

The visit combined sight-seeing and independent travel with formal meetings and brainstorming sessions. Holmes' presentation to the CIIA concentrated on the United Nations and its potential contribution to greater international cooperation. He suggested ways in which the Soviets could become more actively involved in cooperative multilateral ventures and attempted to find common ground with them on questions of northern sovereignty and international peacekeeping. The trip was punctuated by an unexpected experience in one of Moscow's newest hotels. On the final morning at breakfast, just before the group boarded the flight home, Holmes emerged from his room bewildered. It appears that when the hotel's management learned that the Canadians were leaving, someone had arranged for every delegate to receive a late-night phone call from a mysterious woman offering her company. "Leave me alone," Holmes had replied, "I'm too old." The group had a good laugh. John Holmes, the ultimate gentleman, could still bring a smile to anyone's face.[34]

Looking back, the 1980s were challenging for John Holmes. The world was changing, and it became difficult to keep up both personally and professionally. He began to doubt some of his longest-held beliefs about Canada and world order, but he no longer had the energy to sort through the new problems and paradoxes with the same vigour as he had been able to muster as a foreign service officer or CIIA director general. The encouragement of his friends, family, and colleagues kept him unusually active for a man his age, but his years as Canada's leading voice in world affairs had come to an end. It was finally time, he was forced to admit, to retire.

14

Saying Goodbye

By the time that John Holmes reached his seventy-eighth year, there were signs that his life was approaching its end. Having taken out a new insurance policy with the CIIA as his beneficiary, a near crash on a tiny airplane headed for Dartmouth hardly flustered him. His personal health also declined, although he did his best to keep himself, and his family, together. "Death and sickness and distress all around me," he wrote to a new friend and confidant, the acclaimed Canadian poet Patrick Lane: "I am the head of an extensive family, surrogate father, uncle and grandfather, which has had its troubles of late, and mine is the shoulder to lie on." Lane had helped him overcome a bout of depression – what Holmes had called emotional constipation – that November, and their discussions by mail over the next five months provided the emotional outlet he needed in order to continue.[1]

Holmes was mentally exhausted, and he was also physically ill. The trouble began when he arrived home from Moscow in the fall. He was in significant pain, noticeably more than that to which his aging body had become accustomed. Since it was largely in his back, a place that had given him trouble for much of his life (and especially after long flights), he ignored it. His family doctor had also just moved away, and he did not have a regular physician to see even if he had wanted to. The pain intensified, and for a time he walked with a cane. As it became more difficult to function, he was convinced to visit an out-patient clinic that had just been established at Women's College Hospital in Toronto. The doctors suspected a problem with his prostate and made him an appointment with a urologist. Holmes was fairly certain that he had cancer before that Christmas. Once he was sure, he called Al Woytasik, a nephew by marriage and, by that point, one of his most trusted friends. It was Woytasik who initially helped take care of him when he later took ill from the radiation therapy. He was not comfortable with his female relatives seeing him in such a weakened state. Woytasik could also be trusted not to reveal his condition to anyone until after the holidays. Holmes refused to ruin the most important family gathering of the year with his news. After informing his closest relatives, he continued to deny his condition to most friends and colleagues. At times, however, he could not help himself. Just before another set of treatments began, Mark Anshan was at his apartment and the two gazed out the window of his living room towards the Rosedale Valley. In a fit of frustration, Holmes raised his voice, "Dammit, why is this happening to me?" Anshan was shocked by the uncharacteristic outburst; only then did he begin to realize the pain that his mentor was feeling. It was not just the physical disability: it was the loss of control over his life, the uncertainty, the general sense of helplessness.

Officially, the diagnosis was metastatic cancer caused by an enlarged and malignant prostate. The doctors removed it successfully in late March 1988, and Holmes was told that he would live for months, if not years. He probably would have, had the initial diagnosis come sooner. Instead, back in London visiting family, the pain returned, and this time it spread to his leg. Not long after, the Holmeses, Beers, and Skinners made plans to see a movie, and Uncle John, looking much thinner than usual, hesitated out of fear that he would not be able to sit through it. Perhaps recognizing his importance to the family's good spirits, he went, and his decision brought smiles to the faces around him. In Toronto, however, there was more disappointing news. The cancer had metastasized to his bones, and there was no cure, only a variety of means of controlling the pain. The spring and early summer of 1988 were divided between London and Toronto. Eventually, his niece, Ann Skinner, returned to Ontario and moved into his apartment to support him as he went in and out of the hospital. By this point, Holmes could no longer enforce his old-fashioned and indeed paternalistic desire that the women in his life – generally his strongest and most capable supporters – be shielded from his grief.

He remained determined and brave. In May, feeling better, and still not having revealed the extent of his illness, he returned to the CIIA. "I am sufficiently recovered to be spending most afternoons in the office," he wrote Harald von Riekhoff. "I expect to be available here a good deal of the time. Let me know when you would like to come and talk about the good old days of foreign policy. I have been working my way through some old papers of late and would be most interested in having you confront me with things I wrote long ago."[2] There was another invitation from Joe Clark to return as special advisor to the Canadian UN delegation in New York, which had to be declined; an interview to complete with Peter Stursberg for a book the journalist was writing about his old friend, Roland Michener; and grades to submit for a pair of student independent study projects that he had agreed to supervise on a volunteer basis at the U of T. He also finished his keynote speech for the inaugural ACUNS conference, worked on a number of book chapters that he had promised to write, and gave his final approval to the first volume of the Department of External Affairs' official history.[3] The visits to the CIIA lasted intermittently until mid-July, allowing him to fulfil the majority of his remaining commitments.

On the days when he lacked the strength to work but still felt strong enough to socialize, he and Skinner welcomed visitors to his apartment. For Kim Nossal, it was surreal: his visit that spring marked the first time he had seen his mentor in pyjamas. For others, it was horrifying: they could not stand to see such a strong man grow so frail. Still more left care packages but could not bear to come in. Nevertheless, Holmes kept his sense of humour. During one of Holmes' longer visits to the hospital, Margaret Doxey, too far away to come by, asked Gayle Fraser if she could send flowers. No, replied Fraser, Holmes would much prefer Belgian chocolate. Not much later Doxey received a note of thanks: "Don't tell the KGB [Committee for State Security (of the former Soviet Union)] where I'm vulnerable," he wrote. Others withdrew altogether, their memories of John Holmes too precious to be staled by the state of his physical decline.

Over time the pain became worse. He avoided taking morphine for as long as he could because he could not stomach living his final days with his faculties inhibited. There were times when this meant sitting up all night, but the struggle was preferable to intellectual incoherence. His selfless nature also remained steady. Before he had taken ill, Holmes had agreed to allow one of his great-nieces, Wendy, to spend a long weekend with her friends at his cottage. As his situation deteriorated she wondered whether it would still be appropriate. When he learned that she was having second thoughts he called and insisted that she go. There was no need for others to suffer on his account. Similarly, when his nephew Charles' daughter Stephanie graduated high school that June he insisted on driving into Toronto from the cottage to attend, even though he was too sick to do so comfortably. Viewing the ceremony was so taxing that he missed the celebratory dinner that evening. Later that month he could not give his speech to ACUNS. By July, the number of real conversations that he could sustain had become fewer and further between. The morphine had reduced him to a frail shell of his former self.

Not long before he died, Holmes took Woytasik aside and asked him when the summer course he had been taking at the U of T's Faculty of Education was scheduled to end. It was a strange question, but Woytasik saw no reason to deny that Friday, 12 August, was his last day. Never one to impose or interfere, and forever afraid of becoming a burden, Holmes held on. That Friday evening, after Woytasik's class finished, a helicopter ambulance air-lifted an ailing elderly man from Toronto to London. The hospital in Holmes' home town had an excellent palliative care unit, and it was only two blocks from his sister Isobel and his niece Nancy's apartment. The Holmes family had debated bringing him home earlier, but they had concluded, wisely, that so long as he had his faculties, he would be happiest in his apartment with his friends and his work. Now that his desk at the CIIA was clear, he came back to London and spent his final hours in greater physical comfort. He died the next day. That week, the first Canadian members of a twenty-five-nation peacekeeping force tasked with monitoring a truce in the Iran-Iraq war left for the Middle East. More ironically, at about the same time, the United States House of Representatives voted in favour of free trade.

A visitation was arranged for the following Monday at the Needham Memorial Chapel on Dundas Street. The funeral itself, a private family affair, was set for Tuesday, 16 August. Holmes' relatives mourned their loss in the company of a number of members of the CIIA. Gayle Fraser, who had been on a much needed vacation in Nova Scotia, flew back to Toronto and proceeded to London with Executive Director David Stafford and a number of other loyal workers. It was Stafford who had asked the family's permission to attend the ceremony. That morning, as Fraser and Ann Skinner ate their breakfast at a coffee shop in town, they picked up a copy of the *London Free Press* and read a heart-felt tribute by another former Holmes protégé, Keith Spicer. Holmes had offered advice on Spicer's first book on foreign aid, and the two had remained friends. The article reduced them both to tears.

Spicer's obituary, "John Holmes: A Great and *Good* Man," first printed in the *Ottawa Citizen* on 15 August, was one of many dedications that appeared in newspapers across the country and throughout the North Atlantic community. Beautifully written, it likely affected more than just Fraser and Skinner. "His contribution as diplomat and intellectual to Canada – and to world peace – was rightly assessed as seminal ... Holmes wore the cap of a gentleman with such ease that for many he defined the idea of graciousness ... in his discreet but brilliant way, he led two generations of Canadians to believe that – middle power or little power – they could make a difference in the world." He had faith in both ideas and ideals, Spicer wrote, he welcomed spirited dialogue, he was unflinchingly loyal, and he was generous with his time and spirit.[4]

In an obituary for the *Independent* in the United Kingdom, David Dilks added, "He was described with general acceptance as 'a national resource' but his friendships and influence extended far beyond North America. Sceptical but never cynical, wedded to principle but not ostentatious in parading it, a practical idealist, he remained firmly Canadian, and perhaps did more than anyone else to explain how a power of middle rank should conduct its international relations." According to Bob Reford, "he had the wisdom of experience, and he had the instinctive wisdom of when to act or not to act, when to speak and when to keep silent." In an issue of the DEA journal, *bout de papier*, John Halstead wrote: "John Holmes had the knack of shedding new light on old truths, of going to the heart of the matter and of winning understanding for unpleasant facts with wit and elegance. His simplicity was never oversimplified and his objectivity was never offensive." "Humility was his hallmark," he added, "tolerance was his touchstone and moderation was his motto. All who knew him, either personally or by reputation, will continue to be nurtured by his spirit for long years to come." Denis Stairs called him "the essence of Canadian civilization at its best."[5] Finally, when the Fletcher School of Diplomacy professor, Alan Henrikson, learned of Holmes' death, he wrote to Fraser:

> I felt that one of the lights of North America had gone out, and yet that he had empowered all the rest of us to shine, more brilliantly and especially more warmly, than we ever could have without having known him, and without having had him know us. I am a different person for having met John Holmes. I know it. He knew it. He set high standards for us, and at the same time personified understanding and tolerance. In these essential "human" qualities, quite apart from his unmistakably distinctive wit and style, which no one else could ever imitate, he emanated civilization, of the most universal and eternal kind.[6]

In part because the funeral was a private affair, a more formal memorial service was planned for Toronto. Until then, in lieu of flowers, sympathizers were encouraged to donate to the Holmes Library at the CIIA, and many did. One of Holmes' greatest immediate legacies was the expansion of the institute's academic resources, something that would have made him proud. Two memorial services, both coordinated in part by the CIIA, followed. After the Faculty Council at the U of T passed a resolution regretting Holmes' death, the university agreed to hold the first ceremony in its medical sciences auditorium. On 27 September 1988, over three hundred people crowded into the hall to pay their respects. The venue was so full that the organizers added an overflow room from which attendees could listen to the service through a speaker system. The program was moderated by the CIIA's president, Gary Posen, and included tributes from speakers associated with nearly every aspect of Holmes' professional career. Charles Ritchie knew him first as a junior member of the East Block, Basil Robinson became a friend during the golden period, and Doug LePan was there for the highs and the lows. Gordon Hawkins worked with him at the CIIA; Albert Tucker hired him at York; Kim Nossal was one of his brightest students at the U of T; Bob Spencer was a colleague at the Centre for International Studies; and, finally, David Stafford was a new friend who had developed an appreciation for Holmes and his lifelong contributions to the CIIA and Canadian life during his final years. Ann Skinner, representing the family, read a Shakespearean sonnet (Number 73), and Anne Thompson's flute provided the musical accompaniment that was so important to Holmes' life.

In their comments, his diplomatic colleagues were the most eloquent. To Ritchie, Holmes had been a "touchstone of integrity, astute judgment, and common sense ... He was a man, a good man, good without dullness, tolerant of almost everything except intolerance, who set his standards high, and never let a friend down." Robinson called him "the patient builder, the soul of integrity, with the brilliant mind, the human heart, the kindly courtesies, the wonderful sense of fun, servant of his nation and the world, mentor to so many of us, and very dear friend." Others were equally generous with their praise and admiration.[7] The university's radio station covered what was in many ways a national event. Peter Mueller, a former student, listened to the ceremony as he was driving. Instinctively, he made his way towards Mount Pleasant Cemetery with tears in his eyes. There, he parked his car and cried.

Three weeks later, thanks in part to the support of the DEA, over two hundred people gathered at the Lester B. Pearson Building in Ottawa for a second service. This time Halstead, the chair of the capital branch of the CIIA, played host, and the speakers included close friend Escott Reid, former junior colleague Si Taylor, historian David Farr, and former ambassador to the UN Yvon Beaulne. Not much later, the Americas Society in New York renamed its lecture series in Holmes' honour, and Marshall Leslie, a student at Glendon, spearheaded the establishment of a John Holmes Memorial Fund at York, the proceeds of which supported another annual public lecture on international relations by a noted expert.[8]

Other honours followed. Shortly after their inaugural conference, the ACUNS executive named their annual keynote lecture after John Holmes. In 1989, the Lionel Gelber Foundation awarded the CIIA $15,000 to begin work on archiving his papers. By the time Gayle Fraser finished, it had increased the grant to $23,000. In 1996, thirty years after their first meeting, then Canadian foreign minister Lloyd Axworthy created a foreign policy outreach fund dedicated to John Holmes' memory. The $1 million endowment was meant to strengthen the participation of non-governmental organizations in the policy-making process. Finally, in 2004, the CIIA's *International Journal* launched its inaugural John W. Holmes issue on Canadian foreign policy, a fitting tribute to the man who had been so crucial to the journal's evolution and to writing about Canada's position in the world as a whole.

Holmes' posthumous publications were mixed. His contribution to *Canada and the New Internationalism*, conference proceedings that John Kirton largely edited but for which he insisted that both share the credit, was vague and unhelpful, reflective of an analyst who seemed to be writing only because he had been asked to and could not bring himself to say no.[9] Other pieces were better. His personal reflections on the early Cold War for a collection of essays edited by Norman Hillmer were thoughtful and revealing. A generous review of the Merchant-Heeney Report (twenty years on) for a book edited by Kim Nossal was a reasonable summary of his moderate approach to Canadian-American relations and his disappointment with the Reagan regime. He was both critical and effective in his two studies of the United States for Lansing Lamont of the Council of the Americas, and Lamont became one of a number of academics who dedicated books to his memory in the late 1980s and early 1990s.[10]

Considering his commitment to teaching, it is fitting that the best publication to emerge after his death was included in the second edition of a political science textbook edited by Bob Matthews. "The United Nations and World Order" was a straightforward, accessible summary of the UN and its evolving role on the international stage. It began with a bit of Holmesian wisdom that students would find easy to appreciate: "Conflict among states," he argued, "is natural and not necessarily sinful. Conflicting interests have existed since tribal times, and disputes among states are likely to increase. That is not necessarily a bad thing because it reflects the increased interdependence of peoples and expanding global communications, and is likely to promote a wider sense of responsibility for the international community for resisting the escalation of controversy ... The test of civilization, then, is not in the existence of conflict but in the means of settlement." Holmes went on to make his standard case about the inevitability of the UN as eloquently as he ever had.[11]

On 11 April 1989, Gayle Fraser opened a letter from Roy Cadwell, the director of Lester B. Pearson Peace Park in Tweed, Ontario. Holmes had been awarded the organization's Man of the Year Peace Award in recognition of his outstanding contribution to world order and Canadian unity. Pierre Trudeau was a previous recipient. Although Holmes obviously could not collect this unique honour, he left behind a text that might well have served as a basis for an acceptance speech. His brief essay, "What Peace Means to Me," was never published in a major venue, but it so captures his thinking and general wisdom that it deserves to be considered here in full:

> The search for peace is not an end in itself. Peace is a by-product of harmony, equilibrium and security. It is the ways and means of securing these that should preoccupy us. For the individual there can be peace as a state of grace, and the more who achieve the state the more likely we are to get international harmony. It is a mistake, however, to assume that we can achieve on this awkward planet a state of peace, perfect peace, free of conflict. Conflict is human, inevitable and to a degree healthy. Conflict of interest among the diverse peoples of the world is natural. But, as Canadians have discovered in several centuries of co-habitation with a neighbour who could defeat us militarily in half an hour, the measure of civilization is in the ways and means not of exorcizing conflict but of coping with it by the fairest means possible.
>
> There is no quick fix for peace. It requires infinite travail and patience not only in these dangerous times; it will have to be managed now and ever more. By what means we mortals can manage to keep the peace, at least relatively, is the problem. The agenda is enormous and complex. There is no simple global structure on which we can cast our burdens, and there is no use saying that there ought to be. The best is too often the enemy of the good. Utopians insisting intolerantly on their impossible dreams too often discourage those who labour in the field from building a variegated infrastructure, stone by stone.
>
> The structures are much stronger and more flexible than they were forty years ago. One advantage of having watched the evolution of international

institutions for the past fifty years or so is that I can see the prolific growth
of bodies, national, regional and universal, which manage some of the most
basic requirements of international life, such as communications, so well
that we take them for granted. Some of them are successful, some are not;
some are groping, but on these we build. The pattern is far from neat, and
the waste is prolific. Nevertheless, there is real substance to world order.
Whether there is enough to confront the challenges of the planet is a question, but those who throw up their hands don't help. As a participant in a
Physicians for Social Responsibility meeting I attended recently said, "We
don't achieve much by just going on frightening ourselves to death."

World order is exceedingly volatile, and probably always will be. We have
to keep the earth on as even a keel as possible, and that won't be exactly
even. The concept of balance of power has been discredited, but it was an
imbalance of power that led to the Second World War. There is no substitute
at the moment for the prudent balancing of power, at least until the grim
necessities of planetary control have tamed us into discretion. Call it equilibrium if you prefer. Mutual assured destruction is indeed a MAD way to
keep the peace for long, but when it has become part of the shaky structure
of equilibrium at this dangerous stage we should be wary of upsetting it
unless in the course of transition to something more stable.

Equilibrium requires prudence at all levels, between the super-powers
certainly, but also among the lesser powers of the first, second and third
worlds. Simple preservation of the *status quo* is perilously destabilizing. We
need change and movement under control. That cannot be achieved without multilateral instruments, especially by productive use of the sprawling
United Nations system. The super-powers may have most say on the critical
issues, nuclear weapons, but there will be no equilibrium without movement and balance on all the other issues, most of which are on the agenda
of UN bodies. Economic progress will not automatically bring peace, but
there can be no peace without hope of it. It would be simpler, of course, if
the super-powers could run the world, but they can't, and they have to be
made to face in co-operation with the rest of us the universal problems. We
must, however, understand their responsibilities and not assume that as we
are weaker we are more peaceful.

Shouting and marching for peace does serve a purpose, particularly if it
crosses frontiers, but the danger is that we leave it at that, disdaining from
a high moral posture the laborious work on the nuts and bolts. Too often it
is based on the mistaken notion that, whereas "the people" love peace, politicians and bureaucrats don't. In this nuclear age there must be few political
leaders and even fewer diplomats with any appetite for war. It is they who

have to exercise prudence and seek compromise because the "people" too often make demands that are incompatible with peaceful relations among states. We have to assert our will for peace and reduction of arms to disturb complacency in both high and low places, but our sermons will be more effective if they are preached with due humility and with proposals that do not require miracles.[12]

No other text so effectively captures John Holmes' well-honed approach to world order: his desire – as was reflected in his own life experiences – to resolve conflicts amicably, to approach global politics realistically, and never to give up hope. He was and remains the idealized voice of Canada in the world: firm but fair, demanding yet compassionate, at times depressing but also inspirational. For half a century, he was a tireless servant of his country and the wider world: an excellent planner, exceptional teacher and mentor, non-governmental leader, reliable friend, and general fountain of wisdom. He brought together students, academics, and policy practitioners in ways that enriched the national dialogue and promoted mutual respect and understanding. He would have been the first to admit that he was not perfect, but his overwhelmingly positive attributes reflected the very best of what it means to be Canadian, a perception for which he deserves disproportionate responsibility for shaping around the world. Diplomat, gentleman, Canadian: there will never be another quite like John Wendell Holmes.

Notes

CHAPTER 1: THE EARLY YEARS

1 John Holmes, "Growing Up WASP," n.d., Trinity College Archives, Toronto, John Holmes Papers 002-0001 (hereafter Holmes Papers), box 74, file E/II/7.

2 Ibid.

3 Much of this information is derived from conversations with John Holmes' friends and members of his family. To protect their privacy, further references to these conversations are limited. Academic specialists who are interested in this book for specific research purposes are invited to contact the author privately to discuss the sources of these and subsequent undocumented observations and comments.

4 Holmes, "Growing Up WASP," n.d., Holmes Papers, box 74, file E/II/7.

5 Holmes, "Pro Patria," *Oracle* (1927), London South Collegiate Institute Archives, Peter Telford Papers.

6 Holmes, "Growing Up WASP," Holmes Papers, box 74, file E/II/7.

7 John R.W. Gwynne-Timothy, *Western's First Century* (London, ON: University of Western Ontario, 1978), 251-73.

8 *Occidentalia* (1929), 44, University of Western Ontario Archives, London, Ontario (hereafter UWOA).

9 E.J. Wright, quoted in *Occidentalia* (1930), 41, UWOA.

10 The Editor [Holmes], "Dear Fellow Students," The *Gazette* (9 October 1930): 2, UWOA, *U of W.O. Gazette* 23 (1930-31).

11 Holmes, "The Gazette," *Occidentalia* (1931): 109, UWOA.

12 Deacon to Holmes, 4 April 1932, Holmes Papers, box 67, file 4.

13 Class prophesy by Ruth Hayes and John Kevin O'Connor, UWOA, University of Western Ontario Scrapbook, vol. 5, 1930-32.

14 Holmes to Deacon, cited in Clara Thomas and John Lennox, *William Arthur Deacon: A Canadian Literary Life* (Toronto: University of Toronto Press, 1982), 166. The League for Social Reconstruction (LSR) was founded in 1931 by a group of left-wing intellectuals in

Montreal and Toronto. Although never formally aligned with a particular political party, members' sympathies clearly lay with what became in 1932 the Co-operative Commonwealth Federation (CCF). J.S. Woodsworth, the CCF's first president, was the LSR's honorary president throughout the 1930s.

15 Holmes, "Dedication," 15 August 1985, Holmes Papers, box 89, file G/I/14. Arthur Garrett Dorland Friends Historical Collection, speech at Pickering College.

16 J.W. Holmes, "Valedictory of Class of 1932," UWOA, University of Western Ontario Scrapbook, 5 (1930-32). Class Day Exercises of the Graduating Class of 1932, Friday, 27 May 1932. See also James J. Talman and Ruth David Talman, *"Western": 1878-1953* (London, ON: University of Western Ontario, 1953), 111-51.

17 C.A.M. Edwards, *Taylor Statten: A Biography* (Toronto: Ryerson Press, 1960), 103.

18 Hedley G. "Bill" Dimock, quoted in Liz Lundell, ed., *Fires of Friendship: Eighty Years of the Taylor Statten Camps* (Toronto: Fires of Friendship Books, 2000), 18.

19 H.J. Cody, *University of Toronto: President's Report for the Year Ending 20th June 1933* (Toronto: University of Toronto, 14 December 1933), 4.

20 The consistency between Holmes' views in 1923 and those summarized by colleagues who reflected on his thinking between 1960 and 1988 is striking. See Marion Magee and Charles Pentland, "A Tribute to John W. Holmes," *International Journal* 44, 4 (1989): 741-42.

21 Holmes, "Border Relations between Canada and the United States during the American Civil War" (MA thesis: University of Toronto, 1933).

22 Fox, 21 September 1932; Dorland, 18 October 1932; and Ford, 7 October 1932. All cited in Holmes, "1932 Application for Imperial Order Daughters of the Empire War Memorial Postgraduate Scholarships," Holmes Papers, box 100, CIIA Personal.

23 Holmes to Gilles Gagnon, 13 June 1972, Holmes Papers, box 58, file 4.

24 Kim Richard Nossal, "Canada and the Search for World Order: John W. Holmes and Canadian Foreign Policy," *International Journal* 59, 4 (2004): 753; Denis Stairs, "The Pedagogics of John W. Holmes," *International Journal* 44, 4 (1989): 926.

25 Dorland was on the board at Pickering.

26 J. McCulley, "A Personal Word," *The Voyageur* 7 (1934): 17, Pickering College Papers (hereafter Pickering Papers).

27 Joseph McCulley, "Reflections of a Headmaster," *The Voyageur* 10 (1937): 16, Pickering Papers.

28 Charles Ritchie, *Storm Signals: More Undiplomatic Diaries, 1962-1971* (Toronto: Macmillan of Canada, 1983), 56.

29 J. McCulley, "A Personal Word," *The Voyageur* 7 (1934): 17, Pickering Papers.

30 Holmes, "Growing Up WASP," n.d., Holmes Papers, box 74, file E/II/7.

31 Holmes, "On the Art of Punning," *The Voyageur* 7 (1934): 6, Pickering Papers.

32 "Going Holmes," *The Voyageur* 11 (1938): 22, Pickering Papers.

33 Holmes to Buzzie, 1 October 1938, Nancy Skinner Papers (hereafter Skinner Papers), John W. Holmes folder, 1938, letters to his family. See also Holmes to Mom and Pop, 23 and 29 September 1938, Skinner Papers.

34 Holmes to Family, 18 October 1938, Skinner Papers.

35 Holmes to Mother and Dad, 15 and 25 October 1938, Skinner Papers; Holmes to Buzz, 19 and 29 October 1938, Skinner Papers.

36 Holmes to Mother and Dad, 18 November 1938, Skinner Papers.

37 Holmes to Bets, 4 December 1938, Skinner Papers, John W. Holmes folder, 1938, letters to his family. See also the letter dated 19-21 November 1938.

38 British Council Dominion Scholarship Application Form (1939), Holmes Papers, box 72, file E/I/16. See also Holmes to Buzz, 15 September 1939, Skinner Papers, John W. Holmes folder, 1939, letters to his family.

39 Holmes to Mother and Dad, 23 January 1939, Skinner Papers, John W. Holmes folder, 1939, letters to his family. On his approach, see Magee and Pentland, "A Tribute to John W. Holmes," 741.

40 John Wendell Holmes, "The American Civil War and Canada Today," *Saturday Night*, 19 August 1939, 2.

41 Holmes to Mother and Dad, 14 February 1939, Skinner Papers, John W. Holmes folder, 1939, letters to his family.

42 Ibid., 25 June 1939.

43 Ibid., 4 September 1939.

44 Ibid., 23 September 1939.

45 Holmes twice mused about completing his degree, most seriously in 1960 and again when he turned seventy-five. In neither case was there any real chance that he would be willing to commit the time and energy necessary.

46 On Reid, see Greg Donaghy and Stéphane Roussel, eds., *Escott Reid Diplomat and Scholar* (Montreal and Kingston: McGill-Queen's University Press, 2004).

47 Tarr to John R. Baldwin, 11 August 1939, in Library and Archives Canada (hereafter LAC), Canadian Institute of International Affairs Papers, MG28 I250 (hereafter CIIA Papers), vol. 1, Edgar J. Tarr, CIIA, World Affairs, correspondence, 1939/41. See also minutes of the 2nd meeting [1940] of the [CIIA] National Executive Committee, 18 March 1940, LAC, CIIA Papers, reel M-4619, vol. 4, minutes, 1939-40.

48 J.M. Macdonnell to F.P. Keppell, 18 November 1939, Carnegie Corporation Archives (hereafter CCA), Carnegie Corporation Papers, MS Coll CCNY, Carnegie Corporation, US Foreign Policy (hereafter Carnegie Papers), series IIIA, Grant Files, box 70c, folder 9, CIIA, Info Service, reel 1: 2005-7004; Baldwin to Holmes, 10 May 1940, Holmes Papers, box 67, file 2.

49 Holmes, undated, unlabelled memoirs, Holmes Papers, box 74, file E/II/7. George Raleigh Parkin was a graduate of Oxford and the Royal Military College of Canada who had served in the British infantry and Canadian Artillery and Royal Engineers during the First World War. He went on to a career in the investment department of Sun Life Assurance and was active throughout his life in internationalist causes.

50 Holmes to Gregory Wirick, 10 January 1982, Holmes Papers, box 48, file 5, United Nations Association in Canada; CIIA, *Report on the Work of the Canadian Institute of International Affairs, 1940-1941*, LAC, Brooke Claxton Papers, MG32 B5 (hereafter Claxton Papers), vol. 24, Canadian Institute of International Affairs, printed material, 1938-45; Holmes to Gregory Wirick, 10 January 1982, Holmes Papers, box 48, file 5; Appendix I, minutes of the 13th annual meeting of the [CIIA] National Council, 19 October 1940, LAC, CIIA Papers, reel M-4619, vol. 4, minutes, 1939-40.

51 Holmes, "Bushels to Burn," *Behind the Headline* 1 (September 1940): 11.

52 CIIA, *Report of the Work of the Canadian Institute of International Affairs, 1940-1941*, LAC, Claxton Papers, vol. 24, Canadian Institute of International Affairs, printed material, 1938-45.

53 Holmes, with Philip Child, "Dynamic Democracy," *Behind the Headlines* 9 (May 1941): 7, 23. On his thinking about world order, see also Nossal, "Canada and the Search for World Order"; and Stairs, "The Pedagogics of John W. Holmes."

54 Holmes to Dad and Mother, August [1941], Skinner Papers, folder 42-44. See also F.H. Soward, "Inside a Canadian Triangle: The University, the CIIA, and the Department of External Affairs: A Personal Record," *International Journal* 33, 1 (1977-78): 66-87.

55 Minutes of the 9th meeting of the [CIIA] National Executive Committee, 29 October 1941, LAC, CIIA Papers, reel M-4619, vol. 5, minutes, 1941-42.

56 Much of the correspondence on this issue can be found in LAC, L.B. Pearson Papers, MG26 N1 (hereafter Pearson Papers), vol. 20, file 3, Canadian Institute of International Affairs, 1941-52.

57 Minutes of the 4th meeting [1942] of the [CIIA] National Executive Committee, 11 May 1942, LAC, CIIA Papers, reel M-4619, vol. 5, minutes, 1941-42.

58 Holmes to W.L. [Bill] Holland, 11 April 1985, Holmes Papers, box 52, file 4. More detail on the interaction between the government and the public can be found in Adam Chapnick, *The Middle Power Project: Canada and the Founding of the United Nations* (Vancouver: UBC Press, 2005).

59 Doug Owram, *The Government Generation: Canadian Intellectuals and the State, 1900-1945* (Toronto: University of Toronto Press, 1986), 261.

60 On the links between the CIIA and the Department of External Affairs during this period, see Soward, "Inside a Canadian Triangle"; and Alex I. Inglis, "The Institute and the Department," *International Journal* 33, 1 (1977-78): 88-103.

61 Holmes to Pearson, 22 September 1942, LAC, Pearson Papers, vol. 83, External Affairs Department Personnel, 1942-52.

62 Pearson to Holmes, 26 September 1942, LAC, Pearson Papers, vol. 83, External Affairs Department Personnel, 1942-52.

63 Holmes to Pearson, 1 October 1942, LAC, Pearson Papers, vol. 83, External Affairs Department Personnel, 1942-52.

64 Much of this information can be found in LAC, Public Service Commission Papers, RG 32 (hereafter PSC Papers), vol. 1204, file 1910.06.18. For context, see Don Matthews to John Starnes, March 1944, cited in Starnes, *Closely Guarded: A Life in Canadian Security and Intelligence* (Toronto: University of Toronto Press, 1998), 31.

65 Holmes to W.L. Holland, 11 April 1985, Holmes Papers, box 52, file 4; Holmes to Heeney, 3 July 1950, Holmes Papers, box 66, file 4.

66 J.M. Macdonnell to W.A. Jessup, 28 June 1943, CCA, Carnegie Papers, series IIIA, Grant Files, box 70c, folder 9, CIIA Info Service, reel 1, 2005-7004.

Chapter 2: External Affairs' New Golden Boy

1 Charles Ritchie, quoted in Peter Stursberg, *Lester Pearson and the American Dilemma* (Toronto: Doubleday Canada, 1980), 9. On the atmosphere in the Canadian public service as a whole, see J.L. Granatstein, *The Ottawa Men: The Civil Service Mandarins, 1935-1957* (Toronto: University of Toronto Press, 1998 [1982]). On the Department of External Affairs in particular, see John Hilliker, *Canada's Department of External Affairs*, vol. 1, *The Early Years, 1909-1946* (Montreal and Kingston: McGill-Queen's University Press, 1990); and John Hilliker and Donald Barry, *Canada's Department of External Affairs*, vol. 2, *Coming of Age, 1946-1968* (Montreal and Kingston: McGill-Queen's University Press, 1995).

2 Adam Chapnick, *The Middle Power Project: Canada and the Founding of the United Nations* (Vancouver: UBC Press, 2005), 10-13, 74-75.

3 Roy MacLaren, *Commissions High: Canada in London, 1870-1971* (Montreal and Kingston: McGill-Queen's University Press, 2006), 378.

4 Kevin Wright and Robert Fife to Kevin Doyle, n.d., Trinity College Archives, Toronto, John Holmes Papers 002-0001 (hereafter Holmes Papers), box 100, Brookings Institution Survey for Ford Foundation. See also J.L. Granatstein, interview with John Holmes, 22 June 1971, Clara Thomas Archives and Special Collections, York University, Toronto, J.L. Granatstein Papers, 1974-0271/001, file 4.

5 Holmes to Cadieux, 10 June 1974, Holmes Papers, box 50, file 2.

6 Marcel Cadieux, *The Canadian Diplomat: An Essay in Definition*, trans. Archibald Day (Toronto: University of Toronto Press, 1963 [1962]), 39-40, 81.

7 Holmes to Soward, 19 January 1970, Holmes Papers, box 69, file 5.

8 Holmes, 18 February 1978, quoted in Judith Robertson Papers, Norman Robertson Round Table Transcript. For a complete assessment, see J.L. Granatstein, *A Man of Influence: Norman A. Robertson and Canadian Statecraft, 1929-1968* (Canada: Deneau Publishers, 1981).

9 Marion Magee and Charles Pentland, "A Tribute to John W. Holmes," *International Journal* 44, 4 (1989): 741-42.

10 Holmes, "The British Commonwealth and the United Nations: The Effect of the War on the British Commonwealth," n.d., Holmes Papers, box 61, file 1.

11 Holmes, "Opinion in the Press and Parliament Concerning the Organization of the United Nations and the Role of Canada in Such Organizations," 27 March 1943, Library and Archives Canada (hereafter LAC), Department of External Affairs Papers, RG 25 (hereafter DEA Papers), series G-2, vol. 3227, file 5475-40C. The original analysis was completed on 3 March.

12 Don Munton and Donald Page, "Planning in the East Block: The Post-Hostilities Problems Committees in Canada, 1943-45," *International Journal* 32, 4 (1977): 677-726; Denis Stairs, "The Pedagogics of John W. Holmes," *International Journal* 44, 4 (1989): 930.

13 Robertson, [Holmes File] n.d., LAC, Public Service Commission Papers, RG 32 (hereafter PSC Papers), vol. 1204, file 1910.06.18.

14 Wrong, Report on John Holmes, 11 January 1944, LAC, PSC Papers, vol. 1204, Personnel File.

15 Holmes to Wrong, 15 December 1943, Holmes Papers, box 60, file 2. See also the rest of the file and Holmes to Wrong, 19 February 1944, Holmes Papers, box 61, file 1.

16 Second Report of the Working Committee on Post-Hostilities Problems, 13 January 1944, Holmes Papers, box 60, file 5.

17 Mexico was not taken seriously as a security partner at this time.

18 Post-Hostilities Planning Committee, draft 2, Canadian Defence Relationships with the United States, 18 May 1944, LAC, Privy Council Office Papers, RG 2 (hereafter PCO Papers), series B-2, vol. 18. file W-22-8, part 4.

19 Chapnick, *The Middle Power Project*, 71-72.

20 Holmes to Soward, 31 May 1966, University of British Columbia Archives, Frederick Hubert Soward Papers, file 1-1, Correspondence 1940-84.

21 Churchill, BBC radio transcript, 11 May 1944, quoted in Massey to Smith, 17 May 1944, LAC, DEA Papers, vol. 5757, file 62(s); Blair Fraser, "Backstage at Ottawa," *Maclean's*, 15 June 1944, 14.

22 Holmes to Family, 12 May 1944, Nancy Skinner Papers (hereafter Skinner Papers), folder 42-44.

23 Ibid.

24 See, for example, Holmes to Wrong, 27 October 1944, Holmes Papers, box 61, file 1; Holmes, "Draft: The Dumbarton Oaks Conference on World Organization: Canadian Interests," 18 September 1944, LAC, DEA Papers, vol. 5708, file 7V(s), part 3.

25 Holmes to Wrong, 17 October 1944, Holmes Papers, box 66, file 6. On the politics of functionalism, see Adam Chapnick, "Principle for Profit: The Functional Principle and the Development of Canadian Foreign Policy, 1943-1947," *Journal of Canadian Studies* 37, 2 (2002): 68-85.

26 Holmes to Mother and Dad, 17 October 1944, Skinner Papers, folder 42-44.

27 Massey to Robertson, 24 November 1944, LAC, PSC Papers, vol. 1204, Personnel File.

28 Maitland to Freese-Pennefather, 28 December 1944, National Archives of England, Wales, and the United Kingdom, Foreign Office Papers, FO 371/50365.

29 Gilles Lalande, *Studies of the Royal Commission on Bilingualism and Biculturalism*, vol. 3, *The Department of External Affairs and Biculturalism* (Ottawa: Queen's Printer, 1969), 81-86; Hilliker, *The Department of External Affairs*, vol. 1, 280.

30 On the development of the University of the East Block, see Holmes to R. Gordon Robertson, 30 November 1944, LAC, DEA Papers, Vol. 2814, file 1086-40, part 2, and subsequent correspondence from the same file.

31 John Lownsbrough, "The Quiet Diplomat," *City and Country Home*, August 1987, 10-14 provides the most thorough coverage of this incident.

32 Holmes to Family, 30 April 1945, Skinner Papers, John W. Holmes folder, 1945, letters to his family.

33 David Dilks, "A View on two Squares: John Holmes in London and Moscow, 1944-1948," *Canada House Lecture Series* 48 (1991): 9; Holmes, *Conversation between Professor John Holmes and Professor David Dilks on Friday, 28 June 1985 at the University of Leeds* (Toronto: CIIA, n.d.); Holmes to Reid, 3 March 1988, LAC, Escott Reid Papers, MG31 E46 (hereafter Escott Reid Papers), vol. 34, Holmes, John W., 1980-88.

34 Holmes to Hillmer, 18 September 1986, Holmes Papers, box 20, file 7; Holmes, "Our Man in London," *Today Magazine*, n.d., cited in Holmes Papers, box 4, file 7.

35 Chapnick, *The Middle Power Project*, 16, 34, 67.

36 Holmes, memorandum, 28 February 1945, LAC, PCO Papers, vol. 30, file U-10-11.

37 Holmes to Family, 8 April 1945, Skinner Papers, John W. Holmes folder, 1945, letters to his family; Vincent Massey, diary entries, May-June 1945, University of Toronto Archives, Toronto, Canada (hereafter UTA), Vincent Massey Papers, B87-0082 (hereafter Massey Papers), box 312, diary, 21 February 1945-14 July 1945.

38 Holmes to Family, 8 and 9 May 1945, Holmes Papers, box 68, file (H); and Holmes to Family, 17 December 1945, Skinner Papers, John W. Holmes folder, 1945, letters to his family.

39 Holmes, "The Bomb: Where the World Went Wrong," *Toronto Star*, 11 September 1982, B4; Holmes to Family, 8 August 1945, Skinner Papers, John W. Holmes folder, 1945, letters to his family.

40 For Holmes' view on Pearson, see Holmes, "The Unquiet Diplomat," with introduction and edited by Adam Chapnick, *International Journal* 62, 2 (2007): 289-309.

41 Draft memo for Pearson from Holmes, attached to Ignatieff to Wrong, 11 September 1945, Holmes Papers, box 61, file 1. See also Holmes to Wrong, 1 September 1945; Wrong to Holmes, 20 September 1945; and Holmes to Pearson, undated and not sent; all in Holmes Papers.

42 Holmes to Family, 10 December 1945, Skinner Papers, John W. Holmes folder, 1945, letters to his family.

43 On these matters, see LAC, PSC Papers, vol. 1204, file 1910.06.18.

44 Holmes to Family, 18 January 1946, Skinner Papers, John W. Holmes folder, 1946, letters to his family.

45 Holmes to Professor Gérard Bergeron, 1 October 1986, Holmes Papers, box 49, file. 4.

46 See, for example, Holmes to Glazebrook, 23 June 1945, Holmes Papers, box 63, file 1; Holmes to Glazebrook, 3 October 1945, Holmes Papers, box 66, file 11.

47 On this incident, see Holmes to Secretary of State for External Affairs (hereafter SSEA), 29 November 1945, and Terry [MacDermot] to Holmes, 7 January 1946, both in Holmes Papers, box 66, file 4. The scholarly debate on this question is considered in Don Page and Don Munton, "Canadian Images of the Cold War, 1946-47," *International Journal* 32, 3 (1977): 577-604; and David J. Bercuson, "'A people so ruthless as the Soviets': Canadian Images of the Cold War and the Soviet Union, 1946-1950," in *Canada and the Soviet Experiment*, ed. David Davie, 89-103 (Toronto: Canadian Scholars Press, 1994).

48 See, for example, Holmes to John English, 31 August 1987, Holmes Papers, box 20, file 7; Holmes to Wrong, 23 February 1946, and Wrong's response, 1 March 1946, both in Holmes Papers, box 102, folder: no label; Massey, diary entries, 2 and 6 February 1946, UTA, Massey Papers, box 313, diary, vol. 58. On Gouzenko, see Robert Bothwell and J.L. Granatstein, eds., *The Gouzenko Transcripts: The Evidence Presented to the Kellock-Taschereau Royal Commission of 1946* (Ottawa: Deneau Publishers, 1982).

49 Peter Mangold, *Success and Failure in British Foreign Policy: Evaluating the Record, 1900-2000* (New York: Palgrave, 2001), 8.

50 On the Commonwealth issue see, for example, Holmes to Wrong, 1 May 1946, enclosed in Wrong to Heeney, 8 May 1946, LAC, PCO Papers, vol. 107, file U-10-11.

51 Holmes to Betty, 9 July 1946, Skinner Papers, John W. Holmes folder, 1946, letters to his family; Holmes, Memorandum for the High Commissioner on a Visit to Italy, 24 July 1946, Leeds University Library, Special Collections, MS 884/3.

52 Holmes to Family, 4 June 1946, Skinner Papers, John W. Holmes folder, letters to his family; Wrong to Pearson, 20 May 1947, LAC, PSC Papers, vol. 1204, Personnel File; Holmes to MacDermot, 8 May 1947, LAC, PSC Papers, vol. 1204, Personnel File; Pearson to Robertson, 14 April 1947, LAC, Pearson Papers, vol. 32, External Affairs Department Personnel, 1946-48.

53 Holmes to Pearson, n.d. [1946], LAC, Pearson Papers, vol. 6, Nominal Pres8 Files, Holmes, J.W., Canada, E.A.

54 Holmes to Buzz, 11 January 1947, Skinner Papers, file: London, 1947.

55 Wrong to Pearson, 12 February 1947, LAC, Pearson Papers, vol. 32, External Affairs Department Personnel, 1946-48.

56 Robertson to Pearson, 27 March 1947; Pearson to Robertson, 14 April 1947, LAC, PSC Papers, vol. 1204, Personnel File.

57 Holmes to Terry MacDermot, 1-3 May 1947 and 8 May 1947, LAC, Pearson Papers, vol. 83, External Affairs Department Personnel, 1942-52.

58 Pearson to Felix Walter, 21 June 1947, LAC, Pearson Papers, vol. 32, External Affairs Department Personnel, 1946-48. See also Hector Mackenzie, "An Old Dominion and the New Commonwealth: Canadian Policy on the Question of India's Membership, 1947-1949," *Journal of Imperial and Commonwealth History* 27, 3 (1999): 82-112.

59 Department of External Affairs, FSO 4, Personnel Report, 2 July 1947, LAC, PSC Papers, vol. 1204, Personnel File.

60 Wrong, cited in Holmes to Mother and Dad, 31 August 1947, Skinner Papers, file: London, 1947.

61 Holmes to SSEA, 1 August 1947, Holmes Papers, box 66, file 5; and Holmes to D.C. [Colin] Robertson, 8 September 1980, Holmes Papers, box 34, file 3.

62 Germany was divided into three, and then four, zones of occupation at the end of the war. Headquartered in Frankfurt, the American zone was originally in the southeast and included Bavaria, Hesse, and parts of what is now Baden-Württemberg.

63 Holmes, untitled, 21 August 1947, Holmes Papers, box 74, E/II/7.

CHAPTER 3: THE RISING STAR

1 K.P. Kirkwood to Pearson, 2 January 1947, Library and Archives Canada (hereafter LAC), L.B. Pearson Papers, MG26 N1 (hereafter Pearson Papers), vol. 32, External Affairs Department Personnel, 1946-48.

2 Holmes to Dad, 5 October 1947, Nancy Skinner Papers (hereafter Skinner Papers), file London, 1947. See also Holmes to MacDermot, 13 October 1947, LAC, Public Service Commission Papers, RG 32 (hereafter PSC Papers), vol. 1204, Personnel File.

3 MacDermot to Acting High Commissioner, Canada House, 3 October 1947, LAC, PSC Papers, RG 32, vol. 1204, Personnel File.

4 Holmes, "Russia Revisited," 28 February 1956, Trinity College Archives, Toronto, John Holmes Papers 002-0001 (hereafter Holmes Papers), box 70, file D/IV/3. See also "John W. Holmes, Moscow 1947-48: A Memoir of His Tour of Duty as Canadian Chargé d'Affaires," n.d., Leeds University Library, Special Collections, MS 826; Frederick J. McEvoy, "Our Men in Moscow: Canadian Diplomats Behind the Iron Curtain," *The Beaver* 72, 6 (December 1992-January 1993): 40-46; Nayantara Saghal, *From Fear Set Free* (London: Victor Gollancz, 1962), 56-60; Walter Bedell Smith, *Moscow Mission 1946-1949* (Melbourne: William Heinmann, 1950), 26-96; and Peter Roberts, *George Costakis: A Russian Life in Art* (Ottawa: Carleton University Press, 1994), 91-115.

5 Holmes, "Moscow Under Stalin," January 1978, Holmes Papers, box 4, file 7.

6 See Don Page and Don Munton, "Canadian Images of the Cold War, 1946-47," *International Journal* 32, 3 (1977): 577-604.

7 Holmes to SSEA, 14 November 1947, Holmes Papers, box 63, file 3.

8 For details, see the entire November 1947 correspondence in Holmes Papers.

9 See Denis Stairs, "The Pedagogics of John W. Holmes," *International Journal* 44, 4 (1989): 926.

10 Pearson to Reid, 8 December 1947, LAC, Pearson Papers, vol. 32, External Affairs Department Personnel, 1946-48; Pearson to Robertson, 26 December 1947, ibid.

11 Holmes, "I Remember Stalin," *Globe and Mail Weekend Magazine*, 4 March 1978; Holmes to Pearson, 24 February 1948, Holmes Papers, box 63, file 3.

12 Holmes to Pearson, 3 March 1948, Holmes Papers, box 63, file 3.

13 Holmes, "Soviet Culture," February 1948, Skinner Papers, 47-48.

14 Holmes to Reid, 1 April 1948, Holmes Papers, box 63, file 3. See also Holmes to Family, 22 January 1948, and Holmes to Buzzy, 18 March 1948, both in Skinner Papers, 47-48.

15 Holmes to Pearson, 9 April 1948, Holmes Papers, box 63, file 3. See also "Memories of Prime Minister Pearson in an interview with Peter Stursberg," 30 June 1978, LAC, Peter Stursberg Papers, MG31 D78 (hereafter Stursberg Papers), vol. 29, John Holmes, 1978.

16 Wilgress to Pearson, 25 May 1948, Holmes Papers, box 63, file 3. There is further evidence to suggest that Wilgress was never entirely impressed with Holmes' performance. He later accused Holmes, at least indirectly, of relying too much on "casual impressions" and having "only superficial knowledge of the country." See Wilgress to Ford, 9 October 1950,

LAC, Robert A.D. Ford Papers, MG31 E73, vol. 2, file 12, correspondence diplomatic, 1950-72.

17 See, for example, Andrew Cohen, *While Canada Slept: How We Lost Our Place in the World* (Toronto: McClelland and Stewart, 2003).

18 Holmes to Pearson, 21 May 1948, Holmes Papers, box 63, file 3.

19 Holmes to Pearson, 26 May 1948, and Holmes to SSEA, 25 June 1948, both in Holmes Papers, box 63, file 3.

20 Holmes to SSEA, 5 July 1948, Holmes Papers, box 63, file 3.

21 Holmes to Family, 8 July 1948, Skinner Papers, 47-48.

22 Holmes to Pearson, 23 July 1948, Holmes Papers, box 63, file 3.

23 Ibid. For a documentary record on the controversy over Canadian participation, see *Documents on Canadian External Relations*, vol. 14, *1948*, ed. Hector Mackenzie (Ottawa: Minister of Supply and Services Canada, 1994), 783-832.

24 Holmes to Family, 22 June 1948, Skinner Papers, 47-48; Holmes to Reid, 21 June 1948, LAC, PSC Papers, vol. 1204, Personnel File.

25 Robertson to Pearson, 23 July 1948, LAC, PSC Papers, vol. 1204, Personnel File.

26 Holmes to Reid, 2 September 1948, Holmes Papers, box 62, file 5, part 2.

27 Holmes to Family, 9 September 1948, Skinner Papers, folder 1948.

28 Bob Ford to Holmes, 22 October 1948, Holmes Papers, box 63, file 2.

29 Holmes to Family, 24 October 1948, Skinner Papers, folder 1948.

30 On McNaughton, see John Swettenham, *McNaughton*, 3 vols. (Toronto: Ryerson Press, 1968-69).

31 Holmes to Family, 6 November 1948 (includes enclosures for 13 and 14 November), Skinner Papers, folder 1948. For context, see Robert A. Spencer, *Canada in World Affairs: From UN to NATO, 1946-1949* (Toronto Oxford University Press, 1959), 142-52; and Anne Trowell Hillmer, "'Here I am in the Middle': The Origins of Canada's Diplomatic Involvement in the Middle East," in *The Domestic Battleground: Canada and the Arab-Israeli Conflict*, ed. David Taras and David H. Goldberg, 125-43 (Montreal and Kingston: McGill-Queen's University Press, 1989).

32 Holmes to Family, 6 November 1948 (includes enclosures for 13 and 14 November), Skinner Papers, folder 1948.

33 Ibid.

34 Holmes to Donald Barry, 28 April 1971, Holmes Papers, box 35, file 15, part 1.

35 Holmes to Family, 6 November 1948 (includes enclosures for 13 and 14 November), Skinner Papers, folder 1948.

36 Susan Lightstone, "The Observer," *Ottawa Magazine*, March 1991, 27-30.

37 Lester Pearson vacated the office of under-secretary to become a Cabinet minister on 10 September 1948. The next day, Reid was temporarily promoted to fill his duties until a permanent replacement could be found. Arnold Heeney, the secretary to the Cabinet, was assigned the position in January 1949 and took over formally on 17 March, at which point Reid became his deputy.

38 Sidney Freifeld, *Undiplomatic Notes: Tales from the Canadian Foreign Service* (Toronto: Hounslow Press, 1990), 182.

39 "J.W.H.," Holmes Papers, box 70, file D/V/IV/3.

40 Holmes, "University of the East Block: *Reports: General*," 18 March 1950, Holmes Papers, box 68, file (H).

41 Peter Dobell and Robert Willmot, "John Holmes," *International Journal* 33, 1 (1977-78): 106. See also Reid to Holmes, 10 May 1951, Holmes Papers, box 65, file 1.

CHAPTER 4: JOHN HOLMES' GOLDEN AGE

1 Escott Reid appears to have been the first to use the term "golden age." See his "Canada in World Affairs: Opportunities of the Next Decade," address to the Annual Dinner of the Canadian Centenary Council, Château Laurier, 1 February 1967, 4.

2 The material that follows is drawn largely from Holmes to Colonel H.F. Wood, 15 January 1963, Trinity College Archives, Toronto, John Holmes Papers 002-0001 (hereafter Holmes Papers), box 59, file 2; Holmes to R.E. [Ralph] Collins, 4 July 1950, Holmes Papers, box 65, file 1; Holmes to Dr. Juraj Andrassy, 4 April 1967, Holmes Papers, box 49, file 1; Holmes "Pearson as Quarterback," review of *The Diplomacy of Constraint: Canada, the Korean War, and the United States* by Denis Stairs, *Canadian Forum* 54, 646 (1974): 55-56; Holmes to Alfred Pick, 23 June 1951, Holmes Papers, box 61, file 2; Holmes, draft, "The Role of the United Nations in the Maintenance of Collective Security," 8 August 1951, Holmes Papers, box 65, file 1.

3 President Truman was also motivated by domestic political considerations.

4 The communists had recently all but defeated the nationalists to end the civil war, forcing the National Party leader, Chiang Kai-shek, to flee to Formosa (Taiwan) and establish a much smaller Republic of China. Because there was no official end to the war, both governments could claim legitimacy.

5 Pearson to All Missions Abroad, 28 June 1950, *Documents on Canadian External Relations* (hereafter *DCER*), vol. 16, *1950*, ed. Greg Donaghy (Ottawa: Minister of Supply and Services Canada, 1996), 31.

6 Extract from minutes of heads of divisions, 23 October 1950, *DCER*, vol. 16, *1950*, 455-57.

7 Holmes, "Relations between Canada and the United States in the United Nations," 26 March 1951," Holmes Papers, box 66, file 1. Escott Reid had to virtually force Holmes to write the memorandum. In fact, Holmes slammed the door as he stormed out of Reid's office before he started writing. Reid claims that Holmes was too modest and felt that he was not the right person to draft the document. It is more likely that Holmes was frustrated with the way that his position had been ignored. See Escott Reid, quoted in "John Holmes: An Appreciation," *Behind the Headlines* 46, 1 (1988): 17.

8 Lester Pearson, "Canadian Foreign Policy in a Two-power World," speech delivered on 10 April 1951 and reproduced in L. Pearson, *Words and Occasions* (Toronto: University of Toronto Press, 1970), 107.

9 Holmes to Reid, 15 May 1951, *DCER*, vol. 17, *1951*, ed. Greg Donaghy (Ottawa: Minister of Supply and Services Canada, 1996), 166.

10 Holmes to SSEA, 7 November 1951, *DCER*, vol. 17.

11 Lois McIntosh to Holmes, 5 June 1951, Holmes Papers, box 65, file 1. See also Holmes to McIntosh, 11 May 1951, in ibid.

12 Holmes to Shelagh Grant, 8 December 1987, Holmes Papers, box 52, file 1.

13 Holmes to Cadieux, n.d., Library and Archives Canada (hereafter LAC), Public Service Commission Papers, RG 32 (hereafter PSC Papers), vol. 1204, Personnel File.

14 It is uncertain whether Holmes knew that Norman had indeed been a communist during his student days overseas. Regardless, he had been a loyal public servant throughout his career.

15 Holmes to Reid, 21 May 1951, Holmes Papers, box 64, file 6. On the problems with morale in the East Block, see J.L. Granatstein, *A Man of Influence: Norman A. Robertson and Canadian Statecraft, 1929-1968* (Canada: Deneau Publishers, 1981), 281. Wrong was in Washington and Robertson was in the midst of a miserable experience as clerk of the privy council and secretary to the cabinet.

16 Holmes to MacDermot, Labour Day 1951, Bishop's University Archives (hereafter BUA), T.W.L. MacDermot Papers, MG 023 (hereafter MacDermot Papers), file 54, label M34 B21.

17 "Holmes, John Wendell," n.d., LAC, PSC Papers, vol. 1204, file 1910.06.18.

18 Holmes was promoted once again just before he arrived at NDC (to FSO 6), making this suggestion questionable.

19 Holmes to MacDermot, 28 January 1952, BUA, MacDermot Papers, file 54, label M34 B22.

20 Ibid.

21 Not long after the group departed, Talal had to resign because of his schizophrenia.

22 "An Informal Report on the Tour of the National Defence College to the Near East, Middle East and North Africa, 1952," Holmes Papers, box 70, file D/IV/4; Holmes to MacDermot, 11 June 1952, BUA, MacDermot Papers, file 54.

23 Holmes to Family, 16 January 1953, Skinner Papers, John W. Holmes folder, 1953, letters to his family. The colleagues were Bob Rothschild and Murray Lester.

24 Holmes to Terry [MacDermot], 10 June 1953 [in letter began on 23 March], BUA, MacDermot Papers, file 54.

25 More detail can be found in John Hilliker and Donald Barry, *Canada's Department of External Affairs*, vol. 2, *Coming of Age, 1946-1968* (Montreal and Kingston: McGill-Queen's University Press, 1995), 87-92 as well as in the notes of 21 February 1952, and 18 March and 13 April 1953, all in LAC, PSC Papers, vol. 1204, Personnel File.

26 Personnel Division release on John W. Holmes, 1 October 1953; and Evan Gill to Charles Ritchie [acting under-secretary], 12 June 1953, both in LAC, PSC Papers, vol. 1204, Personnel File.

27 For a sense of the time and of Holmes' stature, see Arthur Andrew, *The Rise and Fall of a Middle Power: Canadian Diplomacy from King to Mulroney* (Toronto: James Lorimer, 1993), 15-17.

28 The name Killers' Row came from Holmes' close friend, C.E. McGaughey, known to most as McGuff, who used it "to denote the place where bright ideas met untimely deaths." See Hilliker and Barry, *Canada's Department of External Affairs*, vol. 2, 49.

29 Granatstein, *A Man of Influence*, 293.

30 L.B. Pearson, "H. Hume Wrong," *External Affairs* 6, 3 (1954): 74-78; Holmes to Mother and Dad, n.d., 1954, Skinner Papers, John W. Holmes folder 1954, letters to his family.

31 On the departmental situation, see Hilliker and Barry, *Canada's Department of External Affairs*, vol. 2, 88-92. See also Holmes to Don Page, 5 January 1982, Holmes Papers, box 37, file 3, part 3.

32 Tribute by James H. Taylor, CIIA, "In Memoriam: John Wendell Holmes, 1910-1988," transcript of memorial held at Lester B. Pearson Building, 17 October 1988, cited in LAC, Escott Reid Papers, vol. 34, Holmes, John W. Memorial (6), 1988.

33 Holmes, "Canadian Foreign Policy," speech to Canadian Army Staff College (Kingston), 19 March 1954, Holmes Papers, box 60, file 2.

34 Holmes, cited in Peter Stursberg, *Lester Pearson and the American Dilemma* (Toronto: Doubleday Canada, 1980), 86. As much as Holmes abhorred the Mao Tze-tung regime,

the nationalists' banishment to Formosa established the chairman as the legitimate ruler of the Chinese mainland. Thinking pragmatically, and recalling his Moscow experience, he concluded that it was best to engage potential enemies to minimize the chances of any misunderstandings expanding into full-blown conflicts.

35 Holmes to MacKay, 20 January 1954, Holmes Papers, box 64, file 5.

36 Holmes to Family, 23 April 1954, Skinner Papers, John W. Holmes folder 1954, letters to his family.

37 For Holmes' own account of the experience, see his "Geneva 1954," *International Journal* 22, 3 (1967): 457-83.

38 Holmes, "Chester Ronning," 27 January 1985, Holmes Papers, box 69, file (R).

39 Stursberg, *Lester Pearson and the American Dilemma*, 125n.

40 Holmes to Escott Reid, 16 February 1967, LAC, Arnold Danford Patrick Heeney Papers, MG30 E144 (hereafter Heeney Papers), vol. 6, Canadian Institute of International Affairs, Correspondence, 1963-68. See also Douglas A. Ross, *In the Interests of Peace: Canada and Vietnam 1954-1973* (Toronto: University of Toronto Press, 1984), 10-14.

41 Holmes to R.M. Macdonnell, 26 August 1954, Holmes Papers, box 64, file 1.

42 Holmes to Ronning, 19 October 1954 and Holmes, [draft] "Policy in Indochina," 15 November 1954, both in Holmes Papers, box 64, file 1; Holmes, "Vietnam and Canada," 6 November 1970, speech to Canadian Association for American Studies, Montreal, Holmes Papers, box 9, file 15; Holmes, Policy on Freedom of Movement in Vietnam," 5 April 1955, Holmes Papers, box 64, file 2; Holmes to Heeney, 2 May 1955, Holmes Papers, box 64, file 5. On Canada's "qualified impartiality," see Ramesh Thakur, *Peacekeeping in Vietnam: Canada, India, Poland, and the International Commission* (Edmonton: University of Alberta Press, 1984), 185.

43 Robertson to Pearson, 8 March 1955, LAC, Pearson Papers, vol. 32, Pearson, L.B., Subject Files, Pre-1958 Series, External Affairs, Heads of Mission Appointments, 1951-57.

44 Holmes to Family, 22 May 1955, Skinner Papers, John W. Holmes folder 1955, letters to his family; Robertson to Pearson, 8 March 1955, LAC, Pearson Papers, vol. 32, Pearson, L.B., Subject Files, Pre-1958 Series, External Affairs, Heads of Mission Appointments, 1951-57.

45 Ross, *In the Interests of Peace*, 163. Holmes to SSEA, "Prospects in Indochina," 11 July 1955, Holmes Papers, box 64, file 1; Saul Rae to Holmes, 15 August 1955, in ibid.

46 Holmes to USSEA, 2 September 1955, Holmes Papers, box 64, file 1.

47 Holmes to Ramesh Thakur, 20 March 1978, Holmes Papers, box 38, file 3, part 2. See also box 64, file 1, as well as Ross, *In the Interests of Peace*, 164.

48 See note by Jules Léger appended to Holmes to Léger, 8 March 1956, *Documents on Canadian External Relations*, vol. 22, *1956-1957*, part 1, ed. Greg Donaghy (Ottawa: Minister of Public Works and Government Services, 2001), 5.

49 Holmes to SSEA, 11 October 1955, Holmes Papers, box 66, file 2; Holmes, "Russia Revisited," 28 February 1956, Holmes Papers, box 16, file 32; Holmes to Pearson, 19 October 1955, LAC, Pearson Papers, vol. 6, Nominal Pre58 Files, Holmes, J.W., Canada, E.A.; Holmes, interview with Peter Stursberg, 30 June 1978, LAC, Stursberg Papers, vol. 29, John Holmes, 1978; Holmes, interview with Robert Reford, 21 October 1955, Holmes Papers, box 66, file 3.

50 Others have suggested that Geoffrey Murray was the original author. See Hilliker and Barry, *Canada's Department of External Affairs*, vol. 2, 121.

51 Holmes to Saul Rae, 5 December 1955, Holmes Papers, box 64, file 1.

52 Holmes to Conor Cruise O'Brien, 13 January 1988, Holmes Papers, box 55, file 4. The only thorough account of the Martin initiative can be found in Greg Donaghy and Donald Barry, "Our Man from Windsor: Paul Martin and the New Members Question, 1955," in *Paul Martin and Canadian Diplomacy*, ed. Ryan Touhey, 3-20 (Waterloo: Centre for Foreign Policy and Federalism, 2001). An earlier account is included in James Eayrs, *Canada in World Affairs, October 1955 to June 1957* (Toronto: Oxford University Press, 1959), 214-26.

53 Holmes, "Canada Comes of Age," *Globe and Mail*, 25 October 1986, D1; Geoffrey Murray, "The 1956 Suez War," interviewed by James Sutterlin, 10 January 1991, United Nations Dag Hammarskjöld Library, UN Oral History Project (02)/M8; Terrence Robertson, *Crisis: The Inside Story of the Suez Conspiracy* (Toronto: McClelland and Stewart, 1964); Holmes to Pearson, 6 December 1956, LAC, Albert Edgar Ritchie Papers, MG31 E44 (hereafter A.E. Ritchie Papers), vol. 2, file 22; Holmes, "Situation in the Middle East: Conversation with the Egyptian Representative," 12 November 1956, LAC, Pearson Papers, vol. 63, UN, general, 1947-57; Holmes, "Principle and Practices of Canadian Foreign Policy: The Role of a Middle Power," speech to Trinity Historical Society, Duke University, 7 April 1960, Holmes Papers, box 7, file 10.

54 John Holmes is hardly mentioned, for example, in John Melady, *Pearson's Prize: Canada and the Suez Crisis* (Toronto: Dundurn Group, 2006).

55 Holmes to Saul Rae, 26 November 1956, Holmes Papers, box 63, file 4. See also "Interview with Mr. John Holmes [by Howard Lentner]," 30 January 1975, LAC, Howard H. Lentner Papers, R11 232-0-9-E, vol. 2, Holmes, John W., 1974-75.

56 Holmes to Pearson, 19 December 1956, LAC, Pearson Papers, vol. 6, Nominal Pre58 Files, Holmes, J.W., Canada, E.A.

57 Holmes to Léger, 15 December 1956, Holmes Papers, box 63, file 4.

CHAPTER 5: DESCENDING THROUGH THE DIEFENBAKER ERA

1 See, for example, Maxwell Cohen, "A New Responsibility in Foreign Policy," *Saturday Night*, 19 January 1957, 5-6, 28.

2 Trevor Lloyd, *Canada in World Affairs: 1957-59* (Toronto: Oxford University Press, 1968), 1.

3 Holmes was paid $12,500, the deputy under-secretary $13,500, and the under-secretary of state for external affairs $18,000.

4 Allan Gotlieb, *The Washington Diaries 1981-1989* (Toronto: McClelland and Stewart, 2006), 591.

5 Lincoln P. Bloomfield to Gayle Fraser, 9 September 1988, Trinity College Archives, Toronto, John Holmes Papers 002-0001 (hereafter Holmes Papers), box 101, file November 10; Walter Crocker to Alexander Brady, 31 January 1961, Holmes Papers, box 67, file 3.

6 For details, see Holmes Papers, box 57, file 2.

7 See, for example, Holmes to Pearson, 18 July 1957, Holmes Papers, box 69, file (P/Q).

8 Patrick H. Brennan, *Reporting the Nation's Business: Press-Government Relations During the Liberal Years, 1935-1957* (Toronto: University of Toronto Press, 1994), ix.

9 Shortly after John Diefenbaker took office, he began to actively discourage civil servants from speaking publicly. Although this might have reduced Holmes' obligations somewhat, it took away two of the real joys of his job – speaking and teaching.

10 Kevin Wright and Robert Fife to Kevin Doyle, edited transcript of interview with John Holmes, n.d., Holmes Papers, box 100, Brookings Institution, survey for Ford Foundation.

11 The best summary of the Pearsonalities issue is John F. Hilliker, "The Politicians and the 'Pearsonalities': The Diefenbaker Government and the Conduct of Canadian External Relations," *Canadian Historical Papers* 19, 1 (1984): 151-67.

12 Diefenbaker was in a minority situation, and reaching out to the Opposition made strategic sense. Furthermore, the speaker gave up the right to vote, except to break ties.

13 Kevin Wright and Robert Fife to Kevin Doyle, edited transcript of interview with John Holmes, n.d., Holmes Papers, box 100, Brookings Institution, survey for Ford Foundation; Holmes, interview with Peter Stursberg, 30 May 1988, Library and Archives Canada (hereafter LAC), Peter Stursberg Papers, MG31 D78 (hereafter Stursberg Papers), vol. 45, file 38. 1988.

14 Holmes to Arnold Smith, 18 April 1957, Holmes Papers, box 65, file 6.

15 Holmes to Charles Ritchie, 27 June 1957, Holmes Papers, box 66, file 11; Holmes to Albert Legault, 28 January 1987, Holmes Papers, box 53, file 5.

16 On the declining state of the department, see Hector Mackenzie, "Recruiting Tomorrow's Ambassadors: Examination and Selection for the Foreign Service of Canada, 1925-1997," in *Diplomatic Missions: The Ambassador in Canadian Foreign Policy*, ed. Robert Wolfe (Kingston: Queen's University School of Policy Studies, 1998), 111.

17 See, for example, J.L. Granatstein, *Canada 1957-1967: The Years of Uncertainty and Innovation* (Toronto: McClelland and Stewart, 1986), 102-5.

18 Holmes to Robertson, 1 August 1957, LAC, Norman Robertson Papers, MG30 E163 (hereafter Robertson Papers), vol. 3a, personal correspondence, 1957-58.

19 Holmes to Allan McGill, 19 August 1957, Allan McGill Papers. See also Holmes to R.H. Roy, 5 December 1972, Holmes Papers, box 34, file 1; Holmes to Peyton Lyon, 17 January 1978, Holmes Papers, box 53, file 6; Holmes to Air Marshal C.R. [Larry] Dunlap, 5 April 1967, Holmes Papers, box 50, file 6; and Joseph T. Jockel, *No Boundaries Upstairs: Canada, the United States, and the Origins of North American Air Defence, 1945-1958* (Vancouver: UBC Press, 1987). Holmes' desire to keep his distance from Diefenbaker is particularly clear in an anecdote revealed by former colleague Tom Delworth. Holmes was once asked to contribute some thoughts to a speech that the prime minister was to deliver to a group of United Baptists. Diefenbaker loved what he wrote. When Delworth heard this, he and Holmes' secretary, Pauline Sabourin, crafted a note, to which they affixed Diefenbaker's signature, expressing the prime minister's pleasure with Holmes' work and asking him to become his personal speech writer. Holmes was absolutely horrified. In fact, he was so concerned that Delworth had to admit what he had done and apologize almost immediately.

20 The Canadian delegation to the UN's summary of the twelfth session of the General Assembly was revealing: "the twelfth session was no model of United Nations achievement ... There was a noticeable weariness among the experienced hands of the active delegations." See Extract from the Final Report of the Twelfth Session of the General Assembly in New York," n.d., *Documents on Canadian External Relations* (hereafter *DCER*), vol. 24, *1957-1958*, part 1, ed. Michael D. Stevenson (Ottawa: Minister of Public Works and Government Services, 2003), 30.

21 For an early draft of these ideas, see Holmes, "The Role of the United Nations," 20 March 1957, LAC, L.B. Pearson Papers, MG26 N1 (hereafter Pearson Papers), vol. 63, UN, general, 1947-57.

22 Holmes to Léger, 22 October 1957, Holmes Papers, box 63, file 4.

23 On the UNOGIL, see United Nations Department of Public Information, *The Blue Helmets: A Review of United Nations Peace-keeping*, 3rd ed. (New York: UN Department

of Public Information, 1996), 115-21; and Sean M. Maloney, *Canada and UN Peacekeeping: Cold War by Other Means, 1945-1970* (St. Catharines, ON: Vanwell Publishing, 2002), 90-96. Maloney is more positive about the outcome of UNOGIL.

24 Holmes' views on the Middle East during this period are best captured in Holmes Papers, box 63, file 4. See especially Holmes to Léger, "Some Reflections on the Geneva Agreements of 1954 and the Possibilities of a Settlement in the Middle East," July 1958.

25 Holmes to Alfred Pick, 23 June 1951, Holmes Papers, box 61, file 2.

26 Holmes, "Draft Memorandum," 27 January 1959, *DCER*, vol. 24, part 1, 61.

27 He was at least somewhat successful but only because Prime Minister Diefenbaker took foreign aid seriously.

28 See Ryan Touhey, "Canada and India at 60: Moving beyond History?" *International Journal* 62, 4 (2007): 738-39.

29 Holmes to Ronning, 26 July 1957, and Holmes to Far Eastern Division, 24 October 1957, both in Holmes Papers, box 64, file 1; Holmes, "Memorandum for the Minister," 29 August 1957, John G. Diefenbaker Centre for the Study of Canada, University of Saskatchewan (hereafter DC), John G. Diefenbaker Papers, MG01/XII/F/232, vol. 113, Foreign Aid: Colombo Plan; Holmes, note attached to Glazebrook to Holmes, 17 October 1957, LAC, Department of External Affairs Papers, RG 25 (hereafter DEA Papers), vol. 7128, file 9126-40, part 10.1; and Holmes to Reid, 21 January 1958, LAC, Escott Reid Papers, MG31 E46 (hereafter Escott Reid Papers), vol. 33, file 60, Holmes, J.W., 1951-69.

30 Holmes to USSEA, 8 November 1957, LAC, Albert Edgar Ritchie Papers, MG31 E44 (hereafter A.E. Ritchie Papers), vol. 2, file 22.

31 Holmes to USSEA, 17 February 1958, Holmes Papers, box 63, file 4.

32 Holmes to Peter Campbell, 10 February 1958, Holmes Papers, box 64, file 2.

33 Allan Gotlieb, *Romanticism and Realism in Canada's Foreign Policy* (Toronto: C.D. Howe Institute, 2004), 8. A conversation with Mr. Gotlieb confirmed his continued disappointment. For Gotlieb's original response, see A.E. Gotlieb to Cadieux, 18 December 1958, *DCER*, vol. 24, part 1, 206-12. For Holmes' recollection, see Holmes, "Draft Memorandum, in ibid., 59.

34 Holmes to Rae, 25 March 1958, Holmes Papers, box 64, file 1; Holmes to Robertson, 20 February 1958, LAC, Norman Robertson Papers, vol. 3a, personal correspondence, 1957-58; Holmes to USSEA, 24 March 1958, Holmes Papers, box 66, file 2.

35 Holmes, "The Canadian Role in International Affairs," 3 April 1958, Holmes Papers, box 16, file 32.

36 The official Canadian contribution to the development of the Commonwealth Scholarship Programme is captured in a series of documents in *DCER*, vol. 24, part 1, 844-79. On Holmes' specific contribution, see George F. Curtis to CIIA Library, 24 April 2002, and "The Commonwealth Scholarships: A Personal, Informal Account," both in CIIA Library, John Holmes Biographical Clipping File.

37 Charles Ritchie, diary entry, 16 October 1958, in Ritchie, *Diplomatic Passport: More Undiplomatic Diaries, 1946-1962* (Toronto: Macmillan of Canada, 1981), 150.

38 Lloyd, *Canada in World Affairs: 1957-1959*, 170.

39 Holmes to David, 11 September 1958, Holmes Papers, box 77, file F/I/5; Holmes to USSEA, 9 December 1957, Holmes Papers, file F/I/4; Peter C. Dobell and Robert Willmot, "John Holmes," *International Journal* 33, 1 (1977-78): 106. There was progress in returning the treasures not stored in Quebec but none in the Duplessis situation. For the complete story, see Gordon Swoger, *The Strange Odyssey of Poland's National Treasures, 1939-1961* (Toronto:

Dundurn Group, 2004). On Holmes' later work, see Holmes, n.d., unlabelled memoirs, Holmes Papers, box 74, E/II/7; and Holmes to Edward McWhinney, 18 January 1980, Holmes Papers, box 54, file 2.

40 Holmes to USSEA, 22 December 1958, Holmes Papers, box 61, file 2; Holmes, "Thirteenth Session of the United Nations General Assembly," 27 January 1959, Holmes Papers, box 65, file 6.

41 CSA Ritchie to USSEA, 6 April 1959, *DCER*, vol. 24, part 1, 66.

42 H. Basil Robinson, *Diefenbaker's World: A Populist in Foreign Affairs* (Toronto: University of Toronto Press, 1989), 58-60.

43 Holmes to Robertson, 14 November 1958, LAC, Norman Robertson Papers, vol. 17, personal correspondence, foreign affairs and staff postings.

44 Holmes to Robertson, 22 November 1958, Holmes Papers, box 64, file 6.

45 Holmes to Robertson, 20 November 1958, LAC, A.E. Ritchie Papers, vol. 2, file 9.

46 Among the many representative letters from this period, see Holmes to Reid, 16 February 1959, LAC, Escott Reid Papers, vol. 33, file 60; Holmes to J.P. Erichsen-Brown, 2 March 1959, Holmes Papers, box 64, file 1; Reid to Holmes, 15 May 1959, Holmes Papers, box 66, file 11; Arnold Smith to Holmes, 9 June 1959, Holmes Papers, box 63, file 4.

47 For Holmes' views, see Holmes Papers, box 64, files 1 and 2. On the decline of their importance, see Douglas A. Ross, *In the Interests of Peace: Canada and Vietnam 1954-1973* (Toronto: University of Toronto Press, 1984), 14.

Chapter 6: Ruin and Recovery

1 Robert Taschereau and R.K. Kellock, *The Report of the Royal Commission to Investigate the Facts Relating to and the Circumstances Surrounding the Communication, by Public Officials and Other Persons in Positions of Trust of Secret and Confidential Information to Agents of a Foreign Power* (Ottawa: King's Printer, 1946), 689.

2 Reginald Whitaker, "Origins of the Canadian Government's Internal Security System, 1946-1952," *Canadian Historical Review* 65, 2 (1984): 168.

3 St. Laurent, quoted in "The Public Servant and the Loyalty Problem," in J.E. Hodgetts and D.C. Corbett, *Canadian Public Administration* (Toronto: Macmillan of Canada, 1960), 426.

4 Commission of Inquiry Concerning Certain Activities of the Royal Canadian Mounted Police, *Freedom and Security under the Law*, 2nd report, vol. 2 (Ottawa: Minister of Supply and Services Canada, 1981), 782.

5 John Sawatsky, *Men in the Shadows: The RCMP Security Service* (Toronto: Doubleday Canada, 1980), 125. See also John Hilliker and Donald Barry, *Canada's Department of External Affairs*, vol. 2, *Coming of Age, 1946-1968* (Montreal and Kingston: McGill-Queen's University Press, 1995), 191; Cabinet Directive [29], "Security Screening of Employees," 21 December 1955, Library and Archives Canada (hereafter LAC), Department of External Affairs Papers, RG 25 (hereafter DEA Papers), vol. 5919, file 50207-A-40, part 3.2, AI request A-2005-00434 / cf.; Commission of Inquiry Concerning Certain Activities of the Royal Canadian Mounted Police, *Freedom and Security under the Law*, 782; and Daniel J. Robinson and David Kimmel, "The Queer Career of Homosexual Security Vetting in Cold War Canada," *Canadian Historical Review* 75, 3 (1994): 319-45.

6 Hillenkoetter, quoted in J.L. Granatstein and David Stafford, *Spy Wars: Espionage and Canada from Gouzenko to Glasnost* (Toronto: Key Porter Books, 1990), 104.

7 R.B. Bryce to Diefenbaker, 1 July 1957, John G. Diefenbaker Centre for the Study of Canada, University of Saskatchewan (hereafter DC), John G. Diefenbaker Papers, MG 01/XII/A/18, Cabinet Documents, vol. 1.

8 J.M. Bella to Commissioner, 29 April 1960, G 355-9-1-15, "Homosexuality within the Federal Government Service," in Canadian Lesbian and Gay Archives, Declassified Documents re: Employment of Homosexuals in Federal Civil Service, folder 93-033.

9 On 5 April 1945, the RCMP also chose not to secure "evidence of character" about Holmes because he had served in the department for over two years. See LAC, Public Service Commission Papers, RG 32 (hereafter PSC Papers), vol. 1204, file 1910.06.18.

10 Holmes to Terry [MacDermot], Labour Day 1951, Trinity College Archives, Toronto, John Holmes Papers 002-0001 (hereafter Holmes Papers), box 89, file G/I/9.

11 Undated, unlabelled press clipping, LAC, RCMP Papers, RG 18, Access to Information Request A-2005-003111/cf. Holmes discussed the Watkins issue with journalist Dean Beeby shortly before he died.

12 See the letters included in University of Regina, Archives and Special Collections (hereafter URA), Patrick Lane Papers, 90-102 (hereafter Lane Papers), box 2, file: correspondence, writers, Holmes, John W., 1987-88.

13 D.F. Wall, Security Panel Document SP-199, Memorandum to the Security Panel: Security Cases Involving Character Weakness, with Special Reference to the Problem of Homosexuality, 12 May 1959, LAC, Canadian Security and Intelligence Services Papers, RG 146 (hereafter CSIS Papers), ATIP Request no. 12, files 117-91-88; 117-92-61; 117-92-57.

14 F.H. Soward to Holmes, 30 September 1959, Nancy Skinner Papers (hereafter Skinner Papers), letters to Holmes. See also Morley Scott to Chester Ronning, 7 July 1960, University of British Columbia Archives, box 6, file 2, correspondence.

15 Watkins to Holmes, 23 October 1959, Holmes Papers, box 69, file John Watkins; Léger to Holmes, 9 November 1959, Skinner Papers, letters to Holmes.

16 Holmes to Chester Ronning, 27 October 1959, Holmes Papers, box 69, file R.

17 John Starnes, *Closely Guarded: A Life in Canadian Security and Intelligence* (Toronto: University of Toronto Press, 1998), 53-54; 92-94.

18 Minutes of 68th meeting of the Security Panel, 6 October 1959, LAC, CSIS Papers, ATIP Request no. 12, files 117-91-88; 117-92-61; 117-92-57.

19 Four years later, close colleague Chester Ronning still thought that Holmes might return to the East Block. See Ronning to Holmes, 25 March 1963, Holmes Papers, box 18, file 10.

20 Holmes to Gordon Cox, 11 December 1959, Holmes Papers, box 67, file 3.

21 Holmes to W.B. Nesbitt, 16 December 1959, Holmes Papers, box 68, file M/N.

22 L.B. Pearson to Holmes, 13 January 1960, Holmes Papers, box 56, file 1, part 2, miscellaneous correspondence (Pearson).

23 [Report on] Interview, KWT [Thompson], John W. Holmes, 22 January 1960, in Rockefeller Archive Center (hereafter RAC), Rockefeller Foundation Papers, Collection RF (hereafter Rockefeller Papers), RG 2-1960 (general correspondence), series 427, reel 41, page 0256.

24 Holmes to Mother, 1 February 1960, Skinner Papers, John W. Holmes, letters to his family, 1960.

25 Holmes later claimed that he made his final decision at colleague Thomas Stone's farm one weekend in March. He saw how the stresses of the foreign service had deprived his close friend of his exuberance and energy and decided to leave before the same thing happened to him. It would be more accurate to say that he came to grips with a decision that he had already made at that time. See Holmes to James Boyd, 26 April 1966; Holmes to Joseph

I. Wearing, 4 May 1966; and Holmes to Norman Robertson, 21 September 1966, all in Holmes Papers, box 39, file 2, part 2, miscellany (Stone Memorial Fund).

26 McGuff to Holmes, 11 April 1960, Skinner Papers, letters to Holmes.

27 Holmes to Mama, 4 February 1960, Skinner Papers, John W. Holmes, letters to his family, 1960.

28 Holmes to Cadieux, 10 February 1960, LAC, Marcel Cadieux Papers, MG31 E31, vol. 3, file 2.

29 Holmes, "Principle and Practices of Canadian Foreign Policy: The Role of a Middle Power," Speech to Trinity Historical Society, Duke University, 7 April 1960, Holmes Papers, box 7, file 10. One might note the similarities to Kim Nossal's analysis in his "Canada and the Search for World Order: John W. Holmes and Canadian Foreign Policy," *International Journal* 59, 4 (2004): 759.

30 CIIA, 2nd meeting of the National Executive Committee, 15 March 1960, LAC, Canadian Institute of International Affairs Papers, MG28 I250 (hereafter CIIA Papers), reel M-422, fol. 12, minutes, 1959-61.

31 Holmes to Robertson, 23 March 1960, LAC, PSC Papers, vol. 1204, personnel file.

32 Robertson to Holmes, 28 March 1960, Skinner Papers, letters to Holmes.

33 "Termination of Employment," n.d., LAC, PSC Papers, vol. 1204, file 1910.06.18.

34 Watkins to Holmes, 14 April 1960; Cadieux to Holmes, 20 February 1960; Klaus to Holmes, 4 May 1960; Soward to Holmes, 5 April 1960, all in Skinner Papers, letters to Holmes. There are countless others. For an international response, see Stephen H. Stackpole, memorandum, 4 August 1960, Carnegie Corporation Archives (hereafter CCA), Carnegie Corporation Papers, MS Coll CCNY, Carnegie Corporation, US Foreign Policy (hereafter Carnegie Papers), series IIIA, grant files, box 460, folder 13, CIIA, 1956-71, cited from reel 6, 2005-7009.

35 Smith, "John Holmes' Voice," *Ottawa Journal*, 22 April 1960, cited in LAC, Escott Reid Papers, MG31 E46 (hereafter Escott Reid Papers), vol. 34, Holmes, John W., memorial (6), 1988. See also Blair Fraser to Holmes, 14 April 1960; and Smith to Holmes, 19 April 1960, both in Skinner Papers, letters to Holmes.

36 Holmes to McGuff, 21 April 1960, LAC, PSC Papers, vol. 1204, personnel file; Holmes to Reid, 2 April 1960, LAC, Escott Reid Papers, vol. 33, file 60, Holmes, John W., 1951-69; Holmes, interview with Peter Stursberg, Toronto, 30 June 1978, LAC, Peter Stursberg Papers, MG31 D78 (hereafter Stursberg Papers), vol. 29, John Holmes, 1978; Holmes, *Conversation between Professor John Holmes and Professor David Dilks on Friday, 28 June 1985 at the University of Leeds* (Toronto: CIIA, n.d.). See also Holmes to Thompson, 5 May 1960, RAC, Rockefeller Papers, RG 2-1960, series 427, reel 41, pp. 0260-0261.

37 Minutes of the 70th meeting of the Security Panel, 21 June 1963, LAC, CSIS Papers, vol. 107, AH-2000/00205; Minutes of special meeting of the Security Panel, 24 June 1960; and R.B. Bryce to Prime Minister and Minister of Justice, 19 December 1960, both in LAC, CSIS Papers, ATIP Request no. 12, files 117-91-88; 117-92-61; 117-92-57.

38 Minutes of the 70th meeting of the Security Panel, 21 June 1963, LAC, CSIS Papers, vol. 107, AH-2000/00205.

39 Cabinet Directive No. 35: Security in the Public Service of Canada, 18 December 1963, LAC, CSIS Papers, vol. 107, AH-2000/00205.

40 Mulroney, 27 April 1992, Canada, House of Commons, *Debates*, 3rd session, 34th Parliament, vol. 8, 9713. Hector Mackenzie deals with this effectively in his "Purged ... from

Memory: The Department of External Affairs and John Holmes," *International Journal* 59, 2 (2004): 375-86.

CHAPTER 7: HEADFIRST INTO THE CIIA

1 On the state of affairs at the time, see Edgar McInnis to Florence Anderson, 24 June 1960, Carnegie Corporation Archives (hereafter CCA), Carnegie Corporation Papers, MS Coll CCNY, Carnegie Corporation, US Foreign Policy (hereafter Carnegie Papers), series IIIA, Grant Files, box 70c, folder 9, CIIA, Information Service, reel 1: 2005-7004.
2 Holmes to Mama, 14 May 1960, Nancy Skinner Papers (hereafter Skinner Papers), John W. Holmes, letters to his family, 1960. See also Holmes to Cecil R. Evans, 27 July 1961, Trinity College Archives, Toronto, John Holmes Papers 002-0001 (hereafter Holmes Papers), box 51, file 1.
3 Holmes to Escott Reid, 3 August 1965, Library and Archives Canada (hereafter LAC), Escott Reid Papers, MG31 E46 (hereafter Escott Reid Papers), vol. 33, file 60, Holmes, John W., 1951-69.
4 Holmes to Pearson, 12 August 1960, Holmes Papers, box 56, file 1, part 2; Holmes to Joseph E. Johnson, 4 December 1970, Holmes Papers, box 53, file 2.
5 Holmes to Glazebrook, n.d. [mid-April 1962], Holmes Papers, box 35, file 9. See the rest of the file for more detail.
6 Peter C. Dobell and Robert Willmot, "John Holmes," *International Journal* 33, 1 (1977-78): 109-10.
7 Eventually, the CIIA broke off and organized its own meetings separately. The results of the change were mixed. For a time, attendance at the annual conference increased, but the new schedule sacrificed some of the networking opportunities that the Learneds – as the most critical conference of the year for Canadian academics in the humanities and social sciences is known – had provided.
8 Holmes to Norman Robertson, 28 September 1960, LAC, Canadian Institute of International Affairs Papers, MG28 I250 (hereafter CIIA Papers), vol. 20, general, Pacific Affairs, University of British Columbia, 1960-62.
9 Holmes to Reid, 19 August 1960, LAC, Escott Reid Papers, vol. 33, file 60, Holmes, John W., 1951-69.
10 William Taubman, *Khrushchev: The Man and His Era* (New York: W.W. Norton, 2003), 475; George Martell, *Experiment in World Government: An Account of the United Nations Operation in the Congo, 1960-1964* (London: Johnson Publications, 1966), 67-69; Rajeshwar Dayal, *Mission for Hammarskjöld: The Congo Crisis* (Princeton: Princeton University Press, 1976), 92-93.
11 Holmes, "Mr. Khrushchev and the United Nations," CBC Mid-week Review, 5 October 1960, LAC, Escott Reid Papers, vol. 33, file 60, Holmes, John W., 1951-69.
12 Denis Stairs, "The Pedagogics of John W. Holmes," *International Journal* 44, 4 (1989): 926,
13 The *Forum* article can be found in Holmes Papers, box 1, file 11. See also Holmes, "The United Nations in the Congo," *International Journal* 16, 1 (1960-61): 1-16.
14 CIIA, minutes of meeting of National Research Committee, 19 October 1960, LAC, CIIA Papers, reel M-4622, vol. 12, minutes 1959-61.
15 Holmes to Lower, 14 January 1943, Queen's University Archives, Arthur Lower Papers, Coll. 5072, box 47, section 12, folder C52.

16 Holmes to Joseph E. Johnson, 14 February 1961, LAC, CIIA Papers, vol. 13, conferences, Bilderberg Conference, 1961; Holmes to Nik Cavell, 21 April 1961, Holmes Papers, box 50, file 2, miscellaneous correspondence (Ca).

17 CIIA, 1st meeting of the National Council, 9 June 1961, LAC, CIIA Papers, reel M-4622, vol. 12, minutes, 1959-61.

18 Holmes to Herbert O. Moran, 6 September 1961, LAC, CIIA Papers, vol. 11, conferences, Conference on Canadian Overseas Assistance, general, 1961-62.

19 Holmes to CIIA Branch Chairmen and Secretaries, 20 November 1961, LAC, CIIA Papers, vol. 8, conferences, 28th Annual Study Conference, 1960-61.

20 Minutes of 2nd meeting of the National Executive Committee, Bank of Nova Scotia, 7 March 1962, CIIA Library, minutes, vol. 13, 1962-64. For details on the conception and evolution of the monthly reports, see the Stephanie Reford Papers, specifically the letters between Holmes and Reford in 1961-62.

21 Holmes to Howard Green [draft], n.d. [February 1961], Holmes Papers, box 74, file E/II/8; CIIA, 1st meeting of the National Executive Committee, 15 February 1961, LAC, CIIA Papers, reel M-4622, vol. 12, minutes, 1959-61. See also Holmes to W. Fred Bull [Canadian Ambassador to Japan], 16 February 1961, Holmes Papers, box 74, file E/II/8. In 1962, Holmes spoke to the City of Toronto's Social Planning Council on the importance of changing national attitudes towards immigration and new immigrants.

22 Robertson to Green, 24 February 1961, LAC, Department of External Affairs Papers, RG 25 (hereafter DEA Papers), file 6386-C-40, part 11. There does not appear to be any additional correspondence in the files of the Department of External Affairs.

23 Holmes to LePan, n.d., Thomas Fisher Rare Book Library, University of Toronto, D.V. LePan Papers, MS. Coll. 104, box 50, file 7; Holmes to Conor Cruise O'Brien, 13 January 1988, Holmes Papers, box 55, file 4; Holmes to Mark Zacher, 11 March 1970, Holmes Papers, box 39, file 1; and Holmes, "In Memoriam: Dag Hammarskjöld," speech to Toronto Women's Branch of CIIA, 20 September 1961, Holmes Papers, box 16, file 31.

24 Holmes to James S. Duncan, 2 May 1961, LAC, CIIA Papers, vol. 13, conferences, Bilderberg Conference, 1961.

25 Holmes to M.W. Duckworth, 20 April 1961, LAC, CIIA Papers, vol. 18, conferences, United Nations Seminar, Mt. Allison University, 1960-62.

26 On middle powers, see Adam Chapnick, "The Middle Power," *Canadian Foreign Policy* 7, 2 (1999): 73-82; and Chapnick, "The Canadian Middle Power Myth," *International Journal* 55, 2 (2000): 188-206.

27 Holmes, "The Politics of Independence," 7 August 1961, Holmes Papers, box 7, file 7; James M. Minifie, *Peacemaker or Powder-Monkey* (Toronto: McClelland and Stewart, 1960); Holmes, "Canada's Role," with Duff Roblin and James Eayrs, in *Diplomacy in Evolution*, ed. D.L.B. Hamlin, 112-25 (Toronto: University of Toronto Press, 1961); I. Norman Smith, "Neutrality, Says John Holmes, Is 'Excessively Logical,'" *Ottawa Citizen*, 4 October 1961, cited in Holmes Papers, box 2, file 1.

28 Holmes, "Canada and the United States in World Politics," *Foreign Affairs* 40, 1 (1961): 109, 113.

29 Holmes, "Negotiating with the Russians," *Commerce Journal* (February 1962): 7-12.

30 Brian Lapping, *Apartheid: A History*, rev. ed. (New York: George Brazziler, 1989 [1987]), 138-39.

31 On this issue, see Robert Bothwell, *Alliance and Illusion: Canada and the World, 1945-1984* (Vancouver: UBC Press, 2007), 142-44; H. Basil Robertson, *Diefenbaker's World: A Populist in Foreign Affairs* (Toronto: University of Toronto Press, 1989), 174-79; and Denis Smith,

Rogue Tory: The Life and Legend of John G. Diefenbaker (Toronto: Macfarlane, Walter and Ross, 1995), 353-66.

32 Holmes, "The Commonwealth as Idea and Prophesy," *Canadian Commentator* 5, 5 (1961): 4-7, at 4.

33 Transcript of CBC's *Weekend Review*, 4 June 1961, Holmes Papers, box 21, file 2, part 3.

34 Holmes, "The Impact on the Commonwealth of the Emergence of Africa," *International Organization* 16,2 (1962): 302; Holmes to Ed Ritchie, 2 November 1961, LAC, CIIA Papers, vol. 12, conferences, World Peace Foundation, Montreal conference, 1961; Holmes, "Political Implications of the European Economic Community," *Queen's Quarterly* 69, 1 (162): 1-10; Holmes to James S. Duncan, 5 April 1962, Holmes Papers, box 50, file 6.

35 Holmes to Reid, 2 April 1962, LAC, Escott Reid Papers, vol. 33, file 60, Holmes, John W., 1951-69.

36 J.M. Macdonnell to Holmes, 19 March 1962, Holmes Papers, box 54, file 1.

37 Stairs, "The Pedagogics of John W. Holmes," 936.

38 Minutes of first meeting of the National Council, 8 June 1962, CIIA Library, minutes, vol. 13, 1962-64.

39 Minutes of 4th meeting of the National Executive Committee, 28 June 1962, CIIA Library, minutes, vol. 13, 1962-64.

40 Educated at Stanford and Cornell, she had recently moved to Toronto with her husband. Clinton Rossiter, a Cornell professor of American government and politics, sent a letter of introduction to the CIIA, and Holmes hired her almost immediately. He found room for her next to his office, and the two developed an excellent rapport. They remained close after Schoeffel left the CIIA to pursue other interests.

41 CIIA, "Report on Expenditures by the Canadian Institute of International Affairs of a Grant from the Ford Foundation, 1963-1967," 22 April 1968, LAC, CIIA Papers, vol. 18, conferences, University of Guelph, Conference on China, 1966-68; Holmes to Paul Martin (Sr.), 24 April 1963, Holmes Papers, box 54, file 4, part 1; minutes of 2nd meeting of the National Council, 8 December 1962, CIIA Library, minutes, vol. 13, 1962-64.

42 Holmes to Mother, 26 January 1963, Skinner Papers, John W. Holmes, letters to his family, 1963.

43 Holmes to Michael Brecher, 27 August 1963, Holmes Papers, box 18, file 10; minutes of the 5th meeting of the [CIIA] National Executive Committee, 3 October 1962, CIIA Library, minutes, vol. 13, 1962-64. Holmes also personally hosted six sessions of the University Abroad series, which enabled faculty to discuss their international research projects on the CBC.

44 Harald von Riekhoff, *NATO: Issues and Prospects* (Toronto: CIIA, 1967). Subsequent postdoctoral fellowships were awarded to such talented researchers as Henry Wiseman, Carsten Holbraad, Guy Gosselin, and Carl Jacobsen.

45 William Diebold, quoted in "John Holmes: An Appreciation," *Behind the Headlines* 46, 1 (1988): 2. See also Holmes to Chairmen, 4 June 1962, LAC, CIIA Papers, vol. 8, conferences, 29th Annual Study Conference, 1962.

46 On the development of the conference, see LAC, CIIA Papers, vol. 9, conferences, Banff Conference on World Development, 1962-64.

47 Minutes of 2nd meeting of the National Council, 7 December 1963, and minutes of 3rd meeting of the National Executive Committee, 29 April 1964, both in CIIA Library, minutes, vol. 13, 1962-64. See also LAC, CIIA Papers, vols. 13 and 16, conferences.

48 CIIA rules limited media coverage and precluded participants from being quoted directly during or after a private, sponsored event.

49 Minutes of 5th meeting of the National Executive Committee, 1 August 1963, CIIA Library, minutes, vol. 13, 1962-64.

50 Holmes, "Canadian External Policies Since 1945," speech to American Historical Association, Chicago, 28 December 1962, Holmes Papers, box 7, file 4.

51 Holmes, "Canadian External Policies Since 1945," *International Journal* 18, 2 (1963): 137-47; Holmes, "The Diplomacy of a Middle Power," *Atlantic Monthly* 214, 5 (1964): 106-12. On Holmes' insistence on the use of the term "middle power," see Holmes to A.M. Halpern, 28 September 1964, Holmes Papers, box 18, file 10.

52 Holmes to Crocker, 12 December 1962, Holmes Papers, box 3, file 15.

53 For representative examples, see Holmes, "Can the Commonwealth Survive? Canadian Answer," *The Round Table*, 213 (December 1963): 12-16; Holmes, "The Commonwealth Faces 1964," *The Times* (London), cited in Holmes Papers, box 4, file 5; and Holmes, "Present Realities of the Commonwealth," speech to the National Conference on Canadian Goals [sponsored by the Progressive Conservative Association of Canada], 9-12 September 1964, Holmes Papers, box 7, file 14.

54 Bothwell, *Alliance and Illusion*, 167-68.

55 For a summary from a Canadian perspective, see Bothwell, *Alliance and Illusion*, 166-69; and Peyton V. Lyon, *Canada in World Affairs, 1961-1963* (Toronto: Oxford University Press, 1968), 27-64.

56 Holmes, "Are Canadians Really Friends of the United States," speech to Bowling Green University, 26 October 1962, Holmes Papers, box 6, file 8.

57 Holmes, "The Unequal Alliance: Canada and the United States," *Fourth Seminar on Canadian-American Relations* (Windsor: University of Windsor, 1962), 249, 265.

58 Holmes, "Let's Drop Our Jealous Attitude," *Toronto Daily Star*, 11 June 1963, cited in Holmes Papers, box 5, file 5.

59 See Holmes, "Canada in Search of its Role," *Foreign Affairs* 41, 4 (1963): 659-72.

60 Lincoln P. Bloomfield to Gayle Fraser, 9 September 1988, Holmes Papers, box 101, file November 10, DEA Delegation.

61 Holmes, "The Atlantic Community: Unity and Reality," speech given to the Atlantic Treaty Association, 15 September 1964, cited in Holmes Papers, box 11, file 13. See also, among many, Holmes, "Why an Atlantic Community," CBC's *Weekend Review*, 26 May 1963, Holmes Papers, box 21, file 2, part 2.

62 Holmes, quoted in CBC's *Weekend Review*, 15 September 1963, in ibid.

63 Holmes, "Peacekeeping in Asia," speech to the Institute for Strategic Studies, 20 September 1964, Holmes Papers, box 11, file 16.

64 Holmes to Nik Cavell, 9 October 1962, Holmes Papers, box 50, file 2. See also Holmes to Brigadier D.C. Cameron, 15 February 1963, Holmes Papers, box 8, file 8, part 3.

65 Holmes, quoted in CBC Pre View Commentary, 27 January 1964, Holmes Papers, box 21, file 2, part 2.

66 Denis Stairs is more forgiving. See his "The Pedagogics of John W. Holmes," 935-36.

67 Watkins to Holmes, 19 February 1963, Holmes Papers, box 69, file (John Watkins).

68 Holmes to Arthur Campbell, 22 October 1963, Holmes Papers, box 35, file 8. For details on the rest of the experience, see the rest of the file.

69 Holmes, Lecture No. 1: The Qualities of the Profession, n.d., Holmes Papers, box 35, file 8.

70 Holmes, "Notes on a Visit to Australia, March 1-12, 1964," Holmes Papers, box 6, file 14.

71 Holmes to Arnold Smith, 23 October 1964, Holmes Papers, box 57, file 5.

72 Holmes to Arthur Campbell, 15 December 1964, Holmes Papers, box 35, file 7; Holmes to Mother, 3 December 1964, Skinner Papers, John W. Holmes, letters to his family, 1964.

CHAPTER 8: A DIPLOMAT IN ACTION

1 During this period, he finally began to turn down requests to speak, to write, and to participate on committees. The evidence can be found throughout his papers in the 1965-67 years and stands in contrast to his less critical attitude towards similar offers just a couple of years earlier.

2 Holmes, quoted in CBC's *Weekend Review*, 10 January 1965, Trinity College Archives, Toronto, John Holmes Papers 002-0001 (hereafter Holmes Papers), box 21, file 2, part 1. His comments reflected long-held views that he had publicly expressed in 1955. See Holmes, "Lecture on the United Nations to Be Delivered to the Annual Meeting of the United Nations Association, Toronto," 5 May 1955, Holmes Papers, box 14, file 20.

3 Abraham Rotstein, *The Precarious Homestead: Essays on Economics, Technology, and Nationalism* (Toronto: New Press, 1973), preface.

4 Holmes, "Canada and Vietnam," quoted in CBC's *Weekend Review*, 21 February 1965, Holmes Papers, box 21, file 2, part 1; Holmes to Pearson, 28 April 1965, Holmes Papers, box 56, file 1, part 2; Holmes, "What the World Expects of Canada," speech to the Hamilton Canadian Club, 29 April 1964, Holmes Papers, box 7, file 8.

5 Holmes, "Canada and the Western Alliance: Aspirations and Realities," speech to Hamilton Association, 13 February 1965, Holmes Papers, box 8, file 1; Holmes, "What the World Expects of Canada," speech to Montreal Canadian Club, 22 February 1965, Holmes Papers, box 10, file 6.

6 Holmes to Léger, 5 February 1955, Holmes Papers, box 77, file F/I/4. See also Holmes [signed by Pearson] to High Commissioner in London, 2 March 1955, Holmes Papers, box 65, file 5; and Holmes, "International Cooperation: The Hard Way," speech to London Council of Women, 20 April 1965, Holmes Papers, box 9, file 4.

7 Arnold Heeney and Livingston T. Merchant, *Canada and the United States: Principles for Partnership,* 28 June 1965, 49.

8 J. King Gordon, "Foreword," in *Canada's Role as a Middle Power*, ed. J. King Gordon (Toronto: CIIA, 1966).

9 Charles Hanly, "The Ethics of Independence," in *An Independent Foreign Policy for Canada?* ed. Stephen Clarkson (Toronto: McClelland and Stewart, 1968), 27.

10 Holmes to Paul M. Eisele, 3 August 1965, Holmes Papers, box 51, file 1; Holmes to Terry MacDermot, 3 August 1965, Holmes Papers, box 54, file 3.

11 Denis Stairs, "The Pedagogics of John W. Holmes," *International Journal* 44, 4 (1989): 936.

12 Holmes to Peter Scott, 20 August 1965, Holmes Papers, box 57, file 4; Holmes to Robert Chaput, 2 November 1965, Holmes Papers, box 50, file 3; Holmes to Alvin Gluek, 16 December 1965, Holmes Papers, box 7, file 12; and Martin L. Friedland, *The University of Toronto: A History* (Toronto: University of Toronto Press, 2002), 527-28. The US official eventually withdrew from the session after learning that his counterpart representing the Vietnamese was going to be an American rather than a member of the Viet Cong.

13 Holmes, "Is There a Future for Middlepowermanship," in Gordon, *Canada's Role as a Middle Power*, 14, 18, 28.

14 Arnold Heeney, "Dealing with Uncle Sam," in Gordon, *Canada's Role as a Middle Power,* 97, 100.

15 On this issue, see Philip Massolin, *Canadian Intellectuals, the Tory Tradition, and the Challenge of Modernity, 1939-1970* (Toronto: University of Toronto Press, 2001), 12-20, 277-84.

16 Holmes to Alvin Gluek, 1 September 1965, Holmes Papers, box 7, file 12. See also Holmes to Robert Campbell, 2 September 1965, Holmes Papers, box 6, file 4; Holmes to Brian

Crane, 10 September 1965, Holmes Papers, box 50, file 5; and Holmes to Norman Harper, 20 September 1965, Library and Archives Canada (hereafter LAC), Canadian Institute of International Affairs Papers, MG28 I250 (hereafter CIIA Papers), vol. 9, conferences, Banff Conference on World Development, 1964-67.

17 Holmes to Lloyd Axworthy, 3 September 1965, LAC, CIIA Papers, vol. 9, conferences, Banff Conference on World Development, 1964-67. Jim Arnett was a graduate of the University of Manitoba who was then taking a law degree at Harvard and had met Holmes while doing research on continental defence. After turning down an offer to work at the CIIA, he went on to a distinguished career as a business lawyer.

18 Lloyd Axworthy to Holmes, 23 September 1965, LAC, CIIA Papers, vol. 9, conferences, Banff Conference on World Development, 1964-67.

19 Holmes to Paul Martin Sr., 2 March 1967, Holmes Papers, box 54, part 4, file 1. The final version of the Russell chapter included a paragraph that read, "One of the requisites for Canada's playing any distinctive role, other than that of a satellite, is the maintenance of a considerable degree of independence. The strength and vitality of its nationalism is an important element of its independence. Without a sense of identity, pride, attachment to his own group, the citizen becomes too susceptible to external influences to sustain a national foreign policy. Nationalism itself is, in part, a function of what a nation accomplishes in international society. So the foreign policy of Canada must be designed as to bolster Canadian nationalism and in doing so Canadian independence." See Holmes, "Nationalism in Canadian Foreign Policy," in *Nationalism in Canada*, ed. Peter Russell (Toronto: McGraw-Hill Ryerson, 1966), 214. Axworthy had written: "the foreign policy of Canada should be so designed as to bolster Canadian independence – otherwise we perish or at least dwindle." See Axworthy to Holmes, 23 September 1965, LAC, CIIA Papers, vol. 9, conferences, Banff Conference on World Development, 1964-67.

20 Holmes to D. Roland Michener, 2 June 1964, Holmes Papers, box 55, file 1, part 1; minutes of the 1st meeting of the National Council, 12 June 1964, CIIA Library, minutes, vol. 13, 1962-64.

21 Mayo to Holmes, 9 October 1963 and 10 March 1965, both in Holmes Papers, box 54, file 4, part 2; Holmes to Bissell, 3 March 1965, Holmes Papers, box 49, file 5; Holmes to Peyton Lyon, 21 June 1965, Holmes Papers, box 53, file 6.

22 Holmes to Heeney, 9 March 1965, LAC, Arnold Danford Patrick Heeney Papers, MG30 E144 (hereafter Heeney Papers), vol. 6, Canadian Institute of International Affairs, 1963-68.

23 Minutes of the 5th meeting of the CIIA National Executive Committee, 11 May 1965, CIIA Library, minutes, vol. 14, 1965-67.

24 Holmes to Robert Clark, 19 May 1965, Holmes Papers, box 50, file 3; John Barfoot Macdonald, *University of British Columbia: Report of the President for the Academic Year, 1964-1965* (Vancouver: University of British Columbia, 1966).

25 Appendix B, "Preliminary Report: The Special Committee of the Future Role of the Institute," appended to minutes of the 1st meeting of the CIIA National Council, 11 June 1965, CIIA Library, minutes, vol. 14, 1965-67.

26 One year earlier, James Eayrs resigned from the CIIA because of a controversy involving institute rules, which precluded him from inviting the CBC to cover a guest lecture by one of his colleagues. Eayrs stayed on as editor of the *International Journal*.

27 Holmes to Henry E. Langford, 24 June 1965, LAC, CIIA Papers, vol. 13, conferences, World Peace Foundation, Boston Conference (1965); Holmes to Heeney, n.d., LAC, Heeney

Papers, vol. 6, Canadian Institute of International Affairs, 1965-69, correspondence and memoranda on the future of the institute; minutes of 2nd meeting of the CIIA National Council, 3-4 December 1965, CIIA Library, minutes, vol. 14, 1965-67.

28 Holmes to Claude Bissell, 19 May 1964, and Bissell to Holmes, 28 May 1964, both in Holmes Papers, box 30, file 3, part 2; Holmes to George Connell, 2 April 1986, Holmes Papers, box 41, file 4, part 1; and Holmes to Heeney, n.d., LAC, Heeney Papers, vol. 6, Canadian Institute of International Affairs, 1965-69, correspondence and memoranda on the future of the institute.

29 Holmes, private memorandum to Heeney, Langford, Brady, Wright, Armstrong, and Gibson, 3 January 1966, LAC, Heeney Papers, vol. 6, Canadian Institute of International Affairs, 1965-69, correspondence and memoranda on the future of the institute.

30 Wright to Heeney, 25 January 1966, and Heeney to Langford, 26 January 1966, draft summary of results of meeting of 18 February 1966, all LAC, Heeney Papers, vol. 6, Canadian Institute of International Affairs, 1965-69, correspondence and memoranda on the future of the institute.

31 Langford to Heeney, 21 February 1966, Holmes to Langford, 24 February 1966, Holmes to Heeney, 16 March 1966, all in LAC, Heeney Papers, vol. 6, Canadian Institute of International Affairs, 1965-69, correspondence and memoranda on the future of the institute.

32 Holmes to Wright, 4 March 1966, and Holmes, draft memo to Pratt, 9 March 1967, both in Holmes Papers, box 30, file 3, part 2; R.C. Pratt to Holmes, 24 June 1966, LAC, Heeney Papers, vol. 6, Canadian Institute of International Affairs, 1965-69, correspondence and memoranda on the future of the institute; Holmes to Pratt, 21 December 1967, Holmes Papers, box 30, file 3, part 1; Holmes to J.E. Smyth, 8 March 1967, Holmes Papers, box 30, file 1, part 2.

33 Holmes, "Canada and Pan America," *Journal of Inter-American Studies* 10, 2 (1968): 173; Holmes, "A Common 'Third World Policy for the West," 14-18 October 1965, Holmes Papers, box 6, file 5; "Canada and the United States in the World Economy: Summary of the Meetings Jointly Sponsored by the CIIA and the World Peace Foundation," 22-24 October 1965, LAC, CIIA Papers, vol. 134, conferences, World Peace Foundation, Boston Conference, 1965.

34 Holmes, "An Open Question: Has the Commonwealth a Future?" *Optima* 16, 3 (1966), 121, 126; Holmes, "Canada and the Commonwealth," *Jeune Afrique* (December 1966), cited in Holmes Papers, box 3, file 1; Holmes, "The Commonwealth and the United Nations," in *A Decade of the Commonwealth, 1955-1964*, ed. W.B. Hamilton, Kenneth Robinson, and C.D.W. Goodwin, 349-65 (Durham, NC: Duke University Press, 1966).

35 Holmes, "Canada as a Middle Power," *Centennial Review* 10, 4 (1966): 435. This article was based on a speech delivered to the Conference on Canadian-American Relations sponsored by the Committee for Canadian-American Studies at Michigan State University.

36 Holmes, "Alliance and Independence," in *La Dualité Canadienne À L'heure des Etats-Unis*, ed. Raymond Morel, (Quebec: Les Presses de l'Université Laval, 1965), 55-56; Holmes, "NATO: A Peacekeeping Agency," cited in Holmes Papers, box 1, file 9; Holmes, "The Role of Middle Powers in the World," speech to United Nations Association in Dublin, Ireland, 21 November 1966, Holmes Papers, box 7, file 9; Holmes, "Canada's Role in the United Nations," *Air University Review* (May/June 1967): 18-27.

37 Holmes to Harvey, 10 May 1967, Holmes Papers, box 52, file 3.

38 Holmes to Martin (Sr.), 17 June 1965, 10 May 1966, and 29 June 1967, all in Holmes Papers, box 54, file 4, part 1.

39 Holmes to Stanley Tupper, 21 September 1965, Holmes Papers, box 58, file 4; Holmes
    to Marcel Cadieux, 11 January 1966, LAC, CIIA Papers, vol. 14, Conferences, Carleton
    University Conference, the Future of NATO, 1966; Holmes to Peter Campbell, 15 August
    1966, Holmes Papers, box 50, file 2.

40 Holmes to Arnold Heeney, 21 September 1965, Holmes Papers, box 39, file 2, part 2;
    International Assembly on Nuclear Weapons, Final Report, 23-26 June 1966, LAC, CIIA
    Papers, vol. 17, conferences, Conference on Nuclear Proliferation (Proposed), 1966, no.
    1, 1965-66; Holmes to Don M. Cornett, 28 June 1966, in ibid.; Holmes to King Gordon,
    7 September 1966, LAC, CIIA Papers, vol. 10, conferences, Banff Conference on World
    Affairs, part 1, 1966-67; Holmes to James L. Cooper, 1 April 1969, Holmes Papers, box 50,
    file 4.

41 Holmes to Emily Stone, 6 February 1967, Holmes Papers, box 39, file 2, part 2.

42 Holmes to Claude Julien, 28 March 1967, Holmes Papers, box 102, Camp, Dalton; Holmes
    to Jean Chapdelaine, 28 March 1967, in ibid; and Holmes to Leonard Beaton, 3 April 1967,
    Holmes Papers, box 47, file 7. On the connection with Pearson, see Holmes to Ed Ritchie
    and Holmes to Pearson, both on 3 February 1967, Holmes Papers, box 2, file 1; Holmes
    to Emily Stone, 6 February 1967, Holmes Papers, box 39, file 2, part 2. On Nyerere, see
    Holmes to David Reece, 23 May 1967, Holmes Papers, box 37, file 1, part 2.

43 Holmes to Reid, 27 June 1967, Holmes Papers, box 13, file 15. The authors were Escott
    Reid, Doug LePan, and Wynne Plumptre.

44 For examples, see Holmes to Pamela Arnold, 28 February 1967, Holmes Papers, box 11,
    file 8; and Holmes, "Conscience in Canadian Foreign Policy," 28 February 1967, Holmes
    Papers, box 13, file 14. The article that was reproduced is Holmes, "Fearful Symmetry: The
    Dilemmas of Consultation and Coordination in the North Atlantic Treaty Organization,"
    International Organization 22, 4 (1968): 821-40.

45 Holmes, "Address on Volunteer Participation in the Formulation of Public Policy," speech
    to the UN Association in Canada, 2 June 1967, Holmes Papers, box 10, file 3.

46 On his relationship with the military colleges, see Holmes Papers, box 46, file 2, and box
    13, file 3, part 2.

47 Holmes, "A Canadian Viewpoint: Vietnam Is Your War, Not Ours," *Los Angeles Times*, 9
    October 1966. Most, if not all, of his *Times* articles can be found in Holmes Papers, box
    5, file 5.

CHAPTER 9: 1967: A YEAR OF TRANSITION

1 Pearson, quoted in Bill McNeil, *John Fisher: "Mr. Canada"* (Markham, ON: Fitzhenry and
   Whiteside, 1983), 50.

2 Escott Reid, "Canadian Foreign Policy, 1967-1977: A Second Golden Decade?" *International
   Journal* 22, 2 (1967): 172.

3 Holmes, quoted in Pierre Berton, *1967: The Last Good Year* (Toronto: Doubleday, 1997), 39.

4 Holmes, "A New Century and a New Confidence," *LA Times*, 17 December 1967, Trinity
   College Archives, Toronto, John Holmes Papers 002-0001 (hereafter Holmes Papers), box
   5, file 5.

5 Holmes, "Canada's Role in the World," Holmes Papers, box 1, file 16; Holmes to J.W. Duf-
   frin, 4 January 1967, Holmes Papers, box 1, file 12 (see entire file for more detail); Holmes,
   "The Necessity of Nationalism," Holmes Papers, box 1, file 17. On his continued academic

engagement, see, for example, Holmes, "Key Issues in Canadian Foreign Policy," in *Peace, Power and Protest*, ed. Paul Evans, 200-16 (Toronto: Ryerson Press, 1967).

6 Holmes to Roland Michener, 26 May 1964, Holmes Papers, box 39, file 3, part 2. The rest of the file (parts 1 and 2) covers the entire story in detail. A conversation with Mr. Dobell provided some clarification. See also minutes of the 2nd meeting of the National Council, 12 December 1964, CIIA Library, minutes, vol. 13, 1962-64.

7 Marcel Cadieux, *The Canadian Diplomat: An Essay in Definition*, trans. Archibald Day (Toronto: University of Toronto Press, 1963 [1962]).

8 Outside of the Holmes Papers cited earlier, more coverage of the later developments of the Parliamentary Centre can be found in CIIA Library, minutes, vol. 14, 1965-67.

9 Dobell to Holmes, undated Christmas card, Holmes Papers, box 67, file 4.

10 Holmes, "The American Civil War and Canada Today," *Saturday Night*, 19 August 1939, 2.

11 Holmes to Jacques Garneau, 24 August 1962, Library and Archives Canada (hereafter LAC), Canadian Institute of International Affairs Papers, MG28 I250 (hereafter CIIA Papers), vol. 8, conferences, 30th Annual Study Conference, 1963.

12 Holmes to Trudeau, 27 November 1962, Holmes Papers, box 58, file 4; minutes of the 2nd meeting of the National Council, 8 December 1962, and minutes of the 1st meeting of the National Council, 8 June 1963, both in CIIA Library, minutes, vol. 13, 1962-64.

13 Holmes to Duncan Campbell, 1 September 1965, Holmes Papers, box 50, file 2.

14 Holmes to Herb H. Lank, 25 November 1968, Holmes Papers, box 24, file 23. See also Holmes, appendix to minutes of 2nd meeting of CIIA National Council, 27 September 1966, CIIA Library, minutes, vol. 14, 1965-67; Holmes to Carroll L. Wilson, 7 March 1967, LAC, CIIA Papers, vol. 13, conferences, World Peace Foundation, Quebec City Conference, 1968, along with subsequent correspondence in the same file; and Holmes to Pratt, 28 December 1967, Holmes Papers, box 55, file 5, part 2.

15 This story is recounted in Holmes Papers, box 16, file 35, parts 1 and 2.

16 John Holmes, *The Better Part of Valour: Essays in Canadian Diplomacy* (Toronto and Montreal: McClelland and Stewart, 1970), vii.

17 Quoted in introduction to Hume Wrong, "The Canada-United States Relationship 1927/1951," *International Journal* 31, 3 (1976): 529.

18 J. Holmes and M. Cadieux, "The Late Norman Robertson," *External Affairs* 20, 9 (1968): 351, 350.

19 Holmes to Brian Urquhart, 6 February 1973, Holmes Papers, box 21, file 8, part 1.

20 Holmes to Norman Robertson, 21 May 1968, Holmes Papers, box 56, file 1, part 1. Holmes' proposal can be found in "Draft Working Memorandum with Regard to the Relation of the Institute and Mr. Pearson," 12 February 1968, in ibid. The rest of the file provides greater detail on the entire experience.

21 Holmes to A.D. Dunton, 12 July 1971, Holmes Papers, box 56, file 1, part 1.

22 Denis Stairs, *The Diplomacy of Constraint: Canada, the Korean War and the United States* (Toronto: University of Toronto Press, 1974).

23 G. Bruce Doern and Brian W. Tomlin, *Faith and Fear: The Free Trade Story* (Toronto: Stoddart, 1991).

24 Charles Pentland, "Mandarins and Manicheans: The 'Independence' Debate on Canadian Foreign Policy," *Queen's Quarterly* 77 (Spring 1970): 99-103.

25 Paul M. Evans, *John Fairbank and the American Understanding of Modern China* (New York: B. Blackwell, 1988).

26 John F. Sokol, "Lest We Forget: In Memory of John W. Holmes," *bout de papier* 9, 1 (1992): 4. Kaplan was in business at the time and was in Mexico to better link the Canadian embassy there to his dealings.

27 Denis Stairs, "Intellectual on Watch: James Eayrs and the Study of Foreign Policy and International Affairs," *International Journal* 62, 2 (2007): 229.

28 Holmes to Eayrs, 8 February 1962, Holmes Papers, box 51, file 1.

29 See his negotiations for a position in March 1967, Holmes Papers, box 30, file 1, part 2.

30 Holmes to Bloomfield, 31 March 1966, Holmes Papers, box 49, file 5. See also Martin L. Friedland, *The University of Toronto: A History* (Toronto: University of Toronto Press, 2002), 468.

31 Holmes to Ford, 31 July 1967, Chuck Ruud Papers.

32 Bruening, quoted in John W. Holmes, *Four Introductory Lectures* (Toronto: Trinity College, n.d.).

33 Holmes, introduction, *Four Introductory Lectures*.

34 Holmes, "The Era of Confederation," *Four Introductory Lectures*, 3, 18.

35 Holmes, "Canada in the Age of Imperialism: 1870 to 1918," *Four Introductory Lectures*, 15.

36 Holmes, "The Second World War and After," *Four Introductory Lectures*, 21, 25.

37 See, for example, John English, "A Fine Romance: Canada and the United Nations, 1943-1957," and Denis Stairs, "Realists at Work: Canadian Policymakers and the Politics of Transition from Hot War to Cold War," both in *Canada and the Early Cold War, 1943-1957*, ed. Greg Donaghy (Ottawa: Department of Foreign Affairs and International Trade, 1998), 73-89, 91-116.

38 Friedland, *The University of Toronto*, 527.

39 Berton, *1967*, 364.

CHAPTER 10: BREAKING FREE FROM THE INSTITUTE

1 On the Stone Memorial Fund, see Trinity College Archives, Toronto, John Holmes Papers 002-0001 (hereafter Holmes Papers), box 39, file 2, parts 1 and 2.

2 On the Order of Canada, see Christopher McCreery, *The Order of Canada: Its Origins, History and Development* (Toronto: University of Toronto Press, 2005).

3 On the departmental grant, see Holmes to Arthur Menzies, 16 December 1968, Holmes Papers, box 54, file 4, part 2.

4 Holmes to James Gibson, 4 April 1968, Holmes Papers, box 38, file 2, part 3.

5 Holmes to Heeney, Holmes Papers, box 40, file 1, part 2.

6 The project seems to have been cursed from the beginning. The first person asked to take charge of the grant, Richard Tait, was not interested. The second, Michael Sherman of the Parliamentary Centre, hurt his back just before the funding arrived and therefore could not start right away.

7 Peter C. Dobell and Robert Willmot, "John Holmes," *International Journal* 33, 1 (1977-78): 109.

8 Holmes to Pearson, 28 June 1968, Holmes Papers, box 56, file 1, part 1.

9 Minutes of 5th meeting of the National Executive Committee, 15 October 1970, CIIA Library, minutes, vol. 15, 1968-70. He repeated this defence to the National Council the following year. See Minutes of the 2nd meeting of the National Council, 5-6 November 1971, CIIA Library, minutes, vol. 16, 1971-73.

10 CIIA guest speakers had what is commonly known as a privileged platform from which to speak. The audience, including any invited members of the media, was not allowed to

make specific reference to their comments outside of the room. This policy takes its name from London's Royal Institute of International Affairs and is often referred to as Chatham House Rules.

11 See, for example, minutes of the 2nd meeting of the National Executive Committee, 8 February 1966, CIIA Library, minutes, vol. 14, 1965-67.

12 Holmes to Harbron, 16 October 1967, Holmes Papers, box 52, file 2; Holmes to Robert Hurlburt, 11 February 1971, Holmes Papers, box 52, file 5.

13 Holmes to Harbron, 22 November 1967, Holmes Papers, box 52, file 2.

14 Holmes to Smith, 23 May 1968, Holmes Papers, box 50, file 4.

15 Holmes to Members of the CIIA Research Committee, 14 September 1970, CIIA Library, minutes, vol. 15, 1968-70.

16 Holmes to King Gordon, 25 January 1968, Library and Archives Canada (hereafter LAC), Canadian Institute of International Affairs Papers, MG28 I250 (hereafter CIIA Papers), vol. 10, conferences, Banff Conference on World Affairs, 1968.

17 Holmes to Wright, 9 March 1968, and Wright to Holmes, 12 March 1968, LAC, Arnold Danford Patrick Heeney Papers, MG30 E144 (hereafter Heeney Papers), vol. 6, Canadian Institute of International Affairs, 1963-68, correspondence.

18 Holmes to Heeney, 12 March 1968, LAC, Heeney Papers, vol. 6, Canadian Institute of International Affairs, 1963-68, correspondence.

19 Ibid., 26 August 1968.

20 Holmes, *Article for International Conciliation* [first draft], Holmes Papers, box 2, file 3. The paper was published as Holmes, "Mediation or Enforcement," *International Journal* 25, 2 (1970): 388-404. See also Holmes to Reid, 25 July 1969, LAC, Escott Reid Papers, MG31 E46 (hereafter Escott Reid Papers), vol. 33, file 61.

21 "Report of the Director General," in *CIIA Annual Report 1970-71*, CIIA Library, minutes, vol. 16, 1971-73.

22 Its successor, the *Canada among Nations* series, is ongoing.

23 CIIA minutes, 20 February 1969, Holmes Papers, box 1, file 2.

24 Holmes to Frank Milligan, 26 September 1969, Holmes Papers, box 18, file 2. See also the rest of the file.

25 Holmes to Jean Lengellé, 27 October 1971, Holmes Papers, box 18, file 2.

26 For a defence of their position, see Stephen Clarkson, "The Choice to Be Made," in *An Independent Foreign Policy for Canada?*, ed. Stephen Clarkson, 253-69 (Toronto: McClelland and Stewart, 1968).

27 Holmes, "Canada and the Pax Americana," speech given at Victoria College, Toronto, 30 January 1968, and St. Francis-Xavier University, 8 February 1968, Holmes Papers, box 6, file 2.

28 Holmes, "The Political Aspects of Interdependence," in *Canadian-American Interdependence: How Much?* Proceedings of the 10th Annual University of Windsor Seminar on Canadian-American Relations 1968, ed. R.H. Wagenberg (Windsor: University of Windsor Press, 1970), 5. See also Holmes to Andrew Bewin, 25 November 1968, Holmes Papers, box 49, file 6; Holmes to Gil Winham, 12 July 1972, Holmes Papers, box 34, file 2.

29 Holmes, "The American Problem," *International Journal* 24, 2 (1969): 232.

30 On Trudeau, see J.L. Granatstein and Robert Bothwell, *Pirouette: Pierre Trudeau and Canadian Foreign Policy* (Toronto: University of Toronto Press, 1990); and Ivan Head and Pierre Trudeau, *The Canadian Way: Shaping Canada's Foreign Policy, 1968-1984* (Toronto: McClelland and Stewart, 1995).

31 Holmes to Ivan Head, 5 April 1971, Holmes Papers, box 52, file 4.

32 Holmes to Johnson, 28 February 1966, Holmes Papers, box 24, file 19.

33 Holmes to Pelletier, 9 April 1968, LAC, CIIA Papers, vol. 13, conferences, World Peace Foundation, Quebec City Conference, 1968.

34 Holmes, "There's a New Canadian Accent," *LA Times*, 18 April 1968, cited in Holmes Papers, box 5, file 5.

35 Head and Trudeau, *The Canadian Way*, 64, 320n1.

36 Ibid., 105. See also Holmes to Pelletier, 9 April 1968, LAC, CIIA Papers, vol. 13, conferences, World Peace Foundation, Quebec City Conference, 1968.

37 Notes on the meeting of September 28 in Ottawa between the Secretary of State for External Affairs and Representatives of Organizations Interested in Foreign Policy Research, 28 September 1968, LAC, CIIA Papers, vol. 19, general, foreign policy review, Department of External Affairs, 1968-69. See also Holmes to Hawkins, 1 October 1968, in ibid.; and Sharp to Holmes, 6 September 1974, Holmes Papers, box 57, file 4.

38 Holmes to Campbell, 17 January 1969, LAC, CIIA Papers, vol. 19, general, foreign policy review, Department of External Affairs, 1968-69. The rest of the file is also helpful. See also Peter C. Newman, "Outsiders Shape Policy," *Montreal Star*, 3 December 1968, 9.

39 See, for example, Holmes to Dalton Camp, Holmes Papers, box 102, Camp, Dalton.

40 Holmes to James E. King, 20 March 1969, Holmes Papers, box 53, file 3.

41 Both quotations from Holmes to Ivan Head, 11 April 1969, Holmes Papers, box 52, file 4.

42 Holmes to Gordon S. Smith, 25 November 1969, Holmes Papers, box 57, file 5; Holmes, "Notes for a Speech," 26 June 1969, Holmes Papers, box 9, file 7.

43 Holmes to Harvey, 17 February 1970, Holmes Papers, box 52, file 3. See also Holmes, "Canada and the World," speech at Brescia College, London, Ontario, 17 February 1969, Holmes Papers, box 9, file 1.

44 Holmes, "The White Paper: The United Nations," CBC International, 2 July 1970, Holmes Papers, box 21, file 2, part 1; Holmes to Ed Ritchie, 22 July 1970, Holmes Papers, box 56, file 3.

45 Holmes, "Canada and the United States: Political and Security Issues," *Behind the Headlines* 29, 1-2 (1970): 1. See also Holmes, "Focus on the Constant Dilemma of US-Canadian Relationships," *International Perspectives*, May/June 1972, 3-14; and Holmes, "Continental Dilemmas," speech at University of Maine, Orono, 18 April 1972, Holmes Papers, box 10, file 16.

46 Holmes to François Duchêne, 11 May 1970, Holmes Papers, box 46, file 5, part 2.

47 Holmes, "Lines Written for a Canadian-American Conference," in *The Star-Spangled Beaver*, ed. John H. Redekop (Toronto: Peter Martin Associates, 1971), 97.

48 Holmes, "After 25 Years," *International Journal* 26, 1 (1970-71): 3. See also Holmes, *Canadian Resources and Canadian Foreign Policy* (Toronto: CIIA, 1971); and Holmes to Walter Laqueur, 19 July 1972, Holmes Papers, box 5, file 3.

49 Holmes to Bruce Hutchison, 7 April 1971, Holmes Papers, box 52, file 5.

50 Holmes to Donald M. MacFarlane, 4 December 1970, Holmes Papers, box 30, file 1, part 1.

51 Holmes to Ed Ritchie and Holmes to C.E. McGaughey, both on 23 July 1970, Holmes Papers, box 54, file 1.

52 James Eayrs, *In Defence of Canada*, vol. 5, *Indochina: The Roots of Complicity* (Toronto: University of Toronto Press, 1983), 224, 283. In a conversation, Eayrs noted that the indictment has haunted him ever since.

Chapter 11: Freedom, Passion, and Frustration

1 Holmes, "UWO Convocation Address," London, 7 June 1973, Trinity College Archives, Toronto, John Holmes Papers 002-0001 (hereafter Holmes Papers), box 8, file 13.
2 Minutes of the 2nd meeting of the CIIA National Council, 30 November-1 December 1973, CIIA, minutes, vol. 16, 1971-73.
3 Holmes to Crane, 4 December 1972, Holmes Papers, box 100, CIIA personal.
4 Holmes to Gordon Robertson, 7 May 1975, Holmes Papers, box 36, file 4, part 1. The Niagara Institute "was founded on the idea that human values and values clarification could be powerful forces for leadership insight and development and could provide important perspectives on the difficult issues that challenge our society's major constituencies, in particular business, government and labour." See Lyle Masvolsky to Holmes, 24 June 1985, Holmes Papers, box 36, file 4, part 1.
5 The situation was actually quite amusing. Visitors arrived at Holmes' south Rosedale apartment to find the door unlocked. He would be lying flat on his back with a telephone by his side and rather unique prism spectacles on his face. These glasses allowed him to look straight up but still see the black-and-white television that he had moved onto a chair close by.
6 Holmes, "Canadian Foreign Policy (outline of project and requirements for further research)," August 1972, Holmes Papers, box 60, file 1. See also Blanchette to Holmes, 29 February 1972, and Holmes to Annette Baker Fox, 23 May 1972, Holmes Papers, box 17, file 6, part 1.
7 Davidson to Holmes, 6 September 1973, Holmes Papers, box 17, file 3. Much of the rest of the information on this period can be found in Holmes Papers, box 17, file 6, parts 1 and 2.
8 Holmes to Davidson, 10 February 1975, Holmes Papers, box 17, file 3.
9 Ibid., 20 April 1976.
10 Davidson to Holmes, 28 October 1976, Holmes Papers, box 17, file 3.
11 Alyson King, "The Glendon College Experiment," in *Escott Reid: Diplomat and Scholar*, ed. Greg Donaghy and Stéphane Roussel, 101-21 (Montreal and Kingston: McGill-Queen's University Press, 2004); Albert Tucker, quoted in CIIA, *In Remembrance of John Wendell Holmes, 18 June 1910-13 August 1988* (Toronto: CIIA, 1988), 5.
12 Holmes to G.B. Shand, 20 August 1973, Holmes Papers, box 27, file 8.
13 Holmes, "Convocation Address," Lakehead University, 26 May 1973, Holmes Papers, box 13, file 1.
14 Holmes to Ed R. Appathurai, 6 March 1973, Holmes Papers, box 27, file 6.
15 Holmes to J.E.G., Hardy, 19 August 1974, Holmes Papers, box 27, file 2. For an old syllabus, see Holmes Papers, box 27, file 4; Holmes to Roger Wickwood, 17 July 1974, Holmes Papers, box 29, file 9; Inis Claude Jr., *Swords into Ploughshares: The Problems and Progress of International Organization*, 3rd ed. (New York: Random House, 1964).
16 Holmes to Allan S. McGill, 27 September 1975, Holmes Papers, box 27, file 3; Albert Tucker to Holmes, 11 April 1975, Holmes Papers, box 27, file 2; Holmes to Arnold Smith, 24 January 1975, Holmes Papers, box 57, file 5.
17 For examples of his encouragement, see Holmes to Gordon Cullingham, 11 June 1987, Holmes Papers, box 2, file 6; and Holmes to Eric Wang, 11 June 1975, Holmes Papers, box 27, file 2.

18 Peter G. Mueller and Douglas A. Ross, *China and Japan: Emerging Global Powers* (New York: Praeger, 1975).

19 Douglas A. Ross, *In the Interests of Peace: Canada and Vietnam 1954-1973* (Toronto: University of Toronto Press, 1984).

20 Holmes, *Canada: A Middle-Aged Power* (Toronto: McClelland and Stewart, 1976), v; Gordon Fairweather, "Ah, Middle Age – Liberating, Exhilarating," *Globe and Mail*, 27 March 1976, 34; Granatstein, "Getting Older and Better?" *Canadian Forum*, June-July 1976, cited in Holmes Papers, box 17, file 2; Soward, "Holmes on the Range," *Vancouver Sun*, 1 October 1976, cited in ibid.

21 Holmes, "Canada and Pacific Security," *Pacific Community* 3, 4 (1972): 742-55; Holmes, "Focus on the World, 1975," draft, n.d., Holmes Papers, box 5, file 1, part 2.

22 Holmes to Stacey, 15 August 1973, Holmes Papers, box 21, file 5; Holmes, review of *Policy by Other Means: Essays in Honour of C.P. Stacey*, cited in ibid.

23 Holmes, "Impact of Domestic Political Factors on Canadian-American Relations: Canada," *International Organization* 28, 4 (1974): 612; Holmes, "Cross-Currents in the US and Canadian World View," speech at the International Press Institute, 21 February 1974, Holmes Papers, box 13, file 9. See also Holmes, "In Praise of National Boundaries: The Case against Creeping Continentalism," *Saturday Night*, July 1974, 13-16.

24 Holmes, "Canada and the Crisis of Middle Powers," *Worldview* 15, 6 (1972): 25; Holmes "Former Diplomat Says Canada Has a Duty to Supervise Truce," *Toronto Star*, 24 January 1973, 10. See also Holmes, "The View from Canada," *Louisville Courier Journal Times*, 5 August 1973, cited in Holmes Papers, box 2, file 6.

25 Holmes to R. Harry Jay, 22 May 1973, Holmes Papers, box 27, file 6.

26 Holmes, "The World: Despite What You Read, the UN Still Works Well," *Saturday Night*, July/August 1975, 13; Holmes, "Introduction to International Affairs," speech to Canadian Forces Staff College, 15 January 1973, Holmes Papers, box 13, file 3, part 2; Holmes "Canada and Collective Security," speech to National Defence College, 19 April 1973, Holmes Papers, box 8, file 8, part 2; Holmes to James P. [Pat] Sewell, 1 February 1974, Holmes Papers, box 57, file 4; Holmes to D.L. McQueen, 30 August 1974, Holmes Papers, box 27, file 4.

27 Holmes, "Sadder but Wiser: The UN at Thirty," *International Perspectives*, November/December 1975, 22.

28 Holmes, "The United Nations at Thirty," speech to Canadian Club, 1 December 1975, Holmes Papers, box 13, file 8.

29 Holmes to J. King Gordon, 5 December 1975, Holmes Papers; Crowe, 27 April 1977, Holmes Papers. See also other letters in the same file.

30 Holmes, Letter from Toronto, 15 March 1976, Holmes Papers, box 36, file 1, part 1; Holmes to Wrong, 1945 [unsent], Holmes Papers, box 63, file 4; Holmes to B.N.D. Rodal, 3 May 1988, Holmes Papers, box 56, file 4; Holmes to Edward G. Lee, 19 February 1979, Holmes Papers, box 53, file 5.

31 This author views the 1944 pronouncement "we have preferred not to be classed with niggers" as one reflecting a degree of ignorance that was a product of its time. The comments that follow cannot be justified the same way. See Holmes to Wrong, 4 August 1944, in *Documents on Canadian External Relations*, vol. 11, part 2, *1944-1945*, ed. John F. Hilliker (Ottawa: Minister of Supply and Services Canada, 1990), 1194.

32 Holmes to Charles P. Pearse, 12 April 1985, Holmes Papers, box 55, file 5, part 1.

33 Holmes to Howard Palmer, 12 December 1986, Holmes Papers, box 57, file 3.

34 In order to subsidize eastern and central Canadian consumers, the National Energy Program deprived western energy-producing provinces from capitalizing fully on the recent dramatic increase in the price of oil.

35 Holmes to Peyton Lyon, 12 August 1975, Holmes Papers, box 53, file 6; Holmes to David Taras, 3 November 1980, Holmes Papers, box 32, file 5.

36 Holmes to J. King Gordon, 25 June 1980, Holmes Papers, box 67, file 7; Holmes to Tom Hockin, 31 January 1986, Holmes Papers, box 11 file 3.

37 Holmes, "Morality, Realism, and Foreign Affairs," *International Perspectives*, September/October 1977, 20, 21; Holmes, "Disunity in Canada: The Safeguard of Democracy," n.d., Holmes Papers, box 72, file E/I/22; Holmes to Dilks, 27 October 1986, Holmes Papers, box 30, file 6, part 1; Holmes, "Canada's Postwar Policies towards Japan," speech to International University Symposium on Japan and Postwar Diplomacy in the Asia-Pacific Region, 18-19 March 1983, Holmes Papers, box 13, file 2.

38 For further elaboration, see Denis Stairs, "The Pedagogics of John W. Holmes," *International Journal* 44, 4 (1989): 921-36; and Kim Richard Nossal, "Canada and the Search for World Order: John W. Holmes and Canadian Foreign Policy," *International Journal* 59, 4 (2004): 749-60.

Chapter 12: Older and Wiser

1 Sandra Gwyn, "Where Are You Mike Pearson, Now That We Need You: Decline and Fall of Canada's Foreign Policy," *Saturday Night*, 3 April 1978, 34, 27.

2 Holmes, "Convocation Address," 22 October 1976 [University of Waterloo], Trinity College Archives, Toronto, John Holmes Papers 002-0001 (hereafter Holmes Papers), box 14, file 27.

3 Holmes to Robin Ranger, 11 October 1977, Holmes Papers, box 48, file 2; Margaret Doxey, "John Holmes: An Appreciation," *Behind the Headlines* 46, 1 (1988): 7.

4 Holmes to Martha and Mark [Anshan], 28 September 1978, Holmes Papers, box 49. file 1; Holmes to Margaret Doxey, 25 September 1978, Holmes Papers, box 26, file 10; Holmes to Norman Penner, 25 January 1980; Holmes to Philippe Garigue, 26 January 1981; and Holmes to Albert Tucker, 8 March 1987, all in Holmes Papers, box 26, file 8.

5 Kim Richard Nossal, ed., *The Acceptance of Paradox: Essays on Canadian Diplomacy in Honour of John W. Holmes* (Toronto: CIIA, 1982).

6 Holmes to Don, Kim, Doug, Dan, Michael, Frank, Clarence, and Peter, 8 April 1980, Holmes Papers, box 31, file 6.

7 Pickering College Papers (hereafter Pickering Papers), Wall Inscriptions [22 May 1981].

8 Holmes, "Moscow under Stalin," *Weekend Magazine* (January 1978), cited in Holmes Papers, box 4, file 7.

9 For examples of revisionist scholarship, see William Appleman Williams, *The Tragedy of American Diplomacy*, new ed. (New York: W.W. Norton, 1988 [1959]); and Joyce and Gabriel Kolko, *The Limits of Power: The World and United States Foreign Policy, 1945-1954* (New York: Harper and Row, 1972).

10 R.D. Cuff and J.L. Granatstein, *Ties That Bind: Canadian-American Relations in Wartime from the Great War to the Cold War*, 2nd ed. (Toronto and Sarasota: Samuel Stevens Hakkert, 1977). See also their "Looking Back at the Cold War," *Canadian Forum* 52 (July/August 1972): 8-11; and "Looking Back Once More – A Rejoinder," *Canadian Forum* 52 (December 1972): 19-20.

11 Holmes, "Moscow under Stalin," cited in Holmes Papers, box 4, file 7; Holmes to Arnold Smith, 15 October 1976, Library and Archives Canada (hereafter LAC), Arnold Cantwell Smith Papers, MG31 E47, vol. 87, file 31. It is worth noting that Holmes' relationship with the noted historian John English developed in earnest after Holmes congratulated him for his trenchant critique of Canadian revisionist scholarship.

12 Holmes, *The CIIA and Canadian Foreign Policy: Hits and Myths* (Toronto: CIIA, 1978), 5, 9, 14.

13 Holmes, *The Shaping of Peace: Canada and the Search for World Order, 1943-1957*, vol. 1 (Toronto: University of Toronto Press, 1979), 308.

14 Holmes, *The Shaping of Peace: Canada and the Search for World Order, 1943-1957*, vol. 2 (Toronto: University of Toronto Press, 1982), 378.

15 Holmes to Menzies, 26 October 1981, Holmes Papers, box 43, file 8; Gotlieb to Holmes, n.d. [August 1978], Holmes Papers, box 43, file 8; Holmes to Soward, 14 December 1978, Holmes Papers, box 69, file (S); Holmes to Reid, 4 December 1978, LAC, Escott Reid Papers, MG31 E46 (hereafter Escott Reid Papers), vol. 33, file 63.

16 Holmes, "Towards a Foreign Policy for the 1980s," speech to the Progressive Conservative Conference at the Guild Inn, 26 January 1979, Holmes Papers, box 12, file 14.

17 Holmes to I. Norman Smith, 19 February 1979, Holmes Papers, box 58, file 3; Holmes to Arnold Smith, 19 February 1979, Holmes Papers, box 12, file 14; Holmes to Rufus Smith, 14 June 1979, Holmes Papers, box 57, file 5.

18 Robert Bothwell, *Alliance and Illusion: Canada and the World, 1945-1984* (Vancouver: UBC Press, 2007), 360-62.

19 On Lévesque's thinking at the time, see his *An Option for Quebec* (Toronto and Montreal: McClelland and Stewart, 1968).

20 John Holmes, "Canadian Unity: The International Dimension," *Transactions of the Royal Society of Canada*, ser. 4, 17 (1979): 99, 101, 102.

21 Holmes to Spencer, 25 May 1978, Holmes Papers, box 41, file 4, part 3. See also related papers in the same file. A conversation with Robert Spencer was also helpful.

22 A significant proportion of the funding was contingent upon the centre raising an additional $75,000 on its own.

23 Minutes of the [CIS] Executive Committee, 13 June 1978, Holmes Papers, box 42, file 1, part 2.

24 Holmes, "Introduction: The IJC and Canada-United States Relations," in *The International Joint Commission: Seventy Years On*, ed. Robert Spencer, John Kirton, and Kim Richard Nossal (Toronto: Centre for International Studies, 1981), 4.

25 CIS, "Donner Canadian Foundation Grant," 31 March 1978, Holmes Papers, box 41, file 4, part 3; minutes of the Executive Committee [CIS], 13 June 1978, Holmes Papers, box 42, file 1, part 2. Boxes 41 through 43 are replete with references to the CIS and its sponsored colloquia.

26 Holmes to Maxwell Cohen, 18 June 1979, Holmes Papers, box 43, file 4; Holmes to Edward G. Lee, 3 November 1980, Holmes Papers, box 41, file 2, part 2.

27 Holmes to Gayle Fraser, 2 October 1979, Holmes Papers, box 31, file 1, part 2; Holmes to Paul Martin and Holmes to George Glazebrook, both on 8 October 1979, Holmes Papers, box 1, file 7.

28 Holmes, *The Changing Pattern of International Institutions* (Leeds: Leeds University Press, 1980), 20.

29 Holmes, "The Changing Nature of International Organizations: The Canadian Perspective," *Canada House Lecture Series* 8 (1979); Holmes, "The Way of the World," *International*

Journal 35,2 (1980): 211-25; Holmes, "How the UN Tries to Keep This Wayward World on Course," *Times Higher Education Supplement*, 18 January 1980, cited in Holmes Papers, box 31, file 1, part 1.

30 Holmes to Gregory Wirick, 10 April 1980, Holmes Papers, box 48, file 5.

CHAPTER 13: REGRETS AND RENEWAL

1 That these ideas are not discussed in Kim Richard Nossal, "Canada and the Search for World Order: John W. Holmes and Canadian Foreign Policy," *International Journal* 59, 4 (2004): 749-60, indicates how exceptional they were in Holmes' history.

2 Holmes to Middlemiss, 8 April 1980, Trinity College Archives, Toronto, John Holmes Papers 002-0001 (hereafter Holmes Papers), box 31, file 5; Holmes to Basil Robinson, 27 August 1987, Holmes Papers, box 57, file 3; Holmes to Lois Beattie, 31 January 1980, Holmes Papers, box 18, file 1; Holmes to Don Munton, 26 June 1980, Holmes Papers, box 55, file 1, part 2.

3 Holmes, "Stop Signs for a Military Trip," *Maclean's*, 1 June 1981, 9; Holmes, "The Canadian Foreign Service at Middle Age," n.d. [November 1982], Holmes Papers, box 8, file 11; Holmes, "The Future of Yesterday," April 1983, Holmes Papers, box 7, file 13; Holmes, "The World According to Ottawa," 8 May 1983, Holmes Papers, box 11, file 5; Holmes, "Safely in the Middle: The Eccentric Views of a Middle Power," in *Security, Conflict, and Survival: Perceptions of a Middle Power*, ed. Nils Ørvik (Toronto: Standing Conference of Atlantic Organizations, 1983), 3; Holmes, "The World According to Ottawa," in *Mackenzie King to Philosopher King: Canadian Foreign Policy in a Modern Age*, ed. Peter St. John (Winnipeg: St. John's College, 1984), 22.

4 Holmes, "Most Safely in the Middle," *International Journal* 39, 2 (1984): 38.

5 Holmes, "Canada and the United Nations: The Way We Were: Reflections of a Junior Founding Father," *Bulletin [Journal of the UN Association in Canada]* 7, 4 (1981-82), 6, 10; Holmes, "The United Nations in Perspective," *Behind the Headlines* 44, 1 (1986).

6 Holmes to Menzies, 24 August 1981 and 5 January 1982, both in Holmes Papers, box 43, file 8.

7 Holmes to Murray Thomson, 4 December 1984, Holmes Papers, box 46, file 3; Holmes to Reid, 1 March 1982, Holmes Papers, box 46, file 3. See also Holmes to Gabriel I. Warren, 8 July 1983, Holmes Papers, box 24, file 8; Holmes, "Canada under the Dove," in *Canada from Sea unto Sea*, ed. Charles J. Humber, 222-39 (Mississauga: Loyalist Press, 1986).

8 Quotations from Holmes, "Canadian Foreign Policy and International Law," in *International Law and Canadian Foreign Policy in the 1980s* (Ottawa: Canadian Council on International Law, 1980), 1; and Holmes to Stephen Woollcombe, 30 March 1984, Holmes Papers, box 42, file 3. See also Holmes, "Energy Track: The First Global Conference on the Future," 22 July 1980, Holmes Papers, box 13, file 6; Holmes to Woollcombe, 13 December 1983, Holmes Papers, box 42, file 3; Holmes to Dr. Roland List, 29 March 1983, Holmes Papers, box 42, file 5, part 2; Holmes to Allan MacEachen, 8 July 1983, Holmes Papers, box 54, file 1; Holmes, "With the Best of Intentions: Interdependence and Freedom," in *And He Loved Big Brother: Man, State and Society in Question*, ed. Shlomo Giora Shoham and Francis Rosenstiel (London, UK: Macmillan, 1985), 39-46.

9 Holmes, *No Other Way: Canada and International Security Institutions* (Toronto: Center for International Studies, 1986), 7, 151; Holmes to Ian Burton, 25 June 1987, Holmes Papers, box 43, file 6; Holmes to David Nolan, 21 October 1987, Holmes Papers, box 27, file 10.

10 Holmes, "Trudeau Speaking for the Many," *International Herald Tribune*, 16 December 1983, cited in Holmes Papers, box 5, file 5; Holmes to Dr. E.M. Chossudousky, 18 January 1984, Holmes Papers, box 37, file 2. A critical, but not entirely contradictory, interpretation of the peace mission can be found in J.L. Granatstein and Robert Bothwell, *Pirouette: Pierre Trudeau and Canadian Foreign Policy* (Toronto: University of Toronto Press, 1990), 365-76.

11 Holmes to General Gerry Thériault, 18 May 1984, Holmes Papers, box 48, file 6; Holmes to John Higginbotham, 3 November 1987, Holmes Papers, box 23, file 21; Holmes to Ernie Regehr, 18 December 1987, Holmes Papers, box 56, file 3; Holmes, "The Dumbbell Won't Do," *Foreign Policy* 50 (Spring 1983): 3-23; Holmes, "Vive La Différence," speech to Canada House, London, 11 November 1982, Holmes Papers, box 9, file 5; Holmes to Gwynne Dyer, 4 March 1987, Holmes Papers, box 50, file 6.

12 Holmes to May, 2 March 1987, Holmes Papers, box 43, file 7. See the rest of the file for greater detail.

13 Spencer to Holmes, 10 December 1979, Holmes Papers, box 28, file 5, part 1.

14 Holmes, *Life with Uncle: The Canadian-American Relationship* (Toronto: University of Toronto Press, 1981), 105.

15 Kazuhiko Okuda, "How Canada Handles the United States: Alliance Politics and John W. Holmes," *Bulletin of the Graduate School of International Relations. International University of Japan* 3 (July 1985): 143-58.

16 Davidson to Holmes and Spencer, 27 October 1981, Holmes Papers, box 18, file 3. See also rest of file and Holmes to Annette Baker Fox, 28 October 1981, Holmes Papers, box 10, file 10.

17 Walter Young, review of *Life with Uncle* by John Holmes, *Canadian Journal of Political Science* 15, 3 (1982): 610. *The New Romans* was published in 1968.

18 For an English translation of the introduction to the Japanese edition, see Holmes, English Introduction, January 1985, Holmes Papers, box 18, file 3. See also Kazuhiko Okuda, "How Canada Handles the United States: Alliance Politics and John W. Holmes," *Bulletin of the Graduate School of International Relations. International University of Japan* 3 (July 1985).

19 Holmes to Tamara and Howard Palmer, 5 March 1986, Tamara Seiler Papers.

20 Herbert H. Meyer, "Trudeau's War on US Business," *Fortune*, 6 April 1981, 74-82.

21 Holmes to Clarkson, 20 May 1986, Holmes Papers, box 27, file 12; Holmes to C. William Maynes, 16 October 1980, Holmes Papers, box 28, file 5, part 1; Holmes to Escott Reid, 15 October 1981, Library and Archives Canada (hereafter LAC), Escott Reid Papers, MG31 E46 (hereafter Escott Reid Papers), vol. 33, file 64, Holmes, John W., 1980-88; Holmes to Thomas L. Hughes, 16 September 1981, Holmes Papers, box 52, file 5; Holmes to Gaddis, 11 November 1986, Holmes Papers, box 18, file 3.

22 Holmes, "Reagan's Imperial Measures," *Toronto Star*, 26 November 1983, B1.

23 Holmes to Reid, 30 August 1984, LAC, Escott Reid Papers, vol. 33, file 64, Holmes, John W., 1980-88; Holmes, "Canada and the United States: Closer or Better Relations?" n.d., Holmes Papers, box 8, file 3; Holmes to Tom Axworthy, 7 January 1985, Holmes Papers, box 49, file 2.

24 Holmes, "The Future of the American Empire," 6 August 1987, Holmes Papers, box 7, file 8; Holmes to Thomas L. Hughes, 4 February 1986, Holmes Papers, box 52, file 5.

25 Holmes to Mel Clark, 25 November 1983, Holmes Papers, box 50, File 3; Holmes to Charles Caccia, 4 December 1984, Holmes Papers, box 50, file 2; Holmes to J. Duncan Edmonds, 13 June 1986, Holmes Papers, box 51, file 1; Holmes to Editor, *Globe and Mail*, 10 August

Notes to pages 271-79

Notes to pages 271-79 323

1987, and Holmes to Arthur Andrew, 17 August 1987, both in Holmes Papers, box 7, file 8; Holmes to Stephen Beecroft, 26 March 1987, Holmes Papers, box 50, file 1.

26 His resignation had been mostly ignored by Spencer anyway. See Drummond to Holmes, 6 July 1981, Holmes to Drummond, 20 July 1981; and Holmes to Spencer, 11 August 1982; all in Holmes Papers, box 41, file 1; Report of the Review Committee for the Centre for International Studies, March 1981; and Spencer to Drummond, 27 April 1981, both in Holmes Papers, box 42, file 1, part 1; Holmes to Spencer, 11 June 1981; Spencer to Holmes, 23 August 1982; and Holmes to Spencer, 24 December 1982, all in Holmes Papers, box 41, file 4, part 2.

27 Report of the Five-Year Review Committee for the Centre for International Studies, January 1986, Holmes Papers, box 42, file 1, part 1; Holmes to Connell, 2 April 1986, Holmes Papers, along with the remainder of the file, including specifically Holmes to Graham, Kirton, and Janice Stein, 6 November 1986.

28 Holmes, "The United Nations: Then and Now," address to United Nations Association, University of Leeds, 13 May 1985, Holmes Papers, box 8, file 12. See Holmes, *Conversation between Professor John Holmes and Professor David Dilks on Friday, 28 June 1985 at the University of Leeds* (Toronto: CIIA, n.d.). See also the relevant letters to his family in Nancy Skinner Papers (hereafter Skinner Papers), John W. Holmes, letters to his family, 1985.

29 Reid, "John Holmes: A Tribute," 17 October 1988, LAC, Escott Reid Papers, vol. 34, Holmes, John W. Memorial (6), 1988.

30 Holmes to Robert Cox, 7 November 1986, Holmes Papers, box 50, file 4; Lois Cleveland and Royce Hanson to Holmes, 5 November 1987, Holmes Papers, box 43, file 6.

31 Gene M. Lyons, "Putting ACUNS Together," *ACUNS Reports and Papers* 2 (1999); Holmes Papers, box 44, file 1, parts 1 and 2 and file 2, part 2; Holmes to King Gordon, 27 August 1987, Holmes Papers, box 46, file 3. Outside of ACUNS, Holmes was also involved in a CIIA project called "Introducing: The World" designed by and for young people.

32 Holmes to Paul Martin [Sr.], 2 October 1982, Holmes Papers, box 33, file 3; Holmes to Joe Clark, 22 October 1985, Holmes Papers, box 37, file 2.

33 Holmes, "The UN at 40: An Upbeat Assessment," *Ottawa Citizen*, 8 February 1986, B3; Julian Doranger to Holmes, 9 September 1986, Holmes Papers, box 23, file 22; Holmes to Reid, 7 January 1987, LAC, Escott Reid Papers, vol. 33, file 64.

34 Holmes to Geoffrey Pearson, 15 January 1981, Holmes Papers, box 16, file 34; Holmes to Alan McLaine, 30 September 1987, Holmes Papers, box 23, file 21. See the rest of the file for more detail.

Chapter 14: Saying Goodbye

1 Holmes to Lane, 24 December 1987, University of Regina, Archives and Special Collections (hereafter URA), Patrick Lane Papers, 90-102 (hereafter Lane Papers), box 2, file: correspondence, writers, Holmes, John W., 1987-88. On his emotional constipation, see the letter from the following day.

2 Holmes to von Riekhoff, 17 May 1988, Trinity College Archives, Toronto, John Holmes Papers 002-0001 (hereafter Holmes Papers), box 44, file 1, part 1.

3 For the text of the ACUNS speech, see Holmes, "Looking Backwards and Forwards," *ACUNS Reports and Papers* 1 (1988). See also John Hilliker, *Canada's Department of External Affairs*, vol. 1, *The Early Years, 1909-1946* (Montreal and Kingston: McGill-Queen's University Press, 1990).

4 Keith Spicer, "John Holmes: A Great and *Good* Man," *Ottawa Citizen*, 15 August 1988, cited in Library and Archives Canada (hereafter LAC), J. King Gordon Papers, MG30 C241, vol. 64, file 11.

5 Dilks, cited in LAC, Escott Reid Papers, MG31 E46 (hereafter Escott Reid Papers), vol. 34, Holmes, John W. Memorial (6), 1988; Robert W. Reford, "John Holmes 1910-1988," *International Perspectives*, September-October 1988, 23; John Halstead, "John Wendell Holmes," *bout de papier* 6, 3 (1988): 33; Stairs to Fraser, 1 October 1988, Holmes Papers, box 73, E/II/3.

6 Alan K. Henrikson to Fraser, 11 October 1988, Nancy Skinner Papers, folder, no label.

7 CIIA, *In Remembrance of John Wendell Holmes, 18 June 1910-13 August 1988* (Toronto: CIIA, 1988), 3.

8 The first lecture was given by Sir Brian Urquhart, an esteemed diplomat and old friend.

9 Holmes, "The New Agenda for Canadian Internationalism," in *Canada and the New Internationalism*, ed. John Holmes and John Kirton, 12-23 (Toronto: CIIA, 1988); Holmes to Kirton, 19 January 1987, Holmes Papers, box 42, file 2.

10 Holmes, "Moscow 1947-1948: Reflections of the Origins of My Cold War," in *Nearly Neighbours: Canada and the Soviet Union from Cold War to Détente and Beyond*, ed. J.L. Black and Norman Hillmer, 41-55 (Kingston: Ronald P. Fry, 1989); Holmes, "Merchant-Heeney Revisited: A Sentimental View," in *America's Alliances and Canadian-American Relations*, ed. Lauren McKinsey and Kim Richard Nossal, 180-99 (Toronto: Summerhill Press, 1988); Holmes, "Crises in Canadian-American Relations: A Canadian Perspective," and "The Disillusioning of the Relationship: Epitaph to a Decade," both in *Friends so Different: Essays on Canada and the United States in the 1980s*, ed. Lansing Lamont and J. Duncan Edmonds, 17-31, 308-18 (Ottawa: Ottawa University Press, 1989).

11 Holmes, "The United Nations and World Order," in *International Conflict and Conflict Management: Readings in World Politics*, ed. Robert O. Matthews, Arthur G. Rubinoff, and Janice Gross Stein, 2nd ed. (Scarborough: Prentice Hall, 1989), 492.

12 Holmes, "What Peace Means to Me," n.d, LAC, Escott Reid Papers, vol. 34, Holmes, John W., 1980-88.

Bibliography

PUBLIC ARCHIVES

Canada

Bishop's University Archives (Lennoxville, Quebec)
T.W.L. MacDermot Papers

Canadian Institute of International Affairs Library (Toronto, Ontario)
Death of John Holmes Clipping File
John Holmes Biographical Clipping File
Minutes

Canadian Lesbian and Gay Archives (Toronto, Ontario)
Declassified documents re: employment of homosexuals in federal civil service

Clara Thomas Archives and Special Collections (York University, Toronto, Ontario)
J.L. Granatstein Papers
Edgar Wardwell McInnis Papers

John G. Diefenbaker Centre for the Study of Canada (University of Saskatchewan, Saskatoon, Saskatchewan)
John G. Diefenbaker Papers

Library and Archives Canada (Ottawa, Ontario)

Institutional Papers:
Canadian Security and Intelligence Service Papers
Department of External Affairs Papers
Privy Council Office Papers

Public Service Commission Papers
Royal Canadian Mounted Police Papers

Personal Papers:
Marcel Cadieux Papers
Canadian Institute of International Affairs Papers
Brooke Claxton Papers
Arnold Danford Patrick Heeney Papers
George Drew Papers
Robert A.D. Ford Papers
J. King Gordon Papers
John Halstead Papers
W. Arthur Irwin Papers
Hugh L. Keenleyside Papers
Howard H. Lentner Papers
D.V. LePan Papers
L.B. Pearson Papers
J.W. Pickersgill Papers
Escott Reid Papers
Albert Edgar Ritchie Papers
Norman Robertson Papers
R. Gordon Robertson Papers
H. Basil Robinson Papers
Louis St. Laurent Papers
Arnold Cantwell Smith Papers
Irving Norman Smith Papers
John Kennett Starnes Papers
Peter Stursberg Papers
Hume Wrong Papers

London South Collegiate Institute Archives (London, Ontario)
Peter Telford Papers
Peter Telford Summary

Queen's University Archives (Kingston, Ontario)
T.A. Crerar Papers
Grant Dexter Papers
Donald Gordon Papers
W.L. Mackenzie King Papers
Arthur Lower Papers

Thomas Fisher Rare Book Library, University of Toronto (Toronto, Ontario)
D.V. LePan Papers

Trinity College Archives (Toronto, Ontario)
John Holmes Papers
George Ignatieff Papers

University of British Columbia Archives (Vancouver, British Columbia)
S. Morley Scott Papers
Frederic Hubert Soward Papers

University of Regina Archives and Special Collections (Regina, Saskatchewan)
Patrick Lane Papers

University of Toronto Archives (Toronto, Ontario)
Alexander Brady Papers
George Brown Papers
Vincent Massey Papers

University of Western Ontario Archives (London, Ontario)
Gazette
Occidentalia, 1928-33
Scrapbooks, 1928-33

United Kingdom

King's College Archives (London)
Gerald Graham Papers

Leeds University Library, Special Collections
Manuscripts by John Holmes

National Archives of England, Wales, and the United Kingdom (Kew)
Foreign Office Papers

United States

Carnegie Corporation Archives (New York)
Carnegie Corporation Papers

Rockefeller Archive Center (Sleepy Hollow, New York)
Rockefeller Foundation Papers

United Nations Dag Hammarskjöld Library (New York)
United Nations Oral History Project

PERSONAL COLLECTIONS

Dean Beeby Papers
Margaret Doxey Papers
Annette Baker Fox Papers
J.L. Granatstein Papers
John Harbron Papers
Gordon Hawkins Papers
Barbara Hyatt Papers
Roy MacLaren Papers

Allan McGill Papers
Ingrid Milic Papers
Pickering College Papers
Stephanie Reford Papers
Judith Robertson Papers
Chuck Ruud Papers
Tamara Seiler Papers
Nancy Skinner Papers

Published Documents

Canada. Department of Foreign Affairs and International Trade. "Lloyd Axworthy Announces Outreach Fund Honouring John Holmes." Press Release 80 (26 August 1996). Available at: http://webapps.dfait-maeci.gc.ca/minipub (viewed 22 February 2005)

–. *Documents on Canadian External Relations.* Vols. 9-26. *1942-1959.*

–. House of Commons. *Debates.* 3rd Session. 34th Parliament. Vol. 8. 1992.

The Canadian Who's Who. Vol. 11. *1967-1969.* Toronto: Who's Who Canadian Publications, 1969.

Cody, H.J. *University of Toronto: President's Report for the Year Ending 30th June 1933.* Toronto: University of Toronto, 14 December 1933.

Commission of Inquiry Concerning Certain Activities of the Royal Canadian Mounted Police. *Freedom and Security under the Law.* 2nd report. Vol. 2. Ottawa: Minister of Supply and Services Canada, 1981.

Heeney, Arnold, and Livingston Merchant. *Canada and the United States: Principles for Partnership,* 28 June 1965.

Lalande, Gilles. *The Department of External Affairs and Biculturalism.* Vol. 3. *Studies of the Royal Commission on Bilingualism and Biculturalism.* Ottawa: Queen's Printer, 1969.

Macdonald, John Barfoot. *University of British Columbia Report of the President for the Academic Year 1964-1965.* Vancouver: University of British Columbia, 1966.

Taschereau, Robert, and R.L. Kellock. *The Report of the Royal Commission to Investigate the Facts Relating to and the Circumstances Surrounding the Communication, by Public Officials and Other Persons in Positions of Trust of Secret and Confidential Information to Agents of a Foreign Power.* Ottawa: Kings Printer, 1946.

United Nations Department of Public Information. *The Blue Helmets: A Review of United Nations Peace-Keeping.* 3rd ed. New York: UN Department of Public Information, 1996.

Newspapers, Magazines, and Periodicals

Air Force College Journal
Air University Review
Atlantic Monthly
Behind the Headlines
bout de papier
Bulletin
Canada-United States Law Journal
Canadian Banker
Canadian Business
Canadian Commentator
Canadian Forum
Canadian Historical Papers
Canadian Historical Review
Centennial Review
City and Country Home
Études Internationales
External Affairs

Financial Post
Financial Times
Foreign Affairs
Fortune
Fredericton Daily Gleaner
Globe and Mail
Hamilton Spectator
International Herald Tribune
International Journal
International Organization
International Perspectives
Jeune Afrique
Journal of Inter-American Studies
Kitchener-Waterloo Record
The Lamp
London Free Press
London Times

Los Angeles Times
Louisville Courier Journal Times
Maclean's
Montreal Gazette
Montreal Star
Niagara Falls Review
The Observer
Orbis
Optima
Oshawa Times
Ottawa Citizen
Ottawa Journal
Ottawa Magazine
Owen Sound Sun Times
Pacific Affairs
Pacific Community

Politique Étrangère
Queen's Quarterly
The Round Table
Saturday Night
Seattle Post-Intelligencer
Survival
The Times/News (Thunder Bay)
Today Magazine
Toronto Star
Transactions of the Royal Society of Canada
Vancouver Sun
Wainwright Star Chronicle
Weekend Magazine
Wilton Park Journal
World Today
Worldview

OTHER PUBLISHED SOURCES

Andrew, Arthur. *The Rise and Fall of A Middle Power: Canadian Diplomacy from King to Mulroney*. Toronto: James Lorimer, 1993.

Andrew, Arthur, and John Holmes. "Diplomacy and Foreign Policy." Cassette Recording. *Canadian Contemporary Issues on Tape*. Toronto: Ontario Institute for Studies in Education, 1974.

Axworthy, Thomas S. "New Bottles for Old Wine: Implementing the *International Policy Statement*." In *Canada among Nations 2005: Split Images*, ed. Andrew F. Cooper and Dane Rowlands. Montreal and Kingston: McGill Queen's University Press, 2005.

Beeby, Dean, and William Kaplan, eds. *Moscow Despatches: Inside Cold War Russia*. Toronto: James Lorimer, 1987.

Beecroft, Stephen. "Canadian Policy Towards China, 1949-1957: The Recognition Problem." In *Reluctant Adversaries: Canada and the People's Republic of China, 1949-1970*, ed. Paul M. Evans and B. Michael Frolic. Toronto: University of Toronto Press, 1991.

Bercuson, David J. "'A people so ruthless as the Soviets': Canadian Images of the Cold War and the Soviet Union, 1946-1950." In *Canada and the Soviet Experiment*, ed. David Davie. Toronto: Canadian Scholars Press, 1994.

Berton, Pierre. *1967: The Last Good Year*. Toronto: Doubleday Canada, 1997.

Bissell, Claude. *The Imperial Canadian: Vincent Massey in Office*. Toronto: University of Toronto Press, 1986.

Bothwell, Robert. *Alliance and Illusion: Canada and the World, 1945-1984*. Toronto: UBC Press, 2007.

–. *Laying the Foundation: A Century of History at University of Toronto*. Toronto: Department of History, University of Toronto, 1991.

–. *The Penguin History of Canada*. Toronto: Penguin Canada, 2006.

Bothwell, Robert, and John English. "The View from Inside Out: Canadian Diplomats and their Public." *International Journal* 39, 1 (1983-84): 47-67.

Bothwell, Robert, and J.L. Granatstein, eds. *The Gouzenko Transcripts: The Evidence Presented to the Kellock-Taschereau Royal Commission of 1946*. Ottawa: Deneau Publishers, 1982.

Boulding, Kenneth E. "National Images and International Systems." In *International Politics and Foreign Policy*, ed. James M. Rosenau. New York: The Free Press, 1969.

Brennan, Patrick H. *Reporting the Nation's Business: Press-Government Relations during the Liberal Years, 1935-1957.* Toronto: University of Toronto Press, 1994.

Burney, Derek H. *Getting It Done: A Memoir.* Montreal and Kingston: McGill-Queen's University Press, 2005.

Cadieux, Marcel. *The Canadian Diplomat: An Essay in Definition.* Trans. Archibald Day. Toronto: University of Toronto Press, 1963 [1962].

"Canada's Engagement with the World: 75 Years of CIIA." Video recording. CIIA: Toronto, 2003.

Canadian Institute of International Affairs. *In Remembrance of John Wendell Holmes, 18 June 1910-13 August 1988.* Toronto: CIIA, 1988.

Chapnick, Adam. "The Canadian Middle Power Myth." *International Journal* 55, 2 (2000): 188-206

–. "The Middle Power." *Canadian Foreign Policy* 7, 2 (1999): 73-82.

–. *The Middle Power Project: Canada and the Founding of the United Nations.* Vancouver: UBC Press, 2005.

–. "Principle for Profit: The Functional Principle and the Development of Canadian Foreign Policy, 1943-1947." *Journal of Canadian Studies* 37, 2 (2002): 68-85.

Clarkson, Stephen, ed. *An Independent Foreign Policy for Canada?* Toronto: McClelland and Stewart, 1968.

Claude, Inis, Jr. *Swords into Plowshares: The Problems and Progress of International Organization.* 3rd ed. New York: Random House, 1964.

Cohen, Andrew. *While Canada Slept: How We Lost Our Place in the World.* Toronto: McClelland and Stewart, 2003.

Cohen, Maxwell. "A New Responsibility in Foreign Policy." *Saturday Night*, 19 January 1957, 5-6, 28.

Cole, Taylor. *The Canadian Bureaucracy: A Study of Canadian Civil Servants and Other Public Employees, 1939-1947.* Durham, NC: Duke University Press, 1949.

Cooper, Andrew F. *Canadian Foreign Policy: Old Habits and New Directions.* Scarborough, ON: Prentice Hall Canada, 1997.

Cuff, R.D., and J.L. Granatstein. *Ties That Bind: Canadian-American Relations in Wartime from the Great War to the Cold War*, 2nd ed. Toronto and Sarasota: Samuel Stevens Hakkert, 1977.

Dayal, Rajeshwar. *Mission for Hammarskjöld: The Congo Crisis.* Princeton: Princeton University Press, 1976.

Dilks, David. "A View on Two Squares: John Holmes in London and Moscow, 1944-48." *Canada House Lecture Series* 48 (1991).

Dobell, Peter C., and Robert Willmot. "John Holmes." *International Journal* 33, 1 (1977-78): 104-14.

Doern, G. Bruce, and Brian W. Tomlin. *Faith and Fear: The Free Trade Story.* Toronto: Stoddart, 1991.

Donaghy, Greg, ed. *Canada and the Early Cold War, 1943-1957.* Ottawa: Department of Foreign Affairs and International Trade, 1998.

Donaghy, Greg, and Don Barry. "Our Man from Windsor: Paul Martin and the New Members Question, 1955." In *Paul Martin and Canadian Diplomacy*, ed. Ryan Touhey. Waterloo: Centre on Foreign Policy and Federalism, 2001.

Donaghy, Greg, and Stéphane Roussel, eds. *Escott Reid: Diplomat and Scholar*. Montreal and Kingston: McGill-Queen's University Press, 2004.

Drouin, Marie-Josée, and Harald B. Malmgren. "Canada, the United States and the World Economy." *Foreign Affairs* 60, 2 (1981/82): 393-413.

Dyment, David M. "Canada-US Relations: Lessons from *Life with Uncle*." *International Insights* (CIIA Occasional Paper) 2, 1 (2004).

Eayrs, James. *Canada in World Affairs: October 1955 to June 1957*. Toronto: Oxford University Press, 1959.

–. *In Defence of Canada*. Vol. 5: *Indochina: The Roots of Complicity*. Toronto: University of Toronto Press, 1983.

Edwards, C.A.M. *Taylor Statten*. Toronto: Ryerson Press, 1960.

English, John. *Shadow of Heaven: The Life of Lester Pearson*. Vol. 1: *1897-1948*. Toronto: Lester and Orpen Dennys, 1989.

–. *The Worldly Years: The Life of Lester Pearson*. Vol. 2: *1949-1972*. Toronto: Alfred A. Knopf Canada, 1992

Evans, Paul M. *John Fairbank and the American Understanding of Modern China*. New York: B. Blackwell, 1988.

Ferns, H.S. *Reading from Left to Right: One Man's Political History*. Toronto: University of Toronto Press, 1983.

Freifeld, Sidney. *Undiplomatic Notes: Tales from the Canadian Foreign Service*. Toronto: Hounslow Press, 1990.

Friedland, Martin L. *The University of Toronto: A History*. Toronto: University of Toronto Press, 2002.

Gotlieb, Allan. *Romanticism and Realism in Canada's Foreign Policy*. Toronto: C.D. Howe Institute, 2004.

–. *The Washington Diaries, 1981-1989*. Toronto: McClelland and Stewart, 2006.

Granatstein, J.L. "The Anglocentrism of Canadian Diplomacy." In *Canadian Culture: International Dimensions*, ed. Andrew Fenton Cooper. Waterloo: Centre on Foreign Policy and Federalism, 1985.

–. *Canada 1957-1967: The Years of Uncertainty and Innovation*. Toronto: McClelland and Stewart, 1986.

–. *A Man of Influence: Norman A. Robertson and Canadian Statecraft, 1929-68*. Canada: Deneau Publishers, 1981.

–. *The Ottawa Men: The Civil Service Mandarins, 1935-1957*. Rev. ed. Toronto: University of Toronto Press, 1999 [1982].

–. *Who Killed the Canadian Military?* Toronto: HarperCollins, 2004.

Granatstein, J.L., and Robert Bothwell. *Pirouette: Pierre Trudeau and Canadian Foreign Policy*. Toronto: University of Toronto Press, 1990.

Granatstein, J.L., and R.D. Cuff. "Looking Back at the Cold War." *Canadian Forum* 52 (July/August 1972): 8-11.

–. "Looking Back Once More: A Rejoinder." *Canadian Forum* 52 (December 1972): 19-20.

Granatstein, J.L., and David Stafford. *Spy Wars: Espionage and Canada from Gouzenko to Glasnost*. Toronto: Key Porter Books, 1990.

Gwyn, Sandra. "Where Are You, Mike Pearson, Now That We Need You: Decline and Fall of Canada's Foreign Policy." *Saturday Night*, 3 April 1978, 27-35.

Gwynne-Timothy, John R.W. *Western's First Century*. London, ON: University of Western Ontario, 1978.

Hadwen, John. "John Holmes: Thou Shouldst Be Living at This Hour." *bout de papier* 13, 2 (1996): 4-5.

Halstead, John. "John Wendell Holmes." *bout de papier* 6, 3 (1988): 32-33.

Harrison, W.E.C. *Canada in World Affairs: 1949 to 1950.* Toronto: Oxford University Press, 1957.

Head, Ivan, and Pierre Trudeau. *The Canadian Way: Shaping Canada's Foreign Policy, 1968-1984.* Toronto: McClelland and Stewart, 1995.

Hewitt, Steve. "'Information believed true': RCMP Security Intelligence Activities on Canadian University Campuses and the Controversy Surrounding Them, 1961-71." *Canadian Historical Review* 81, 2 (2000): 191-228.

Hilliker, John. *Canada's Department of External Affairs.* Vol. 1: *The Early Years, 1909-1946.* Montreal and Kingston: McGill-Queen's University Press, 1990.

–. "The Politicians and the 'Pearsonalities': The Diefenbaker Government and the Conduct of Canadian External Relations." *Canadian Historical Papers* 19, 1 (1984): 151-67.

–. "'Sleeping with an elephant': Canada, the United States and Herbert Norman, 1939-1957." In *Changing Japanese Identities in Multicultural Canada*, ed. Joseph F. Kess, Hiroko Noro, Midge Ayukawa, and Helen Lansdowne. Victoria, BC: Centre for Asia-Pacific Initiatives, 2003.

Hilliker, John, and Donald Barry. *Canada's Department of External Affairs.* Vol. 2: *Coming of Age, 1946-1968.* Montreal and Kingston: McGill-Queen's University Press, 1995.

Hodgetts, J.E., and D.C. Corbett. *Canadian Public Administration.* Toronto: Macmillan, 1960.

Ignatieff, George. *The Making of a Peacemonger: The Memoirs of George Ignatieff.* Toronto: University of Toronto Press, 1985.

Inglis, Alex I. "The Institution and the Department." *International Journal* 33, 1 (1977-78): 88-103.

Jockel, Joseph T. *No Boundaries Upstairs: Canada, the United States, and the Origins of North American Air Defence, 1945-1958.* Vancouver: UBC Press, 1987.

"John Holmes: An Appreciation." *Behind the Headlines* 46, 1 (1988).

Keating, Tom. *Canada and World Order: The Multilateralist Tradition in Canadian Foreign Policy.* Toronto: McClelland and Stewart, 1993.

Keenleyside, T.A. "Lament for a Foreign Service: The Decline of Canadian Idealism." *Journal of Canadian Studies* 15, 4 (1980-81): 75-84.

Keirstead, B.S. *Canada in World Affairs: September 1951 to October 1953.* Toronto: Oxford University Press, 1956.

Kinsman, Gary. "'Character weaknesses' and 'fruit machines': Towards an Analysis of the Anti-homosexual Security Campaign in the Canadian Civil Service." *Labour/Le Travail* 35 (Spring 1995): 133-61.

–. "Constructing Gay Men and Lesbians as National Security Risks, 1950-70." In *Whose National Security? Canadian State Surveillance and the Creation of Enemies*, ed. Gary Kinsman, Dieter K. Buse, and Mercedes Steedman. Toronto: Between the Lines, 2000.

Kinsman, Gary, and Patrizia Gentile. *"In the interests of the state": The Anti-gay, Anti-lesbian National Security Campaign in Canada. A Preliminary Research Report.* Sudbury: Laurentian University, 1998.

Kolko, Joyce, and Gabriel Kolko. *The Limits of Power: The World and United States Foreign Policy, 1945-1954.* New York: Harper and Row, 1972.

Lapping, Brian. *Apartheid: A History*. Rev. ed. New York: George Brazziler, 1989 [1987].

Lévesque, René. *An Option for Quebec*. Toronto and Montreal: McClelland and Stewart, 1968

Lightstone, Susan. "The Observer." *Ottawa Magazine*, March 1991, 27-30.

Lloyd, Trevor. *Canada in World Affairs: 1957-1959*. Toronto: Oxford University Press, 1968.

Lownsbrough, John. "The Quiet Diplomat." *City and Country Home*, August 1987, 10-14.

Lunan, Gordon. *The Making of a Spy: A Political Odyssey*. Montreal: Robert Davies Publishing, 1995.

Lundell, Liz, ed. *Fires of Friendship: Eighty Years of the Taylor Statten Camps*. Toronto: Fires of Friendship Books, 2000.

Lyon, Peyton V. *Canada in World Affairs, 1961-1963*. Toronto: Oxford University Press, 1968.

Lyons, Gene M. "Putting ACUNS Together." *ACUNS Reports and Papers* 2 (1999).

Mackenzie, Hector. "An Old Dominion and the New Commonwealth: Canadian Policy on the Question of India's Membership, 1947-49." *Journal of Imperial and Commonwealth History* 27, 3 (1999): 82-112.

–. "Purged … from Memory: The Department of External Affairs and John Holmes." *International Journal* 59, 2 (2004): 375-86.

–. "Recruiting Tomorrow's Ambassadors: Examination and Selection for the Foreign Service of Canada, 1925-1997." In *Diplomatic Missions: The Ambassador in Canadian Foreign Policy*, ed. Robert Wolfe. Kingston: Queen's University School of Policy Studies, 1998.

MacLaren, Roy. *Commissions High: Canada in London, 1870-1971*. Montreal and Kingston: McGill-Queen's University Press, 2006.

Magee, Marion E., R.O. Matthews, and Charles Pentland. "A Tribute to John W. Holmes." *International Journal* 44, 4 (1989): 739-42.

Maloney, Sean M. *Canada and UN Peacekeeping: Cold War by Other Means, 1945-1970*. St. Catharines, ON: Vanwell Publishing, 2002.

Mangold, Peter. *Success and Failure in British Foreign Policy: Evaluating the Record, 1900-2000*. New York: Palgrave, 2001.

Mansergh, Nicholas. *The Commonwealth Experience*. London: Weidenfeld and Nicolson, 1969.

–. *Survey of British Commonwealth Affairs*. Vol. 2: *Problems of Wartime Co-operation and Post-war Change, 1939-1952*. London: Oxford University Press, 1958.

Martell, George. *Experiment in World Government: An Account of the United Nations Operation in the Congo, 1960-1964*. London: Johnson Publications, 1966.

Martin, David C. *Wilderness of Mirrors*. New York: Harper and Row, 1980.

Martin, Paul. *A Very Public Life*. Vol. 1: *Far from Home*. Ottawa: Deneau Publishers, 1983.

Massey, Vincent. *What's Past Is Prologue: The Memoirs of the Right Honourable Vincent Massey, C.H.* Toronto: Macmillan, 1963.

Massolin, Philip. *Canadian Intellectuals, the Tory Tradition, and the Challenge of Modernity, 1939-1970*. Toronto: University of Toronto Press, 2001.

Masters, Donald C. *Canada in World Affairs, 1953 to 1955*. Toronto: Oxford University Press, 1959.

McCreery, Christopher. *The Order of Canada: Its Origins, History, and Development*. Toronto: University of Toronto Press, 2005.

McEvoy, Frederick J. "Our Men in Moscow: Canadian Diplomats Behind the Iron Curtain." *The Beaver* 72, 6 (December 1992-January 1993): 40-46.

McNeil, Bill. *John Fisher: "Mr. Canada."* Markham, ON: Fitzhenry and Whiteside, 1983.

Melady, John. *Pearson's Prize: Canada and the Suez Crisis.* Toronto: Dundurn Group, 2006.

Meyer, Herbert E. "Trudeau's War on US Business." *Fortune,* 6 April 1981, 74-82.

Minifie, James M. *Peacemaker or Powder-monkey.* Toronto: McClelland and Stewart, 1960.

Mueller, Peter G., and Douglas A. Ross. *China and Japan: Emerging Global Powers.* New York: Praeger, 1975.

Munton, Don, and Tom Keating. "Internationalism and the Canadian Public." *Canadian Journal of Political Science* 34, 3 (2001): 517-49.

Murray, Geoffrey. "Glimpses of Suez 1956." *International Journal* 29, 1 (1973-74): 46-66.

Nossal, Kim Richard, ed. *An Acceptance of Paradox: Essays on Canadian Diplomacy in Honour of John W. Holmes.* Toronto: CIIA, 1982.

Nossal, Kim Richard. "Canada and the Search for World Order: John W. Holmes and Canadian Foreign Policy." *International Journal* 59, 4 (2004): 749-60.

Okuda, Kazuhiko. "How Canada Handles the United States: Alliance Politics and John W. Holmes." *Bulletin of the Graduate School of International Relations. IUJ* 3, July 1985.

Owram, Doug. *The Government Generation: Canadian Intellectuals and the State, 1900-1945.* Toronto: University of Toronto Press, 1986.

Page, Donald, and Don Munton. "Canadian Images of the Cold War, 1946-47." *International Journal* 32, 3 (1977): 577-604.

Pandit, Vijaya Lakshmi. *The Scope of Happiness: A Personal Memoir.* New York: Crown Publishers, 1979.

Pearson, Geoffrey A.H. *Seize the Day: Lester B. Pearson and Crisis Diplomacy.* Ottawa: Carleton University Press, 1993.

Pearson, Lester B. "Forty Years On: Reflections on Our Foreign Policy." *International Journal* 22, 3 (1967): 357-63.

–. "H. Hume Wrong." *External Affairs* 6, 3 (1954): 74-78.

–. *Mike: The Memoirs of the Rt. Hon. Lester B. Pearson.* Vol. 2: *1948-1957*, ed. John A. Munro and Alex I. Inglis. Toronto and Buffalo: University of Toronto Press, 1973.

–. *Words and Occasions.* Toronto: University of Toronto Press, 1970.

Pentland, Charles. "Mandarins and Manicheans: The 'Independence' Debate on Canadian Foreign Policy." *Queen's Quarterly* 77 (Spring 1970): 99-103.

Pincher, Chapman. *Their Trade Is Treachery.* London, UK: Sidgwick and Jackson, 1981.

Reford, Robert W. "John W. Holmes, 1910-1988." *International Perspectives* 17, 5 (1988): 23-24.

Reid, Escott. "Canada in World Affairs: Opportunities of the Next Decade." Address at the Annual Dinner of the Canadian Centenary Council. Château Laurier, 1 February 1967.

–. "Canadian Foreign Policy, 1967-1977: A Second Golden Decade?" *International Journal* 22, 2 (1967): 171-81.

–. *Envoy to Nehru.* Delhi: Oxford University Press, 1981.

–. *On Duty: A Canadian at the Making of the United Nations, 1945-1946.* Toronto: McClelland and Stewart, 1983.

–. *Radical Mandarin: The Memoirs of Escott Reid.* Toronto: University of Toronto Press, 1989.

–. *Time of Fear and Hope: The Making of the North Atlantic Treaty, 1947-1949.* Toronto: McClelland and Stewart, 1977.

Ritchie, Charles. *Diplomatic Passport: More Undiplomatic Diaries, 1946-1962.* Toronto: Macmillan, 1981.

—. *Storm Signals: More Undiplomatic Diaries, 1962-1971*. Toronto: Macmillan, 1983.

Roberts, Peter. *George Costakis: A Russian Life in Art*. Ottawa: Carleton University Press, 1994.

Robertson, Gordon. *Memoirs of a Very Civil Servant*. Toronto: University of Toronto Press, 2000.

Robertson, Terrence. *Crisis: The Inside Story of the Suez Conspiracy*. Toronto: McClelland and Stewart, 1964.

Robinson, Daniel J., and David Kimmel. "The Queer Career of Homosexual Security Vetting in Cold War Canada." *Canadian Historical Review* 75, 3 (1994): 319-45.

Robinson, H. Basil. *Diefenbaker's World: A Populist in Foreign Affairs*. Toronto: University of Toronto Press, 1989.

Ross, Douglas A. *In the Interests of Peace: Canada and Vietnam, 1954-1973*. Toronto: University of Toronto Press, 1984.

Rotstein, Abraham. *The Precarious Homestead: Essays on Economics, Technology, and Nationalism*. Toronto: New Press, 1973.

Roy, Patricia E. *The Oriental Question: Consolidating a White Man's Province, 1914-41*. Vancouver: UBC Press, 2003.

Saghal, Nayantara. *From Fear Set Free*. London: Victor Gollancz, 1962.

Sawatsky, John. *Men in the Shadows: The RCMP Security Service*. Toronto: Doubleday Canada, 1980.

—. *For Services Rendered: Leslie James Bennett and the RCMP Security Service*. Toronto: Doubleday Canada, 1982.

Simpson, Erika. "The Principles of Liberal Internationalism According to Lester Pearson." *Journal of Canadian Studies* 34, 1 (1999): 75-92.

Smith, Denis. *Rogue Tory: The Life and Legend of John G. Diefenbaker*. Toronto: Macfarlane, Walter and Ross, 1995.

Smith, Norman. "Pearson, People, and Press." *International Journal* 29, 1 (1973-74): 5-23.

Smith, Walter Bedell. *Moscow Mission, 1946-1949*. Melbourne: William Heinmann, 1950.

Sokol, John F. "Lest We Forget: In Memory of John W. Holmes." *bout de papier* 9, 1 (1992): 4.

Soward, F.H. "Inside a Canadian Triangle: The University, the CIIA, and the Department of External Affairs. A Personal Record." *International Journal* 33, 1 (1977-78): 66-87.

Spencer, Robert A. *Canada in World Affairs: From UN to NATO, 1946-1949*. Toronto: Oxford University Press, 1959.

Stairs, Denis. *The Diplomacy of Constraint: Canada, the Korean War and the United States*. Toronto: University of Toronto Press, 1974.

—. "Intellectual on Watch: James Eayrs and the Study of Foreign Policy and International Affairs." *International Journal* 62, 2 (2007): 215-39.

—. "The Pedagogics of John W. Holmes." *International Journal* 44, 4 (1989): 921-36.

—. "Present in Moderation: Lester Pearson and the Craft of Diplomacy." *International Journal* 29, 1 (1973-74): 143-53.

Stamp, Robert M. *The Canadian Obituary Record: A Biographical Dictionary of Canadians Who Died in 1988*. Toronto and Oxford: Dundurn Press, 1989.

Starnes, John. *Closely Guarded: A Life in Canadian Security and Intelligence*. Toronto: University of Toronto Press, 1998.

Stursberg, Peter. *Lester Pearson and the American Dilemma*. Toronto: Doubleday Canada, 1980.

Swettenham, John. *McNaughton*. 3 vols. Toronto: Ryerson Press, 1968-69.

Swoger, Gordon. *The Strange Odyssey of Poland's National Treasures, 1939-1961: A Polish-Canadian Story*. Toronto: Dundurn Group, 2004.

Talman, James J., and Ruth David Talman. *"Western": 1878-1953*. London: University of Western Ontario, 1953.

Tamblyn, William Ferguson. *These Sixty Years*. London: University of Western Ontario, 1938.

Taubman, William. *Khrushchev: The Man and His Era*. New York: W.W. Norton, 2003.

Taylor, J.H. "Vietnam: A Year with Uncle Ho." In *Canadian Peacekeepers in Indochina, 1954-1973: Recollections*, ed. Arthur E. Blanchette. Ottawa: Golden Dog Press, 2002.

Thakur, Ramesh. *Peacekeeping in Vietnam: Canada, India, Poland, and the International Commission*. Edmonton: University of Alberta Press, 1984.

Thomas, Clara, and John Lennox. *William Arthur Deacon: A Canadian Literary Life*. Toronto: University of Toronto Press, 1982.

Thornton, Martin. "Lester B. Pearson and John W. Holmes: A Non-Revisionist Relationship." *British Journal of Canadian Studies* 11, 1 (1996): 53-65.

Touhey, Ryan. "Canada and India at 60: Moving beyond History?" *International Journal* 62, 4 (2007): 733-52.

von Riekhoff, Harald. *NATO: Issues and Prospects*. Toronto: CIIA, 1967.

Whitaker, Reginald. "Origins of the Canadian Government's Internal Security System, 1946-1952." *Canadian Historical Review* 65, 2 (1984): 154-83.

Wilgress, Dana. *Memoirs*. Toronto: Ryerson Press, 1967.

Williams, William Appleman. *The Tragedy of American Diplomacy*. New ed. New York: W.W. Norton, 1988 [1959].

Wrong, Hume. "The Canada-United States Relationship 1927/1951." Introduction by John Holmes. *International Journal* 31, 3 (1976): 529-45.

Works by John W. Holmes
(excludes newspaper articles, book reviews, and forewords)

"The Advantages of Diversity in NATO." In *NATO: In Quest of Cohesion*, ed. Karl H. Cerzy and Henry W. Briefs. New York: Frederick A. Praeger, 1965.

"After 25 Years." *International Journal* 26, 1 (1970-71): 1-4

"Alliance and Independence." In *La Dualité Canadienne À L'heure des États-Unis*, ed. Raymond Morel. Québec: Les Presses de L'Université Laval, 1965.

"Alliances in Trouble." *Canadian Forum* 43 (August 1963): 97-99.

"The American Civil War and Canada Today." *Saturday Night*, 19 August 1939, 2.

"American Disappointment with the United Nations." In *National Security and Nuclear Strategy*, ed. Robert H. Connery and Demetrios Caraley. Vermont: Capital City Press, 1983. Reprinted from *Proceedings of the Academy of Political Science* 32, 4 (1977): 30-43.

"The American Problem." *International Journal* 24, 2 (1969): 229-45.

"The Anglo-Canadian Neurosis." *The Round Table* 223 (July 1966): 251-60. Reprinted as "A Canadian's Commonwealth: Realism out of Rhetoric," *Duke University Commonwealth-Studies Center Reprint Series*, no. 17.

"The Atlantic Community: Unity and Reality." *Atlantic Community Quarterly* 2, 4 (1964-65): 528-36.

"Australia and New Zealand at War." (ed.) *Oxford Pamphlets on World Affairs* 9 (1940).

The Better Part of Valour: Essays on Canadian Diplomacy. Toronto and Montreal: McClelland and Stewart, 1970.

"Beyond the Cold War Chessboard." *Worldview* 17, 6 (1974): 21-22.

"Bilateral Bellyaches." *Canadian Business* 54, 11 (1981): 115-26.

"Border Relations between Canada and the United States during the American Civil War." MA thesis, University of Toronto, April 1933.

"Bushels to Burn." *Behind the Headline* 1 (September 1940).

"Can the Commonwealth Survive? A Canadian Answer." *The Round Table* 213 (December 1963): 12-16.

Canada: A Middle-aged Power. Toronto: McClelland and Stewart, 1976.

"Canada and China." In *Policies Toward China: Views from Six Continents*, ed. A.M. Halpern. New York: McGraw Hill, 1965.

"Canada and Pacific Security." *Pacific Community* 3, 4 (1972): 742-55.

"Canada and Pan America." *Journal of Inter-American Studies* 10, 2 (1968): 173-84.

"Canada and the Commonwealth." *Jeune Afrique*, December 1966. Cited from Holmes Papers.

"Canada and the Crisis of Middle Powers." *Worldview* 15, 6 (1972): 23-27.

Canada and the New Internationalism, eds. John Holmes and John Kirton. Toronto: Canadian Institute of International Affairs, 1988.

"Canada and the Pacific." *Pacific Affairs* 44, 1 (1971): 5-17.

"Canada and the Pax Americana." In *Empire and Nations: Essays in Honour of Frederic H. Soward*, ed. Harvey L. Dyck and H. Peter Krosby. Toronto: University of Toronto Press, 1969.

"Canada and the United Nations: The Way We Were – Reflections of a Junior Founding Father." *Bulletin* 7, 4 (1981-82): 6-10.

"Canada and the United States in World Politics." *Foreign Affairs* 40, 1 (1961): 105-17.

"Canada and the United States: Political and Security Issues." *Behind the Headlines* 29, 1-2 (1970). Reprinted in *Atlantic Community Quarterly* 8, 3 (1970): 398-416.

"Canada and the USA: John Chancellor Interviews John Holmes." *The Lamp*, fall 1971, 1-9. Reprinted in *Reader's Digest* under the title "New Patterns in Partnership." Cited from Holmes Papers.

"Canada and the Vietnam War." In *War and Society in North America*, ed. J.L. Granatstein and R.D. Cuff. Toronto: Thomas Nelson and Sons, 1971.

"Canada and the Year of the Diplomats." *Weekend Magazine*, 1 January 1972, 18.

"Canada as a Middle Power." *Centennial Review* 10, 4 (1966): 430-45.

"Le Canada dans le Monde," *Politique Étrangère* 33, 4 (1968): 293-314.

"Le Canada et la Guerre Froide." With Jean-René Laroche. In *Le Canada et le Québec sur la Scène Internationale*. Quebec: Centre Québécois de Relations Internationales, 1977.

"Canada, Estados Unidos y el Hemisferio: El Futuro en Perspectiva." In *América Latina y Canadá frente a la Política Exterior de los Estados Unidos*, ed. R. Barry Farrell. Mexico: Fondo de Cultura Económica, 1975.

"Canada in Search of Its Role." *Foreign Affairs* 41, 4 (1963): 659-72.

"Canada: The Reluctant Power," *Orbis* 15, 1 (1971): 292-304.

"Canada under the Dove." In *Canada From Sea unto Sea*, ed. Charles J. Humber. Mississauga: Loyalist Press, 1986.

"Canada's Involvement in the Pacific Arena." *Air Force College Journal* (1963): 21-27.

"Canada's Role." With Duff Roblin and James Eayrs. In *Diplomacy in Evolution*, ed. D.L.B. Hamlin. Toronto: University of Toronto Press, 1961.

"Canada's Role in International Organizations." *Canadian Banker* 74, 1 (1967): 115-30. Also in *The Role of Canada in North America: Public Lectures of the York Central District High School Board* (Richmond Hill: York Central District High School Board, 1966).

"Canada's Role in the United Nations." *Air University Review* 18, 4 (1967): 18-27.

"Canada's Role in the World." *Century* (1967). Cited from Holmes Papers.

"Canadian-American Relations: Vive La Difference." *The Round Table* 285 (January 1983): 11-24.

"Canadian External Policies Since 1945." *International Journal* 18, 2 (1963): 137-47. Reprinted in J.L. Granatstein, ed., *Canadian Foreign Policy Since 1945: Middle Power or Satellite?* (Toronto: Copp Clark, 1972).

"Canadian Foreign Policy and International Law." In *International Law and Canadian Foreign Policy in the 1980s*. Ottawa: Canadian Council on International Law, 1980.

Canadian Resources and Canadian Foreign Policy. Toronto: CIIA, 1971.

"Canadian Unity: The International Dimension." *Transactions of the Royal Society of Canada*, series 4, 17 (1979): 99-109.

"A Canadian's Commonwealth: Realism out of Rhetoric." *The Round Table* 56 (October 1966): 335-47. Reprinted in W.J. Stankiewicz, ed., *British Government in an Era of Reform* (London: Cassell and Collier MacMillan, 1976).

"The Changing Nature of International Organizations: The Canadian Perspective." *Canada House Lecture Series* 8 (1979).

The Changing Pattern of International Institutions. Leeds: Leeds University Press, 1980.

The CIIA and Canadian Foreign Policy: Hits and Myths. Toronto: CIIA, 1978.

"Clio and I." *Proceedings of the Royal Society of Canada*, series 5, 1 (1986): 251-55.

"Collective Engagement." *Issue Brief* 6, Canadian Centre for Arms Control, 1987, 1-12.

"A Commonwealth Secretariat: New Style." *Canadian Banker* 72, 1 (1965): 63-68.

"The Commonwealth and Africa." *International Journal* 17, 2 (1962): 133-36.

"The Commonwealth and the United Nations." In *A Decade of the Commonwealth, 1955-1964*, ed. W.B. Hamilton, Kenneth Robinson, and C.D.W. Goodwin. Durham, NC: Duke University Press, 1966.

"The Commonwealth as Idea and Prophesy." *Canadian Commentator* 5, 5 (1961): 4-7.

"The Commonwealth Faces 1964." *The Times* (London), 7 January 1964. Cited from Holmes Papers.

"Containment: Forty Years Later." *bout de papier* 5, 3 (1987): 30-35. With George Grande, John Halstead, and George Ignatieff.

Conversation between Professor John Holmes and Professor David Dilks on Friday, 28 June 1985, at the University of Leeds. Toronto: CIIA, n.d.

"Crises in Canadian-American Relations: A Canadian Perspective." In *Friends So Different: Essays on Canada and the United States in the 1980s*, ed. Lansing Lamont and J. Duncan Edmonds. Ottawa: Ottawa University Press, 1989.

"A Critical Look at Europe." *Wilton Park Journal* 26 (December 1961): 3-8.

"Danger of Continental Nationalism." *The Observer*, 18 November 1962. Cited from Holmes Papers.

"The Diplomacy of a Middle Power." *Atlantic Monthly*, 5 November 1964, 106-12.

"The Disillusioning of the Relationship: Epitaph to a Decade." In *Friends So Different: Essays on Canada and the United States in the 1980s*, ed. Lansing Lamont and J. Duncan Edmonds. Ottawa: Ottawa University Press, 1989.

"Divided We Stand." *International Journal* 31, 3 (1976): 385-98.

"The Dumbbell Won't Do." *Foreign Policy* 50 (Spring 1983): 3-23.

"Dynamic Democracy." With Philip Child. *Behind the Headlines* 9 (May 1941).

"The Fallacy of a Common Diplomacy." *The Observer*, 25 November 1962. Cited from Holmes Papers.

"Fearful Symmetry: The Dilemmas of Consultation and Coordination in the North Atlantic Treaty Organization." *International Organization* 22, 4 (1968): 821-40.

"Focus on the Constant Dilemma of US-Canadian Relationships." *International Perspectives* (May/June 1972): 3-14. Reprinted in part as "US-Canada: A View from the North." *Canada Today* 4, 4 (1973): 7-8.

Four Introductory Lectures. Toronto: Trinity College, n.d.

"Frederick Hubert Soward." *International Journal* 40, 1 (1984-85): 203-06.

"From Sea to Sea: Canada's Move from the Atlantic to the Pacific." In *Politics of the Pacific Rim: Perspectives on the 1980's*, ed. F. Quei Quo. Burnaby, BC: SFU Publications, 1982.

"The Future of the American Empire." *International Perspectives* 16 (January/February 1988): 3-7.

"Geneva: 1954." *International Journal* 22, 3 (1967): 457-83. Reprinted in J.L. Granatstein, ed., *Canadian Foreign Policy Since 1945* (Toronto: Copp Clark, 1972).

"Good Reason for Us to Stay." *Financial Post*, 9 May 1964. Cited from Holmes Papers.

"Growing Independence in Canadian-American Relations." *Foreign Affairs* 46, 1 (1967): 151-66.

"Heads across the Border." *Canada-United States Law Journal* 1 (Summer 1978): 145-52.

"How the UN Tries to Keep This Wayward World On Course." *The Times Higher Educational Supplement*, 18 January 1980, 12.

"How the Wheels Go Round." (ed). *Democracy and Citizenship Series* 2, 15 October 1940.

"The Illusion of Europe." *Worldview* 16, 10 (1973): 6-12.

"Impact of Domestic Political Factors on Canadian-American Relations: Canada." *International Organization* 28, 4 (1974): 612-35.

"The Impact on the Commonwealth of the Emergence of Africa." *International Organization* 16, 2 (1962): 291-302. Reprinted in Norman Judson Padelford, ed., *Africa and World Order* (New York: Praeger, 1963).

"In Defence of Nationalism." In *The Decisive Years*. Vol. 5: *1967*, ed. S.M. Philip. Toronto: Barker Publishing, 1967.

"In Praise of National Boundaries: The Case against Creeping Continentalism." *Saturday Night*, 7 July 1974, 13-26.

"Introduction: The IJC and Canada-United States Relations." In *The International Joint Commission: Seventy Years On*, ed. Robert Spencer, John Kirton, and Kim Richard Nossal. Toronto: Centre for International Studies, 1981.

"Is There a Future for Middlepowermanship?" In *Canada's Role as a Middle Power*, ed. J. King Gordon. Toronto: CIIA, 1966.

"Les Institutions Internationales et la Politique Extérieure." *Études Internationales* 1, 2 (1970): 20-40.

"Merrie Canada." In *Stratford Papers on Shakespeare* (Toronto: W.J. Gage, 1965), 73-88.

"Kanadas Außenpolitik im Rahmen der Vereinten Nationen." *Österreichische Zeitschrift für Aussenpolitik* 4, 4 (1964): 195-204.

"Key Issues in Canadian Foreign Policy." In *Peace, Power, and Protest*, ed. Paul Evans. Toronto: Ryerson Press, 1967.

"The Late Norman Robertson." *External Affairs* 20, 9 (1968): 346-57. With Marcel Cadieux.

"Liberty, Equality, and Eternity." *International Journal* 39, 3 (1984): 637-54.

Life with Uncle: The Canadian-American Relationship. Toronto: University of Toronto Press, 1981.

"Lines Written for a Canadian-American Conference." In *The Star-Spangled Beaver*, ed. John H. Redekop. Toronto: Peter Martin Associates, 1971.

"Looking Backwards and Forwards." *ACUNS Reports and Papers* 1 (1988).

"Mediation or Enforcement?" *International Journal* 25, 2 (1970): 388-404.

"Merchant-Heeney Revisited: A Sentimental View." In *America's Alliances and Canadian-American Relations*, ed. Lauren McKinsey and Kim Richard Nossal. Toronto: Summerhill Press, 1988.

"Morality, Realism and Foreign Affairs: Everything Has Its Season – and That Adds to Complexity." *International Perspectives* (September/October 1977): 20-25.

"Moscow 1947-1948: Reflections on the Origins of My Cold War." In *Nearly Neighbours: Canada and the Soviet Union – From Cold War to Détente and Beyond*, ed. J.L. Black and Norman Hillmer. Kingston: Ronald P. Fry, 1989.

"Most Safely in the Middle." *International Journal* 39, 2 (1984): 366-88.

"Mr. Khrushchev and the UN." *Canadian Forum* 40, 478 (1960): 169-71.

"Nationalism in Canadian Foreign Policy." In *Nationalism in Canada*, ed. Peter Russell. Toronto: McGraw-Hill Ryerson Ltd., 1966.

"NATO: A Peacekeeping Agency." *Canadian Business* 39, 5 (1961): 34-38.

"The Necessity of Nationalism?" In *The Decisive Years*. Weston, ON: Baxter Publishing, 1967.

"Negotiating with the Russians." *Commerce Journal* (February 1962): 7-12.

"The New Agenda for Canadian Internationalism." In *Canada and the New Internationalism*, ed. John Holmes and John Kirton. Toronto: Canadian Institute of International Affairs, 1988.

"The New Commonwealth." *Your Canada* 1 (1965). Cited from Holmes Papers.

"New Perspectives of Canadian Foreign Policy." *The World Today* 25, 10 (1969): 450-60. Reprinted in *Survival* 11, 11 (1969): 334-40; and *Relazioni Internazionali* 34, 3 (1970).

No Other Way: Canada and International Security Institutions. Toronto: Centre for International Studies, 1986.

"A Non-American Perspective." In *The Changing United Nations: Options for the United States*, ed. David A. Kay. *Proceedings of the Academic of Political Science* 32, 4 (1977): 30-43. Reprinted in Robert Connery and Demetrios Caraley, eds., *National Security and Nuclear Strategy* (New York: Academy of Political Science, 1983).

"On Our Other Hemisphere: Reflections on the Bahia Conference." *International Journal* 17, 4 (1962): 414-19.

"An Open Question: Has the Commonwealth a Future?" *Optima* 16, 3 (1966): 121-28.

"Opportunities Abroad." In *The Decisive Years*. Weston, ON: Baxter Publishing, 1962.

"Our Man in London," *Today Magazine*, 13 December 1980.

"The Political and Philosophical Aspects of UN Security Forces." *International Journal* 19, 3 (1964): 292-307. Reprinted in Joel Larus, ed., *From Collective Security to Preventative Diplomacy: Readings in International Organization and the Maintenance of Peace* (New York: John Wiley and Sons, 1965), 478-89; and in David Kay, ed., *The United Nations Political System* (New York: John Wiley, 1967).

"The Political Aspects of Interdependence." In *Canadian-American Interdependence: How Much? Proceedings of the 10th Annual University of Windsor Seminar on Canadian-*

American Relations, 1968, ed. R.H. Wagenberg (Windsor: University of Windsor Press, 1970): 3-7.

"Political Implications of the European Economic Community." *Queen's Quarterly* 69, 1 (1962): 1-10. Reprinted in *The Observer* (London) and *Atlantic Community Quarterly* 1, 1 (1963): 23-36.

"La Portée du Nationalisme Québécois dans les Relations Canado-Américaines." In *Le Nationalisme Québécois à la Croisée des Chemins*, ed. Albert Legault and Alfred O. Hero Jr. Laval: Centre Québécois des Relations Internationales, 1974.

"Preface." In Stanley R. Tupper and Doug R. Bailey. *One Continent – Two Voices: The Future of Canada/US Relations*. Toronto and Vancouver: Clarke, Irwin, 1967.

"The Relationship in Alliance and in World Affairs." In *The United States and Canada*, ed. John S. Dickey. Englewood Cliffs, NJ: Prentice Hall, 1964.

"R.J. Sutherland." *Survival* 9, 2 (1967): 67.

"Sadder but Wiser: The UN at Thirty." *International Perspectives* (November/December 1975): 19-23.

"Safely in the Middle: The Eccentric Views of a Middle Power." In *Security, Conflict and Survival: Perceptions of a Middle Power*, ed. Nils Ørvik. Toronto: Standing Conference of Atlantic Organizations, 1983.

"Shadow and Substance: Diplomatic Relations Between Britain and Canada." In *Britain and Canada: A Survey of a Changing Relationship*, ed. Peter Lyon. London: Frank Cass, 1976.

The Shaping of Peace: Canada and the Search for World Order, 1943-1957. Vol. 1. Toronto: University of Toronto Press, 1979.

The Shaping of Peace: Canada and the Search for World Order, 1943-1957. Vol. 2. Toronto: University of Toronto Press, 1982.

"The Significance of Quebec Nationalism for Canadian-American Relations." n.d. Cited from Holmes Papers. Also translated as "La Portée du Nationalisme Québécois dans les Relations Canado-Américaines."

Some Aspects of Mediation: Report of a Conference Sponsored by the European Centre of the Carnegie Endowment for International Peace, Geneva. Talloires, France: Carnegie Endowment for International Peace, 1970.

"Stop Signs for a Military Trip," *Maclean's*, 1 June 1981, 9.

"The Study of Diplomacy: A Sermon." In *The Changing Role of the Diplomatic Function in the Making of Foreign Policy*. Centre for Foreign Policy Studies, Dalhousie University, Occasional Paper, June 1973.

"Techniques of Peacekeeping in Asia." In *China and the Peace of Asia*, ed. Alastair Buchan. London: Chatto and Windus, 1965.

"Toward a History of Canada's Relations with the Soviet Union." Centre for Russian and East European Studies Working Paper No. 1, October 1986.

"The Unequal Alliance: Canada and the United States." Fourth Seminar on Canadian American Relations. Windsor: University of Windsor, 1962.

"The United Nations and World Order." In *International Conflict and Conflict Management: Readings in World Politics*, ed. Robert O. Matthews, Arthur G. Rubinoff, and Janice Gross Stein. 2nd ed. Scarborough: Prentice Hall, 1989.

"The United Nations at 40: An Upbeat Assessment." In *Canadians and the United Nations*, ed. Clyde Sanger. Ottawa: Ministry of Supply and Services Canada, 1988.

"The United Nations in Perspective." *Behind the Headlines* 44, 1 (1986).

"The United Nations in the Congo." *International Journal* 16, 1 (1960-61): 1-16.

"The United Nations: Then and Now." *University of Leeds Review* 28 (1985/86): 165-79.
"The United States and International Organizations: A Canadian Perspective." In *The Reagan Revolution?* Ed. B.B. Kymlicka and Jean V. Matthews. Chicago: Dorsey Press, 1988.
"The United States in the World: A Canadian Comment." In *A Nation Observed: Perspectives on America's World Role*, ed. Donald R. Lesh. Washington, DC: Potomac Associates, 1974.
"The Unquiet Diplomat: Lester B. Pearson." With introduction and edited by Adam Chapnick. *International Journal* 62, 2 (2007): 289-309.
"The View from Canada," *Louisville Courier Journal Times*, 5 August 1973. Cited from Holmes Papers.
"The Way of the World." *International Journal* 35, 2 (1980): 211-25.
"The West and the Third World." *International Journal* 21, 1 (1965): 20-41.
"With the Best of Intentions: Interdependence and Freedom." In *And He Loved Big Brother: Man, State and Society in Question*, ed. Shlomo Giora Shoham and Francis Rosenstiel. London, UK: Macmillan, 1985.
"The World According to Ottawa." In *Mackenzie King to Philosopher King: Canadian Foreign Policy in a Modern Age*, ed. Peter St. John. Winnipeg: St. John's College, 1984.
"The World: Despite What You Read, the UN Still Works Well." *Saturday Night*, July/August 1975, 10-13.
"The Year of Europe," *London Times*, 25 April 1972.
"1945: Reflections from Canada House." *bout de papier* 6, 3 (1988): 16-21.

INTERVIEWS AND CONVERSATIONS

Irving Abella. Telephone. 15 June 2006.
Douglas Anglin. Ottawa, Ontario. 2 February 2006.
Mark Anshan. Telephone. 2 January 2007.
Christopher Armstrong. Toronto, Ontario. 8 February 2006.
Thomas Axworthy. Toronto, Ontario. 8 February 2006.
Louis Balthazar. E-mail. 24 February 2006.
Jane Barrett. Toronto, Ontario. 13 February 2006.
William Barton. Ottawa, Ontario. 1 February 2006.
Dean Beeby. Ottawa, Ontario. 9 March 2006.
Charles Beer. Newmarket, Ontario. 13 May 2005.
James Beer. Telephone. 26 April 2006.
David Bercuson. Telephone. 2 March 2006.
David Blair. Telephone. 26 April 2006.
Michael Bliss. Toronto, Ontario. 1 February 2007.
Robert Bothwell. Toronto, Ontario. 22 March 2006.
Charles Boyd. Newmarket, Ontario. 13 May 2005.
Lee-Anne Broadhead. Telephone. 30 May 2006.
Charles Caccia. Telephone. 1 May 2006.
Robert Cameron. Telephone. 27 April 2006.
Ross Campbell. Telephone. 15 February 2006.
Michel Charrier. Telephone. 9 January 2008.
Stephen Clarkson. Telephone. 22 March 2006.

Robert Cox. Toronto, Ontario. 11 November 2005.
Wilfred Coutu. Telephone. 23 May 2006.
Marshall Crowe. Toronto, Ontario. 24 February 2006.
James Daw. E-mail. 27 May 2006.
Tom Delworth. Telephone. 31 March 2006.
Sandra Demson. Telephone. 18 October 2007.
Jack Denne. Telephone. 20 February 2006.
Peter Dobell. Ottawa, Canada. 7 December 2005.
James Dow. Telephone. 21 April 2006.
Margaret Doxey. Peterborough, Ontario. 9 January 2006.
Daniel Drache. Toronto, Ontario. 20 April 2006.
James Eayrs. Toronto, Ontario. 5 April 2006.
John English. Waterloo, Ontario. 2 March 2006.
Paul Evans. Telephone. 15 March 2006.
David Farr. Ottawa, Ontario. 10 January 2006.
Annette Baker Fox. Telephone. 6 February 2006.
Gayle Fraser. Toronto, Ontario. 10 April 2006.
Allan Gotlieb. Toronto, Ontario. 13 June 2006.
Bill Graham. Toronto, Ontario. 2 October 2007.
Mary Graham. Telephone. 3 January 2006.
Jack Granatstein. Toronto, Ontario. 6 January 2006.
Madeline Grant. Toronto, Ontario. 15 March 2006.
Lois Greaves. Telephone. 29 March 2006.
Frank Griffiths. Telephone. 22 February 2006.
John Hadwen. Ottawa, Ontario. 10 January 2006.
Fen Hampson. Ottawa, Ontario. 6 December 2005.
Peter Hancock. Telephone. 30 March 2006.
John Harbron. Toronto, Ontario. 22 May 2007.
Gordon Hawkins. Toronto, Ontario. 20 November 2005.
Chantal Hébert. E-mail. 22 February 2006.
Alan Henrikson. Telephone. 14 August 2007.
John Hilliker. Ottawa, Ontario. 5 December 2005.
Norman Hillmer. Ottawa, Ontario. 9 March 2006.
Michiel Horn. Toronto, Ontario. 21 February 2006.
Christopher Hume. Telephone. 25 May 2006.
Jack and Barbara Hyatt. Toronto, Ontario. 9 December 2005.
Frank Iacobucci. Telephone. 3 October 2007.
Henry H.R. Jackman. Telephone. 15 March 2006.
Jean M. Johnson. Telephone. 17 October 2007.
Robert Kaplan. Telephone. 15 October 2007.
C.M. Kelley. Ottawa, Ontario. 8 March 2006.
Stanislav Kirschbaum. Toronto, Ontario. 21 February 2006.
John Kirton. Toronto, Ontario. 25 November 2005.
Arthur Kroeger. Ottawa, Ontario. 20 October 2005.
Patrick Lane. Telephone. 7 September 2005.
Alex Langford. Telephone. 14 March 2006.
Albert Legault. E-mail. 23 February 2006.

Marshall Leslie. Telephone. 22 May 2006.
Don LePan. Telephone. 15 March 2006.
Nick LePan. Toronto, Ontario. 15 February 2006.
David Leyton-Brown. Telephone. 13 March 2006.
Peyton Lyon. Ottawa, Ontario. 10 January 2006.
Eugene M. Lyons. Telephone. 10 November 2005.
Donald Macdonald. Toronto, Ontario. 16 May 2006.
H. Ian Macdonald. Telephone. 28 May 2007.
Roy MacLaren. Toronto, Ontario. 27 March 2006.
Marion Magee. Toronto, Ontario. 11 November 2005.
Robert O. Matthews. Toronto, Ontario. 24 January 2006.
Steve McCauley. Telephone. 30 May 2006.
Allan McGill. E-mail. 19 February 2006.
Errington (Ric) McMahon. Telephone. 20 February 2006.
Ray McTavish. Telephone. 20 February 2006.
Arthur Menzies. Ottawa, Ontario. 11 January 2006.
Dan Middlemiss. Telephone. 29 March 2006.
Ingrid Milic. Toronto, Ontario. 21 March 2006.
Pamela Mills. Toronto, Ontario. 21 March 2006.
Ron Moore. Telephone. 20 February 2006.
Martha Moos. Telephone. 17 October 2007.
Maureen Appel Molot. Ottawa, Ontario. 5 December 2005.
Reid Morden. Toronto, Ontario. 10 February 2006.
Peter Mueller. Toronto, Ontario. 21 February 2006.
Don Munton. E-mail. 3 March 2006. Telephone. 6 March 2006.
Janice Murray. Telephone. 20 March 2006.
Kim Richard Nossal. Kingston, Ontario. 12 January 2006.
Joseph Nye. E-mail. 21 March 2006.
Don Page. Telephone. 27 September 2005.
Geoffrey Pearson. Ottawa, Ontario. 17 October 2005.
Patricia Pearson. E-mail. 2 March 2006.
Charles Pentland. Telephone. 16 June 2006.
Jim and Heather Peterson. Toronto, Ontario. 17 April 2006.
Alfred Pick. Telephone. 20 June 2006.
Lois Rae. Toronto, Ontario. 2 June 2006.
Robert Reford. Telephone. 1 February 2006.
Ernie Regehr. Telephone. 30 May 2006.
Don Rickerd. Toronto, Ontario. 20 January 2006.
Elizabeth Riddell-Dixon. Ottawa, Ontario. 31 October 2005.
Robert Riddle. E-mail. 6 October 2005.
H. Basil Robinson. Ottawa, Ontario. 20 October 2005.
Judith Robertson. Toronto, Ontario. 5 October 2005.
R. Gordon Robertson. Ottawa, Ontario. 15 November 2005.
Paul Robertson. Telephone. 1 May 2006.
Hume Rogers. Telephone. 16 March 2006.
Douglas Ross. E-mail. 2 February 2006. Telephone. 3 February 2006.
Abe Rotstein. Toronto, Ontario. 29 April 2006.

Pauline Sabourin. Ottawa, Ontario. 2 February 2006.
A. Edward Safarian. Toronto, Ontario. 24 March 2006.
Jone Schoeffel. Toronto, Ontario. 17 October 2007.
J. Blair Seaborn. Telephone. 18 May 2006.
Tamara Palmer Seiler. Telephone. 17 February 2006.
Martin Shadwick. Telephone. 17 May 2006.
Andrée Sheehan. Telephone. 22 May 2006.
Michael Shenstone. Telephone. 19 June 2006.
Sarah Sigsworth. Telephone. 29 July 2005.
Jill Sinclair. Telephone. 30 May 2006.
Ann Skinner. London, Ontario. 27 June 2005.
Nancy Skinner. London, Ontario. 6 May 2005.
Douglas Small. Ottawa, Ontario. 1 February 2006.
Ian Smart. Telephone. 10 March 2006.
Robert Spencer. Ottawa, Ontario. 11 January 2006.
Keith Spicer. E-mail. 6 April 2006.
Peter St. John. Telephone. 3 May 2005.
David Stafford. E-mail. 21 December 2005.
Denis Stairs. Toronto, Ontario. 11 March 2006.
John Starnes. Ottawa, Ontario. 21 October 2005.
Don Story. Telephone. 6 January 2006.
David Taras. Telephone. 17 February 2006.
James Taylor. Ottawa, Ontario. 10 January and 2 February 2006.
Brian Tomlin. Telephone. 21 December 2005.
Albert Tucker. Toronto, Ontario. 21 February 2006.
Brian Urquhart. Telephone. 10 October 2006.
Harald von Riekhoff. Ottawa, Ontario. 7 December 2005.
Donald Walker. Telephone. 25 May 2006.
Mel Watkins. Telephone. 1 April 2006.
Bernard Wood. Telephone. 6 July 2006.
Albert J. Woytasik and Janet M. Woytasik. Hamilton, Ontario. 29 July 2005.
Wendy Woytasik-Karr. Brampton, Ontario. 28 September 2005.
Gerald Wright. Ottawa, Ontario. 11 January 2006.
Max Yalden. Telephone. 15 June 2006.
Mark Zacher. Telephone. 10 February 2006.

Index

Academic Council on the United Nations System (ACUNS), 273-74, 279-80, 283
Academy of Sciences of the USSR, 275
The Acceptance of Paradox: Essays on Canadian Diplomacy in Honour of John W. Holmes, 248
Acheson, Dean, 70
Algeria, 98, 101
Algonquin Park, 11
American Historical Association, 147, 178
Americanization of Canada, 166-67, 270. *See also* nationalism (Canada)
Americas Society, 282
Amnesty International, 241
Andrew, Geoff, 216
Andreyevna, Vera, 55
Anshan, Mark, 234, 246, 278
anti-Americanism, 92, 100, 149-50, 203, 214, 220, 237, 268-70
anti-Semitism, 240-41
Appathurai, Edward, 233, 238, 246
appeasement, philosophy of, 20. *See also* Second World War
Appel, Maureen. *See* Molot, Maureen
Arbatov, Georgi, 275
armed forces (Canada): First Canadian Infantry Division, 64; funding for, 218, 265; morale, 218

arms control, 252-53, 286
arms race, 167-68, 253, 263
Arnett, Jim, 171, 310n17
Arnold, Matthew, 11
Association of Universities and Colleges of Canada, 216
Atlantic Monthly, 147
Austin, Bunny, 16
Australia, 36, 47, 77, 111, 148, 154
Australian Institute of International Affairs, 154
Austria, 17
Avro Arrow, 105
axis powers, 42
Axworthy, Lloyd, 171-72, 283
Axworthy, Thomas, 145, 171

baby boom, 165-66
Bahia conference on world tensions (1962), 153
Bahrain, 76-77
Bahrain Petroleum Company, 76
Baldwin, John, 22-24
Baltic Sea, 54
Banting, Frederick, 17
Barbados, 153
Barry, Donald, 66
Baryshnikov, Mikhail, 227

346

Printed and bound in Canada by Friesens

Set in Stone by Artegraphica Design Co. Ltd.

Copy editor: Joanne Richardson

Indexer: Megan Sproule-Jones

ENVIRONMENTAL BENEFITS STATEMENT

UBC Press saved the following resources by printing the pages of this book on chlorine free paper made with 100% post-consumer waste.

TREES	WATER	ENERGY	SOLID WASTE	GREENHOUSE GASES
9	**3,150**	**6**	**405**	**759**
FULLY GROWN	GALLONS	MILLION BTUs	POUNDS	POUNDS

Calculations based on research by Environmental Defense and the Paper Task Force. Manufactured at Friesens Corporation